THE SOCIAL CONSCIENCE

'The composition of this book has been for the author a long struggle of escape, and so must the reading of it be for most readers if the author's assault upon them is to be successful – *a struggle of escape from habitual modes of thought and expression.* The ideas which are here expressed so laboriously are extremely simple and should be obvious. *The difficulty lies, not in the new ideas, but in escaping from the old ones,* which ramify ... into every corner of our minds.'

JOHN MAYNARD KEYNES
Preface to *General Theory of Employment, Interest and Money*
13th December, 1935

Michel Glautier's
other books include

Accounting in a Changing Environment (co-author)
Accounting Theory and Practice (co-author)
Accounting Practice (co-author)
Basic Financial Accounting (co-author)
Cost Accounting (co-author)
A Reference Guide to International Taxation (co-author)

THE SOCIAL CONSCIENCE

Michel Glautier

SHEPHEARD-WALWYN (PUBLISHERS) LTD

©Michel Glautier 2007

All rights reserved. No part of this book may be
reproduced in any form without the written permission
of the publisher, Shepheard-Walwyn (Publishers) Ltd

First published in 2007 by
Shepheard-Walwyn (Publishers) Ltd
15 Alder Road
London SW14 8ER

British Library Cataloguing in Publication Data
A catalogue record of this book
is available from the British Library

ISBN-13: 978-0-85683-248-2
ISBN-10: 0-85683-248-0

Typeset by Alacrity,
Banwell Castle, Weston-super-Mare
Printed through Print Solutions, Wallington, Surrey

For Amanda, Jennifer, Louise and Alexandre

Contents

Acknowledgments	viii
Prologue	ix
Introduction	xi

Part I
THE HUMANE CONDITION

1 Living in Our Times	3
2 A Caring Society in a Market Economy	23
3 Policy Objectives for a Caring Society	43

Part II
EMPOWERING A CARING SOCIETY

4 Education for a Caring Society	77
5 Market Behaviour	106
6 Accounting, Accountability and Shareholder Value	137
7 The State, Society and Government	166
8 Citizenship and the Democratic Deficit; Governance and Accountability	193

Part III
THE GREAT DEBATE

9 Authority and Freedom in a Caring Society	231
10 Conflict Resolution and Crime Control	255

Part IV
GLOBAL TRENDS AND PERSPECTIVES

11 Towards the Future: The Dynamics of Change	297
Epilogue	335
Meditation	337
General Reading	339
Index	343

Acknowledgements

MY GRATITUDE goes to my lifelong friend James Shepherd, who gave me so much help when I began writing many years ago, and to Jean Shepherd, whose encouragement, guidance and support was my mainstay when writing this book. She gave me valuable insights, enlarged my perceptions and made significant inputs.

Michael Ashcroft, Leslie Blake, Dr Josef Craven, Brian Hodgkinson and Dr Stephanie Wilson, all scholars in their fields, gave valuable advice and comments, for which I am very grateful.

I have been greatly helped by Margaret Colwell, who edited this work with sensitivity and understanding of the purpose that I wished to achieve.

I am especially indebted to Anthony Werner, not only for undertaking the publication of this work, but also for having invested considerable time and care in improving the argument and its presentation.

Prologue

This book tells of
The past, discusses the present and looks to the future of
A Social Conscience
Founded on only two fundamental principles of life:
The Instinct to Care
The Necessity to Share

Introduction

LIFE IS A manifestation that has appeared as a mystery to the thinking man from time immemorial. So abundant and varied are its forms that, until recent times, man has had the wisdom to accept its unfathomable nature and bow to a mystical Creator having universal sovereign power and knowledge. It remains unfathomable and is an irresistible attraction to thinkers. The scientific age has increased considerably the means available to thinkers to advance knowledge over a wide variety of fronts. As new discoveries are made, some part of the mystery is unravelled. The discovery of the structure of DNA, in particular, with all the possibilities that it has shown for extending and improving physical life, is proof of the intelligence of the human mind. But the discovery of DNA also revealed the wonder and the magic that is the order and harmony that sustains life. The human mind inches forward towards an ultimate goal of understanding the origin of life. But, paradoxically, discovery seems only to deepen mystery, which tauntingly recedes from the grasp of understanding as knowledge advances.

From a religious perspective, an acceptable basis for understanding life is today a matter of personal choice. Relics still exist of prehistoric man's conception of life in the miraculous survival of the Australian aboriginal. Separated by infinite time from other people, they have retained to this day a perception of a pictorial heaven, as seen by the naked eye and interpreted as an imagined 'other' world peopled by mystical beings assuming the shapes of constellations of stars. Physical life is a dream: reality lies in the starry heaven above, the ultimate destination on awakening. Ancient Egyptians, like the Greeks, believed that life on Earth was a preparation for the life to come. They were mystical people and considered that throughout life on Earth, mystical knowledge of the Divine World was potentially available to anyone who wanted it. The preparation for life after death was a crucial aspect of their burial ceremonials. The Christian belief in resurrection also seeks to give life continuity after death. Those troubled by the lack of objective evidence of life after death reject that possibility. The meaning of life and death, as physical experiences, has been the subject of religious interpretation for as long as man has looked up to the skies for locating heaven.

As formal religions have gradually lost their influence in many Western industrial nations, they have been replaced by other beliefs, all seeking to explain or interpret life and being. The French philosopher Jean-Paul Sartre[1] developed the notion of existentialism that explains life as reality in existence. Humanism is a set of beliefs about life that has gained wide adherence. It explains life in terms of physical being and beliefs: there are no supernatural beings; the material universe is the only thing that exists, and science provides the only reliable knowledge of this universe; there is no afterlife and no reincarnation. Humanism rallies atheists and agnostics in placing at the centre of its beliefs a commitment to moral values that are derived from human experience and thought.

This book discusses the 'humane condition'[2] based on moral values. The concept provides us with a meaningful reality within which we can situate ourselves and understand our purpose.

The Ancient World still has useful ideas and guidelines to offer in the difficult and perplexing world in which we find ourselves. Plato is particularly relevant to the argument developed in this book. According to Plato[3] the world has two aspects, the visible, or that which is perceived by the senses and the non-visible or intelligible, which consists of universal, eternal forms or ideas perceived only by the mind. Human experiences of so-called reality are only of visible appearances, and from them can be derived only opinions and beliefs. Genuine reality exists in such Platonic forms as goodness, truth, beauty and justice, which exist in the mind.

This text is concerned with genuine reality as expressed in the ideal forms defined by Plato, which are treated here as absolute values. To those holding religious beliefs, Life, Truth and Love may be understood as absolutes and as symbolic expressions of a Supreme Being, or God.

Life includes all manifestations of existence, in whatever form, and is paramount. From whatever viewpoint it is considered, the absence of life is nothingness. In a scientific sense, life includes man, animals, trees, plants and all things visible to the naked eye as well as the minute particles of matter that are its most elementary forms.

---

1 Sartre, J.-P., *Existentialism and Humanism*, London: Methuen, 1948.
2 The term 'humane condition' is an adaptation of the term 'the human condition' used to emphasise the paramount importance of moral values.
3 See *The Dialogues of Plato*, Jowett, B. (trans.), New York: Random House, 20th edn, 1937.

Truth is a moral value particularly relevant to the activities of the mind that is itself engaged in its eternal search. Truth, expressed in such derivatives as honesty, sincerity, good faith and trust, validates and guarantees the continuity of human relationships and of society itself.

Love is to the heart what Truth is to the mind. Love is a moral value that relates the human experience to all other humans, species and things. It expresses itself in a goodness that binds people together. To many, Love is the greatest of the *desiderata*, and felt as the greatest human need. Love as a moral value is here defined as a sympathetic awareness of another or others. It takes the form of an appreciation of the qualities of others and of the life of all things. It is sensitive to the external and internal beauty of all manifestations of life itself. It is the main motivation in the creation of harmonious relationships and of happiness, which is one of man's most constant searches.

To those who are existentialists or humanists, Life, Truth and Love may be accepted as moral values that are central to the human condition. They are all three *sui generis*, that is, they are unique and do not depend on other conditions

The argument for a caring society finds its justification in moral values. It relies on two simple propositions. The first proposition is that caring is not only an instinct present in nature, but is a moral value in itself. It is an expression of Love, and it is also through caring that genuine reality comes into the experience of Life. It takes very little for the caring instinct to manifest itself, whoever the other or others are, or whatever other forms of life or indeed objects. The caring instinct is a vehicle for the expression of moral values. It is the central argument of this text that public policy based on explicit moral values makes possible a fuller realisation of the caring instinct.

The second proposition follows from the first: given that caring is an instinct, sharing becomes a necessity. We live our lives as individuals but share them with those with whom the joys and trials of life are experienced. It is in the manner in which life is shared with others that it becomes a meaningful reality. In that sense, sharing is a moral value as well as an existential imperative. Caring may be seen as a self-satisfying experience, and as such it does not conflict with the sense of self biologically instilled through the survival instinct.[4] Sharing, on the other hand, may

---

4 Dawkins, R., *The Selfish Gene*, Oxford University Press, 1976.

conflict with the sense of self and hence be constrained. However, a caring society cannot exist unless the idea of sharing is generally accepted. Why we should willingly accept that view is part of the central argument of this text.

It will be shown that both caring and sharing exist naturally in the notion of the family as the fundamental unit of social structure. The idea that society is an extension of the family provides the springboard from which to discuss the ways in which a caring society may be empowered.

These points are discussed in the Part I, The Humane Condition, the term 'humane' expressing the moral values implicit in caring and sharing. It must be emphasised that the ideas discussed do not constitute an argument in favour of any specific religious belief, or indeed any other set of beliefs such as humanism, or any political credo such as socialism. It seeks to employ moral values as a basis for examining problems of society and evaluating policies aimed at improving the humane condition. One of the most important aspects of this debate concerns the Social Conscience and its role in providing value judgements of social and economic behaviour. Moral values have sovereign authority in all matters of judgement affecting society; they provide the essential jurisprudence for established law and accepted custom. The principal postulate on which this text relies is that the Social Conscience, as expressed in public opinion and in generally accepted beliefs, is and should be the sovereign authority, since it is founded on moral values. Support for this idea is derived from Durkheim who argued that moral laws, defined as social facts, imposed upon individuals a moral obligation to obey rules. Durkheim considered that society is something beyond us and something within us, and that when society is strongly integrated the moral laws (or social facts) hold individuals under its control.[5] The Social Conscience is thus the ultimate law.

The existing social structure reflects the influence of a market economy that has shaped society to the needs of industrial and financial capitalism. Caring and sharing are eroded in such a society. There is, in the collective memory, an experience of social misery, deprivation and brutality associated with the transformation

---

5 Emile Durkheim (1858-1917) is considered one of the founders of modern sociology. He introduced the concept of functionalism, which argues that the basis of an orderly society is the existence of a central value system that imposes common values on all its members. See Lukes, S., *Emile Durkheim, His Life and Work: A Historical and Critical Study*.

of an agrarian economy into a capitalist economy. Marked by this experience, European nations have retained a strong commitment to the idea of a social economy, manifested in government policies addressed to social programmes. The notion of welfare is entrenched in the political debate. In Great Britain, it led to the creation of the Welfare State, for which social objectives were political priorities. Most European countries adopted and still maintain extensive social programmes. Government policies, that are now orientated towards reducing commitments when budgeting expenditure, are tending to consider selective privatisation of some welfare activity. Part II, Empowering a Caring Society, examines how caring and sharing could be implemented in social policies, even within the constraining context of a market economy. The role of education is considered as an important means of bringing about a caring society. The market economy, based on the shareholder value criterion has social consequences that run counter to this aspiration. The role of government and of government policy is another aspect of this debate.

One of the major social problems of our times is the conflict between freedom and authority. Much of recent history reflects man's struggle to be free from oppressive authority. The French Revolution was a culminating point: Liberty, Equality and Fraternity were proclaimed as the moral values on which the new society was to be founded. This was the rallying cry for social change everywhere in Europe. It was most magnificently proclaimed in Beethoven's 9th Symphony, 'Ode to Joy', dedicated to freedom and the brotherhood of man. To this day, these three moral values are at the heart of what the French call *l'esprit républicain* (the republican spirit). That man should be free from oppression is universally conceded, but the need for order within society is also accepted as necessary to good government. Overfed by unthinking populism, freedom has degenerated to some extent into permissiveness, and the expression of authority in a demand for discipline or call to order seems to attract instant opposition. The tension between freedom and authority is an important aspect of the social debate and it is discussed in Part III.

Social change is a continuous process that is inspired by a number of reciprocal factors: the world of ideas, science, and changing technological, material and political circumstances. Are we in control of our destiny or at the mercy of forces beyond our control? Certainly, as the world gets smaller with the globalisation of the market economy, there is a risk that welfare policies will have lower priority than profit-making. The concentration of economic and hence military power in the hands of one nation, that dictates its law to the rest of the world and takes as bounty a wholly disproportionate percentage of all its natural resources for its own excessive consumption, may be seen as an alarming portent of a new form of oppression. The absorption of nations, with their own culture and history, into larger federations or unions governed by remote and bureaucratic authorities adds to concerns about the future of their newly gained freedom and, in some cases, their nationhood. From Communist empire to European Union, some Eastern European nations, such as Poland, worry about how these changes will impact on values for which they have fought, damaging their freedom of expression and sense of identity. Finally, the threat that climate change implies for the survival of life on Earth has created a general sense of foreboding and helplessness. The significance of these trends for caring and sharing in this wider context is discussed in Part IV.

It is hoped that the thoughts expressed in this book will interest the general reader, and that he will find in them a direct link with the keynote ideas that have fascinated so many illustrious thinkers in the past, from Plato, Aristotle and St Thomas Aquinas to Locke, Hume, Rousseau, Kant, Marx and Durkheim *et al.* The book is also addressed to members of religious congregations and those concerned with moral values.

Education is vital to empowering a caring society. There is now recognition of the need to restate the importance of ethics and morality in the teaching curriculum. It is hoped that this book will provide useful material for discussion. Education for citizenship has been adopted as an important orientation of education in schools. This book recognises caring and sharing as two of the most significant educational values. Many professional bodies, such as the British Medical Association, the Law Society and the Institute of Chartered Accountants are concerned with the moral values implicit in governance and transparency. This book may also be useful as a supplement to courses set by professional bodies which have introduced ethics into the curriculum.

PART I

THE HUMANE CONDITION

—1—
Living in Our Times

The expansion of the market economy is assuming global proportions. Insisting on free trade, unrestrained capitalism reaching out to all corners of the world imposes its own values, thereby altering human relationships and the structure of society. A relatively small number of influential financial groups dominate the international capital market and govern the global economy. Devoid of a Social Conscience and with little concern with moral values, it is driven by an obsession for wealth and seeks to gain control of world economic resources. This new world force reasons in terms of 'shareholder value' as the rationale for investing in economic development.

Against these trends, there is a caring society that is embedded in the Social Conscience and which is committed to the belief that wealth should be equitably shared and that the objective of society should be the well-being of all its members. Identity, social cohesion, sovereign authority and moral values are its four pillars. The most important social problems of our time reside in a loss of identity and social cohesion within society, the erosion of traditional moral values and the threat to sovereign authority reflected in the spirit of this age and the excessive permissiveness that abuses the legitimacy of new found freedom.

WE ARE LIVING in bewildering times. Fearful of the direction in which society is going, we are unhappy about many aspects of life, and prey to endless evil and misfortune. A climate of insecurity and agitation exacerbated by the information revolution has reduced the cushioning effects of space and time between events and their public awareness and appreciation. At the forefront of the diffusion of information to the public, the media have been instrumental in creating this climate of anxiety for much of the information that reaches the public emphasises bad rather than good news.

Rapid advances in scientific knowledge and technological progress are acting to change social and working conditions. Full employment has been abandoned as a social policy objective, the hazard of market conditions has created a pervasive sense of job insecurity in all classes of the population and traditional bonds of loyalty between the enterprise and its employees have been eroded.

The dominance of the market economy, its global expansion and the rationalisation of the activities of large multinational and supranational enterprises has, without doubt, had the most far-reaching impact on society. Traditionally the market place existed for the exchange of surpluses, and functioned within and as an adjunct to society. The global market economy, however, aims to produce surpluses, the prime objective being profit as a return on capital employed. Hence the social framework and its traditional values are transformed: they are shaped by money and its commercial logic. The profit imperatives of a relatively small circle of financiers who control the international capital market, and as such are influential in many large business corporations, govern the global economy.

Obstacles to global trade in the form of national boundaries are vanishing as nations are pushed into forming larger markets through economic and political unions. The migration of workers, the freedom of establishment and the transfer of production to low-cost countries create their own peculiar social problems. The development of a large international financial market has concentrated investment funds in the hands of powerful financial institutions, such as pension and investment funds. This new world force reasons in terms of the shareholder value criterion as the unique rationale for managing funds and evaluating business performance. It glorifies unrestrained capitalism and places wealth as its sole objective without regard for social and moral values.

Against these trends, there remains deeply embedded in the Social Conscience the notion of a caring society that earlier fought against widespread misery and poverty. This notion witnessed its apogee in the concept of the Welfare State in Great Britain. It represented different shared values and emphasised social justice as the basis for social cohesion. It remains a preoccupation in European political thinking today in the concept of the social economy and a continuing and age-old commitment to the belief that wealth should be shared and that the prime concern of government should be the well-being of all members of society.

As a consequence of the emergence of a global economy, the structure of society is being redefined, instilling different values and sowing the seeds of possible future social conflicts. Four broad sets of problems deserve attention in this context: loss of identity, weakening social cohesion, erosion of traditional moral values, and the blurring of the sovereign authority.

The Four Pillars of Society

Identity, social cohesion, shared moral values and sovereign authority may be seen as the four pillars on which our society is founded. They represent key problem areas within society; they are interdependent and each affects the other.

Identity
Identity is a stem concept for all areas of human knowledge, from the natural sciences to the social sciences, from philosophy to medicine, and from human to market behaviour. In a social sense, the meaning and the relevance of identity invoke a number of questions. As to its meaning, it may be asked whether it is real, substantial, imagined, acquired, created, symbolic, individual, public, shared, transferable and inheritable. All of these attributes may be found depending on the circumstances in which identity is the relevant concept. It is real in a physical sense, when referred to physical attributes. It is also real as a meaning in the Platonic sense. It may also be imagined, when used to define the qualities that it embodies. It may be symbolic when it is used to attach moral values to identity. Thus, identity as a meaning is a complex notion.

The relevance of identity is conditioned by the context in which it is understood and utilised. In this sense, it is also as diverse as the different circumstances in which it is used. As one of the pillars of a caring society, identity is a key concept on four levels. The first level is identity as attached to an individual as such: identity is important to his own sense of self. The second level is identity as attached to the family as the primary social unit in a caring society. The third level is identity of groups: in this connection it will be noted that the market economy, as well as a caring society, relies on identity. The identity of a corporation is separate from that of its owners, its employees and with whom it does business. Through communication of information and choice of brand names, it seeks to establish positive relationships with others, treating these relationships as part of 'goodwill' for its business. Finally, identity is fundamental to nationhood. The nation is the largest social unit with effective means, through the legal and administrative systems of the State, to implement social progress. Whenever identity is used in the context of social action, it signifies adherence to a social group by establishing common cause with its members.

Identity in the context of social theory, and hence in the context of this text, expresses the manner in which common qualitative properties are shared. These cover a wide spectrum of notions ranging from gender and race, to culture and nationality.

Identity expressed through social groupings, is one of mankind's basic needs. It is as necessary and as urgent as the need for affection, for it affords recognition and security. It is found by belonging to and identifying with a group. Problems within society arise whenever the identity of the group itself, or the identification of the individual with the group, is diluted or blurred for any reason so that there is segregation, a rift between those who belong and those who do not. Such problems usually provoke sharp reactions, which may be both defensive and aggressive; by threatening the integrity of the group, they may cause social unrest and instability, which will persist until acceptable and viable solutions are found. For the individual, these problems may lead to alienation or exclusion, resulting in insecurity as well as loss of economic advantages. Many social problems of our times arise from discrimination, segregation and exclusion, actual or perceived.

The compelling need for identity is as pervasive today as discrimination, and it takes as many forms as there are social groups. Nature, through parentage, creates a primary identity with immutable characteristics, such as race, colour and gender. It is evident that no moral judgement can be attached to identification based on these criteria. However, although such identification is a perfectly innocuous process in itself, it may bear the stigma of moral or value judgements. It is these judgements that typically lead to segregation and discrimination on the grounds of race, colour and gender, as well as religious, political or moral beliefs. They are the root causes of some of the most difficult problems in our society.

The family structure determines the social group into which the individual is born and with which he has his closest contact during the formative years of his life. If the family is a secure social group in which the father and the mother structure their lives and integrate their children, it will have a major influence on him in a variety of ways. From it he will derive a sense of physical well-being and self-confidence; it will determine his behaviour, beliefs and culture. For good or ill, the relationship within the family will have a psychological impact on the individual. A sense of alienation from the family is often an important factor in mental illness and social problems.

Beyond race, gender, colour, citizenship and family, social groups are mostly a matter of individual choice, insofar as circumstances allow choice. They may be groups of people with shared religious or political views, members of social, sporting and professional clubs, as well as groups with physical disabilities, or groups of the excluded and disadvantaged such as the poor and unemployed.

Once identification is established, an individual is grouped with others sharing the same characteristics. This enables the projection of a smaller group identity into a larger group identity, such as national identity, which Bloom[1] has characterised as:

> that paradigm condition in which a mass of people have made the same identification with the national symbols – have internalised the symbols of the nation – so that they may act as one psychological group when there is a threat to, or the possibility of enhancement of, these symbols of national identity.

It has been said that territory, culture, language, law, religion, history and race may all be factors in the creation of national identity. The universal tendency to develop collective identities, common to all forms of social groups, expresses a primal need for loyalty or cohesiveness as protection against external threats. The nation state, the largest grouping, offers its members a stronger sense of protection, belonging and even personal identity than any alternative large group. It may be suggested that misgivings in these regards among citizens of member countries of the European Community with the prospect of further integration through a European Constitution, which threatens national identity by attempting to create a European identity. The fear of loss of nationhood, together with the perception of the European Commission as an autocratic body pursuing its own policies and objectives, and which appears undemocratic, has made that body distrusted and disliked by most citizens of member nations. In addition, the enlargement by a group of Eastern European nations, with the prospect of the inclusion of Turkey, an Islamic nation, has magnified the sense of physical and economic insecurity in the Western European group.

Social identity, of which national identity is one specific grouping around qualitative facts, not only integrates individuals sharing common characteristics but also imposes on them an expected behavioural response, or a behavioural initiative, to given

---

1 Bloom, W., *Personal Identity, Group Identity, National Identity*, Cambridge University Press, 1990.

circumstances that conform to national symbols. Groupism, therefore, is a central aspect of human evolutionary psychology. Nations and societies are in-groups on the largest scale, formed by multiple subsidiary groups. They will regard other nations and societies as out-groups.

Social identity plays an important role in in-group/out-group relations, the distribution of resources, self-categorisation and expectations of behaviour. It is an automatic redefinition of 'self' in terms of shared group membership.

Ethnic grouping, or the formation of groups with genetic similarities, is a central source of values and a mechanism for providing individuals with identity. Such groups cannot be absorbed through integration with other ethnic groups in a nation state.

It follows that identity in a social context is a significant bonding between individuals acting as a group, from which flows a number of behavioural implications. It results in an immediate mutual recognition of each in the other, a recognition that extends to all members of the group. This mutual recognition of the self in the others bonds the members of the group through an instinctive acceptance of each other. To identify with another person or a group of persons is also a commitment, which includes sharing the beliefs, symbols or purposes that are subsumed in the identity. It is this acceptance that will incite and support a unified group behavioural response. It is this acceptance that will motivate the instinct to care and the commitment to share and so contribute to nationhood.

The awareness and recognition of the dynamics of group behaviour is a very large area of research, covering many different areas of interest. Groupism, as a primary human behavioural pattern, is the readiness to form groups round any perceived or imagined differences in bodily or mental characteristics, and to this end almost any pretext will serve. Those who consider themselves similar in some respect tend to aggregate, to form a herd or flock, and in so doing are immediately distinguished from those who identify themselves with other groups.

The market economy has also found the concept of identity of great strategic importance to corporate business, for creating employee and customer loyalty and a sympathetic awareness of corporate action in a community context. At the same time, it serves in competing against other corporations in the same area of business. Corporate identity is reflected in the corporate image that it seeks to communicate and in the brand names attached to products. Considerable expenditure is devoted annually by big business to publicity aimed at creating a favourable public image. The objective of corporate directors is the successful management of business with a view to maintaining and improving shareholder value. Shareholder value is significantly influenced by the value of the goodwill attached to the corporate identity and to its brands by the public, as reflected in the share price quoted on the Stock Exchange.

It follows that group identity has two sets of distinct and opposing influences on social behaviour. The first is a unifying influence, creating groups with identical characteristics and motivations; the second is an incitement to segregation into different groups through a process of discrimination and thus alienation.

Group identification leads into inter-group competition, which is another aspect of group psychology. Implicitly, a permanent fracture in the social fabric caused by the co-existence within one state of different ethnic groups is a considerable obstacle to the creation of a political state with a unified political programme, particularly with respect to social harmony. Many states are the historical consequences of wars that have redefined boundaries established on racial or cultural factors as determinants of nationhood. Internal conflicts attributable to such fractures persist in many countries. The resolution of these conflicts, through a political intra-group consensus, even if superficial, has enabled most states to survive. In others, civil conflict and wars have erupted into hatred and bloodshed rendering reconciliation a near-impossible mission.

According to Anderson,[2]

> unlike smaller groups, nations are imagined communities, because members of even the smallest nations do not know most of their fellow-members, they will never meet them ... even hear from them, and yet in the mind of each member of a nation lives the ideal of national togetherness.

The existence of a nation is an awareness of a shared virtual reality. This leads to an interesting paradox, which is that the real influence on behaviour is an imagined or unreal condition. Having imagined a state on which to base identity, and in which to invest allegiance, there follows an imagined and symbolic justification for such allegiance, framed in terms of the moral values attached to the 'national character'. National character is a strong and unified set of beliefs about behaviour, especially expected behaviour, that

---

2 Anderson, B., *Imagined Communities: Reflections on the Origin and Spread of Nationalism*, Amsterdam: Centre for Asian Studies, 1983; and *Long Distance Nationalism: World Capitalism and the Rise of Identity Politics*, Amsterdam: Centre for Asian Studies, 1992.

adds morality to the logic of reason in making an identity classification. It claims the benefits of the higher moral ground for the nation by virtue of the moral values reflected in the national character, compared with those of others nations. Consequently, the other out-groups are invariably disadvantaged when comparisons are made. This strengthens the motivation towards in-group thinking or parochialism, rather than towards out-group concerns, such as internationalism or universalism. This sentiment is very strongly present in the English, French and Germans, who have warred with each other for most of the last thousand years and who continue to perpetuate their peculiar symbolisms.[3] In an international context, in which some congruence is needed in behaviour, the attempted creation of a European identity has the appearance of superlative comedy as national characters act out excruciatingly funny theatrical performances that would have gratified Shakespeare himself. Thereby is the sublime reduced to the ridiculous.

As Crick[4] has pointed out, the sense of nationhood represented in moral values, the notion of citizenship that is attached to English history and English institutions, and the role of schools in creating social cohesion through the teaching of citizenship, have implications for the current debate about identity within the European Union. The influence of history on identity and nationhood cannot be shared with other nations and subsumed in a new European identity. The Economic and Social Research Council[5] recognised the special relevance of history to identity and nationhood in setting up the BRISHIN (British Island Stories: History, Identity and Nationhood) project in 2001.

The large movements of populations during the last century caused by wars, persecution, poverty and a desire for a better life, have brought into prominence the social problems consequent on integrating immigrants into societies with a strongly established sense of identity based on race, tradition, culture and history. Generally immigration has provoked discrimination against

---

3 It is noteworthy that, some sixty years after the end of World War II, the portrayal of the German soldier as a goon still serves to delight English audiences.
4 Crick, B., 'The Sense of Identity of the Indigenous British' in Parekh, B. (ed.), *British National Identity in a European Context*, New Community special issue, Vol 21, No. 2, 1995, pp.167-82.
5 The central aim of BRISHIN is to explore empirically and theoretically the conceptual relationship between history, nationhood and state-formation, and to consider the implications for the re-configuration of British national identity. The project engages with contemporary debates across Britain on history, identities, nationalism, school history teaching, citizenship, heritage and the role of the press.

newcomers and the process of integration has been hampered by the tendency of some immigrant groups to retain their own identity. This may be observed in older host countries populated through immigration, sometimes through open-door policies, as was the case in the USA and Australia, sometimes through a tradition of accepting refugees as happened in France. Migrants with pronounced differences from the host population, particularly of race or colour, have had much more difficulty in integrating, than those with attributes similar to the host population. Their relative exclusion has remained evident over a prolonged period of presence. Anti-discrimination laws and initiatives favouring minorities in housing, employment and social welfare have often served to worsen anti-immigrant sentiments in the host population. Such laws and policies may create a reverse sense of discrimination when the host population is made to feel disadvantaged compared to migrants. The resulting tension may break out as public violence and lead to the creation of no-go areas and ghettoes. Where immigrant groups are strongly identified with a particular faith such as Islam or Judaism, identity may lead to long-lasting discrimination through the reverse process by which such groups voluntarily preserve their own identity and refuse to integrate in a social and cultural sense.

It has taken the USA at least two centuries to build a nation through immigration. By contrast, the Europe Union is attempting to create one in a relatively short period of time by uniting countries that have their own strong identities. There remains in member countries a sentimental relic of long-lasting hostility and suspicion which may not be eradicated for many years. The desire of political leaders to press ahead with the creation of a European nation, sometimes without the democratic consent of the populations concerned, and frequently in the face of substantial opposition from public opinion, may eventually lead to popular revolt by groups such as farmers who see in European expansion a threat to their own existence and livelihood. This occurred in 2005 when the people of France and the Netherlands, called upon to vote in referendums on the proposed European Constitution backed by their political leaders and elites, rejected the proposal to the astonishment of the other member states.

This crisis has revealed the fragility of the European Union itself. Such is the disparity of culture and tradition in the enlarged European Union that one wonders where and when a break-up point will be reached. Integration is being forced through at such a pace that nations feel and fear the loss of their identity within a new nation. This dilution of national identity may well be the fatal flaw in the European ambition.

At a micro-level, the fragmentation of the family and the prevalence of divorce have shattered the security found traditionally in the family. Historically, an important social distinction existed between the formal marriage, that guaranteed the continuity of the family and the transmission of property to heirs in a continuum of succession, and a simple concubinage, that had no legal substance and existed outside the family structure. The Romans had a clear view of the importance of family and recognised the two forms of relationship. Property and civil rights preserved the family much as divorce laws have destroyed it by facilitating separation and divorce and providing for the redistribution of family property and alimony rights. The formal marriage, which our judicial system inherited from the Roman *Jus Civile*, was intended to preserve the identity of the family. Property rights and the legal protection that it afforded to its members were the hallmarks of family identity. Concubinage is replacing marriage among the younger members of society, who are rejecting the rigorous obligations of marriage as a long-term commitment. As a result, the long-term integrity and stability of the family unit is being replaced by relationships which have their initial logic in sexual attraction, often intense but of short duration, and susceptible to termination without legal process or enduring obligations. The resulting deprivations experienced in the mono-parental family, both parent and child, but particularly the child, are widely recognised as major ills of our times.

Social Cohesion
As we have seen, identity is of primary importance in understanding the nature and psychology of social groups, showing the reasons why they are formed. Since man is fundamentally a social being, the manner in which members of a social group relate to each other, how their common interests are shared, and how the group functions in effectively attaining its goals depends very much upon the level of social cohesion within the group.

The term 'cohesion' in a social context is currently as widely discussed as the concept of identity. The reason for such an intensity of interest lies precisely in the sense of loss of identity and of social cohesion created by the mass migration of people of different race, history, tradition, culture, religion and language.

Homogeneity has ceded to pluralism; latent conflicts exist within social groups, with a potential for open violence. This important problem is extensively discussed in Chapter 8. The pressure for merging national identity into wider concepts, such as a European identity has also served to exacerbate the general feeling of insecurity. Finally, the concentration of global economic and military power into the hands of the USA. and its espousal of a new political philosophy which brings an aggressive neo-conservatism to foreign policy, in which a doctrinal war on terrorism is being waged, has thrown the entire world into the reality of a new form of conflict.

There are few precise definitions of social cohesion. It is generally assumed that its meaning is implicit in the context of the discussion. *The Oxford English Dictionary* states that the root verb, 'to cohere', 'indicates to cleave or stick together, said of parts or of mass ... to unite or remain united in action ... to be congruous or consistent. Cohesion is the action or condition of cohering.' In a scientific sense, 'cohesion is the force with which like molecules of a body cleave together'.

The relationship between identity and social cohesion may be explained as consisting of realities or attributes that are alike in individuals and that bind or hold them together by the mutual attraction of their common or shared likeness, a force that is called cohesion. Unlike the law of magnetism under which like poles repel and unlike poles attract, social cohesion exerts a converse influence. The presence of unlikeness or absence of identity prevents cohesion; at best it will lead to indifference, at worst to rejection through segregation and conflict. The economic, social and political problems that are manifest in pluralist societies imply establishing limits for social cohesion and finding ways of reducing conflict through mediation.[6]

Shared moral values, acting through the Social Conscience, act naturally to foster social cohesion. Social cohesion reflects the qualities of fair play and sharing in relationships between individuals or between groups. It also guarantees the stability and durability of the ties that create and maintain co-existence within groups. But the fundamental moral value implicit in fair play and sharing is that of caring for others, as reflected in both personal behaviour and public policy at a national level. A highly significant

---

6 For a fuller discussion see Berger, P.L. (ed.), *The Limits of Social Cohesion: Conflict and Mediation in Pluralist Societies*, Colorado, Westview Press, 1999.

aspect of identity, derived from parentage and associated with nationality, that affects social cohesion is the sense of citizenship. A commitment to citizenship as a moral value is significant for social cohesion. But, the greater force in making for social cohesion is the instinct of caring.

At the family level, cohesion exists in the bonding of husband and wife, which is the cement holding the family together in a happy, stable and permanent environment in which children can grow and develop their own personalities under the most propitious conditions. The caring family shares basic needs such as food and other essentials of life. It acts against exclusion that is consequent upon individual poverty. It may extend beyond the basic unit of parents and children to the concept of the extended family, which includes grandparents, brothers and sisters and their children and even more distant cousins. Its effectiveness as a social unit lies in the sense of belonging to a group that has a high sense of social responsibility to its members, and the moral obligation of caring and sharing which is also the essence of a welfare society. The kith and kin relationship effectively integrates its members, granting to each customary rights and imposing on each customary duties. Importantly, authority resides in the shared collective memory and consensus for punishing wrongdoing. In some extended families elderly members enjoy the confidence and respect of younger members, and when problems arise their counsel is sought and observed. In effect, there exists a rudimentary form of government, albeit non-democratic in the modern sense.

Economic progress, through the market economy, has in many different ways significantly eroded family ties and altered the very nature of family relationships. The shift from rural life to industrial life marked the beginning of this process. The dependence of family members on employment and on earned income to cover basic needs has steadily grown as these have increased. Media advertising today fuels consumerism to such an extent that the family is enslaved to a level of spending which earlier generations could never have imagined.

Until recent times, the father provided for the needs of his family by being employed while the mother stayed at home to care for the children. This was considered as conforming to the nature of man and woman, and the best way for bringing up children within a happy and caring family. Today one income is often insufficient to provide for family needs, compelling mothers to seek work to balance the family budget. This may take its toll: an absent father, a working mother and children abandoned to the care of others or to their own devices are destructive to family life. It may also be a root cause of a host of social problems.

Whilst many women have welcomed the chance of having a career that continues beyond marriage, the financial independence they gain through the market economy may be detrimental to family relationships. Firstly, some women have been made less tolerant of the burden of caring for others that married life imposes on wives and mothers. Secondly, the wish to have a child is no longer subordinated to the economic and social need of being married. Many single mothers and divorced women are bringing up children by themselves. The economic and social forces that united men and women in marriage no longer compel it.

Undoubtedly the breakdown of marriages, under the pressure of consumerism and changing expectations with respect to married life, has resulted in increasing divorce rates, facilitated by legal systems that have responded to demands for easier, less costly and more rapid divorces. A divorce, however, is a legal solution in which there are no winners: all are losers. Legal costs, property arrangements and maintenance obligations are heavy burdens. The survivors live as fathers who have lost daily contact with their children and as mothers struggling to bring up a family alone. Children may be scarred somewhere in their psyche by the loss of one important formative influence – the love of a father for his children or the love of a mother for her children, and that love which thrives in a happy family.

Children, as they grow into adolescence, may lack a sense of personal security, self-discipline and self-respect. The problem of authority over children at home and at school is one which daily concerns parent and teachers. In some of the worst affected cases, there is a risk of a slide into homelessness, alcoholism, drug abuse and a life blighted by delinquency. Numerous authoritative studies indicate that widespread drug-taking, violence, dishonesty and other criminal behaviour is pervasive throughout society and symptomatic of the pressures that are exerted on adults by consumerism.

Another serious threat to the traditional family concept is the newly legislated right for same-sex couples to enjoy the benefits of legal marriage and with it the right to bring up children in an unnatural sexual environment. In the case of a lesbian couple, there would be two women, one with the behavioural role of a male, the other as a natural female; in the case of a male homosexual couple there would be two males, one with the behavioural role of a female, the other as a natural male. In either case, an innocent child is submitted to a blurred sexual environment and may well be handicapped emotionally as a result of difficulties of identification. Whether same-sex relationships are the right context for bringing up children is a moral issue that should be judged by the criterion of the well-being of the children. However, in the present climate of political correctness, the demand for rights over children from a vocal minority is succeeding. Legislators are betraying the evident moral rights of children, by throwing them without their consent into such ambiguous parental situations. Political expediency and a distorted concept of political correctness will have deprived children of future generations of their natural rights

At national level, social cohesion is often referred to the concept of nationhood. Crick[7] has argued in favour of the citizenship concept in this regard. Clearly this concept looks beyond existing pluralism to an overriding unifying force that lies in a common acceptance of citizenship. It should be noted that the concept of national identity through a sense of nationhood, however defined, can be a potent force for evil as well as for good. In the strong form of aggressive nationalism, it has been a major cause of wars for centuries. The belief in the *Herrenvolk* or master race that Hitler inspired in the German population certainly created a high level of social cohesion, but led to intensive discrimination and persecution of 'non-Aryan'[8] people.

The key to the effective functioning of a society that comprises different races and cultures, all sharing a common economic and social environment, is obedience to the same moral values and an adherence to accepted and common rules of law. This condition is much more complex and may require the sharing of beliefs, such as religious and political commitments. Where similar beliefs exist, there is a social consensus expressed in shared moral values that gives stability to society. Where there is disagreement within society as to moral values or other beliefs, there is likely to be conflict, the depth of such conflict depending on the strength of commitment to those beliefs. Dissent gathers under demands for religious freedom and political rights. History is strewn with the experience of religious conflicts and this problem seems to be

---

7 Crick, B. (ed.), *Citizens: Towards a Citizenship Culture*, The Political Quarterly Publishing Co., Ltd, 2001.
8 Among the infamous tests of Aryanism or Germanic racial purity were physical attributes such as the shape of heads and other facial characteristics.

recurring today as fundamental elements in religious groups become fanatical in their political actions.

Moral Values
Those attributes that have to do with the culture of society, its humanity and the quality of its civilisation, as manifested in the actions of its leaders and the behaviour of its members, are the moral values that are mutually shared and observed. Arguably the most important social problem of our times resides in the spirit of this age, its moral values and its sense of being. Identity and social cohesion may be seen as concerned with society in a structural sense. By contrast, shared moral values reflect the spiritual quality or moral climate. Insofar as these values relate to social groups, their cohesion and the identification of members with the group and with each other, they may be described as the Social Conscience. These moral values are enshrined in law and in custom that determine expectations as to conduct.

The Social Conscience of groups associated with different cultures is found embedded in religious teachings that establish clear moral values for the conduct of daily life in obedience to Divine Law. Holy Books, such as the Old Testament, the New Testament and the Koran provide detailed lessons and precepts that reflect the Social Conscience in its continuity from early times to the present day. The Ten Commandments handed down to Moses not only define the relationship of obedience to God but also those basic social rules, which have retained their authority under law to this day. By defining God as Infinite Goodness or Love, the first commandment, to have no other God, means that the absolute moral rule is the expression of Love, or goodness in action, which is fundamental to the Social Conscience.

From a religious standpoint, God may be perceived as embodying Life, Truth and Love, from which are derived the fundamental values that form the Social Conscience. At the heart of social relationships are truth, honesty, sincerity, love and caring for one's neighbour. The taking of life, stealing and other dishonesty are all severely punished as transgressions of the fundamental values that form the Social Conscience.

Truth, honesty and sincerity are imperative rules in all relationships of whatever nature. In the conduct of business in the market economy, or in disputes arising in any context, verifying that these rules have been observed is the first step in formalising a judgement. The attestation may be in the form of swearing an oath in legal proceedings, or signing to confirm the sincerity of a tax declaration, or any other statement used by another in reliance upon its truth, for example, the audit certification issued by auditors of published financial statements by corporate entities. The absence of truth, honesty or sincerity is a fatal flaw carrying severe penalties.

Religious teachings are clearly more than exhortations to respect the fundamental moral values relating to truth, honesty and sincerity. They are remarkable for their concern with those moral values that remain at the heart of our Social Conscience today, namely, seeking after good, loving our neighbour and obeying the moral law. They extend the notion of love for others in the duty of care in its multifarious legal forms. They are also at the root of the notion of a caring society that has its expression in government policies concerned with social welfare. They also reflect concern that behaviour in a market economy should not transgress the Social Conscience.

Until relatively recent times, the Church was the major actor against poverty. In modern times, states have formally recognised social rights to health care, housing, education, employment and pensions. The Welfare State, as established in the United Kingdom in the aftermath of World War II, was without doubt the most powerful expression of social concern and the concept of caring in society.

However, the Welfare State has not survived the 20th century unscathed. The partial retreat from it began with the first oil shock to strike Western industrial society following the Yom Kippur War of 1973. An embargo by the oil-producing nations resulted in a sevenfold increase in the oil price from about $4 a barrel to some $30 a barrel in a few weeks. The resulting financial crisis marked the restoration of profitability as the unique objective of the business firm. Eventually, this notion was enshrined in the concept of shareholder value, which has became the criterion for evaluating business decisions in terms of their impact on the value of the firm to shareholders. Governments once committed to social welfare programmes as central to their political platforms are adopting different views of their social role in a market economy. The market economy demands less government and more private enterprise. Social programmes are being submitted to the logic of the market economy. Some governments, concerned with the financial burden of welfare programmes, are actively considering their transfer to the private sector through privatisation. Access to education, health, housing and pensions may in future be limited by the ability to pay. The Social Conscience is in a state of crisis and the gap between rich and poor, the winners and losers, is becoming disturbingly visible.

Sovereign Authority
The role of sovereign authority is to recognise and render effective the Social Conscience, not only in the manner in which it acts as a governing body but also in the rules of law that are enacted under its authority. Sovereign authority exists within society as its Social Conscience: it acts to ensure the protection of its identity and the maintenance of social cohesion which, when moral values are shared, creates strong ties within groups. Society at large and social groups of whatever nature, seek to establish rules of conduct based on consensus. To ensure that behaviour conforms to the Social Conscience, groups delegate regulatory powers to a representative authority, in which such powers are vested. In small social units, such as the family, this representative authority is the head of the family, who traditionally was the father. The representative authority concept is found in all social units – the tribe has a chieftain, the enterprise has a president or chief executive officer and the nation has a head of state. The trust placed by society in the representative authority that reflects the Social Conscience is also associated with the belief that, not only will it be the ultimate arbiter for settling conflicts, but also that its action will take a benevolent form and be for the good of society. Accordingly, that authority has delegated powers to create rules as the need arises, but, in carrying out its regulatory functions, there is the expectation that it will act as a trustee for the Social Conscience with respect to shared moral values. Should this perception change, then relations between the representative authority and social groups could become strained, leading to political problems and social instability.

Many social problems have their origin in the manner in which society relates to the representative authority, and how consensus is reached and enforced. At the family level, for example, the concept of the head of the family as residing in the ultimate authority of the father may be contested. This development has been strongly marked in Western society with its debate over women's rights. The fragmentation of authority within the family has had a serious impact on its cohesion and has weakened one element of identity important to the well-being of its individual members. Likewise, at national level, when the link between the population as a defined social group and its representative authority weakens or is blurred for any reason, there emerge problems of identity, consensus and trust in the commitment of the representative authority to the interests of its constituency.

Movements of populations across national boundaries are fragmenting the cohesion of traditional social groups, particularly those based upon racial identity as well as cultural tradition. At the same time there has been a revival of strong religious affiliations as the basis for social identification.

The coexistence of groups with their own strong religious identity undermines national social cohesion, and the problem of integration becomes even more difficult when racial and religious elements are combined to create barriers between different social groups. European countries that have recently experienced relatively high levels of immigration are facing real difficulties in trying to integrate migrants. When racial and religious identification is pervasive and strongly defined, migrant communities may not understand, recognise and fully respect the laws and values of the host country.

A major global problem affecting many nations is the emergence of conflict, often in a violent form, particularly conflict between social groups based on religious identity. On a much larger scale, it threatens to divide the world's population across religious boundaries. The expansion of a radical form of Islam, drawing on a constituency in Arab and Asian populations representing nearly a quarter of the world's population, has brought about a state of war with the much smaller population that identifies its interests with the USA.

The coalition and coalescence of a large number of states within the framework of large political and economic units, such as the expanded European Union, threatens to disrupt completely the link between individual representative authorities and their populations. The fundamental need for an identifiable authority, the need for it to be representative of the social group from which it derives its powers, the need for consensus over the sphere of delegation and the manner in which power is delegated and the need for transparency in its actions and answerability for them, are all essential elements of social cohesion.

Conclusion
We are witnessing in our times radical and profound changes in the moral environment that characterised society for much of its

history as regards the concepts of caring for others, loving our neighbours and observing the moral law that is implied in these values. The changes in the moral climate brought about by the globalisation of the world economy have enshrined shareholder value as the cornerstone of business policy, have endowed it with moral justification and have made economic growth, defined as expanding income, the *summum bonum*. The translation and expression of well-being only in this singular dimension of expanding income has given money and the culture associated with it a central place in our world of ideas, and made it the measure of success in personal experience.

The market economy and the shareholder value concept by which it is driven have undermined the notion of the caring society. The diktats of the market economy have dehumanised the business enterprise by eliminating from the process of decision-making those human considerations that are so much part of man's emotional and psychological well-being.

The real crisis of living in our times may be seen as a weakening of the four pillars of society: identity, social cohesion, shared moral values and sovereign authority. The tendency for national unity to fracture into sub-groups with their own specific interests, which is natural to larger and expanded social units such as the nation, has become more marked with uncontrolled and uncontrollable immigration. Traditional points of fracture, such as class distinctions created groups that were otherwise homogeneous with respect to race, colour, history, language, culture and shared moral values. The differences were of manageable proportions. In particular, national symbols, such as King and Country, the Flag and shared beliefs in national virtues and national pride, were effective in gathering together different groups in a strong sense of national unity. The loss of a sense of nationhood in pluralistic societies, in which conflict characterises contact between peoples, who see themselves as distinctively different and form strongly entrenched subcultures, has made it difficult to establish a unifying social consensus. Attention is concentrated on observed differences as causes of dissent and conflict. Much social effort is diverted towards explanation and debate which fail to convince and are ineffective in overcoming entrenched antagonisms. Social cohesion has ceded to social conflict, in which all parties justifiably claim to be victims of discrimination. Moral issues and their influence on the Social Conscience are fudged. The links between different subgroups which once established effective and enduring social cohesion, expressed in the notion of nationhood, are no longer effective in overcoming divisiveness. It is, however, the loss of faith in political leaders as trustees of the Social Conscience that has severely damaged the respect for representative authority. The persistent betrayal of the Social Conscience by political elites, the corruptive abuse of political influence for personal interests, and the prevalence of government spin to manipulate information with the sole intent to deceive, have served to rupture the vital link between nation and government: political leaders are no longer the trusted representative authorities for the Social Conscience.

—2—

A Caring Society in a Market Economy

The co-existence of a caring society within a market economy poses two fundamental questions. Can a caring society exist in a market economy? Is a market economy sustainable, where it denies man's fundamental nature and need to care and to share? These moral values are enshrined in family life.

The origin of this dilemma lies in the English Enlightenment and its beliefs about human nature. Adam Smith declared that 'man, led by an invisible hand and pursuing his own interests, frequently promoted that of society, an end that was no part of his intention'. In arguing for free trade, Bentham pleaded that 'every man was the best judge of his own advantage and should be allowed to pursue it without hindrance'. The social ills that were the consequences of 'laissez-faire' eventually led to state intervention to reconcile individual freedom with the social objectives of a caring society, reviving in this way Rousseau's concept of the social contract and leading to the notion of the Welfare State. The enduring nature of a caring society is that caring is a natural sentiment. For that reason, the resolution of the dilemma posed in this chapter is to discover how it may be released as an effective force in social action.

LIVING IN OUR TIMES is conditioned by a set of complex problems that earlier societies did not experience and which are themselves largely the product of technological changes and the rapid evolution of the market economy. The problematical question that needs to be addressed is: 'Can a caring society exist in a market economy?' A further question of importance falls for discussion: 'Is a market economy sustainable when it denies man's fundamental nature and need for caring and for sharing?'

The advent of capitalism, as an economic system, focuses on capital, its deployment and management in the production of goods and services within a market economy, and the distribution of income that attributes profit to capital. It has resulted in a dichotomy in society between what has been described as the market economy and the social economy, reflecting the differing and opposing interests of those engaged in profit-seeking and those concerned with welfare and moved by broader social and human considerations.

The earlier development of capitalism in Western society provoked a conflict with the ruling and pervasive religious ethic. That ethic was essentially catholic in character and much concerned with the provision of moral rules for a human experience sublimated to God's intentions for man. In particular, for nascent markets of the time, this conflict centred on such problems as the notion of the 'just price' and the practice of usury. Prior to the conversion of Rome to Catholicism under the Emperor Constantine, Aristotle had written on these problems, which remained much under discussion throughout the Middle Ages, the writings of St Thomas Aquinas being significant as regards the early development of commercial capitalism occurring at that time. The Reformation and the Protestant ethic freed Western society from such considerations and England, which underwent successive economic revolutions, such as the enclosure movement of the 16th century and the Industrial Revolution of the 18th century, rapidly grew in wealth and prosperity.

If capitalism resulted in economic progress and the increase in the wealth of the nation, it also had distressing social effects on society itself and in particular through the cruel and widespread poverty that it inflicted on the working classes. It is not surprising that, whereas England successfully achieved great economic power under capitalism, the social conditions that had prevailed in a heretofore agrarian and stable society underwent a dramatic change. The rise of the towns and factories, urban poverty, workhouses and child labour were the cruel features of a society that neither Thomas More could have anticipated in his *Utopia*, nor Milton have imagined as his thoughts moved him from *Paradise Lost* to *Paradise Regained*.

Those 'dark satanic mills', which were the torture chambers of generations of textile workers in Lancashire's pleasant land, inspired horror and protest. To this day, the tales of Charles Dickens vividly remind us of man's fate during this period, when unprotected from and exposed to rapacious capitalism. Public opinion among the middle classes inspired early discussions about the nature of society under capitalism. Alternative production methods, such as workers' co-operatives and work methods introduced experimentally by philanthropic manufacturers, as well as concern for education and health of the working classes, were manifestations of opposition to the social ills associated with capitalism. The Socialist ethic had its earliest expression in England, with the writing of E. Jones, and later with those of Marx and Engels. During the same period, Newman and others sketched out the core elements of what later became the concept of social welfare. It was also during this period that the working classes began to unite in the form of Combinations, that later took the legal form of Trade Unions. The Co-operative movement, born in Rochdale, was another aspect of the search for a social alternative to capitalism that went on to extend its influence into the heartland of capitalism through the mutualism movement and the development of mutual insurance companies and the Penny Banks. Some industrialists tried to give capitalism a social character by associating their employees with them in their enterprise and men such as Ruskin created the concept that was later developed in labour laws as the principle of worker participation. They inscribed their name in the history of their time and left the legacy of a hope as yet unfulfilled. By the beginning of the 20th century, these social movements lent united support to the emergence of the Labour Party that reflected a Social Conscience strongly rooted in a caring and sharing society. Socialism is now a major political force in most European countries. Its core philosophy is the need for a strong social economy and state intervention to control the excesses of capitalism.

Today, the country that offers the most divisive model for choice between capitalism and socialism is the USA, where in the midst of wealth and abundance, a substantial proportion of society lives below the subsistence level and has a restricted access to basic social services. Those Eastern European countries that are currently moving from a socialist economy to a capitalist economy are also seeing the appearance of similar social problems.

Living in our times is proof that progress in knowledge and science has not solved the real problem of society, namely people living together in the human experience of sharing and caring. The realisation of a social utopia is a dream that continues to inspire social reformers.

For the purpose of this chapter, the segregation of man's social environment, characterised by the interdependence of each with the other within society, from his economic environment, characterised by a conflicting relationship with the other for the resources essential to life, represents a dramatic schism that is the first important cause of social conflict.

The Nature of a Caring Society
The family is the primary form of a society based on caring and sharing. This notion of caring takes place in an affectionate context, which is an expression of mutual concern and a vital emotional need for all individuals.

The traditional family assumes a social character in which there exists a natural hierarchy of relationships. To this day, in many cultures there is an ordered interdependence between family members looking for leadership and guidance from an elder, who has the moral authority over individual members and is able to ensure discipline within the group and so ensure social harmony.

In most parts of the world, the influence of the traditional family remains considerable. In particular, the extended family system holds sway in most of the developing world. Founded on the notion of caring and sharing, its members share family resources and enjoy its protection in a manner that even the Welfare State in Britain and similar systems in other European countries have not been able to achieve.

It is in recent times and only in Western societies that the family structure has undergone radical change. The ties that maintained the extended family as an effective social unit have weakened considerably. As a social unit, the extended family in Western society has been replaced by the nuclear family, limited to the micro-social unit defined by the coexistence of a father, mother and their children.

The traditional family provides the best illustration for understanding the human and social needs within society. In that sense, the family may be considered as the basic element of a social structure and society at large as merely its extension. It follows that the twin notions of caring and sharing, which act to bind the family together, should be at the philosophical core of political and social objectives for enhancing the sense of community in society and for the promotion of welfare policies. Thus, these notions suggest that the family is the ideal micro-model for conceiving a national social framework based on welfare. The understanding of living in our times begins with the family that widens into larger structures that are at the roots of nationhood.

Focusing on the family structure as a model for developing nation-wide welfare policies based on the principle of caring and sharing is helpful also in understanding a further important aspect of family relationships of dependence and interdependence. In effect, although man lives as a social being within the family, he is also conditioned by his biological self, which is instinctive and influences his behaviour towards others.

The first step towards a caring and sharing society depends on the existence of a sense of community and willingness to care for and share with others. Religious teachings explain that God, manifested as Love, is the supreme influence and the greatest good. Love, as realised at the human level, is seen by many as the greatest happiness that life can offer. Romantic literature and popular music place love at the heart of its concerns. Love may also be defined as an attitude of sympathetic awareness for others. It is neither angelism nor evangelism that motivates the argument that seeking good is a social objective of the first importance. Rather, it is a conviction that it is the overriding purpose in living and its most worthy cause.

The strongest biological instinct attached to life itself is the survival instinct. It is noteworthy that the action of the family is to unite a group of individuals who may be so self-driven that the potential conflict between the self of one member and the other selves within the family is sublimated to the interest of the grouped selves, namely the family. An understanding is needed of the reasons and the manner in which this sublimation is achieved through a sense of community and of how a caring society is able to function effectively in the interest of all its members. This poses the question: 'What is the compelling force that leads the self to sublimate its own interest to the interest of another or others?'

It is the survival or the self-interest aspect of man's behaviour upon which capitalism is founded as a social system. From this perspective, it may be argued that the very success of a market economy based on capitalism is the appeal to self and the creation of a competitive society in which each competes with the other for economic resources. Rousseau saw the origin of inequality as arising when man began to form society and men competed with each other. Life then becomes a lottery in which the strongest and the most able command the greater share. The weakest and the less able attract attention only by reason of their poverty and eventually may rely only on what is left of charitable sentiment. Hobbes saw society as a covenant against savagery; Plato and Rousseau believed that a just society was one in which everyone was in his right place. Rousseau argued further that men might recover their freedom through a social contract.

It is because the family instils an affectionate and reasoned awareness of others that the basic biological instinct is converted into a social force that ensures the well-being and survival of the family.

Such is the belief in the market economy, based on capitalism, in Western industrial society that it would be rare to find a political platform arguing in favour of a caring society based on the sacrifice of self to the benefit of others. Clever politicians have long realised that the winning platform that attracts most votes is that which promises to give most to voters and demands the least by way of sacrifice. Political success is based on the winning force of selfishness and not on love for others. This suggests that the political viability of a caring society depends on the alternative that it presents when the market economy is ultimately submerged and overcome by the social problems that are the consequences of its inevitable expansion. Plato himself saw this problem when discussing the popular rejection of a society governed by an oligarchy of wealth. Every sign of this possibility is manifest today in the way in which international financial markets are governing the global economy. Marx foresaw that,

> along with the constantly diminishing number of the magnates of capitalism, who usurp and monopolise all advantages of this process of transformation, grows the mass of misery, oppression, slavery, degradation, exploitation; but with this there also grows the revolt of the working class. *(Das Kapital)*

In the preceding chapter, it is argued that the four pillars of a caring and sharing society are identity, social cohesion, sovereign authority and shared moral values. In line with this argument, the affectionate and reasoned awareness of others for an effective caring society is found in the intensity of identification with others in society, the resulting social cohesion and the action of a sovereign authority that is conducive to the creation and maintenance of such a society. Ultimately, it is the presence and action of shared moral values that provides the unifying bond. Accordingly, a caring society is the result of these shared moral values that result in a set of social circumstances that create a bonding within social groups and a sympathetic awareness between its members.

A Caring Society and a Market Economy
The caring society predates the market economy that owes its origins to the way in which society developed in relatively recent times. The discussion of a co-existence between a caring society

and a market economy is a matter of appreciating the importance of moral values that historically have played a dominant role in man's thinking and behaviour. It is also a matter of accepting that the logic that determines market behaviour centres on the role of money in society. Since money of itself does not have the ability to express moral and ethical values, it is the manner in which money is obtained and applied that determines the morality test.

History shows that moral values have played a dominant role in society and continue to provide the reference base for arbitration and judgement regarding whatever choice man has to make. They are at the root of social relationships and constitute the very foundation of jurisprudence. The invention of money and the adoption of money as a medium of exchange and as a standard and a store of value were crucial to the appearance of a full-blown market economy, which dates from relatively modern times.

Moral values are expressed in religious beliefs and their force in the strictures and commandments with which they are associated, for example, the Ten Commandments. If the influence of religion has waned over recent times, moral values retain their full influence in those normative judgements that qualify behaviour as good or reprehensible. The social economy is governed by uncontested acceptance of those rules: the market economy incurs the opprobrium attached to the rule of money when it denies moral values.

A naive view that a caring society may comfortably co-exist in a market economy is almost the same as saying that socialism and capitalism are compatible with each other. Early socialists were motivated by an ideal of a caring society expressed in the manner in which social problems could be resolved by community action. Interpreting those problems as having their source in industrial capitalism, Marx was moved to declare that the means of production and distribution conditioned the nature of society. Hence, bringing the means of production and distribution under social or state control was an imperative for the resolution of social problems. This implied that the existence of a caring society was completely dependent on state intervention, requiring the public control of the means of production and distribution and relying on a bureaucracy that excluded freedom and choice at the individual level. Communism, as the extreme form of socialism is known, did not secure the improvement in the material conditions of life that the progress in scientific knowledge and technology brought to those countries that had espoused political and economic systems based on capitalism. Nonetheless, within those countries that have recently moved to a market economy and have rid themselves of communist regimes, the newly found freedom and the market economy has brought into its train high levels of unemployment and the pauperisation of a large section of the population.

The Market Economy: The Moral Dilemma
A caring society implies that moral values act to regulate relationships between individuals in such a way that the well-being of society as a whole is optimised. This means that individuals, who by nature may be driven by self-interest, are persuaded to find their self-interest optimised in that of society. Modern economic theory does not bring moral values into the analysis of market behaviour and accordingly does not attempt to reconcile market behaviour with the social objectives of a caring society.

Man's economic environment may be defined as the context in which social groups ensure their survival, through access to the essential resources of life. In basic terms, this means the availability of food and shelter needed to sustain life. For primitive groups such as apes and monkeys, the economic environment is freely given by nature and consensually shared in accordance with group customs. For man, his intelligence has expanded his needs beyond what nature has provided.

Significantly, for the purposes of defining man's economic environment, neo-classical economists, following Malthus, have adopted as a first and deterministic concept the notion of scarcity of resources. Once this notion is accepted as applicable to man's social existence, it follows that competition within society for access to limited resources is the primary cause of conflict. Such conflict may be in a violent form, such as war, or the use of political influence, or through more peaceful competition. The conflict for scarce resources through peaceful competition takes place in the context of relationships defined in the notion of markets, in which they are exchanged and in which demand for and the supply of scarce resources are reconciled through a price mechanism. These very simple notions are well known to first year students of economics.

History records that markets have existed from time immemorial. Agrarian society resorted to markets for the purpose of exchanging surpluses for goods and commodities of which they were in short or non-existent supply. In this sense, markets dealt with the basic economic problem, namely, scarcity, which was solved through the process of exchange based on a valuation expressed as a price. The market price was that price at which the seller was willing to sell and the buyer willing to buy. It dealt with the surplus/scarcity situation by regulating the quantities demanded and supplied.

Traditionally, agrarian societies were in a state of sustainable equilibrium and largely self-sufficient with respect to basic needs. Economic activity was marginal in that respect and in the absence of money, commerce took the form of barter. As markets developed, the conflict between buyer and seller drew the attention of moral authorities, such as the churches and philosophers, to the need for a 'just price'.

In this sense, the economic system was incorporated into the social environment by the notion of a price that was morally justifiable and socially acceptable. As mentioned previously, early Greek philosophers such as Plato and Aristotle, and others later such as St Thomas Aquinas, were much concerned with this problem. The churches, as moral and legal authorities, established and maintained moral rules for society. Most of these rules were incorporated into law and can be seen in the *ratio decidendi* of court decisions to this day.

Moral codes that had their source in religious teachings have other very significant features. Acceptance that man has fallen from grace was and remains a core philosophical and psychological factor in the appreciation of man's relationship with the Creator and with himself. Moral and religious teachings exerted considerable influence on society itself by prescriptions on such matters as usury and the notion of just price. Catholic teachings that had their roots in Aristotle acted to prevent economic progress and social change. As R.H. Tawney and Max Weber explained, the Reformation and the rise of the Protestant ethic had an important influence on the emergence of capitalism and the Industrial Revolution by breaching the hegemony of Catholic teachings and allowing the emergence of a new social order in which *laissez-faire* was the founding concept. Essential to this change was a moral justification in favour of man's action rather than the imposition of religious dogma.

Philosophers such as de Mandeville, Adam Smith, Bentham, and subsequently David Ricardo and John Stuart Mill, contributed significantly to the debate on the moral problems that arose with early industrialisation and the development of a market economy. Adam Smith sanctified the beneficence of the natural law under which man, led by an 'invisible hand' and pursuing his own interest, frequently promoted that of society, an end that was no part of his intention. Bentham led the argument for free trade, declaring that every man is the best judge of his own advantage and it was desirable that he should be allowed to pursue it without hindrance in the form of tariff barriers which favour some sections of society at the expense of others.

It is also interesting to note that morality influenced modern economic thought in attempting to provide reconciliation between the social and the economic environment that maintained the concept of social harmony in daily existence. Thus, de Mandeville in his celebrated *Fable of the Bees* took up Leibniz's argument in comparing society to a beehive – each bee, selfishly seeking for herself, contributes to the welfare of the entire hive. Hence, economic efficiency becomes social efficiency and the moral problem is resolved. Adam Smith, widely recognised as the father of modern economics, took up de Mandeville's hypothesis and described in his *Wealth of Nations*, the nature of markets and their social importance.

The switch in philosophical focus that this revolution of thinking produced had a considerable impact on society. From a religious conviction of the omniscience of God, found in the natural law, and the influence of the 'invisible hand' working through a market economy, there was and remains to this day the fundamental problem of how and where to reconcile authority, based on the intervention of law expressing moral values and *laissez-faire*, that would limit to a minimum all forms of state intervention.

Economic Efficiency and Laissez-Faire

The Bethamite doctrine that inspired the *credo* on which modern capitalism is based undoubtedly was persuasive on thinkers of his age and enshrined the *laissez-faire* principle in its theory of markets. *Laissez-faire* gave rise to the Free Trade doctrine that England espoused in the 19th century and retained substantially throughout the 20th century and to this day.

However, Mill and others had reservations with respect to the unlimited freedom that Bentham claimed for individuals in a market economy and in particular the moral implications that such freedom implied. The influence of religious teaching and in particular the doctrine of Original Sin and the Fallibility of Man remained sufficiently strong to oppose Bentham's claims. After all, Bentham was writing in a period when the relief of misery and poverty, the provision of hospices for the poor and the founding of schools were solely financed by charitable institutions and philanthropists motivated by Christian beliefs. Who can forget Scrooge's poignant conversion to charitable giving in Dickens' *A Christmas Carol* that reflected then as it does now, the spirit of caring for others that is strongly present in shared moral values? It was left to Keynes to state that 'the political problem of mankind is to combine three things: economic efficiency, social justice and individual liberty'.[1]

The market economy consists of all those enterprises in the market that obtain and manage economic resources. These enterprises are financed by funds provided by their owners in the form of capital, usually invested permanently in the form of share capital. According to neo-economic theory, the sole objective of the enterprise should be the maximisation of profits for shareholders, this being the strict condition for economic efficiency in the use of resources by the enterprise. Profit is entirely attributable to shareholders and distributed to them, usually in the form of dividends as a return on capital. According to the theory of finance and the efficient market hypothesis, the allocation of available funds to enterprises in the market is optimised when made on the basis of return on capital. Under simple accounting rules, profit is calculated on a periodic basis by matching periodic revenues and periodic expenses, the resulting difference between the arithmetical surplus or deficit being the net profit or net loss, as the case may be.

Enterprises structured on the basis of share capital may be under private ownership or may allow the public at large to buy through a public offering. Most large corporations obtain the right to have their shares quoted on a stock exchange. Stock exchanges act under market conditions as regards share pricing, namely the demand and supply for shares of a given corporation on a daily or quoted basis. The value of shares so determined is a function of market sentiment, which will reflect not only past and current profitability, but also expectations of future profitability and expected future returns to shareholders. Shareholder value is the description given to the number resulting from this valuation process. It emerges as the price that a willing buyer will pay and a willing seller will obtain at the moment when shares are transacted on the market.

It is this set of reasons that has brought into prominence the term 'shareholder value' to redefine the objective of enterprises as

---

1 Keynes, J.M., *End of Laissez-Faire*, London: Macmillan, 1919, p.311.

being the optimisation of shareholder value in the long-term. It calls for a management philosophy giving priority to the overall objective of improving shareholder value in management decision-making. It follows that decisions relating to current operations, investment decisions, asset and debt management decisions, should all be taken with this objective in mind.

The cost of using other factors of production, such as land (rent) and labour (wages) employed by the enterprise in its activities, are treated as expenses. These are deemed to have been incurred by the enterprise and they are brought into the calculus of the profit attributable to shareholders, in accordance with generally accepted accounting principles (GAAP). For this purpose, two important distinctions are made: those expenses that are regarded as resulting in the acquisition of assets, susceptible of providing an enduring advantage for more than one year, are capitalised and may be written off against annual profits through depreciation: those expenses that are regarded as exhausted completely in the activities of the current year are treated as costs and are brought directly into the calculation of annual profit. In this analysis, the human factor is treated as a cost and not as an integral part of capital. Its contribution to profits is measured in terms of the market price paid for labour on a current basis, that is, daily, weekly or monthly, as may be the hiring conditions. As the enterprise simply obtains labour services, it has no further obligations to individuals, once the services have been rendered and paid, save such obligations as have been imposed by law.

Socialist theories, such as those propounded by Marx and, in particular, the Labour Theory of Value as restated by Rosa Luxemburg, based on the philosophical argument that it is the work of man that creates all value, is rejected in the Theory of the Firm. Hence, business managers and employees are locked into a permanent relationship that is contentious and in which their different interests are opposed. Managers seek to improve profit performance by reducing costs, and in particular labour costs, and employees seek to increase their income through salary increases. Negotiations between managers and employees regarding salary adjustments, taking account of inflation or of improved productivity, can be acrimonious with deadlocks resulting in strikes.

The substantial reason for this conflict lies in the nature of present society itself and in the resentment at the dehumanising of man under capitalism and of his exploitation by the enterprise. Capitalism has not been able to modify itself or adjust to a different social context than that prevailing at its origin, namely, the existence of a society divided into two main classes, as noted by Marx – the wealthy who controlled society and the poor who were under the control of the wealthy and contracting out their services.

Corporate financial reports announcing improved profitability and dividends to shareholders and substantial profit related bonuses to top management are heralded in the Press. At the same time, profit improvements resulting in part from labour cost savings obtained through staff reductions and the transfer of work to lower labour cost countries are hardly conducive to stable and happy industrial relations.

Attempts to mitigate the dysfunctional effects of capitalism on the social economy have taken various forms with little real success. Attempts to take account of human resources as assets on corporate balance sheets led nowhere. Attempts to develop a theory of corporate enterprise reflecting a broader social context, through the notion of stakeholders as replacement for shareholders, did nothing to alter the economic reality. The extension of corporate disclosure requirements, such as the Corporate Report in the United Kingdom and the Social Report in France, did not change the fundamentals of corporate financial management with respect to the shareholder value imperative. These extended disclosure requirements did not require business corporations to undertake social programmes, nor effectively to encourage them to adopt social objectives other than profit making. Considerable investments by the corporate sector in media advertising vaunting corporate social contributions and the commitment to corporate social responsibility did not convince a sceptical public opinion.

Economic efficiency under free market conditions refers to the financial optimisation of economic resources, seen as a return on capital, expressed in the notion of shareholder value. The success of the market economy for generating economic activity, increasing national income and national wealth is undoubted. Its vigour, as an economic system, is being considerably reinforced and enhanced with the development of global markets.

Social Justice and Intervention
Marx, as a social philosopher, predicted the collapse of capitalism because of the economic and social problems that it created. Keynes, as an economist, accepted capitalism as a social system,

but had to face the problem of economic efficiency insofar as unemployment levels had created a grave social problem in itself. The *laissez-faire* doctrine had already resulted in recessions and serious unemployment prior to the Great Depression of the early 1930s that incidentally followed the Stock Exchange collapse in 1929.

Keynes' *General Theory of Employment, Interest and Money* published in 1936 was written towards the end of the Great Depression, associated in the public mind with the misery and social injustice of massive unemployment. It reopened the debate about capitalism under *laissez-faire*, arguing for state intervention in the market economy to deal with the problem of unemployment through the management of the level of demand, using budget deficits to this end. It should not be forgotten that the Russian Revolution of October 1917 had considerably weakened the confidence of Western industrial countries in the ability to maintain their own political systems through the backwash created by the collapse of Imperial Russia. The human losses during the Great War already had awakened some revolutionary fervour and the depression of 1919 in the United Kingdom had already raised the question of 'a land fit for heroes to live in'. The fear of a revolutionary contamination in the United Kingdom existed and King George V had already trembled briefly on his throne at that time.

Social justice is a much larger notion than Keynes might have envisaged in the rescue of the market economy from depression and the restoration of employment levels. The aftermath of the Great Depression was fertile ground for new thinking on economic problems as revealed in Keynes' work. But it was Beveridge who made the most significant contribution to new thinking on social problems in Britain. The Beveridge Reports (1941-4) defined public policy objectives for a society concerned with social welfare. The Welfare State that resulted from Beveridge's work was a landmark in the progress towards a caring society, which looks beyond a welfare state and is concerned with the human conditions and values of society itself.

According to Beveridge, the five important areas for public social policy objectives were: full employment, family allowances for all children up to the age of fifteen years, comprehensive health care for the whole population, a unified national scheme of social insurance run by the State and the safety net of a unified scheme of social assistance aimed at eliminating want and poverty. These objectives were given effect by the Labour Government in the immediate post-war years in a heavy programme of social legislation that included the National Health Services Act 1948, the National Insurance Act 1948 and other accompanying legislation. As regards employment, the full employment target was fixed at 97.5% of the working population, the maximum acceptable unemployment being 2.5%.

The concept of a caring society is deeply embedded in the Social Conscience and the collective memory that attaches mankind and society to that infinite quest, namely seeking after 'good'. The set of values that determine the Social Conscience in that sense do likewise define the nature of social justice. The Social Conscience also resides in the sense of community that inspires a caring society. Social justice, like justice itself, has two facets – giving and receiving.

Social justice is brought about in the market economy by state intervention through the legal system and the process by which laws are made. Whether through the influence of custom in Common Law countries and the embedded notion of natural law in other forms of jurisprudence, the law is a statement of jurisprudence based on a judgemental and argued appreciation of 'what is right'. Under capitalism, social injustice lies in the inequality in the distribution of income and wealth associated with the market economy. Historically, the Social Conscience has manifested itself in the market economy as a slow burning awareness of injustice expressed in public opinion. Popular democracy renders effective public opinion, albeit to a limited extent, through elected governments. It has brought about a changing context for the market economy through the process of state intervention.

State intervention acts in a number of ways to give effect to social justice in a market economy. First, by imposing legal obligations on business enterprises, to give effect to public demand for actions of a welfare nature towards employees. These include a spectrum of measures ranging from physical working conditions (heat, lighting and other facilities) to contractual obligations under labour contracts, such as hours worked, pension and retirement plans, salary negotiations and representation, if not participation, in management decision-making.

Second, by intervening in the distribution of income and wealth associated with enterprise activity. This is realised in a wide variety of ways, from setting minimum wage levels to the taxation of corporate profits and, in some countries, the taxation of corporate capital for the purpose of funding a social economy that is under state management.

Third, social justice is sought through state intervention in the market economy by bringing under state control and management activities of a public or welfare nature. The extent of state intervention may take the form of a monopoly in the provision of public services, such as transport, postal services, electricity and gas supplies to the provision of a minimum level of social service substantially free of charge to users, such as education, health care and resident homes for the aged and infirm. The social economy consists of all these various forms of state-managed activities. Funding is obtained through the taxation system that redistributes income from the market economy to the social economy.

The extent of the market economy and the size of the social economy may depend on particular circumstances and existing political climate. In some European countries having a strong tradition of state control and an attachment to socialist principles, such as France or other Latin countries, there is a public commitment to the maintenance of an extensive public service and a social economy providing high levels of service. In some respect, the market economy is in the form of a mixed economy, with a substantial industrial and service sector under government control or influence and state participation in the share capital. In other countries with a strong historical attachment to *laissez-faire* and individual freedom, the reverse is the case and the social economy is of minimal size. Industrial and commercial activities providing public services are in the control of publicly quoted corporations managed in terms of the 'shareholder value' criterion. Likewise, the provision of services of a social nature, such as education and health care, may be undertaken by business interests offering services under competitive conditions with respect to quality and pricing. In countries, such as the United Kingdom and the USA, there exists considerable social injustice in the disparity of social services available to poorer classes that by reason of insufficient income or poverty cannot access the level and quality of social services available on a paying basis.

Countries politically committed to a large social economy are obliged to resort to high levels of taxation to finance the big state budget deficits attributable to this sector. In particular, education and health care are characterised by huge financing needs. The fiscal burden that is imposed on the market economy and in particular on corporate enterprises, through high flat-rate levels of corporation tax is considered as weakening competitiveness in world markets as compared to those countries that offer business enterprises a more favourable taxation climate. The pursuit of economic growth and hence economic efficiency has been the dominating concern over the last decades and there is a strong public debate over the privatisation of the social sector and the withdrawal of the State from welfare activities. The case for lower business taxation, in particular, is argued as an incentive to foreign investment and to economic growth. The economic strength and resilience of countries that are returning to the principle of *laissez-faire* and a free market economy are persuading other countries to follow suit. The pendulum appears to be swinging against a social economy based on welfare principles.

The Social Contract and Individual Freedom
It remains to deal with the third political problem raised by Keynes, namely the reconciliation of individual freedom with the social objectives of a caring society. It presupposes a relationship of interdependence between society and the individuals of which it is composed. One of the most important problems of society that has been at the core of the development of law is the concept of freedom under law.

The law is the authority that defines individual freedom in a social context through legal rules that impose rights and obligations upon an individual with respect to other members of society. Such legal rules may be both prescriptive and proscriptive, that is, imposing a duty by prescribing a rule to be observed and proscriptive by a prohibition to act freely in a given case. Thus, it is fallacious to believe that individual freedom is other than a limited freedom under law. To believe otherwise, is to accept anarchy and social disorder. It is also interesting to note that the notion of care is enshrined in jurisprudence. In many aspects of the Law of Tort, and in particular in the Law of Negligence, there is prescribed a duty of care, often explicit and sometimes implied, towards others. Likewise in Criminal Law, behaviour that exhibits a lack of care is prohibited and sanctioned, for example, careless driving under the Road Traffic Acts and the failure to warn others of possible danger where it exists.

The law is fundamentally a social phenomenon concerned with the regulation of behaviour by establishing order in accordance with legal rules backed by the imposition of authority. If we accept that the validity of legal rules in jurisprudence is the moral values to which they seek to give effect, it must then follow that those values, through their general acceptance by the Social Conscience, constitute the authority under which individual freedom is constrained.

Hence, the essential character of the social contract is the respect for the law and obedience to the rules of law. Individuals are expected to conform to these rules, to obey the police as agents of the law and to abide by the decisions of the courts in the event of disputes. The extent to which a community is law-abiding may be gauged from crime statistics.

In addition to the rules enshrined in law, there are within all societies sets of rules of behaviour that are generally accepted and expected with respect to the behaviour of individuals or groups of individuals in public and as between individuals in their personal relationships. In judgemental terms, these rules may be understood as relating to the notion of caring and sharing, expressed in terms of respect for others. As such, these customary rules may be modified by changes in social formalities, such as the recent habit of addressing others by first names. The extent to which behaviour affronts others is a function of general acceptance within society. There is an evident distinction made between civility and incivility in the reaction that incivility provokes. It remains offensive to the British public to have men urinating in public view, whereas responding to physical needs in this case does not offend a more tolerant French public.

The social contract is a much larger concept than simply obedience to law or respect for custom. Rousseau's contribution to today's social problems remains as pertinent as it was when he wrote *The Social Contract* in 1762, a few decades prior to the French Revolution that was to shatter the social order in Europe. It laid the foundations of modern democratic society based on the notions of Liberty, Equality and Fraternity that continue to resonate with even greater force today. Essentially sentimental and romantic in his view of man and society, Rousseau trusted these emotions to guide him into a perception of life that has endeared him to his followers. His observations and teachings have confirmed him as the most influential social philosopher of his time and a continuing inspiration to those searching for solutions to today's problems.

Rousseau approached the social contract from the viewpoint of freedom. To him we owe the declaration 'man is born free, but everywhere he is in chains'. It is evident that his social contract has to do with individual freedom. He argued that if a civil society or

State were to be based on a genuine social contract, man would receive in exchange for independence a better kind of freedom, namely true political freedom. Rousseau defined society as an artificial person consisting of a set of individuals united by a genuine will, *la volonté générale.* Society owes its existence to the pledge that brings it into being as a pledged group. Rousseau considered the Republic to be the creation of the general will in each and every member to further the public, common or national interest even though it may conflict at times with personal interest.

However, Rousseau was a man of his time, when philosophers were concerned with the problems of government and with freedom from oppression. The French Revolution was within shot. The turmoil among intellectuals and politicians was its harbinger. But, as time has proved, the notion of political freedom and popular democracy has not fulfilled the hopes that were implied in the social contract. As defined by Rousseau, the social contract is not a concept natural to man. Its effectiveness lies in the willingness of people to implement its conditions. Therein lies one of its major failings. However, the principal reason why a society based on Rousseau's social contract is unrealisable lies in the notion of freedom expressed as political freedom. As G.B. Shaw explained with great emphasis in the Preface to his play *Major Barbara*, it is not possible to ask a man to address his mind to ideas belonging to the realm of belief and religion, when it is preoccupied with the emptiness of his stomach. Political freedom has not itself freed man from hunger, unemployment and solitude in distress. Herein lies the difference between the social contract as providing an effective structure for society and the concept of a caring society based on the notion of the family, which is natural to man and, by extension, is natural to society itself.

Conclusion
Many would be of the view that the notion of a caring society has its essential justification in a reasoned and sympathetic view of life itself. It rests on the implicit acceptance within society of duties and obligations deemed to exist between the State and the individual. For example, the protection of the citizen is one of the most important responsibilities of the State. Likewise, the bond of loyalty between the State and the individual imposes upon the individual a duty of giving support to the State, whenever and however such support is required. Again, most of such duties and obligations are enshrined in law. The Welfare State extended the

relationship between the State and the individual to protecting the individual from want in its various forms.

The caring society goes beyond the concept of a social contract and of the Welfare State to place the relationships between individuals, and between individuals and the State, on the footing of caring and sharing such as would occur naturally within a family. The question that remains is how such a naturally occurring phenomenon may be released as an effective force in social action.

—3—

Policy Objectives for a Caring Society

A caring society implies that the driving force of the 'self' instinct is modified from a concern with self to a caring attitude towards others: the closer the relationship with another or others, the stronger the caring instinct. This shows that it is a natural sentiment in human nature. It motivates a willingness to share. Caring and sharing are moral values that are embedded in the Social Conscience. The Social Conscience may be argued to be the sovereign authority in judgements relating to society and to social behaviour. It is the point of reference in the debate over capitalism and socialism as social models. It is seen in government policy that seeks to reconcile economic efficiency, social justice and individual liberty. The process by which a caring society may be made more evident in human experience may be seen in the conditions that are found in family values. The policy objectives of a caring society go beyond those of a welfare state and associate economic welfare and social justice with social harmony driven by moral values.

THIS CHAPTER examines the extent to which the caring instinct, that is naturally present in social relationships, may be released as an effective force to improve the sense of humaneness in society and between people through an acceptance of the necessity of sharing. Two basic instincts are seen to condition human behaviour in social groups; the 'self' instinct and the 'caring' instinct. The 'self' instinct, which psychologists describe as the survival or the self-preservation instinct, appears as dominant in nearly all circumstances, whereas the 'caring' instinct appears to reduce the driving force of the self instinct by shifting the concern with self to a care for others. We have described this concern as a sympathetic awareness of the other or others. The caring instinct appears to be stronger in social relationships as the degree of dependence is intensified.

The substance of the argument in the first chapter is that the concept of the family is useful and pertinent to seeing society from the viewpoint of one that places caring at the centre of its concern and action. It is not far-fetched, therefore, to imagine that the family concept may be taken as a model for seeing the problems of society in our times from that viewpoint and to imagining that a better world may be the outcome of a stronger presence of feelings of caring and sharing in society.

The compelling force of the self instinct, both at an individual level and at a social level, was discussed in Chapter 2. It was interesting to note that many philosophers interpreted the self instinct as beneficial to society and, when allowed unimpeded expression, resulted in improved social conditions for all. As mentioned in the previous chapter, Adam Smith sanctified this doctrine in the celebrated statement that 'man, led by an invisible hand and pursuing his own interest, frequently promoted that of society, an end that was no part of his intention'.[1]

There is the special expression of the self instinct through the concept of property and its influence on economic and social behaviour, which remains to be discussed. The distinguishing and critical feature of Western society is the key role played by the concept of property. In tribal societies, all resources are communally held and shared. No one may claim the ownership and control of any object. Historians and philosophers generally agree that the concept of property that identifies rights and objects as susceptible to being brought under personal ownership is the origin of law. It is easy to appreciate that, in the absence of property and where all goods are communally held, the major source of conflict between individuals in social groups is absent. It is also easy to understand that a society based on socialist principles would judge private property to be a significant threat to its existence and would wish to bring all property into public ownership. Finally, it is also easy to see that the self instinct is strongly motivated towards obtaining ownership and the enjoyment of the use of property. Markets exist for the purpose of negotiating property rights and this is the very basis of the market economy. For these several reasons, the reality today of a market economy cannot be questioned, although whether private property rights in the gift of nature should be allowed or whether such rights should be confined to the product of labour is a matter of discussion.

The Significance of Moral Values
The evolution of Western industrial society from a land-based agrarian economy to the market economy of today has been a very long process. The evolution of capitalism itself can be traced back

---

1 Smith, Adam, *Inquiry into the Nature and Causes of the Wealth of Nations*, 1776, Bk IV, Ch. II.

to Roman times. Roman authors such as Cato, Varro and Columella wrote treatises relative to the management of estates and property. There was some rudimentary industrial activity and markets existed for the exchange of goods.

In the long journey from Roman times to the present, the evolution of modern society occurred through centuries in which moral values marked the nature and features of a civilisation that for long remained contained within the boundaries of Europe and the Near and Middle East. With its earliest roots in Antiquity and later in Ancient Egypt, Greece and Rome, Western civilisation attained its most glorious days during the Renaissance and went on to transform the world by devising a way of thinking called the scientific method that moved it to the Age of Science and to an unlimited expansion of the perspectives open to mankind.

If the frontiers of Western civilisation are seen in a purely geographical sense as established on a racial basis, it is evident that it is limited to a relatively small fraction of the world's total population and this fraction is reducing through time. If these frontiers are seen in an economic sense, it may be said that much of the world's resources are consumed for the benefit and maintenance of that civilisation. If these frontiers are viewed from the perspective of military might, Western civilisation was, is and remains a dominating and even conquering influence.

Most thinkers would say that the quintessence of Western civilisation lies in its moral prerogative and those moral values in which it has its justification. Accordingly, if frontiers are to be found, it may be argued that these frontiers are moral ones. It is the force of these moral values that is perpetuated in the Social Conscience. It insists on the obligation to hold to moral values in the application of scientific knowledge and questions the market economy's reliance on shareholder value as a determining and motivating principle. These values are defining the moral frontiers of the market economy, as scientific and technological advances reduce the world's physical dimensions and bring populations closer together in the logic of the geographical extension of the market economy. Hence, moral values will bring to the fore the inescapable necessity of caring and sharing on the much larger scale of a global economy.

Moral Values and the Political Debate
The problems of society and of government have been the subject matter of an extraordinarily rich philosophical activity of a civilisation that focused on moral values and a broadly based culture

founded on religious beliefs. From Plato and Aristotle to the present day, philosophers directed attention to the role of the sovereign authority, its nature, objectives, structure and mechanisms. Forged on the anvil of time, Western civilisation endured a long period of conflict during which nation states were created and destroyed, recreated and integrated in empires that themselves were destroyed and reappeared in other forms and at other times. The politics of power and of war fascinated the attention of thinkers in a world where the absolutism of political power was unquestioned. But the overriding authority to which the justification for action was sought was moral values. The source of these moral values was a Supreme Authority from which all moral rules emanated and to which the justification for action was referred. In earlier times, the Supreme Authority was represented by several deities or gods that had their own residences and whose presence was attested in the form of statues that represented their nature and character. There were Gods of War, of Love, of Peace etc. Uniquely, the Jewish nation succeeded at a very earlier stage in reducing the number of gods to only one God, namely Jehovah. Western civilisation adopted monotheism as a religious belief in only one God.

In the history of the Jewish people, Jehovah is a fearsome character, an authoritarian tyrant, dispensing rules that had to be strictly observed and who meted out rewards in the form of favours and severe punishment for failings. Jehovah was and remains the embodiment of the moral law and in close and permanent relationship with his people, through regular contact with his Law within synagogues. The moral values inscribed in the Ten Commandments given to Moses by God are the fundamental laws of the Jewish people, as written in the Tablets or the Torah, which is the Word of God. For this reason, it is said that the Jewish people are the People of the Word.

Inspired by a new prophet within the Jewish nation, who claimed to be the Christ and the Son of God, the followers of Jesus of Nazareth founded the Christian religion. At that time, the Roman Empire extended its civilisation over most of Europe and the Middle East, including the land of Israel. Whereas, to this day, Jews have refused to accept Jesus of Nazareth as the Son of God, he was subsequently accepted as such by the Romans themselves, when the Roman Emperor Constantine was converted to the Christian faith in the 3rd century AD. The reconciliation of Rome and Jerusalem on the matter of the personality of Jesus has not so far occurred, and there remains very much present today a difficulty between the Jewish nation and other nations of the Christian faith with respect to this point. However, it is widely accepted that apart from this question, there is unanimity of belief as to the moral values that are the basis of Western civilisation and that have their origin in Judaeo-Christian religious beliefs. The Ten Commandments that are the foundations of the Jewish faith are equally fundamental to all Christian traditions.

The mystification of moral values in order to give them supreme authority is a most interesting phenomenon. The problem of the Personality of God is a curious debate in the sense in which the moral values that are deemed to emanate from God and which are accepted by man seem naturally present in man himself. In purely verifiable and hence in concrete terms, apart from the meeting of Moses with Jehovah on Mount Sinai, there have been no other recorded meetings with God from which the authority of religious beliefs may be confirmed. Jesus of Nazareth's claim of his special relationship to God as his Son offended Jewish Orthodox belief and especially his claim of fulfilling the prophecy of the coming of God on earth. Christians differentiate themselves essentially from Jewish Orthodoxy on this point, accepting that Jesus was the Son of God sent on earth as representative of His Father. Christian Orthodoxy accepts the words of Jesus, as related by the apostles, as direct communications from God via His Son, together with the theology proclaimed by Jesus of the relationship of himself to God and to men in the words, 'I am in my Father, and ye in me, and I in you,' and, 'The kingdom of God is within you.' This allusion to spiritual values as being inherent in man and, as providing an explanation for moral values as existing naturally in man, has long been discussed by theologians, as philosophers concerned with religious beliefs. What is true and much more important than purely doctrinal debate is that moral values, which are used to justify action and behaviour today, are directly expressed in religious beliefs.

For our purposes, however, the most interesting aspect of this debate concerns the origins of the Social Conscience that acts in such a deterministic manner in providing value judgements with respect to social and economic behaviour. Suffice it to say that moral values have acquired sovereign authority on all matters of judgement affecting society and provide the essential jurisprudence for established law and accepted custom.

Accordingly, it may be postulated that, for all practical purposes, the Social Conscience that is found in public opinion and in generally accepted beliefs is and should be the sovereign authority. This postulate is fundamental to the thesis developed in this text, namely that the reality of a caring society is an established fact in the Social Conscience.

An influential school of thinkers in France, of which Durkheim is probably the best known in this respect, argued strongly that moral laws, defined as *social facts*, acted upon individuals as a moral obligation to obey a rule. Durkheim considered that society is something beyond us and something in us, and that, when society is strongly integrated, the moral laws (social facts) hold individuals under its control.[2] Accordingly, the Social Conscience, as it is perceived and expressed, is the ultimate law. In line with this reasoning, the political debate is an extension of the moral problem and must be submitted to the judgment of moral values, as basic law. Western society reached this conclusion during the historical period known as the Enlightenment, that is some three hundred years ago.

Hence, it is easy to understand why Western society reached its great intellectual divide at the time of the Enlightenment. Previously, religious beliefs had focused exclusively on the Word of God and the regulation of society under the authority of a king or royal sovereign, whose authority was hereditary by reason of lineage and was absolute in terms of the doctrine of the Divine Right of Kings. Symbolically, the enthronement of a king was his anointment by a representative of the supreme religious authority through a religious process known as coronation. This practice is still observed today. The anointed sovereign is not only ruler, but also the Defender of the Faith and, most important, the fountain of justice. This remains valid to this day in the laws of England.[3] Equity, which was an important development in English law, evolved from the practice of subjects to appeal to the king, as the fountain of justice, for a rule that did not exist or one that was considered as unjust. The appeal was made to the Lord Chancellor, as the king's representative in these matters. He, being an

---

2 Emile Durkheim (1858-1917) is considered as one of the founders of modern sociology. He introduced the concept of functionalism, which argues that the basis of an orderly society is the existence of a central value system that imposes common values on all its members. See Lukes, S., *Emile Durkheim, His Life and Work: A Historical and Critical Study*.
3 Henry de Bracton (1210-68), the great medieval lawyer and constitutional scholar, declared that 'the King must not be under man, but under God and under the law, because law makes the King.' See Blake, L.L., *The Royal Law*, London: Shepheard-Walwyn (Publishers) Ltd, 2000, pp.35, 41.

ecclesiastical person, acted as the King's conscience to provide a rule of law to meet the stated case. This is a quite fascinating example of the reference to moral values and the notion of the Social Conscience in matters of social behaviour.

The Renaissance, which began in Italy towards the end of the 14th century, marked the start of a series of convulsive developments, which was to move Western Europe from a feudal political system and an agrarian economy to a democratic system and an industrial economy. Those developments were the agrarian revolution beginning in the 16th century, the emergence of commercial capitalism, the Enlightenment and the advent of the Scientific Age, the appearance of industrial capitalism with the Industrial Revolution which has continued to manifest itself in sustained technological progress that finally had brought man to consider outer space as a zone of possible activity. These achievements must be considered as quite remarkable for the species known as *Homo sapiens*, whose antecedents with other primates formed the substance of Darwin's research into the origins of man barely two centuries ago.

This series of developments and cataclysmic changes was also marked by different paths taken by thinkers on the nature of the moral problem and political beliefs with respect to man and society. The dominance of religion on the mores of society up to the time of the Enlightenment meant that social behaviour was tightly constrained by a moral code which has its reason in the teaching of the New Testament and the Christian faith. The political question and the problem of government were examined in the same light.

The Age of Enlightenment, as it occurred in England, was a break with the past with respect particularly to the notion of self-interest and hence with individual freedom. As we saw in the preceding chapter, this debate was led by such intellectual giants as Locke, Hume, Hobbs, Bentham and others in England, Leibniz, Kant and Hegel in Germany and Rousseau, Saint-Simon and Comte in France. In France, the debate was much more diverse. Whereas Rousseau also preached the doctrine of individual freedom, many French philosophers were rationalists, for example Descartes and Diderot. The break with the feudal past in France was much more violent than elsewhere in Europe. It destroyed the existing political and social system and replaced it through a bloody and popular revolution by a republican system that had 'Liberty, Equality and Fraternity' as a rallying cry.

With its nascent industrial activities effectively frustrated and destroyed by the wars that were to follow the Revolution, French society was reformed on rationalist lines determined by Bonaparte, a Corsican who eventually succeeded in usurping the republican revolution and installing himself as a new Emperor with imperial powers.

The significance of the French Revolution and the adoption of the Napoleonic system remains highly relevant to the determination of the future of the European Union as it consolidates itself into a European nation state. The orientation of the French political system, which is also highly influential in other European nations that have followed the same political development, confirms the priority of the interests of the State over those of the individual. Hence, much of the philosophical debate is concerned with political theory and government.

England was to remain in the more tranquil contemplation of self-interest and individual freedom, and the importance of those concepts for the development of laws and government. Self-interest was translated into the doctrine of *laissez-faire* and a much reduced influence of the sovereign in the daily life of society. Driven by self interest and a commitment to *laissez-fair* through the doctrine of free trade, England was to become a formidable industrial and military power and an exceedingly rich nation. the UK remains committed to the liberalism that sustains market forces. It is this commitment that is at the root of what may be called the European schism. It will remain an enduring disagreement between Britain and its Continental neighbours and will prevent its successful participation in the European Union.

The political debate in Western Europe carried over into the New World, which was won over to the English conception of society. The American Constitution adopted the French wording, but substituted the English meaning, in its laws and governmental practices.

The European schism today is part of a much wider area of difference between two dominant cultures that have co-existed in Europe for centuries, and more so since the time of the Reformation in England.

Continental Europe has a system of jurisprudence that is drawn from Roman Law and from Canon Law. It is codified and has no natural flexibility. It is the result of government action in the form of state decrees and does not result from public consensus. Hence, it only indirectly reflects the Social Conscience. Judges are appointed and paid by the Government and are effectively public servants. The interference of politicians in the judicial process is one of the most worrying aspects of the legal system in Europe, as it places the impartiality of judges in doubt. This creates a special difficulty with respect to the relations between individuals and the sovereign authority. It will be recalled that this relationship is one of the four pillars of a caring society.

England has a system of Common Law that originated directly from popular consultation with the people through the assize system. Its clear reference basis is the Social Conscience. It is not codified, except to the extent to which parts of the Common Law have been consolidated by statute. It remains flexible in that judges are able to develop law through the interpretation of rules of Common Law and establish new precedents. Finally, the independence of judges guarantees the notion of freedom under law. Hence, the possibilities open for implementing a caring society appear more evident in those countries having a political system derived from the English experience.

The foregoing review of the history of the political debate has crucial implications for situating the policies of a caring society in a context where political traditions dictate the manner in which political choices are made and decisions are reached.

The concept of the caring society is closer to the English tradition in which society forms its jurisprudence from the bottom up, through the importance of customary rules and their integration into law through the assize system. Equally important is the manner in which English society has been shaped by the conflict between the sovereign authority (Social Conscience) and the despotic powers claimed under the doctrine of the Divine Right of Kings (King's conscience), modified as early as Magna Carta in 1215, and later the Bill of Rights in 1689. The Bill of Rights established the supremacy of Parliament and allowed England to become a parliamentary democracy much earlier than other nations.

Therefore, the possibilities that English society has of adopting the caring society organically from the basis of the family concept would be in keeping with the natural way in which English society has evolved.

Alternative Political Systems
Political systems are founded on theories that are concerned with the nature of government, its structures and orientations and its methods. Politics, as a social science, examines differing viewpoints

with respect to the function of government as a relationship within a society of individuals and the manner in which that relationship is established and maintained. The science of politics goes much further than this simple statement, but, for the purpose of this discussion, suffice it to say that politics has been emphatically concerned with choice as regards the nature of that relationship.

The caring society is an all-embracing concept that seeks to unify economic, social and moral values in a holistic manner through a harmony between these several aspects. Much of political philosophy has been focused on theories implying choice between mutually exclusive forms of society. Discussion has been polarised as between capitalism and communism as two extreme forms of society, one based on private property and personal freedom, the other on public property and personal freedom limited by the sovereign authority.

Today, some two centuries after Bentham, the schism between these two concepts of society remains. The caring instinct expresses itself more naturally in the theory of socialism as a form of society and as a basis for organising economic activity. The self instinct is the basis of a form of society that is known as the market economy and which sees society as organised on the basis of capitalism and individual action. These two forms of society are essentially mutually exclusive. Hence, if the policy objectives of a caring society are to be realised, they must be accommodated within the extant political system. As will be argued in subsequent chapters, the reforms necessary to accommodating a vibrant market economy to the imperatives of a caring society lie in three areas of reform, namely the education of the next generation, the social context in which the market functions, and the political context in which government policies are determined and implemented.

The Three Principal Political Objectives
Keynes defined the political problem of mankind as combining economic efficiency, social justice and individual liberty. This classification was used to structure the discussion in the previous chapter that considered the caring society within the context of the realities of a market economy. It was in this sense that Keynes saw the political problem as one stemming from the market economy. This declaration in 1911, made long before Beveridge, defined the objectives of a welfare state in terms of a practical plan for Government action. It was implemented by a socialist government in the years immediately after the Second World War.

The passage of time is constantly changing the nature of the problems facing society, and is also changing the perception of these problems. Wars, for example, impact the Social Conscience through the disgust that death and destruction and shattered lives instils in the public mind. The end of both World Wars in the last century interestingly provoked a very similar reaction: a wish to create a new society. At the end of the First World War, the cry was for a 'land fit for heroes to live in'. At the end of World War II, the cry was similar, but the influence of the Great Depression of the inter-war years manifested itself in a demand for a caring society with a more precise definition of social objectives, in particular full employment, national health insurance, housing, education and provisions for retirement. Essentially, those were the recommendations of the Beveridge Report, as adopted in the United Kingdom. Throughout Europe, populations turned to socialism and to communism, believing that such was the path to a fair and just society in which governments would and could play the leading role in placing public welfare at the centre of policy.

The failure of governments throughout Europe to maintain welfare at the centre of policy and action may be judged to be a failure of democracy, if democracy is defined as government for the people, by the people and with the people, for the demand for a caring society remains manifest at the popular level. This may be seen in the concern for employment, health, education and housing, which remains very high and to which political parties unceasingly pay lip service.

The failing support by successive governments in the United Kingdom for a Welfare State in the form proposed by Beveridge and the demand for a caring society, as expressed in public opinion, may also be judged to be a failure of elective democracy as a form of government. For example, nations are led into wars by political leaders, and often only one political leader, who succeed in usurping the principles of democratic government by a political process that results in the concentration of power into their own hands. Recently, Tony Blair, who was elected by popular vote as Prime Minister of what is claimed to be the oldest democracy in the world, succeeded in taking Britain into war in Iraq and in the process was said to have ignored the views of his key ministers. as well as those of his own generals. Standing virtually alone, he succeeded in ignoring public opinion and public protest and continued with a policy of aggression against another state, in defiance of international law and the United Nations. This example shows that, if emperors and kings had absolute powers over people in former times, it is clear from much of what is seen today, that democracy has been perverted into the personal glory and into the effective tyranny of the personal power wielded by political leaders. It is said, with a measure of truth, that freedom under democracy is the right to express opinion only at periodic elections. More nations than we care to think are in the hands of dictators and most dictators in power today were elected through popular vote and subsequently have elected themselves as leaders for life.

Moreover, reconciling the policy objectives of a caring society with the realities of a market economy requires a balanced assessment of the evident contributions that capitalism has made to improving economic well-being through raising the standard of living of successive generations. This has been achieved by the mobilisation of capital by the owners of wealth towards the production of goods and services rather than the profligate spending on luxury that was the hallmark of earlier times. It is the structure and methods of modern capitalism, as expressed in the market economy, as well as the theory of modern capitalism, manifested in the shareholder value criterion, that is so divisive. It leads the market economy to manifest a total lack of concern for moral values and to discount the significance of the impact of its actions on society.

Science and modern technology have given ample proof that the seeming impossibility of ambitious projects should not be a barrier to endeavour. Success is always in some measure translating the impossible into the realisable. This is a particularly important lesson for the establishment of a caring society that faces such seeming impossibility in breaking the stranglehold that a market economy has on humanity, through the morass of materialism, selfishness, personal greed and the corruptibility of political leaders

From the foregoing, it follows that policy objectives for a caring society are more fundamental than they may appear on the surface and go much beyond those of a welfare state. They are directed to those three essentials concerns that are economic welfare, social harmony and moral values. Although this formulation has a certain resemblance to Keynes' views, it reflects a humanistic shift towards seeing society as inspired by caring and seeing its operating mechanism in the act of sharing. Hence, the determination of policy objectives for a caring society should not be seen as a political problem involving negotiating mechanisms, but rather at seeing how man's natural instinct for caring in a social structure based on the family concept may release itself as a spontaneous recognition of the necessity to share. This approach reflects Rousseau's philosophy and his concept of natural freedom. It may be noted that Rousseau saw society itself as being the origin of inequality. In less prosaic terms, Rousseau probably would have agreed with an interpretation of the policy objectives of a caring society as concerned with providing its members with the wherewithal to live decently, in a society that protects and enhances the quality of life of all its members and that sustains mankind in its humanity by the support of moral values translated into human experience by the force of law.

Looking at the world as a whole, the problems of Western industrial society may be seen as exceptional in their significance and dimension and are discussed as the problems of the developed nations, as distinct from the rest of the world categorised as developing countries. This is a classification that pleases economists for it is relevant to the analysis of economic growth and development. Another classification of the same thing is the distinction between the haves and the have-nots. Looking further into segmental grouping, there are more complex distinctions that are created by historical and religious factors. Far from being homogenous in its concerns, humanity is heterogeneous in its many facets. The Arab or Jew may well be in his counting house counting out his money, when not far away the Bedouin is in his desert shifting his tent and camels and looking for water. Indeed, humanity has evolved in so many different ways as to make the observation of human society the source of enriching reflection. If the market economy is to maintain its expansion across the world with the globalisation of capitalism, it is evident that the need for a caring society will become more insistent.

Moral Values as Originating from Caring Relationships
The lengthy discussion of the origins of moral values as stemming from philosophical reflections or even religious beliefs derived from a mystical relationship with a Divine Creator underlines the importance that society has always attached to moral values. The reasons why human society is a moral society may perhaps always remain a mystery, unless a more scientific or rational explanation for the existence and influence of moral values on human behaviour is discovered.

If it is accepted that the family concept is the kernel from which society has developed, an interesting hypothesis may be developed as to the source of moral values. They may appear naturally in family groups conditioned by the necessity of sharing life together. In this interpretation, caring and sharing assumes a new importance with respect to the reliance on moral values for regulating social relationships. Here, the argument is turned upside down, for instead of moral values being used as externally imposed values originating in religious beliefs that man has not inspired, it may be considered that man himself has inspired those moral values from within himself in the context of a family relationship that nature has made necessary to his survival. But this would fit the hypothesis that man created God in his image and likeness, rather than the other way round. However, such a heresy is offensive with regard to the marvellous mystery that is the nature of life itself, as scientists discover daily and which is so evident in the natural perfection and harmony that is revealed in nature. Accordingly, a more reasonable expression of the mystical relationship of God and man that would also be pertinent to this discussion of the origin of moral values is that there is a divinity in man that explains that understanding of his being. This romantic and appealing argument was strongly expressed in the romantic literature of the 19th century, for example in many of Wordsworth's poems. In line with this sentiment, the ultimate destiny of man as found in the nature of his relationship with God is expressed by Shakespeare in the statement that 'There's a divinity that shapes our ends,/Rough-hew them how we will.'[4]

The explanation of the causal factors or, social facts as defined by Durkheim, that bring the individual and the Social Conscience to knowing that there is a difference between right and wrong may arguably be the gateway to the ultimate unravelling of the mystery of origins of morality. For all practical purposes, man seems naturally equipped with the knowledge that seeking after what is right is the golden rule for decisions that have to be made, in conformity with the morality of perfection that lies in the sublime harmony seen everywhere in nature.

The discussion of the source of moral values as being found in man himself, for whatever reason, is also justified by reference to the manner in which it has been the special talent of the English nation to create its own system of Common Law out of a jurisprudence based on popular custom. The moral laws that people developed for their own use in their family and social relationships, the

---

4 Shakespeare, W., *Hamlet*, Act 5 Sc 2.

validity of which had been tested in use, by their translation into the Common Law of England, provided that country with an easily enforceable system of justice, since legal rules had been accepted prior to being formalised into recognised law. England did not need democracy, nor indeed had heard of it, at the time that Common Law was created by popular consent.

Accordingly, the process by which a caring society may be made more manifest in the human experience may be simplified, much in the same way as Common Law was adopted as the basis of jurisprudence. This inspires the following questions:

(a) What are the conditions seen as imperatives to a caring society?
(b) What are the moral values that are determinants of behaviour between family members?
(c) How is the life of the family structured in an ordered way?
(d) What are the responsibilities that determine the obligations that exist between family members?
(e) How is discipline enforced through effective rules reflecting moral values?
(f) What are the conditions that determine the survival of the family unit?

A social theory based on answers to these questions would amply meet the need to define the policy objectives of a caring society that would contribute at the same time to solving many of the social problems facing mankind. In this analysis, political theories, political parties and political leaders appear not only as redundant, but also as perverse in confusing the truth that is the distinction between right and wrong.

Conditions that are Imperative for a Caring Society
Founded on Family Values
These conditions were discussed in Chapter 1, as the four pillars of society, namely, identity, social cohesion, sovereign authority and moral values. Interpreted as imperatives for family life, these conditions are not simply environmental, but are fundamental to the very existence of the family and to a meaningful appreciation of the primary need, which is the need for security.

Accordingly, the first and crucial policy objective from the viewpoint of the family is the need for security. By extension, it is also the *sine qua non* for a caring society. Security manifests itself most significantly as the impulse to protect and to preserve.

The family exists as an entity within which a number of individuals identify themselves as members of a social unit, in which their interests and vital concerns are reflected and merged in collective action. It originates in the act of procreation and by the laws of inheritance; the family will have racial characteristics. Nations are constituted of groups of families that have historically located themselves in defined geographical zones and, for these reasons, have shared the same historical experience and have the same collective memory. Importantly, they share the same language of communication and within that language, as Wittgenstein explained, there are different levels of communication within the common understanding of the ideas and the sentiments communicated in speech. Through the historical experience, families have the same collective memory, a common speech and shared moral values.

Environmental threats to the security of a society based on the collective of families may be external or internal to society itself. External threats may be direct in the form of military attacks aimed at the conquest of the territorial rights and the seizure of the members and property of the invaded population. It is one of the most frequent occurrences in the history of nations and to this day is an aspect of foreign policy that remains in current use, as for example, the recent invasion and conquest of Iraq by USA and UK forces. All three countries involved were members of the United Nations, an assembly designed to promote peace in the world and to avoid conflicts in the nature of wars. The General Assembly of the United Nations, representing all nations in the world, by a vast majority were unable to prevent the invasion that took place, which effectively brought to nought the hopes that humanity had placed in international law, as the supreme authority for the family of nations. Nonetheless, it is evident that the Social Conscience holds the USA and the UK as guilty of aggression. Although the Statute of Rome created an International Criminal Court, there is no effective international jurisdiction as yet capable of bringing the leaders of these two countries to justice. Moreover, the failure of international law has resulted in a wide and perhaps long-lasting sense of insecurity stemming from the political ambitions and the military capabilities of two nations that started war that was morally repugnant to a world committed to peace, when the possibility of a peace settlement had not been exhausted.

Internal threats stem from the weakening or the disintegration of cohesion within society. It may be the result of the peaceful but unabsorbed immigration by foreign peoples often having a strong sense of family, or the loss of control over its affairs, or the acceptance of allegiance to other sovereign authorities. These different factors have a similar result, namely the weakening of identity and of social cohesion. The sense of loss of security is heightened, when the relationship with the sovereign authority is weakened by diminished trust or when that sovereign authority is usurped in the interest of minorities. These various factors all combine, for moral values are no longer commonly shared. These internal threats have become very present in Western society, though the impact of immigration differs as between nations.

English society, as a cultural tradition, is visibly disintegrating as several indicators reveal. A major reason is that the substantial immigration of recent years is quite different from historical immigration that came from neighbouring countries, sharing the same racial origins, culture and moral values. This historical immigration originated from conquest, for example the Anglo-Saxon, Viking and Norman invasions, causing the earlier Britons to retreat westwards into what is now Wales. A new nation was formed which had no choice but to accept the Duke of Normandy as King and his laws and government. Scholars of Anglo-Saxon culture prior to the Norman Conquest of England note its richness and point out that the Anglo-Saxon King Alfred was the closest that the country ever had to a philosopher king. When King Harold II was slain by William of Normandy at the Battle of Hastings in 1066, England as it then was, disappeared and was eventually absorbed into a feudal state ruled by Normans. French became the official language and English nobles were replaced in the social hierarchy by Norman barons. The legend of Robin Hood 'riding through the glen with his band of men, feared by the bad and loved by the good, robbing the rich to give to the poor' tells of the social conflict of this unhappy period for English culture. Anglo-Saxon nobles, dispossessed of their estates and castles, had the forest as refuge and as the only honourable alternative to collaboration with the conquering enemy. During this period, 'Presentment of Englishry' was admitted in Norman courts as a mitigating circumstance in crimes of murder.[5] The indomitable

---

5 After the Norman Conquest, to deter local communities from a continuing habit of killing Normans, a heavy fine was levied on any village where a dead body was discovered, the presumption being Norman unless it could be proved to be English. The fine was known as the 'Murdrum', from which the word 'murder' is derived. As the system developed, many of the early coroners' inquests dealt with the 'Presumption of Normandy', which could only be rebutted by the local community, and a fine thus avoided, by the 'Presentment of Englishry'.

courage of the English was seen again in the defiance of another English nobleman, direct descendant of the Duke of Marlborough, Winston S. Churchill, who in 1940 vowed to defend his country against continental invaders by fighting them on the beaches.

The recent and massive immigration into Britain, particularly from India, Pakistan and the West Indies is racially different and has lifestyles that are and remain foreign to the host population. With the exception of West Indians, they have different mother tongues, share different religious faiths and live in larger families. The greatest difficulty that this immigration presents to the host population is that it does not, cannot and will not integrate with the host population and is likely to constitute a separate society. This immigration has tended to concentrate in geographical areas that are the larger towns and cities, replacing the former population by one that is by and large industrious, imaginative and successful in business. In this way, and over a relatively short period of time, Asian migrants have populated large areas of central and northern England. Some London boroughs now have white English populations as minorities. The wealth which they have succeeded in creating is invested in the acquisition of residential properties at prices that are beyond the means of members of the traditional population. It is not unrealistic to foresee that traditional England in time may be transformed into an Asian country through peaceful conquest.

Given the strength of the family concept among Asians, the richness of Asian cultures and the virtues of its people, it may well be that the heritage that Asian immigrants bring with their conquest of England will result in a changed nation. The politicians and social reformers of the 1950s and 1960s, who saw in the end of empire an opportunity and a need to create a multiracial state, and who glorified its merits, are now in their graves. They could not know that the dream of multiracialism was a mirage that would not resist the concentric forces of identity and social cohesion which will act inexorably with the force of time and ineluctably forge a new society with a single and dominant culture.

French society has experienced over the centuries a substantial immigration in much the same way as England. Immigration from Eastern and Central Europe was successfully absorbed and, as in England, enriched the host country is many ways. Recent immigration also has different racial, religious and cultural characteristics. It also has concentrated in geographical zones. Contrary to the English experience, it has been the will of the French people expressed through successive governments that immigrants must conform to the language, culture and moral values of the French people. French society insists that, as new French citizens, immigrants must integrate under the same *valeurs républicaine*, or republican values. These republican values may seem exotic and incomprehensible to the English. Of fundamental importance to republican values is the doctrine of *laïcité*, or secularity. The Republic arising from the French Revolution was not only a revolt against the King but also against the Church. Since 1792, France has described herself as *républicaine et laïcque*, that is republican and secular. The teaching of religion in state schools remains forbidden in terms of this doctrine, which has recently been extended in the law forbidding the wearing of religious symbols within schools. This law is aimed, in particular, at the new immigration from Islamic countries, but also it applies to the wearing of the *kippah*; it is a sweeping declaration that France will remain French as regards the education of its children. In this sense, France is adopting a national policy that has the objective of compelling the integration of immigrants into the mores, language and cultural habits of the host population. Unlike England, it appears that France has the will and the intention to remain French.

Moral Values as Determinants of Behaviour
Life, Truth and Love are a trilogy of symbolic terms that are invariably and uniquely stated together. They are often found in religious texts to provide meaning to the spiritual values that are associated with man's understanding of divinity. Their symbolism is used in an extended way to identify and determine those moral values that not only underpin the relationship of man to God, but which are also enjoined upon man as the moral justification for his actions. They are accepted universally in civilised society as the respect for life in all its forms, the adherence to truth in all circumstances and in the expression of love towards one's neighbour as motivating social action.

Life is the first symbol within the trilogy and is also the first in importance in moral law, and for the preservation of the family. 'Thou shall not kill,' is one of the Ten Commandments. The protection and the preservation of life in all its forms, and in particular the life of human beings, is the most imperative of the three symbols that defines the totality of moral values. It is the *alpha* and *omega* of all rules, for without life there is nothing. It is hardly surprising that the medical profession, that has the prime concern of looking after health, requires its new members to state their commitment to the preservation of life in terms of the Hippocratic Oath, which forbids doctors from terminating the life of patients even when great suffering is present and hopes of recovery are nil. The discussion of euthanasia in this context poses an exceptionally difficult moral problem for the medical profession, for it imposes the most awful decision and responsibility that may be imposed on a person, namely the ultimate decision regarding the life of another person. Taking life unlawfully is the most serious of crimes and carries the most severe penalties under law. The most ghastly events of recent years have been war crimes, crimes against humanity, genocide, the extermination of people through ethnic cleansing and the mass murder of populations through wars conducted with weapons of mass destruction, as well as conventional weapons of exceptional destructiveness, used indiscriminately in areas of dense civilian population.

Proud of the level of civilisation that Western nations have reached, of the magnificence of its culture and the progress of science, the dark side is the high civilian death toll as collateral damage incidental to bombardment using the most advanced weaponry in wars that are political in motivation and inspired by politicians. This indicates the moral depth to which Western civilisation has sunk in its contemptuous disregard for principle and sacredness of life. In like terms, there is a universal condemnation by decent people of any form of violence and cruelty towards human and animal life in all species. Concern for the environment reflects the importance attached to the value of life as reflected in the simple fact of existence.

Life-threatening symbolism has become an important medium of expression to an entertainment and film industry, replicated in modern theatre and in art forms that seek to draw attention and to obtain recognition through the propagation of gratuitous violence, killing, cruelty and insane destruction. Images of violence that denigrate the respect for life, and to which the public at large is inescapably exposed, have had a corrupting influence on social behaviour generally, and in particular on the behaviour of the young, and is an affront to traditional family values. The pretended right to unrestricted freedom of expression and routine violence, as well as a climate of political correctness, seem to have cowed society into the toleration of the intolerable. The responsibility of a caring society clearly is to restore the respect for life, and for others, as the first moral obligation and the highest ranking moral value.

Truth is the second symbol in the trilogy of basic moral values that ranks immediately after life in its importance. Its significance is that it provides the unique reference in establishing justification for thought and action. It is the foundation of the Social Conscience and underpins it in all respects. Truth has the characteristic of being *sui generis*, that is it stands alone and is unique in itself. In terms of logic, only two possibilities exist, truth and falsehood. The truth cannot be established from the standpoint of what is false. It exists simply as truth and as a condition; it cannot be verified or tested from the basis of what is false. By contrast, what is false is judged and destroyed by reference to what is true. In absolute terms, it is a *credo* that absolute truth cannot be reached by man and belongs only to God. The search for truth is the key problem for man in his intellectual endeavours and in the activities that have transformed his experience of life through the idea of progress in all its manifestations and particularly in the development of science and technology.

Truth, as justification, is the foundation of the Social Conscience that has its most important social use in defining rules of law and upholding those rules in society. It provides the framework for determining acceptable behaviour. Truth in this sense is justice. As determinant of behaviour and in all forms of relationships between people, truth is expressed most obviously through two of the moral values that are directly derived from it, namely, honesty and sincerity. Truth holds society together. Truth is the basic condition for all lasting and beneficial relationships and in this sense is the cement that holds families together. Honesty and sincerity, as Truth expressed through the evidence of behaviour, are moral values that are apparent and are used as tests to validate conduct. There is a widespread demand today for transparency in matters affecting the conduct of government and business affairs. This is no more and no less than a requirement for honesty and sincerity and proof of these moral values in the information that is provided about the conduct of affairs of such public importance. The practice of spinning to manipulate information to make it appear and be accepted as true, when in fact it is false, is a means that has become routinely employed by governments in explaining policies and actions to their constituents, pretending in this manner to comply with the requirement of transparency while at the same time perpetrating wrongdoing in government.

Truth, as expressed in honesty and sincerity, is vital to the existence of another key aspect of durable and beneficial relationships, namely the need for trust between people. Without trust there cannot be a relationship. It is the very basis of each and all relationships. It brings into focus the need for security between people in the way they relate to each other. Trust is the measure of faith in another's intentions and actions. Trust in another person is the certitude of the benevolence that is the supreme expectation of the outcome of the relationship with that other person. Once destroyed, trust is peculiar in that it cannot be recreated. Truth, as a moral value, leads to another moral value, which is the need to appreciate the content and the manner in which truth is present in any given circumstance or problem. A perception of the existence and extent of truth is essential in the acquisition of knowledge. It is interesting to note that truth is frequently associated with light, which is one of the five basic elements of life. The term enlightenment indicates its importance in the reduction of ignorance and the advancement of knowledge. Thus the truth is fundamental for scientific research.

From the foregoing, it is clear that truth, expressed as honesty and sincerity which create trust, is vital to the preservation of the family and to the understanding of the concept of a caring society as knowledge with a direct bearing on life.

Finally, there is Love, which comes as the third symbol in the trilogy of moral values. Love, ranks as equal *inter pares* with life and truth. However, it adds a particular dimension to the sets of moral values that have been discussed above and considered as being derived from life and truth. If the justification for a caring society lies in the moral values that are its foundations, love inspires the very heart and soul of its motivation. Love belongs to life and truth in an indivisible whole in which all three symbols are combined to express the qualities of the same creative force from which the spirit of humanity emanates. Beyond life and truth, however, love has the unique and distinguishing virtue of conveying the sentiment that is the dearest and the most precious to man, namely, that affection that draws and binds people together in an atmosphere of caring in the reciprocity of loving sentiments. Love is symbolic of that most desirable moral value that transforms social relationships from a sympathetic awareness of another or others into the reason for giving expression to the natural impulse to form a family as the basic structure of a caring society.

Love is a rich source of moral values. Creative of a sympathetic awareness of others, it manifests itself in generosity as a moral value. It is the outgoing towards others that is the nature of caring. The heart and mind notion, which is invoked to express the duality of life as an experience of feeling and thinking, often shapes an ultimate decision under the influence of the heart, rather than the mind. This reveals another special feature that constitutes the strict and necessary condition for a caring society, associated with generosity, namely forgiveness. Forgiveness is necessary in social relationships and acts to eliminates conflicts.

Love, as a sympathetic awareness of others, is also a liberating force allowing individuals to discover an extended notion of freedom in a caring society. Freedom in this sense becomes an important moral value in society and for the preservation of the family. Rousseau made much of this point in his discussion of the social contract, through which he argued that man finds real freedom in society.

Finally, a sympathetic awareness of others instils an ability to appreciate qualities and virtues. The context of a loving relationship between couples is one in which beauty as a physical attribute and also as an attribute of mind forms the basis of attraction. Beauty, however perceived, becomes a moral value. Often, it is perceived in the notion of harmony which is itself beautiful. Thus, seeking to express beauty and harmony may be judged to be also determinants of behaviour.

The Family as a Social Unit Structured in an Ordered Way
Order may be defined as a rationalisation of behaviour between members of a social unit that has the main objective of creating harmony. Order is essential in enabling society to reach the objectives that it has defined for itself, by integrating its members by reference to their personalities, attributes, skills and needs which are situated in a holistic context with the good of all as the ultimate aim. In a normative sense, order ensures the integration of each member by ascribing to each a stated role. Hence, order prevents exclusion, ensures and strengthens the sense of identity and social cohesion.

Order stems from the acceptance of harmony as a moral value and the rejection of chaos, which are the absence of order and the supremacy of disorder. The *a priori* condition for a family structure that reflects both order and harmony is the acceptance by all its members of the authority that is vested naturally in parents, by virtue of the responsibilities that they have with respect to children. This authority is commonly known as 'parental authority'.

In extended families, elders have an important influence not only by virtue of the respect that they are accorded in traditional families, but also by their role as trustees with respect to the management of family property and finances. As well as being custodians of customs, their accumulated experience of life and wisdom acts as a permanent and accessible basis of reference with respect to family matters and hence to broader social issues. This type of parental influence remains, to an extent, in modern Western and Eastern European countries, particularly where Catholicism remains an important social influence.

The Protestant ethic played an important role in the rise of capitalism and it is in those countries in which Protestantism is the predominant religion and, in particular, in post-Reformation England, that capitalism had its most marked impact on the social structure. The market economy and consumerism place enormous pressures on family life. The present social crises in Western society may be directly attributable to this pressure, by contributing to the disintegration of the extended family and even the nuclear family unit restricted to a couple and their children. Survival in the market economy depends on social flexibility, such as the ability to move to where jobs or business opportunities exist. The market economy also thrives on individualism in social action and concern for self impedes the ability to care for others.

Parental authority has been and is seriously challenged, as are family values and the family unit, by the ethos of the market economy. The focus on the self that the market economy promotes and encourages undermines the integrity of the social structure that is the family. In addition the associated demand for individual freedom in all its manifestations within the family, has seriously impaired parental authority.

The weakening of parental authority may be attributed to a variety of other factors. Although parental authority is an authority shared by both parents, traditionally mothers have relied on fathers to have the last say. Fathers, as males, have that capability necessary to impose discipline upon children, particularly boys who would challenge parental authority as part of the natural process of discovering themselves. Often, testing the limits of parental authority is part of the game play of growing up and it is in testing those limits that enables parental authority to provide children with a sense of personal security. This sense of personal security is possibly one of the most important gifts that parents can grant to children. The role of fathers has been considerably constrained by the rights that women have acquired in recent times in matrimonial affairs and the freedom given to marry in haste and to divorce with like convenience and rapidity. The loss of a sense of security that existed in the notion of permanence of marriage has affected not only children, but parents as well.

Children's rights legislation aimed at extending the protection of children against abuse has, in its wake, also undermined considerably the authority of parents, teachers and others involved in the upbringing of children, and the influence that they have over children. With the support of the law and by virtue of the new social order inspired by liberal thinkers, parental authority effectively has been replaced by children's rights. The authority that flows from these rights has given way to a generation of children which feels free to do as they like and who have scant respect for adults, be they their parents, teachers or any other adult person, whether policeman, bus conductor or simple citizen, who are routinely subjected to juvenile incivility. Among the many and perverse consequences of this development is the generalisation of undisciplined behaviour in children at home, in the street and at school. In believing that they are free to do as they like and in the reticence of adults, either as parents or as teachers, to guide and instruct behaviour through the imposition of discipline, what should be a precious period of adolescence is a grim experience of generalised unruliness, incivility, delinquency, violence and drug abuse. The will of parents to impose authority has been replaced by a sense of resignation and the abdication from their duties and responsibilities.

Parental responsibility and authority and the sense of security that children derive and enjoy in the context of a caring family may also be judged in the context of the higher living standards that economic progress has conferred upon this generation. Many parents now have a natural concern for their children's development into successful and responsible adults.

Certain communities which have migrated to Western European countries, for example Asians from the Indian sub-continent and China, have succeeded in maintaining family traditions and values, which have enabled them successfully to establish themselves in market societies. Others communities that have not had this background have floundered relatively and found themselves living in socially deprived areas. Although it is in the behaviour of children from deprived areas that the loss of parental authority and the effects of social and personal insecurity are most evident, problem children are not restricted to those from so-called deprived areas. Children and young persons across a broad spectrum of social classes have become involved in drugs, crime and other antisocial behaviour.

Social policy objectives for promoting a caring society should be concerned with restoring family values to alleviate and reduce the difficulties that adolescents experience. School education can play a positive role in this regard, but it cannot replace the role of parents and the loss of parental authority does not assist the school in its mission.

The Responsibilities that Determine the Obligations Existing between Family Members

Our forebears had the wisdom to determine for us the obligations which family members have towards each other. An early source of codified family law is Roman Law, which deals extensively with the regulation of family life and family property. Roman Law provided the fundamental rules in these regards that time has done little to change. The authority of the *paterfamilias* has been eroded, but the duties and responsibilities of husbands and fathers are substantially unchanged. Legislation regarding matrimonial matters and property echoes the Roman *Jus Civilis* with remarkable fidelity, particularly in those countries that adopted Roman Law as basic law.

The concept of the family in a corporate sense with respect to the protection and enjoyment of property rights is fundamental to understanding the nature of Western society as a property owing democracy. Family units are created on the basis of legal contracts that deal emphatically with property rights. The community of property created by the marriage contract rested on a contractual promise by the husband in the form, 'With all my worldly goods I thee endow.' The concept of the dowry also formed part of traditional unions and represented that property which the woman brought into the marriage. In Roman Law, it was paid by the father of the bride and represented his responsibility towards the maintenance of his daughter on the transfer of this responsibility to her husband. The concept of the bride price remains current in certain societies to this day, for example, in the *lobola* system employed in Southern Africa, in which the husband compensates the father for the loss of the services of his daughter. It is also a guarantee of good behaviour, or freedom from vice, for it is returnable by the father in the event of the husband not being satisfied with the marriage.

The concept of the corporate property-owning family was also fundamental to the succession in title to property and particularly to land, by laws of inheritance by legally recognised heirs, namely, children born in wedlock. In effect, far from being a relationship directed to optimising personal and sexual happiness, the family is in reality an economic unit. That reality is made evident in the maintenance rights that parties and children have under matrimonial law.

As to the other obligations that the family structure imposes on its members, these may be found in natural law, that is, by deduction from what may be observed in nature. Gender differentiation is basic to nature and to many of the functions that are gender determined. It is in the nature of the male to protect and feed his family; it is in the nature of the female to give birth to children and to care and nourish them and in this regard to have the help and support of the male. It is the duty of both parents to provide their children with suitable education. It is in nature for children to be dependent on their parents and in this context to respect and obey their wishes. The caring family is a creation of natural law and this is the reason for its existence, its permanence and the distribution of obligations.

Man-made or social laws have sought to modify some of the basic aspects of both the corporate family and natural law. By and large, however, family obligations have been maintained and are recognised in the event of divorce or legal separation. Marriage 'in community of property' or 'without community of property' have become formulae of choice, rendered necessary to limit the financial risks associated with high divorce rates. Marriage has become an unstable and short-term relationship, in which a constant search for marital bliss strongly experienced in sexual gratification is routinely accepted as the most significant objective for marriage and *a contrario* for seeking divorce. It is clear from the disputes as to property rights and maintenance that arise on the rupture of marriage that the corporate concept remains a core family value. As to the distribution of roles and social obligation within marriage, the market economy has had some influence as may be seen in the debate as to the sharing of roles. In the sense that caring is at the heart of family life, whether a husband does or does not do the dishes does not constitute an important philosophical problem, even though it may be a matter of family dispute. However, if the wife is obliged to work as well as look after the children, the husband may be asked rightly to accept a larger share of domestic duties.

Social laws favouring children's rights to education have lengthened the period of obligatory maintenance on parents beyond the age of legal majority, that is, when a child becomes fully adult in law and no longer dependent upon parents for maintenance. The right to education has not been accompanied by any criteria as to the exercise of that right. Education or training having a direct relationship to future employment would constitute such a criterion, as would assiduity in the efforts made towards success in obtaining relevant qualifications. Many educational programmes do not have obvious vocational objectives and serve to conceal hidden unemployment or unemployability.

Obligations of children towards parents are rarely expressed in social legislation. However, some interesting differences exist between Common Law and Roman Law countries in this regard. These differences are not generally known, but they are significant to family obligations. In countries such as France, children once adult are responsible for their parents, in the event of need. In other words, legal maintenance obligations go both ways. Parents have maintenance obligations towards children during infancy; children have maintenance obligations for parents when they become dependent through age or infirmity. The primary obligation of care rests upon the children. If impecunious old parents need institutional care and cannot be looked after by their children, the financial costs of such care must be met by the children to the extent of their own assets, and only thereafter will the State take over that responsibility. Thus, the concept of the caring family is an extended notion. Likewise, with respect to laws of succession and inheritance, heirs inherit financial liabilities as well as financial assets. A debt-burdened inheritance could be a financial catastrophe. French law also recognises the rights of grandparents to access to their grandchildren, which is not the case in English law. This right extends beyond the divorce of parents and is inviolate.

Family Discipline Enforced through Effective Rules based on Moral Values

Following Durkheim's[6] theory of functionalism, the influence of a central value system based on socially recognised moral values is determinant in instructing social behaviour. Embedded in the

---

6 Lukes, S., *Emile Durkheim, His Life and Work: A Historical and Critical Analysis.*

Social Conscience, moral values are intuitively understood in shared meaning. The process through which shared moral values are transmitted from generation to generation starts at birth, for no sooner is the child born than the mother seeks to guide the child in the right way with watchful and loving care.

Reference to moral values in the course of daily conversation, remarks, judgements, praise and criticism of behaviour of members is so much part of family life as to pass virtually unnoticed. It is deeply embedded in the Social Conscience of the family, as well as the society or culture with which it is identified. Its authority rests in the general and uncontested acceptance of moral values and in the expectation that behaviour must conform in all situations to the supreme judgement, namely, doing and being seen to do the right thing.

The right thing embraces all moral values. Speaking the truth, being sincere, caring for others, helping others, working hard, being generous, being steadfast in loyalty to others as well as true to oneself, facing difficulties with courage and fortitude, respecting others in all circumstances, these are the many and various aspects of behaviour that express that all-embracing moral value, doing the right thing.

Despite much seeming evidence to the contrary, we live in a moral world and ours is a moral society. Embedded moral values act to discipline behaviour both unconsciously and as conscious self-control. They act as an effective *ex ante* discipline. The observance and the consciousness of conformity to morally approved behaviour is critical to self-esteem and hence to a sense of personal security.

Moral values naturally and instinctively discipline behaviour through the awareness of wrongdoing by reference to doing right. It is the uncomfortable sense that wrongdoing provokes that corrects behaviour through the sense of guilt to which wrongdoing gives rise. Formal penalties for wrongdoing, both in terms of Criminal and Civil Law, may act as deterrents, but self-condemnation occurs as the *ab initio* knowledge of guilt. Restoring the self-esteem of wrongdoers, whether as juvenile delinquents rebelling against authority, or as convicted criminals bearing for life the stigma of wrongdoing, may be arguably the most significant treatment for the redemption of offenders and their reintegration into society.

The Conditions that Determine the Survival of the Family Unit
It is self-evident that the survival of the family unit is dependent on the persistence of family values. The family unit is a natural

phenomenon which arises out of the need for the continuance of the species and is exemplified in the mating instinct that unites male and female of most species in the act of procreation and the protection of the young, until they are able to fend for themselves. What distinguishes the species that is our own, namely *Homo sapiens*, from other species is the intelligence that drives imaginative enquiry as to existence and its justification. It has pushed reflection towards a transcendental and mystical relationship with a creative spiritual force to which all life is credited. That unique and special relationship is present in all cultures and throughout the history of man, from Ancient Egyptians to Australian Aboriginals, from Incas to Hindus and from Muslins to Christians. The endeavour to bridge the experience of physical life with that of a spiritual life has been treated generally in religious teachings and religious dogmas. 'Our Father which art in Heaven,' is a postulate that the logic of reason would contest as to meaning and as to reality. It is supported by faith, for it is only through faith that its reality may be experienced.

Without necessarily attempting to bridge the unbridgeable between the physical and spiritual in terms of a continuum of life as an experience, another postulate regarding spirituality argues that the divinity of God is manifest in the divinity of Man. This notion of reflection is also found in religious teachings and in the dogmas that have been projected. To try to define the nature of the divinity of God through the divinity of Man made in His image and likeness has collided with the insistence of scientific enquiry on the need for observable evidence susceptible of being validated by proof. However objectionable to reason it may appear to be, another postulate that tries to circumvent this difficulty offers the possibility that man has created God in his own image and likeness. Indeed, wherever formal religious organisations exist, their ceremonies and ceremonials are replete with physical statues of the unseen God. Prior to monotheism, earlier religions felt the need for more than one god to fill the realm of imagination. The Greeks and Romans, from whom we have derived so much of our civilisations in terms of knowledge as science and as beliefs, had the need to ascribe different spiritual purposes to different gods. This has not diminished in any sense the richness of their contribution to our own experience of life.

The mysticism that is present in mankind's thinking about the meaning and purpose of life is likely to persist, even though science may well succeed in piercing all the secrets of creation with logical and scientifically acceptable explanations, following the remarkable discovery of the structure of the DNA achieved in 1953 by Francis Crick, Rosalind Franklin, James Watson and Maurice Wilkins.

Beyond nature and beyond science, there is another aspect of human life which belongs to the realm of mystery and of mysticism. It is that curious and inexplicable presence of moral values in society and their close association with family values. Whether believer or whether agnostic or atheist, there is unanimity with respect to the supremacy of moral values and with regard to the humane conditions which should qualify social behaviour in a well-ordered society. To most, this is the true meaning of life, namely, enjoying the experience of life in civilised society.

Given that the family and family values are fundamental realities of our civilisation, both are *sine qua non* to any discussion of the future of society. It is inconceivable that the family unit should cease to exist as such. Attempts that have been made, through collectivism and communism in Communist Russia and in the *kibbutz* in Israel, to create grouped social units in which parents and children are indiscriminately related, have not inspired any real desire for emulation. On the contrary, the desire to create a family unit in which caring and sharing enriches sentiments and emotions in the cohesiveness of relationships based on close identity, remains strongly present even when threatened, as we have noted, by the pressures exerted by the market economy and radical movements reflecting minorities views.

Hence, it is in the persistence and in the supremacy of moral values, expressed in the Social Conscience that the conditions for the survival of the family unit will endure.

Conclusions
A caring society is an all-embracing concept that seeks to unify economic, social and political action in a holistic manner by their harmonisation through shared moral values. The sovereign authority on which a caring society relies is its Social Conscience, made manifest in the constant desire to define action in accordance with the supreme moral test, namely conformity with the notion of 'what is right' and accordingly doing what is right.

The existence of a caring society is a present reality, the evidence of which resides in the instinct to care and the necessity to share that are the moral laws or *'social facts'*. These, acting as the sovereign authority of the Social Conscience, impose their hold on individuals. As explained by Durkheim,[7] the existence of a central value system that imposes common values on all its members is the basis of an orderly society.

The conditions of Kant's logic of reason as a basis for order in society are fully met in the understanding of the functionality of moral values. Doing what is right implies the *ex ante* question, 'What is right?' as well as its *ex post* implementation, so that doing what is right is at once a policy objective and a social action.

Religious beliefs, jurisprudence and custom find common cause in the Social Conscience, and its universality as seen in instinctive caring, which is the cement of family life and, by extension, the founding and permanent bond that provides cohesiveness to society and harmony through social order.

Speculation as to the existence of God, the relation of God and man and the meaning of life itself transcends two worlds, the unseen and the visible world. Such moral precepts as may be postulated from this speculation are contested by the evolution of scientific thought and the rigorous testing of postulates by the application of the scientific method for validation. By contrast, the Social Conscience is a constant and its presence is self-validating.

The Social Conscience is a mysterious phenomenon, not only in its tendency to determine behaviour, but also in the general acceptance of its central value system, which is authoritative as a determinant of action. So embedded are moral values in the Social Conscience that, even though they may not prevent wrongdoing, they succeed in creating the sense of wrongdoing through a sense of guilt. Looking guilty is the transparent evidence of wrongdoing. Making amends is the recuperation of individual conscience and being at peace with oneself.

Policy objectives for a caring society are moral answers to social problems broadly defined over the range of political, economic and social action. Empowering a caring society in a market economy means the reconciliation of market objectives with the Social Conscience.

---

[7] Lukes, S., *Emile Durkheim, His Life and Work: A Historical and Critical Analysis.*

PART II

EMPOWERING A CARING SOCIETY

PART I considered the human condition in the context of society and in particular through the nature of relationships within society implied in living together in social groups. It was argued that, because the family structure is one which is so fundamental and so important to the simple act of living, it is the basic social group with which to begin to explore social relationships. By extension, it is the most useful and relevant structure from which to discuss the problems that arise in larger social groups and in particular those of nations or states. The very existence of the family as a social unit depends on two essential and interdependent conditions, namely the presence of caring which is a natural phenomenon existing within a family environment and the accepted necessity of sharing which is implicit in caring. Caring and sharing are noble sentiments and they impact on the nature of the 'human condition' in a specific manner. It is for this reason that Part I is addressed to what could be called the humane condition.

Caring and sharing, as motivating behaviour, depends on the intimacy and closeness of relationships for they condition the way in which self is rendered aware of others. A sense of common identity and social cohesion are requirements for a caring society. A caring and sharing society exists also when there is present a sympathetic awareness between members. This implies that they are able to appreciate each other through shared moral values and can establish a harmonious way of living together through an ordered structure, in which reason assists in defining the role and function of each member. A caring society looks to a sovereign authority for empowering its policy objectives, and the relationship with that authority is a determinant to its well-being.

We live in a market economy, which fosters a competitive spirit between people and accentuates the concern for self and for self-gratification. The market economy has favoured economic growth at the cost of considerably damaging the social fabric, creating divisions between people and nations everywhere and fomenting social ills of many different forms.

The objective of Part II is to see how two such unlike situations as a caring society and a market economy could be reconciled by empowering a caring society, whilst preserving the economic advantages that the market economy evidently offers. This problem is considered as having three distinct aspects or dimensions. First, it will be argued that education has a key role in providing the inspiration, the willingness and the capabilities of people to empower a caring society. Second, it will be argued that the market economy can be adapted to serve the needs of a caring society, if a democratic will exists that is sufficiently strong to make the market economy subservient to society rather than the reverse, which seems now to be the case. Third, the will and the means necessary to empower a caring society is a task for government, for it is by the action of government that harmony may be created between the current conflicting objectives of a market economy with those of a caring society, which represents the larger national constituency. These three different topics are the subject matter of the following three chapters.

—4—
Education for a Caring Society

Education for a caring society should be adopted as an educational policy objective. It is through education that caring and sharing may be made effective in reforming society. There are three ways in which this may be achieved; by instilling into educated persons the knowledge and the moral values necessary for a civilised society, in providing the market economy with managers able to incorporate moral values in business decisions and ensuring that citizens are conscious that they have a personal as well as a collective responsibility for the well-being of all members of society. Education is not limited to formal schooling, but includes all the influences that shape the whole person. These include the family, the successful integration of a child as a school member, the influence of the social environment that sets the moral values for the peer group with which the child has a social life out of school, as well as the religious community to which a child belongs. All these influences are involved in the transmission of those moral values that are at true foundations of a caring society.

THERE ARE THREE dimensions to the role of education with regard to its contribution towards empowering a caring society. First, at the level of the education of the person; the challenge may be stated as being to reform society through the schooling system. Education for a caring society should be adopted as an educational policy objective.[1] Second, through management and professional education, to reform the business community with respect to its social role, so that business leaders adopt a responsible and broadly caring attitude towards all parties with whom they are involved in business activities. The concern for employees, customers, suppliers and the public at large is a wide social responsibility. It includes the protection of the environment, public social responsibility as well as moral standards with respect to their own conduct. Third, to influence general thinking towards a caring society through all the various forms of education, so that those who enter political life and become political leaders do so with a

---

1 Education for a caring society should be distinguished from education for citizenship, the former having an emphatic social orientation whilst the latter may be judged to have an orientation towards nation-building.

personal sense of mission, sublimating personal ambition for power to a personal ambition to serve.

The family concept and what may be called family values nowadays seem less prized than heretofore. It is true, however, that they remain very much present in the hopes for happy and permanent unions, for contented homes and the joy of having and bringing up children. In this perspective, education should place emphasis on family values, social values being an extension of family values.

Relationships in a caring society express family values and that sympathetic awareness between individuals, which fosters caring as a sentiment. Inspiring such a vision of society depends on two conditions. The first is obtaining a consensus that such a vision is desirable and should be a policy objective. The second is to have the means to realise that vision and render it effective. One naturally thinks of education as being necessary to both these conditions, in bringing about the reforms implied in moving to a society that changes its views about social problems and social relationships. Hopes for betterment are placed on education in modern times with the fervour that hopes of ultimate redemption were placed on religion in former times. A humane society, in this view, results from the quality of the education of its people.

The importance that our forebears attached to the education of children as one of the first duties of government has retained its priority in public opinion and in the political debate today. Schools are intended to educate children who will:

(a) create families, raise and care for the next generation;
(b) become the future workers committed to the market and social economy;
(c) be the future citizens with responsibilities to the wider community.

These differing end-objectives invoke a number of questions, for example, do they involve the same educational values, do they involve the same moral values, should these values be specified and how could they be made explicit in the curriculum?

Reforming Society through Education
Education may be seen as comprising four distinct areas of activity.

(a) General education up to the age of 16 years, which is a legal requirement in most developed countries. It is aimed at preparing children for adult life, through the acquisition of basic knowledge, such as reading, writing and counting, as well as knowledge pertaining to the national culture. It also seeks to develop the ability to think critically as well as promoting understanding. The end of this period is marked by the award of a school leaving certificate, usually containing some form of performance evaluation.

(b) Further and vocational education, which enables those seeking to enter particular fields of activity to acquire more specific knowledge, as a prerequisite for employment. It may be part of a scheme of apprenticeship into a trade, such as plumbing, painting, as well as a wide variety of commercial skills. In all cases, it involves full or part-time study at a recognised teaching institution. The successful completion of a course is marked by the award of a diploma, usually also with some form of performance evaluation. Further education not only prepares a person for a specific job function, but offers a guarantee to an employer that a new recruit does possess the basic knowledge needed for the job.

(c) Higher education at universities is usually restricted to those satisfying entry requirements which are selective. University degree courses commonly are defined in a strict and progressive curriculum, which is aimed at extending the depth of existing knowledge. In particular, they foster an intellectual life, in which research and the advancement of knowledge is the ultimate objective.

Centres of learning have existed since ancient times. Plato specified seven liberal arts that should form the basis of education, namely, grammar, rhetoric, dialectic, arithmetic, geometry, harmony and astronomy. According to Aristotle, the first three are to do respectively with formulating, communicating and discovering truth. As to the remaining four, they constitute the study of natural philosophy or the study of the physical laws of creation; arithmetic being concerned with number at rest, geometry with magnitude at rest, harmony with number in motion and astronomy being magnitude in motion. These areas of knowledge under different descriptions are still to be found at the core of university studies. Newman[2] was at the forefront of the radical developments that occurred in England in the late 19th century. These were the increased influence of universities and the Education Act

---

2 Newman, J.H., *The Idea of a University*.

1871 that led to the introduction of general education through schools. Recently, university education has expanded to include new areas of knowledge and their applications, as they have appeared on the intellectual firmament. Traditionally, universities prepared students for entry into the higher professions such as medicine, law and architecture. Today, a wide panoply of new professional subjects is taught as areas of specialisation. The teaching profession itself has flourished through the training of teachers through specialist institutions within universities.

(d) Postgraduate educational courses that allow higher levels of specialisation. They include all forms of postgraduate research degrees, such as doctoral degrees necessary for eventual university appointments. Mostly conducted within universities, some postgraduate research is performed in specialised independent research establishments. A recent and important development has been management education leading to MBA degrees and to management careers within the market economy. Finally, professions, such as the medical, legal and accounting professions, admit new members into professional practice on the basis of a qualifying examination prior to the award of a practicing certificate.

Seen in the light of these activities, education may play a crucial role in reforming society towards the concept of caring and sharing in preparing individuals in the following three ways:

(a) Helping to produce educated persons equipped with the knowledge and moral values necessary to maintaining a civilised society;
(b) Providing the market economy with individuals who are knowledgeable and are influential in management decision making and able to include moral as well as economic value judgements in business decisions;
(c) Insuring that citizens are conscious that they have a personal as well as a collective engagement with respect to the well-being of all members of society and promoting in this way the ideals of a caring society as a family of citizens.

This chapter focuses on the general education of the population. Further and higher education, as well as postgraduate research will be discussed, as appropriate, in following chapters.

It will be argued that the higher the proportion of educated persons in society, the greater is the chance that society will become increasingly humane with social relationships characterised by caring and sharing. The argument in favour of a strong national commitment to education and the justification for a high level of both public and private sector financial investment in education is that the expected outcomes are in the guarantees for a future world of economic progress, higher levels of social well-being and the permanence of political stability.

The Meaning of Education

According to Peters,[3] 'in exploring the concept of education a territory is being entered where there are few signposts ... the "logical geography" of concepts in the area of education has not yet been mapped'. It follows that the processes that might be involved in education lack equally that degree of clear expression in relation to the definition of an end result. It may be useful to attempt to obtain an agreed view of what is 'an educated person', but there is no particular process that seems to be directly related and strictly necessary to that achievement. As stated by Peters,[4] 'Education ... refers to no particular process; rather it encapsulates criteria to which any one of a family of processes must conform ... To be educated is not to have arrived; it is to travel with a different view.'

Peters[5] further states that the main criteria which must be satisfied by an educated person are as follows:

> (i) An educated man is one whose form of life – as exhibited in his conduct, the activities to which he is committed, his judgements and feelings – is thought to be desirable.
> (ii) Whatever he is trained to do, he must have knowledge, not just knack, and an understanding of principles. His form of life must also exhibit some mastery of forms of thought and awareness which are not harnessed purely to utilitarian or vocational purposes or confined to one mode.
> (iii) Knowledge and understanding must not be inert either in the sense that they make no difference to his general view of the world, his actions within it and reactions to it *or* in the sense that they involve no concern for the standards immanent

---

3 Peters, R.S., 'What is an Educational Process?', in *The Concept of Education*, Peters, R.S. (ed.), London: Routledge & Kegan Paul, reprinted 1987.
4 *Ibid.*
5 *Ibid.*

in forms of thoughts and awareness, as well as the ability to attain them.

The criteria stated above do not attempt to provide end-objectives or functions in society for an educated person. They indicate that an educated person is one who enjoys a state of being that has a particular value content, but does not relate that state of being to an impact on society. It is left to supposition as to what the presence of a high proportion of educated persons in society might lead to with respect to the social characteristics of society as manifested in social relationships.

The need for a definition is that it provides a meaning that is reliable, useful and constructive in relation to the purpose being discussed. Society is a term that is definable in relation to a group of people that shares life as a community. Hence, it is possible to discuss the purpose of education in terms of its significance to objectives or purposes that are considered as desirable states for society. It is also possible to define what those desirable states should comprise in value terms and in the advantages that they are capable of creating. In other words, it is possible to talk about education in terms of moral values and to evaluate society in terms of the moral values that are present.

If education is defined only as an end result, to talk about education is to refer to an achievement. This does not help in defining the means necessary for that achievement. Indeed education, in this case, has an apparent clarity of meaning that has every aspect of a mirage. The more one seeks a clear understanding, the more difficult it seems to obtain a precise definition as a meaning and in particular relating it to an end that is desired.

The absence of a satisfactory definition of the concept of education can be compensated by reference to a structured discussion of a range of questions that are related to its problems. Thus, it has become the practice to discuss the problems of education as relating to aims, content and methods. This supposes that education is itself a structured process. If that were so, it would be possible to conduct all educational processes entirely in a formal manner and under perfect control with respect to the relation of tasks to performance. Cause and effect would be perfectly integrated and predictable.

According to Kant,[6] 'a man can only become a man through education. He is nothing more than what education has made him.'

---

6 Kant, I., *On Pedagogy*.

Reconciling this comment with Peters' definition of an educated man, it is reasonable to deduce that the aims of education could be reduced to the single dimension of producing an 'educated person'. This avoids getting into a controversial argument about the aims of education and leaves open enquiry into the nature of education itself, which provides greater scope for more profound understanding.

The discussion of formal education as involving a family of processes that have their outcome in an 'educated person' is of relatively recent origin. According to the *Oxford English Dictionary*, the term 'educated', as referring to the all-round development of a person in moral and intellectual terms, only emerged in the 19th century.

The truth may lie elsewhere, for if one considers all the influences that make a man and that therefore constitute education, it is evident that all life's influences are part of what is education, confirming that education is an ongoing process throughout life as a conscious experience.

It is relevant and useful at this stage to refer back to Plato's dialogue in *Laws*, Bk 1, where he enjoins us:

> ... let us not quarrel with one another about a word, provided that the proposition ... holds good: to wit that those who are rightly educated generally become good men. Neither must we cast a slight upon education, which is the first and fairest thing that the best of men can ever have and which, though liable to take a wrong direction, is capable of reformation. And this work of reformation is the great business of every man while he lives.

Formal and Informal Education
We referred earlier to four levels of education, each of which is aimed at different age groups and having different educational objectives. Their common feature is that they form part of formal education conducted through schools and other educational institutions. Considering education in the broad sense indicated above, formal education is only one aspect of education. If education is defined as the set of social influences that shape the being of an individual in an existentialist way, such that the result is the emergence of an individual with a high moral value content in his personality and with knowledge appropriate to making a contribution of value to society, it follows that a formal institution such as the 'school' is only one of the influences in the education of the person. Other informal influences are those that are present in his personal

life, such as the family, the beliefs that he shares with others and that may be excluded from the 'school', such as religious beliefs, clubs and associations in which he discovers and enjoys other forms of knowledge and other social experiences that are usually outside the stated objectives of the school as an organisation.

Seeing education as consisting of both formal and informal influences on the emergence of an educated person implies giving an appropriate recognition to the impact of those influences that originate from other sources. Education becomes a question of identifying the source of various influences that shape a person, the structures within which those influences act as well as the nature and effects that they may be assumed to have in the making of a person.

It is also useful to think of education not simply in terms of an end product defined as an educated person, but to amplify that term to relate it to the notion of a caring society. This notion emphasises the humane quality of a being who has been educated, so as to express those moral qualities that mark in a special and particular way the term 'educated person'.

A child becomes a human being discernible as such through relationships that have particular meanings. According to Oakeshott,[7]

> Being human is recognising oneself to be related to others ... in virtue of participation in multiple understood relationships and in the enjoyment of understood historic languages of feelings, sentiments, imaginings, fancies, desires, recognition, moral and religious beliefs, intellectual and practical enterprises, customs, conventions, procedures and practices; canons, maxims and principles of conduct, rules which denote obligations and offices which specify duties.

If education is considered in terms of the very broad perspectives stated above, it follows that life itself is a set of processes that consists of both formal and informal education. Formal education may be defined as that which has stated aims that has agreed content and that is conducted in a structured manner in accordance with prescribed and approved methods. Formal education through schooling is regulated under law and administered through a state authority that has delegated powers with respect to schools in general. Informal education may be defined as all other activities that occur outside formal schooling and is a prevalent form of

---

[7] Oakeshott, M., 'Education: The Engagement and its Frustration', in *Education and the Development of Reason*, Dearden, Hirst and Peters (ed.), London: Routledge & Kegan Paul, 1972.

education, relevant and purposeful in contributing to the making of an educated person. Many of its activities have high moral value content, stimulating the mind and sensibilities, broadening cultural horizons and beneficial to society. In line with this view, informal educational processes may be assumed to include music, theatre, literary works, art forms, cultural activities in all their variety, social activities, sporting activities etc., that add to human experience as forms of education and particularly by being identified as having moral values.

From the foregoing discussion, four separate sources may be seen as having distinct influences on education, namely, formal education through the schooling system, the family as an educative context, society itself acting through different ways in developing broadly based knowledge and moral values and, finally, organised religion, which continues to provide both formal education in denominational schools as well as upholding moral values through religious teachings.

General Education

General education, as provided formally in schools is a basic human right for all children in developed countries. The philosophy of education has been a major strand in the history of concern with society, the role of government, the importance of the individual as such and as a member of society. From Plato and Aristotle through a long and distinguished line of famous thinkers, such as Locke, Hume, Leibniz, Rousseau, Kant, Durkheim and recently Dewey, the debate about education has continued and its importance has not ceased to increase. Many social problems are assumed to result from failings in education and many of their solutions are assumed to be found in educational reform.

The role of the school and the influence of society are clearly linked in the notion of education as seen in a formal process of schooling under state authority and structured under three aspects, namely aims, content and methods.

By general consensus, content in the form of knowledge is a major matter of educational concern. Such knowledge may be specific in relation to doing something that has a stated purpose, such as reading, writing or counting. The acquisition of basic skills is one of the first stages in childhood development, often associated with play. Learning through play is inspired by a natural curiosity which leads to the acquisition of knowledge through discovery and an appreciation of its usefulness and relevance. This is an important part of the development of the thinking person but it does not necessarily mean that such a person is an educated person. A higher primate, such as an ape or indeed one of the more intelligent mammals such as a dolphin, through the process of structured learning or schooling could become a thinking being in the manner that has been described. There is much evidence in support of this belief.

Beyond the acquisition of knowledge that leads to intellectual development and to rationalised thinking, that is, thinking that links cause and effect, there are two fundamental areas related to knowledge that account for a thinking person becoming an educated person.

The first is the ability to make a critical evaluation of knowledge in the context of a current use and to make an accept/reject decision in that context and to embark upon the discovery of new knowledge following that decision. This is called critical analysis and it is the basis of judgement. Knowledge without judgement is knowing without knowing why.

The second is the ability to formulate a judgement that has a determining qualitative content. This implies that the judgement will or will not be rendered effective by implementation, if its use or the resulting ends are unacceptable by reference to a standard of quality. This qualitative standard could be one of the quality level or it could be a judgement that is an accept/reject decision based on morality, that is, an understood difference established by reference to what is considered good or bad. A simple illustration is the accept/reject decision that is made by a vegetarian with respect to protein intake. Protein is a food element essential to the body. A major source of protein is meat. To consume protein in that form requires the killing of a being of species, such as a cow. A vegetarian opposes this use of life as being immoral for it offends the sanctity of life. Consequently, he makes an accept/reject decision on the basis of a moral value. Concern for the moral importance of life has changed perceptions of the manner in which even those who accept the consumption of meat insist the breeding of animals for slaughter and the act of slaughter must be humane. Cruelty as regards breeding conditions and slaughter is forbidden under regulations enforced by law. This is a good example of the manner by which a caring society concerned with moral values effectively opposes an industrial activity conducted upon competitive market conditions and designed to manufacture meat at lowest possible cost. It is the reliance on moral values for making decisions with respect to both current and new knowledge that is the essential characteristic of the educated man. Hence, it is the most important determinant in defining the nature of education itself.

If education is defined only as a performance result associated with the formal process of schooling, then it follows that a person formed specifically in accordance with those aims, will be a product result of the process. He will be given a formal certificate of authenticity as to his educational level and performance achievement. Equally, the individual who has failed to meet the performance levels required for the award of certificate of educational performance will bear a stigma for the rest of his life and will join the ranks of those excluded from many opportunities that society offers to those deemed as successful within limited sets of criteria.

Rousseau stated that individuals are born equal and it is society that creates inequality but there exists an infinite variety of talents that nature has bestowed on individuals and that account for differences between them. Performance standards that are based on narrow sets of criteria that reduce all individuals to a simplified and common standard may be dysfunctional with respect to society's own needs for integrating individuals in a harmonious and useful manner into its activities.

The educational system may be considered as having a responsibility for creating inequality, if it should fail to treat the individual in the context of his own personal merits, or in any way that restricts his potential or exposes him to performance standards that may be inappropriate.

The standards that are used by schools to evaluate performance reflect in many ways those performance standards used in society generally and in particular at the workplace. One of the aims of schooling clearly is the preparation of the individual for work, as a means for earning a living and also creating for himself a way of living through work or activity.

The manner in which schooling may be judged to fail the individual in respect to performance evaluation may be considered in two ways. First, by restricting schooling to a set of disciplines or subjects deemed to constitute the body of knowledge relevant to education, children who have special gifts that cannot find expression in that context may be penalised. Second, because performance evaluation is of necessity always made on a comparative basis, since ranking of performance is an inescapable feature of assessment, the inequality of performance of one individual results from comparison with a deemed better performance of another individual. This is an effective cause of inequality that will have an impact throughout life through the opportunities that are offered by the market economy that demand such evaluations for selecting employees. It is also an effective cause of inequality that results in long-term harm to the individual by creating within his sense of being a feeling of inadequacy and hence a feeling of inferiority. For a teacher to say, 'John is better behaved than Peter,' and by inference a better child, is not simply an evaluation, it stigmatises Peter.

The acquisition of basic knowledge, such as reading, writing and counting, as well as knowledge pertaining to the national culture and instilling in children the ability to think critically and develop understanding were and remain major objectives in school education. By tradition, an important element of general education in school was the development of team spirit, in which the sharing of the experience of learning under a teacher's leadership and involvement was conducted in a climate of mutual exchange. The synergy that resulted from this cross fertilisation of experiences and views was the substantial added value of school.

Today, the extensive reliance on computer and multimedia systems in schools has had two deleterious effects on education. First, the isolation of individuals working with computers has eroded completely the value that a shared learning environment created. Second, the role of the teacher as leader and guide in the learning situation has been diminished and made subservient to an interactive technology that is inert in terms of human values. The teacher has been reclassified to the new and fundamentally different role of facilitator, thereby altering his former role in co-ordinating a team or class of learners. In the new-speak that has accompanied the recent evolution in educational thinking, even the role of head of the school has been reduced to an administrative one as a coordinator and has lost the traditional school leadership role. Within the school, the segregation of roles and functions has had an alienating effect by reducing the importance of each of its members in a community sense. Moreover, the isolation of the individual from the peer group of learners is exacerbated by out-of-school obligations in terms of homework and project work conducted in the home environment, in which he is again isolated with the computer and lives as a hermit within his own home, glued to a computer screen and wired up by earphones.

Schools also contributed significantly to the team spirit through group and sporting activities within the school curriculum. In particular, the emphasis was on sporting activities intended to develop that courage both physical and mental, needed to face the challenges of life. It also placed a premium on physical well-being. The obese child was an exceptional case, well outside the norm in the peer group and unable fully to participate in its activities. The computer culture has supplanted those group activities both in and out of schools for the majority of children. This new culture of watchers and listeners has little time to devote to out-of-school sporting activities requiring significant physical effort. Obesity, through overeating and the lack of physical activity has become a serious health problem. The obese child is no longer the exception; he has become the normal child.

Given our assertion that education has a crucial role in reforming society to the ideals of one based on caring and sharing, the foregoing discussion indicates that education is in itself in a state of crisis with respect not only to traditional objectives implicit in its socialising function, but also to those of teachers in their teaching function. There is no denying the advantages that the computer-based information revolution has brought to modern society; there is no denying that it has brought in its train considerable changes in living patterns; there is no denying that the future cannot be made subordinate to the past and that new conditions must be integrated in an harmonious manner to the ideals that education aims to achieve.

A humane society founded on the principles of sharing and caring and in a sense of community based on moral values will expect such principles and values to be fully reflected in educational philosophy, processes and teaching methods. Education is a human and humane experience involving a continuous dialogue between teachers and pupils in an ongoing exchange of beliefs and views in which an eventual consensus is forged. It leads to a sense of community through the friendship that eliminates isolation. It absorbs an obsessive sense of self in a sense of community that fosters a sympathetic awareness of others and makes the idea of caring and sharing a natural and community fellowship.

The hopes and expectations attached to education for reforming society are entrusted to those having the political authority and the leadership role for making value judgements and establishing policy objectives. The reliance on modern computerised management systems facilitates the central administration of the schooling system as a social service. The gathering of data is standardised, but when data has been transformed into information, it will have been modified by judgemental considerations and may be infected by bias. Computers facilitate the transmission of information for management purpose in a very broad sense, from setting performance standards to performance evaluation, relying on reporting and control systems, which are comparable to those used for enterprise management. However, they are perfectly inert with regard to moral value judgements, which are the most important concerns in education. A quantitative evaluation of performance of the schooling system, even if it gives an output view of the numbers of children processed and their attainment on measurement scales based on examination results, cannot provide a perception of true performance. The effectiveness of general education may be appreciated only in terms of the proportion of children who have benefited from education and in some measure are educated persons. Statistics relating to improvements in numeracy and literacy may or may not be indicative of the output performance of the general educational system. However, statistics relative to truancy rates, juvenile delinquency, drug-taking, incivility and unemployment among adolescents certainly reflect the relative loss of influence of moral values and the failure of schools in their designated mission of producing the next generation of educated persons.

Education and the Family
The family is to education a total experience that covers both informal and formal education and consists of a set of relationships adapted to the transmission of a heritage of knowledge and of moral values.

The family is especially significant and important in the upbringing of children and may be seen as the cradle of education. The quality and the stability of family life have rightly been prized by all generations as offering an optimal structure for living happily and successfully growing up within a caring environment. In most areas of the world, the family remains the keystone of society. In Western European and mostly Protestant countries, the family concept has become less prized. For various reasons, it has suffered a diminution of esteem.

Nevertheless, there remains strongly entrenched within a caring society a sentiment that, under ideal conditions, the family is the best formula for living and maintaining the human race. The love and the care that parents bestow on their children, the joy and the sense of security and protection that children enjoy in the intimacy of the family relationship and the happiness that is shared by and within the family is the most meaningful and touching of all the various facets of life. Within the family structure that nature has provided for all species and which is manifested generally in animal life, as well as human life, parents bring to life the young ensuring in this way the continuity of the species. They impose their authority on the young and teach them how to face the problems of life by showing them what to do and how to do it. Parents pass on to their children the lessons of experience that are invaluable to survival; they also instil in them the ability to distinguish between right and wrong in their manner of behaving. Children are obliged initially by their dependence on parents to respect the parental authority and obey the moral rules that are prescribed by parents, before eventually accepting them as their own, as justified by reason as well as necessity. In these various ways, parents hand over to their children those moral values required to lead harmonious and happy lives in conformity with standards of behaviour in which moral values exert a determining influence.

It follows that an appropriate meaning of the term 'education' in this sense may be understood as a specific transaction that goes on between generations of human beings in which newcomers are initiated into society. In this context, the moral values that are identified and transmitted are those which have gained acceptance through generations as moral commitments that provide the justification for beliefs and the basis of humane relationships.

This invites another perspective of the term 'education' as a transmission of an inheritance of understanding. It takes education beyond the cradle of the family and broadens the vision of its scope to that of society as a whole. Those moral values that are transmitted as an inheritance of civilisation have an enduring validity in their immutable acceptance through generations. For example, truth is unlikely to be rejected as a moral value in favour of lies or untruths. What shocks the Social Conscience at the moment is the immoral manner in which lies are used as expedients to conceal truth. A commitment to truth is an authoritative moral value that prohibits the use of a lie in preference to truth. It is viewed as an essential reference point for the transparency of understanding.

The first stage of initiation into a caring society means learning to live within the family relationship. As such, it is largely one of indoctrination. It involves the child accepting the rules that are imposed and the moral values that they reflect. This process does not offer the child much choice, save that of disobedience. Discipline, as the required observance of moral values and rules of behaviour having general acceptance within society, is fundamental to social order. Parental authority is the first level of authority to which the child is exposed. Discipline, expressed as good behaviour is expected to result in a well-behaved child, namely one that will not disrupt the social order. Socialising through discipline relies on the stick and carrot method to secure consent. Reward and punishment will be contested at a very early stage by the child with an argument that refers to fairness.

The socialising process by which society is created through personal relationships begins almost at birth. It continues with greater intensity as the sphere of relationships expands and persists throughout adult life as a constant need to adapt to others in maintaining harmonious relationships and the good functioning of society. Harmony as a moral value that depends on order, which is the result of discipline, allied to the concept of justice, explained as fairness, form part of the first set of moral values that determine the humane condition. The child becomes aware of these moral values at a very early stage of life in an informal manner in the school of infancy. The caring environment, in which love expressed in the affectionate relationship between the parental authority and the child, comforts the child's submission of self in exchange for a better 'good'. This is, in effect, Rousseau's social contract, in which there is an exchange that leads to a better freedom. It exists naturally in the school of infancy.

Soon, the child adds to the parental relationship a new and expanding set of other relationships. He makes contact with other children. He learns the rules of living with others, the need to share and even the need to give. Especially, he learns the need to avoid hurting others and he learns that caring about others is necessary to avoid hurting others. In the school of infancy, society naturally creates itself through socialising relationships. Awareness of others, sensitivity to others, learning through play to live together is the learning experiences of the school of infancy. Even as a child, he begins to expand his awareness of his responsibility towards others and, in particular, those who are weaker. Learning not to hurt others and not to derive satisfaction through violence is again one of the most important moral values that are learnt at the school of infancy.

The breakdown of parental authority, the rejection of discipline by children in schools, incivility and violent behaviour outside school, result from a generalised abdication of parental, school and state authority as regards enforcing acceptable standards of behaviour. The abandonment of traditional moral values in society is, in part, a consequence of the conflict between freedom and authority in modern Western society, which is discussed in a subsequent chapter.

Societal Influences as Informal Education
The need to have control over the educational processes to ensure that the performance achieved is that which is desired is made explicit in formal education through evaluation procedures and awards of performance certificates, but it is more problematical to evaluate informal education. For example, there has been much debate for many years with respect to the influence of television as a media, particularly upon children. Firstly, it is known that the influence of television on children is real and that the messages that it communicates are perceived and understood. Can the messages transmitted through the medium of the television be defined as informal education? This is largely a matter of circumstances. It is perfectly possible to use the television as a method of teaching as confirmed by the Open University. It is also true that, as people read much less than heretofore and as they rely much more on televised news and information, media derived knowledge has become an important means for acquiring knowledge for the population at large.

It is an uncomfortable truth that many of the messages and understandings communicated through media and entertainment channels appear not only void of moral values but deny moral values, for example, the gratuitous and casual use of violence. Many would judge such content of television programmes as representing the perversion of moral values and as having a negative influence on a society based on moral values.

Television holds the attention of audiences and particularly young persons who are susceptible to influence by messages that emphasise violence, sex, destruction as normal events and casual in their nature. Can it be inferred from Kant, that television is an educational process that makes for violent individuals, obsessed with sex as a way of life and with destruction as an enjoyable and justifiable activity? As a caricature, if education is to be defined by reference to an end that is the educated person, is it possible that reverse processes could operate that would effectively counter the aim of education as stated and produce monsters having knowledge but void of any moral content? Much as this hypothesis may be repugnant, all indices indicate that moral values are on the decline and the criminality in violent and destructive forms seems to be increasing.

Computer games have become a compulsive occupation for an entire generation of young people. Schooled at an early age under the doctrine of learning through play, the association of learning and entertainment may have weakened the notion that learning is also a matter of discipline and effort. Children no longer socialise to the extent of previous generations through team games and sporting activities, but isolate themselves in an intense relationship with their computer. The fashion in computer games is an emphasis on human relations that are violent, on social situations that are evil and on personal behaviour that is destructive. An interactive computer game allows a child the unrestrictive freedom to indulge the reality of visual violence with the sole objective of deriving a thrill for murder, sexual violence, robbery, attacks on the police and all the possible acts of criminal violence. Computer games indulge freely and without penal sanction the type of behaviour that society has been at pains to repress since time immemorial. They act in this sense not only as denials of moral values, but encourage depravity in all its forms. Those providers of this type of informal education do so under the protection of a distorted concept of freedom that permits vice to flourish.

There is no area of knowledge to which access is as easy as that provided by websites and even young children are fully conversant with that form of information technology. The fact that internet security systems now allow for parental control of access to sites is a clear recognition of the moral dangers to which children are exposed through multimedia technology.

Hence informal education may well be in opposition and in contradiction to those that are normally associated with schooling as formal education, which is subject to control as to aims, content and methods.

The influence of television is beyond the control of regulatory authorities, except when censorship may be exercised, usually on moral grounds. There is a further dimension to the regulation and control of informal education, namely the debate over the freedom of expression that strongly opposes censorship. It is, in effect, a debate about moral values. Literary and artistic licence is argued to be a justified and necessary condition and the unrestricted freedom of expression is essential to all art forms. Accordingly, freedom of expression is the sole moral value in question. It is a doctrinal belief that the impact and influence of messages and understandings resulting from this freedom cannot be evaluated under any relevant criteria based on other moral value judgements. In other words, other moral values are all susceptible of interpretation. A painting that is perfectly ugly to one may be perfectly beautiful to another and thus beauty is *per se* a circumstantial appreciation. Hence, meaning and influence are interpreted as susceptible of being infinitely elastic, and, on the basis of this reasoning, censorship constrains imagination. There is a frame hanging in the modern art section of a famous London art gallery in which is stretched a totally blank sheet. It obtained the high commendation by art critics and judges that was needed for its acceptance for permanent exhibition. A callow youth from an educationally deprived area of London could well have been moved to add suitable graffiti to reduce the monotony of the painting's singular uniqueness of colour. Such a gratuitous act would certainly have carried the penalty appropriate to the wilful damage of a work of art, even though a reasonable person would have exonerated the youth on the grounds that his imagination had been fired by the understandable inspiration of finding a use for it.

The problem of freedom generally will be discussed in a subsequent chapter. As far as the role of education and its importance to a caring society, the acceptance that informal education, as defined above, is an important influence in that regard unquestionably raises the problem of evaluation and control. A caring society is one in which moral values are at its heart. Those influences that denigrate such values constitute a direct attack on the concept of a caring society and on civilisation generally. According to Oakeshott,[8] moral values are recognised as being desirable because they inspire gratitude, pride and even the veneration of those who already enjoy them, endowing them with an identity they esteem and are understood as an engagement rather than an heirloom.

Much of the output of the new information technology has a more subtle and insidious objective associated with product marketing and creating a culture of dependence through subliminal advertising. In addition to creating a captive market in this manner, it contributes to the more general purpose of creating a sub-culture among the young based on consumption and self-gratification to the detriment of all other lifestyle considerations, with culture moguls projecting their own pathetic life models on the gullible young.

8 Oakeshott, M., 'Education: The Engagement and its Frustration'.

The Ongoing Debate about Education
The discussion of education in schools has been concerned largely and variously with the notions of aims, content and methods, lending emphasis to one or the other, depending upon the problem being considered. Many new ideas about education have resulted from changing beliefs about aims and content.

Currently, the notion of citizenship as a moral value in itself opposes two extreme theories of education. A caring society focuses upon the individual in the first instance and sees the individual's role in society as a projection into adult life and a defined social role. A caring society is concerned, therefore, with the notion of the 'educated person' discussed earlier in this chapter. It is as an individual that the educated person fulfils three distinct functions in society.

The first is as a family member, who as an adult will have the most important function in life with respect to the procreation of life, as a natural father or as a natural mother, as defined by nature with their special and particular attributes of such roles towards their children. In this sense, education has much to do with both moral values and family values and their importance in society.

The second function of an individual is participating as an adult in work activity. General education is the first level preparation for working life. Further, higher and professional education has the immediate objective of preparing individuals for specific functions that reflect their innate or special skills and motivations. In this context, a caring society remains focused on the individual, on his merits, potential and the many different rewards that may be his or hers to enjoy and to share with others. It is evident that a caring society is concerned with the well-being of its members within the market economy and the welfare of others is implied in all personal working relationships. In addition to the economic rewards that flow from the nature of work itself, there is an important moral value element in the way in which relations at work are structured in an environment in which caring is the guiding principle. Traditionally, further, higher and professional education has not shown a strong interest in moral values, focusing rather on expertise and professional skills and knowledge. Some professions that have a close relationship with human life, such as the medical and allied professions commit their teaching to a moral framework, commonly described as 'deontology'. It enshrines the value of individual life, the moral obligation to protect life and professional responsibility in this regard. The best illustration of this deontology is the Hippocratic Oath. Most other professions are committed to formal standards, but not all of these standards necessarily reflect moral values as a guiding principle. There is a real debate on this problem within the accounting profession and within the financial services industry as a whole. In all cases, professional misconduct is a personal and individual responsibility and disqualification from the right to practice is the most severe penalty that is the right of a professional body to apply to offending members.

The third function of an individual is as a member of that larger family which is the nation, providing at once identification and social cohesion. The concept of a caring society sees the nation as built up from the bottom, that is, the basic family unit. In the first chapter, shared moral values were determined to be the basis of participation in society and the foundation upon which responsibility for government could be delegated by individuals to a governing authority. The democratic principle is deemed to reflect the moral value that should determine the relationship between the State and the individual. The moral values that are shared in democratic societies are also those found within the family unit and form the set of moral values upon which all forms of education are founded. The education of the individual as a citizen is one of the guarantees of individual freedom and of a caring society. Requiring the observance and preservation of those moral values by politicians, to whom the delegation of government is entrusted through democratic elections, is the second guarantee of individual freedom and of a caring society. It is in this regard that there is today a major threat to the integrity of society through the widespread abuse of power and of trust. Politicians of all persuasions seek in all things their personal interests rather than those of society. Clearly, citizen education does have a use in enabling the citizen to develop not only knowledge of a functioning democracy but an ability to make a critical analysis and judgement of the overall performance of government ministers, with particular reference to moral principles manifested in decisions and actions.

Receiving the heritage of knowledge, which is the gift of civilisation transmitted from generation to generation, using that knowledge through the experience of life in all its forms, understanding that knowledge and applying it to useful purposes and to engage in the ongoing commitment to progress through new knowledge is the task that is the privilege of each individual. Knowledge stems from thinking and thinking is that activity of mind that is the essential characteristic of human existence. Living is thinking by means of knowledge; it is also thinking about knowledge in a purposeful way. The initial questions which face each thinking individual in this sense are not only 'What to do?' but 'What is the right thing to do?' These are the most important questions and they are always also moral questions.

We are schooled both formally and informally as regards knowledge and as regards its use. Knowledge is subjected and submitted to the moral imperative which is eternally questioning, 'What is right?' This question is the expression of eternal doubt and as treated in the Cartesian doctrine of systematic doubt found its expression in Descartes'[9] most celebrated statement of the meaning of life: 'I think, therefore I am.'

The moral implication of the question 'What is right?' in a decision context concerning most social situations, involves others or their interests. Hence, what is perceived as right is ultimately an expression of caring. Viewed in a social perspective, the eternal doubt as to what is right spurs a caring society to be open to perpetual self-examination.

What is right is the absolute moral imperative as regards the education of the individual. This question opens and expands the debate about moral values by virtue of the evident truth that education is the process through which the individual is initiated into society, lives within it and shares life with others. Accepting that it is through interaction with others in a social context that the individual is fulfilled, it follows that the debate about moral values in education is also one of justification. Hence, this debate refers to a normative set of ideas that are inexorably based on moral values.

The first question is, then: 'Has education to do with the individual, or has it to do with society?' It seems reasonable to suggest that education has to do with both the individual and with society, since reason and consequences are irretrievably associated in the notion of a caring society. Concern with the aims of education, content and method has long been the subject matter of the philosophy of education. Much of the literature has been about the education of the individual in relation to his being. For example, since man is essentially rational by nature, education ought to be concerned with the development of that characteristic. Another argument stresses the importance of personal relationships and that

---

9 Descartes, R., 'Je pense, donc je suis', in *Le Discours sur la Méthode*, Pt. 4.

therefore education should be a socialising experience. In these discussions, the aim of education is often interpreted in relation to the nature of man and to naturalism is an operative concept. One definition of education states it is a process of 'bringing forth what is in the nature of the person'. In line with this belief, the substance of the person exists in his being; all his talents are already present in the special and unique being that is his natural self. Rousseau[10] tried to show how a natural education, unlike the artificial and formal education of society, enables Emile to become social, moral and rational while remaining true to his original nature.

The self-realisation or the whole person concept of education by itself pays little attention to accounting for the fulfilment or consequential effects of education. By contrast, imposing on the educational process an objective defined strictly in relation to the interests of society, defined as the State, reduces the significance of the individual to that of a function and deprives him of his humanity. This instrumental theory is expressed in Durkheim's[11] definition of education as:

> ... the influence exercised by the adult generation on those that are no yet ready for social life. Its object is to arouse and develop in the child a certain number of physical, intellectual and moral states which are required of him both by the political society as a whole and by the special milieu for which he is specifically destined.

The argument in favour of a caring society is an argument about moral values in society. Education is essential to empowering such a society and, for that reason, it is a matter of public policy and political will. Left to itself as a guiding principle, the education of the 'whole person' has little meaning in that sense, unless it is seen in the context of a social fulfilment. The infinite variety of talents that exists in human nature, as expressed in an infinite variety of different personalities and as manifested and made effective through education, serve to optimise the humane condition that is a caring society.

The discussion of content and methods of education is a large and controversial issue. Focusing on education for a caring society is a matter of reforming a population, so that social behaviour is subjected to the criterion, 'What is right?'

10 Rousseau, J.J., *Emile*.
11 Durkheim, R., *Education et Sociologie* (posthumous publication), Paris: Alcan, 1922, p.49.

The next question is: 'Is there a corpus of moral values that can form the basis of an ethical education?' Some would argue that the inclusion of religious studies or ethical studies in the school curriculum would meet this need. In general terms, the growing public disaffection with religion has acted against religious studies in state schools.

There is a renewed debate about civics in the school curriculum, which has arisen from public concern with the prevalence of a culture of bad manners, lack of respect for authority, incivility, disrespect for property, gratuitous violence, obscenity, dishonesty, gang violence, drunkenness, drug addiction etc. The school is being asked to provide a remedy for the failure of parents to bring up children correctly and for the failure of the State to provide an environment in which people feel secure and may live peacefully. The demand that teachers should act *in loco parentis* with respect to compensating for the inability of the parents of this generation to bring up children correctly is a heavy and inappropriate burden to place on teachers. It is quite understandable that teachers are themselves in some difficulty with respect to their perception of their responsibility in this regard.

The debate about ethical studies has moved in recent years to the concept of 'citizenship' education. In the United Kingdom, the Advisory Group on Education for Citizenship and the Teaching of Democracy in Schools, established by the then Secretary of State for Education under the Chairmanship of Professor Bernard Crick, had the remit of:

> ... providing advice on effective education for citizenship in schools – to include the nature and participation in democracy, the duties, responsibilities and rights of individuals as citizens; and the value to individuals and society of community activity.

This remit carries strong echoes of the influence of Durkheim's instrumental theory of education, referred to earlier, which subordinates education to a limited concept of society, namely, a political society of which education is seen as the image and reflection.

The Crick Report published in 1998 may be judged to have adopted Durkheim's concept of education in its conclusion that 'the teaching of citizenship and democracy is so important both for schools and the life of the nation, that there should be a statutory requirement on schools to ensure that it is part of the entitlement of all pupils'. As such, citizenship education is an extension of a curriculum requirement in general education having the objective of preparing children and adolescents for adult life with citizenship responsibilities.

Education for Citizenship may be viewed as a visionary commitment to political education in democracy having the objective of preparing students 'to participate effectively, actively and responsibly within their communities in adult life'. It has created an international movement in favour of citizenship education, which is gathering pace and growing influence in educational circles. It is loaded with complex and perplexing questions, not the least being those relating to moral values and political objectives. Moreover, highly controversial issues, which are also referred to in a context of political correctness that may act to limit the freedom of expression, may undermine the educational value of citizenship education. How to achieve 'political literacy ... from a position of knowledge and a capacity to identify strategies for action' without falling into the moral error of indoctrination, is surely a major philosophical issue. Big citizenship questions such as power, freedom, justice, equality, protest, rights and fairness may not be as exciting to an average student struggling with spelling and grammar and the logic of simple forms of mathematics as protagonists of citizenship education may imagine. Aiming citizenship education at children aged from five years to adolescents of sixteen to eighteen is a noble objective in principle, but likely to be undermined as a teaching platform by its absence of reality for the child. Indeed, this may be seen in the general apathy of the adult public in most countries towards the democratic process and in the sectarian issues that divide and oppose politicians of different persuasions.

The Role of Religion in Education
The foregoing discussion of the role of education in empowering a caring society has focused on formal education through the schooling system and the informal education that society itself makes available in many different ways.

From earliest times, religion has played a social role of overwhelming importance in a number of ways. By prescribing and requiring the observance of religious rules from which moral values are derived, religion has provided the rules that act as the basis of jurisprudence as well as the Social Conscience. Indeed, even today in many countries, religious courts settle all matters of litigation. Canon Law was the applicable law in England prior to the Judicature Acts of 1875 in matters of private and family law. In the 16th century in England, the Lord Chancellor, who was an ecclesiastical person and acted as the King's conscience, introduced the principles of Equity into English law. This branch of law retains its authority to this day in all Common Law countries. If the influence of religion has waned in Protestant countries, it remains a powerful force in Catholic countries. Similarly, Islamic and Rabbinical law have retained their moral and legal authority among populations of Islamic and Judaic faith.

The concern of all religious authorities is strongly orientated towards family life and family values. Religions of all denominations embody the principles of caring and sharing as cardinal doctrinal commitments. Nowhere is caring more evident in religious action than in the concern for the young. Such education as existed was provided by religious bodies and it is only since the latter part of the 19th century that the State assumed a responsibility for the provision of school education. Most of the oldest universities and schools were established as religious foundations.

Today, the role of religion in education may be discussed under two aspects. First, acquainting children from an early age with the Holy Books, which are the authoritative texts. Both the Old and the New Testaments have been used traditionally in churches of all Christian denominations for the purpose of religious instruction. The history of the Jewish people is replete with tales that are both interesting from an historical viewpoint as well as for the moral teachings that they embody. Some are also valuable from the viewpoint of literature, for example, the Book of Job in the King James Version of the Bible that is universally recognised for the quality of its verse. Even though Jews do not recognise the New Testament, the co-existence of both the Old and the New Testament in the Bible and the access that these Holy Texts provide to an understanding of both the Christian and the Jewish faiths has a social relevance that goes beyond the moral values that are made explicit. Religious beliefs often serve to divide people. However, used in the context of biblical, ethical or religious studies, Holy Books can also serve to create a sympathetic awareness of people of other faiths and hence help to increase social cohesion.

Western civilisation cannot divorce itself from the Eastern world, particularly when they share the same problems. The Koran may also usefully be read and taught, through the moral values that it upholds and which echo those of the Bible. As the global economy expands and integrates all nations under its economic influence, the empowerment of a caring and sharing society through education cannot afford to discount the importance of bridging a seeming but unreal difference in moral values between people of different faiths. Hence, it follows that the school curriculum should include that area of knowledge through which these values are clearly enunciated.

In view of the radicalism that is appearing in the world today and bringing in its train both racial and religious violence, now is not the time to abandon the teaching of religion in schools. Rather, it is the time to use the opportunity which exists through the schooling system to instil in children the sharing of their common heritage, which is the belief in God that is the religious credo. The basis of all religious teaching is the acceptance that we are all children of God and all members of one and the same family.

Many have rejected religion. The impact of socialism in all its expressions and, in particular the influence of the Communist Revolution, has been to encourage atheism among intellectuals, as well as the working classes. Those who are not atheist are, at least, agnostic. The materialism and consumerism of modern times has magnified the immediacy of pleasure and self-satisfaction. These influences also act as obstacles to the emergence of a caring society.

Hence, there is strong opposition in Western society against the teaching of religion in schools and a conviction that state schools should be secular and adopt a neutral position as regards religion. The argument against including religion in the school curriculum is essentially political and motivated mainly from political parties of the left and also by fringe groups reacting against the moral standpoints with which religious authorities are associated. Another argument is that teachers generally are not qualified to teach religion. Moreover, given that recent immigration has resulted in a more polyglot population reflecting a greater spread of religious beliefs, it is felt that the teaching of religion in schools could be conducive to social conflicts.

Nevertheless, it is remarkable that the protagonists of the teaching of citizenship make a case for the use of history to this end and at the same time reject the teaching of religion, when the history of Western civilisation and the moral values that are the basis of citizenship, are of Judaeo-Christian origins.

Second, there is a continuing desire of parents to have their children educated in religious schools or denominational schools, such as Catholic schools, Jewish schools or Islamic schools. These schools are subjected to state supervision and licensing and they continue to flourish and to present an alternative to the state system. From a parental viewpoint, the desire to have their children educated in this manner is clearly a demand for education founded on moral values and a conviction that moral values should be the determinant of choice with respect to general education.

Conclusions
Empowering a caring society begins with reforming the existing beliefs which are pervasive in modern society and that are reinforced by the mores of a market economy, in which competition between individuals in many aspects of life has weakened the awareness of others and stimulated selfishness, greed and acquisitiveness.

It is in children, uncorrupted by the hold that the modern world exercises over beliefs and behaviour, that new ideals may find fertile ground. The hopes for a caring society reside in education and its proximity and influence over children. Teachers being, in spirit, sufficiently distant from the realities of a market economy in their function as teachers, are able to undertake the responsibility of acting as agents in the design and creation of a new society, which reflects those moral values that economic progress and the market economy have stifled. The teaching profession is staffed by a population which frequently has a high level of social commitment and sense of mission. Famous educators have been influential figures in the progress of civilisation.

The education of the whole person, the stimulation of vision and imagination through knowledge and awareness of realities of different forms, the ability to appreciate beauty and harmony in all things and, above all, the acquisition of that degree of sensitivity that leads to sentimental fulfilment are the true educational values.

Empowering a caring society means enabling an educated person to fulfil his or her mission in life by self-realisation in an open society sharing mutual ideals and moral values.

The divide that separates Rousseau from Durkheim is precisely the relative importance that is given to the individual. For Rousseau, it is the education of the individual and the realisation of his natural talents that is the purpose of education. For Durkheim and many others, it is the socialisation of the individual and his integration in society that is the prime objective. In this sense, education is an instrument for nation building and a servant to the market economy.

Viewing education as the means of empowering a caring society does not imply that education is thereby solely a social instrument.

Education for a Caring Society

A caring society sees each individual as benefiting from education and sharing life with others in a society in which individuals are members of one family, united in sympathetic awareness of each other.

—5—

Market Behaviour

The market economy is the vehicle which transformed an agrarian society into a market society, with its particular values and structures. The market economy is not self-regulating and the notion of perfect markets is not sustainable in the face of such economic phenomena as inflation and recession. Market imperfections deny the moral values to which Adam Smith was committed. Marx and Schumpeter both believed that capitalism, which is the economic system on which the market economy relies, leads to the exploitation and oppression of mankind by capitalists and cannot survive because its value system is flawed. Nevertheless, the market economy thrives and considerable improvements in living standards have resulted from its action. The development of the joint stock corporation with limited liability made an important contribution to the expansion of the market economy. The reconciliation of the market economy with a caring society, which is the great divide between capitalism and socialism, must focus on removing inequalities in income distribution and on restoring social justice.

TWO CRUCIAL QUESTIONS face us in resolving the dilemma that lies in the coexistence of a caring society and a market economy:

Can a caring society exist in a market economy?

Is a market economy sustainable that denies man's fundamental nature and needs for caring and sharing?

Having discussed the policy objectives of a caring society in Chapter 3, and examined in Chapter 4 the implication of these objectives for the reform of education, we turn now to discussing the dilemma posed by the foregoing two questions for the reform of the market economy towards a caring society. To this end, it is necessary to understand the nature of the market economy, the social structure that it assumes as necessary to its efficient functioning, its objective and methods and the value system upon which it relies. This chapter will also discuss the social implications of modern industrial society based on capitalism, that is, the private ownership and enjoyment of economic resources, with special reference to the social context created by the shareholder value concept.

A caring society acts in accordance with the Social Conscience that is the authority that it obeys. The market economy is one in which each person present in the market as a buyer or seller is motivated by self-interest in a competitive environment in which the objective is profit-seeking. Markets thrive when there are no barriers of any kind to free trade and trading is free of regulation or constraint.

Markets have existed from time immemorial. The history of civilisation is associated with trading activities conducted through markets or fairs, as they were known in medieval times. The freedom to trade has always been and remains a fundamental human right. The presence of free markets is essential to economic development. The specialisation of labour and concentration of skills under conditions that allow the law of comparative advantages to apply, results in economic growth leading to improved living standards through the exchange of production surpluses.

Markets respond to needs. There are an infinite number of markets. Their business is conducted in accordance with custom and law, reflecting in these ways the Social Conscience and its moral values. Although markets are usually closely identified with economic activity and their behaviour in that sense is considered within the context of economic theory, their impact is equally important in terms of social theory and the manner in which society functions. A recent publication suggests that modern society may be perceived as a market society in which social behaviour is conditioned by the manner in which people act out their economic behaviour in their social behaviour by adopting similar values.[1]

The advent of industrial capitalism in the 18th and 19th centuries in England was made possible by the association of landed wealth that provided the required capital to early entrepreneurs for industrial development. The Joint Stock Companies Acts of 1844 greatly encouraged the industrialisation of England by innovating a legal identity, namely the Joint Stock Company that was separate from that of its owners. It made two very significant contributions to economic growth at this period. First, it provided a structure for channelling to such companies funds provided by investors in such

---

1 See Slater, D. and Tonkiss, F., *Market Society*, Cambridge: Polity Press, 2001.

a way that they retained ownership, but separated ownership from control.[2] The certificates of ownership were and remain in the form of 'shares' and capital provided in this way is described as 'share capital'. It appears as a credit balance in favour of shareholders on company balance sheets. Companies were also able to raise capital by way of long-term and short-term loans, but these loans were debt owed by the company to creditors. Second, to provide financial protection to investors and thereby encourage the development of the Joint Stock Company model, their liability for the company's debts was and remains limited in law to the amount of the capital invested, or the capital agreed to be invested and as yet uncalled.

The Joint Stock Company concept and the principle of limited liability are the central feature of modern capitalist organisation. Companies, sometimes known as corporations, are deemed in law to be owned by shareholders. Generally, they are managed by professional managers, whose responsibilities are to manage them for the benefit of shareholders with the objective of maintaining and improving the value of their shares. The 'shareholder value' principle is the cornerstone of corporate financial management theory that provides the rules for corporate management, as well as the theory of finance concerned with the functioning of financial markets.

The Nature of the Market Economy
The market economy is a system for the exchange of economic resources, goods and services that relies on a price mechanism for regulating the effective level of demand for and the supply of such resources, goods and service. The pricing mechanism determines the market price, which is defined as the price at which buyers are willing to buy and sellers are willing to sell. The pricing mechanism is an automatic control system with respect to demand and supply and continuously responds to changes in demand and supply conditions by adjusting the market price. Under conditions of perfect competition, the pricing mechanism will ensure the efficient allocation of economic resources, goods and service within the market economy. The efficient market hypothesis is one that assumes that perfect competition exists. It ceases to hold good in the presence of market distortions created by imperfect

---

2 Control depends upon the proportion of the share capital held. Legally, it requires having a majority of the issued share capital having voting rights, normally 51% of the ordinary share capital.

competition or monopoly situations that allow either buyers or sellers unduly to influence pricing by their ability to control supply or demand, as the case may be. The tendency towards manipulating markets through limiting competition by influencing demand or supply is strongly present in the market economy. It results in 'unfair competition' and brings the market economy into conflict with the Social Conscience, as it is expressed in the regulatory measures that are either institutionalised by market supervisory authorities or legislated under state authority.

Operators in the market economy, acting either as buyers or sellers, are motivated by the prospect of realising financial gains. In this sense, future expectations of gains that motivate business decisions are the driving force in the market economy. Buyers will not buy now unless they expect to make a profit in the future from their acquisition: sellers will not sell unless they are able to expect a profit from a sale now.

The market economy is a complex economy consisting of many different types of markets. They may exist in relation to types of resources, for example the labour market, or to the type of good, for example the wheat market, or as categories of markets, such as wholesale or retail markets. Markets may have physical locations, for example, Labour Exchanges where unemployed persons may go to seek work, or the Stock Exchange, where shares or other financial instruments may be bought and sold, using brokers as intermediaries. Internet websites are also markets for a variety of goods and services using credit cards to realise transactions. As a concept, a market is almost infinitely flexible. A market can be determined in relation to the timing of exchanges, for example futures markets in relation to currencies, options to purchase or to sell commodities or financial instruments.

In all cases, markets share common features in bringing into exchange relationship buyers and sellers for stated resources, goods or services and using a pricing mechanism for establishing transactions. However, it should be noted that market exchange transactions[3] have a further and distinguishing feature in that they are financial transactions and as such are expressed in

---

3 In some Third World countries, the money economy may be insufficient, as a result of poverty, to support a market economy relying on the monetary settlement of transactions. Markets are able to function on the principle of barter, which is the exchange of goods for other goods on a bilateral basis between an individual buyer and an individual seller. Barter trading may also occur on an international basis between countries.

money terms. The conversion of physical resources, goods and services into financial values is realised in the translation of demand and supply into a market demand price or a market supply price.

The Market Price as an Expression of Value
The need to translate the heterogeneous physical and qualitative characteristics of real things into a surrogate that has only one characteristic, namely an exchange value against money, which is perfectly homogenous to all actors in the market, be they buyers or sellers, limits considerably what the market price can express as value in a broader sense.[4]

In an earlier approach to this problem, economic theory considered value in terms of utility: the utility theory. It will be recalled, from Chapter 2, that the moral value of free trade was that selfish personal ambitions resulted through free markets in the common good. Adam Smith made this principle the core postulate in his *Wealth of Nations*, and Bentham went on to discuss free trade by introducing the notion of utility and focusing upon this notion as a moral value. Defined by Bentham as the tendency of an object or action to increase or decrease overall happiness in the context of market behaviour, J.S. Mill went on to develop the notion of utility into the political doctrine of Utilitarianism for a society that ought to maximise welfare, that welfare consisting of their happiness and seeking 'the greatest happiness of the greatest number'.[5]

Linking the theoretical justification for a market economy based on free trade to a welfare criterion expressed in the maximisation of human happiness combined two central moral values of a caring society, namely the insistence on individual freedom and the happiness of members of society generally. However, rendering effective rational market decisions on the basis of happiness at a time when morality and logic were two major strands in philosophical debate implied a measurement base in which to express the logic of reason. Bentham was discouraged by that difficulty. The search for a utile proved to be futile and whereas money as a

---

4 The concept of value has different interpretations that depend upon the type of decision problems in which used. The market price is an 'exchange' value. Other concepts of value used in decision-making include 'present value' expressing value in use, 'opportunity cost' used in considering alternative decision-choices, 'historical value' used in financial reports, 'replacement cost' and 'current cost' that are also accounting valuations. These will be mentioned as appropriate elsewhere in this chapter.
5 See Mill, J.S., *Utilitarianism*, 1861.

concept had the advantage of being measurable, happiness expressed as utility defied measurement.

Nevertheless, the translation of a version of happiness into a condition of satisfaction to rationalise the process of decision-making in the market was an imperative to the development of market theory. Utility as an expression of satisfaction was and is immensely useful to economic theory, in particular to the problem of market equilibrium as established in the equilibrium of demand and supply through the market price. It was left to Edgeworth[6] to use the concept of utility through a generalised utility function and to develop indifference curve analysis, establishing in this way market equilibrium through the contract curve.

Edgeworth was able to explain that the market price resulted from conditions of indifference, experienced by buyers and sellers, as between holding money and exchanging money for goods and services. Indifference curve analysis explained market equilibrium as a function of a particular and exact level of satisfaction, at which money or goods are held indifferently.

Consequently, the concept of indifference, as expressed in satisfaction or utility, is central to the process of market valuation, measured as a price and expressed in money terms. This is quite a considerable conundrum to face in market decision-making! The process of reaching the point of market equilibrium is influenced not just by satisfaction or indifference as between goods and money. It is absolutely determined by the quantity factor. Herein lies a further enigma, the experience in market behaviour of diminishing utility at the margin, the margin being the last unit at which exchange occurs. The market price in this sense is the marginal price, at which the sum of the indifferences of all buyers and all sellers reaches equilibrium.

The presence of the concept of satisfaction in market theory has social consequences that go far beyond purely economic considerations. In particular, by admitting the concept of welfare as a value judgement and a test of validity, it exposes the totality of extant economic theory to criteria of morality and of moral value judgements. It restores the moral dilemma made explicit in Chapter 3, namely that economic decision-making should result from the determination of 'what is right' in a moral sense.

---

6 Edgeworth, F.Y., *Mathematical Psychic: An Essay on the Application of Mathematics to the Moral Sciences*, 1881.

The moral values relating to money value management in a market economy are consistent with those of a caring society. Considered as the moral need to maintain the level of indifference between money and other goods and services, in a context of price and market stability, there is the other aspect of the constituent elements of indifference, as a factor in market decisions. In other words, is it possible to manipulate the desirability *per se* of other goods and services, rather than that of money, and thus unfairly manipulate the market price? By posing this question in the context of indifference analysis, that is, utility or satisfaction, the problem of the consistence of market values with moral values falls to be considered. Since quantity is accepted as a decision factor in the marginal analysis of market pricing, clearly, manipulating quantities available on the market by limiting supply, will affect market price.

There has been a long and considerable debate in economic theory and in government policy with reference to unfair competition. The doctrine of free trade, as the undeniable human right, is also based on other moral postulates founded on moral values such as honesty and sincerity as conditions in market transactions.

Whereas reconciliation of a market economy with a caring society is effected by the introduction of welfare, as happiness or satisfaction in the calculus of market equilibrium, the measurability of utility remains beyond reach. Edgeworth proposed the use of a 'hedonimeter' for measuring a utile as a unit of satisfaction, but this proposition did not meet the criterion of feasibility. Current research continues to attempt to provide a solution of the measurement problem through its extrapolation into experienced utility.[7]

The Market Economy and Complex Moral Value Choices
The discussion so far indicates that the market economy is not necessarily in conflict with the moral values that reflect the Social Conscience. The action of the market economy favours individual freedom in allowing access to goods and services resulting from the specialisation of labour and enlarges the freedom of choice offered, resulting in a higher level of satisfaction and increased living standards. A further and important moral value is the freedom afforded to expression of self and of personal skills and abilities that an individual may possess. The engagement of these

---

7 See Kahneman, D., Wakker, P. and Sarin, R., 'Back to Bentham? Explorations of Experienced Utility', *The Quarterly Journal of Economics*, 112, 1997, pp.375-406.

qualities in a successful employment experience is made possible by a labour market that offers freedom of choice of employment and of opportunities for personal improvement. In considering the integration of the individual in society, the Social Conscience also accepts that the commitment of an individual to society engages a personal responsibility for individual actions and decisions.

It is generally assumed that perfect markets under conditions of perfect competition and unimpeded access to information will optimise social welfare, as it would be expressed in a concept of added value. Naturally, this requires that there be no distortions or imperfections in the market economy and that the distribution of income is equitable and not biased towards any social groups. However, the market economy does not function on the basis of added social value, but rather on gains individually realised from exchange transactions expressed in money.

In reality, the presence of imperfections is normal in the market economy. These imperfections are different in their nature and in their effects. Some result from actions intended to create disparities through market differentiation. Some rely on distorted information and illicit market manipulations to create unfair competition. Some resort to malpractice, downright dishonesty and culpable criminality to get rich quickly.

The Social Conscience is aware of these imperfections and seeks to intervene to mitigate their effects through regulatory measures. They include the extension of liability under civil and Criminal Law in such diverse areas as product liability for harmful products, manufacturers' liability for defects, liability for errors of omission and commission in the law of contract and tort for negligence, as well as penalties for fraudulent misrepresentation and business crimes generally.

Free Trade and State Intervention
As we shall discuss in Chapter 7, freedom exists under authority. It is authority that grants freedom and protects freedom. The freedom of trade and the concept of free trade are subjected to the authority of the Social Conscience as expressed in law and the customs of trade.

The need for intervention with respect to the market's institutions, infrastructure and business environment has long been accepted. The excessive optimism regarding the virtues of free trade, as expressed by de Mandeville and Adam Smith, was almost immediately questioned by Ricardo and J.S. Mill, and thereafter by pessimism as to its consequence expressed by Malthus, Marx and Schumpeter. The limits to free trade that the market economy has accepted indicate its recognition of the importance of the Social Conscience, the necessity for compatibility of business and social objectives and its inability to solve unaided some of its technical problems.

There are two specific areas in which the compatibility of business and social objectives raises serious moral issues, facing the Social Conscience with a problematic choice. Here the State is able to assist by intervening directly in the market economy.

The first area is the need for stability of monetary values to ensure fairness between actors trading both in the market and through time. It is essentially a matter of ethics and of security. The second area is the need to ensure that the market economy maintains its capacity to provide and improve desired levels of welfare. Under exceptional circumstances, both conditions may be met simultaneously, but generally these objectives conflict and involve a choice at government policy level, which may mean sacrificing the social objective of monetary stability to the social objective of improving employment.

This intervention involves two different aspects of government financial control over the market economy. The first relies on monetary policy for controlling the money supply through interest rate management aimed at preventing monetary inflation. The second acts through fiscal policy to control the level of economic activity by managing the level of aggregate demand in order to avoid economic recession and depression.

Markets are self-regulating and activity is a function of demand and supply. They respond to variability automatically simply through the price mechanism. Markets act out of sentiment and respond to sentiment for developing forecasts of future conditions to incorporate into current behaviour. Under free trade, market behaviour, unlike enterprise behaviour, cannot be planned and controlled strictly under planned objectives. Left to themselves, markets cannot deal with monetary inflation that could be destructive, nor can they deal with mood swings that shift from excessive optimism to depressive pessimism and be equally destructive. These swings are phenomena connected with trade cycles that are repetitive over time and create booms and slumps in market activity levels. Both monetary inflation and economic recession have serious effects on social welfare, and in both of these areas, the market economy has needed the help of state intervention.

Financial Capital and Production Capital in the Market Economy
The market economy functions on the basis of capitalism. It is financed by credit supplied to the business enterprise in the form of share capital, which has two important social consequences, in that ownership of the share capital gives the right of ownership of the enterprise and the right to the profit that it has earned. The enterprise applies the capital obtained in this manner in financing the economic structure in the form of assets used in business operations. Continental European countries define the share capital as the 'social capital' to explain its origin and the assets as the economic capital to explain its use.

Accordingly, a distinction is made between two forms of capital that is determined by the manner of use. Financial capital is provided through financial markets to the business sector and production capital represents funds committed by the business sector to the production of goods and services.

Those involved in financial markets have different objectives and motives from those engaged in production activity through business enterprises. The former are concerned with the financing of business enterprises as their main objective. They specialise in using financial capital in the form of financial assets and financial instruments in financial engineering activities concerned with setting up strategies and financing packages. Their ultimate and sole objective is to use money to make money. In other words, they seek to increase their own wealth by increasing the value of the financial assets that they control. They use business enterprises simply to this end. In technical terms, as shareholders in business enterprise, their objective is the increase in shareholder value, expressed as the increase in the value of their shares in the market.

They achieve this objective in a variety of ways, all of which are part of schemes for making money and increasing their wealth. To this end, they seek the power to control the market economy through the influence of financial market as suppliers of funds. These actors include pension funds, investment funds, banks, insurance companies etc. Their activities are on a global basis. As the USA is the richest and most powerful nation in the world, it is hardly surprising that United States financial interests effectively control the financial market and the global economy. Within the financial market itself, there are a small number of huge pension funds and enormously rich individuals that have a dominating influence over much of world economic activity. Their activities have serious implications for the Social Conscience and for a caring society.

Those involved in employing production capital in enterprise activity are motivated towards the generation of new wealth in the form of goods and services. Instead of simply making money out of money, they seek to manage production capital in the most efficient manner for the purpose of optimising profits, their objective being to accumulate greater and greater profit-making capacity through investments in innovation. Economic growth and improvement in living standards and social welfare depend on their ability to maintain economic progress through industrial transformation that accompanies radical innovation. Successful and high performing economies are those in which 'creative destruction'[8] occurs at a high rate. Corporate managers are concerned with profitability, both with respect to current operating profits and to returns on investment, expressed in such concepts as the internal rate of return (IRR) and the rate of return on investment (ROI).

In recent years notions of corporate profitability have been subsumed in the growing influence of financial markets mobilising funds from various institutions to take up substantial positions in the financial capital of corporate enterprises. The consolidation of corporate enterprises by mergers and acquisitions, through which financial markets have extended their influence on the market economy, has made the concept of 'shareholder value' the chief criterion for evaluating corporate financial performance and corporate managerial performance.

The problem of imperfections in the market economy, the nature of the problems within the market economy necessitating state intervention and the impact of market behaviour on the Social Conscience have to be examined in accordance with the different motivations of those involved with financial capital management as distinct from the management of production capital. These differences have major implications for the two fundamental questions postulated at the outset, that is, whether a caring society can exist in a market economy and whether a market economy is sustainable that does not conform with the Social Conscience.

8 Schumpeter coined this expression to explain the nature of the forces that sustain long-term economic growth by destroying methods, products, processes and ideas that had outlived their relevance by radical innovations that necessarily involved the destruction of existing technology and ideas. See Schumpeter, J.A., *Capitalism, Socialism and Democracy*. This same philosophy is found in Kuhn's theory of the necessity of destruction through revolution for the progress of scientific knowledge. See Kuhn, T.S., *The Structure of Scientific Revolutions*.

In particular, the idea of making money out of money has been viewed as immoral from very early times. Plato and Aristotle, who were concerned with moral values, saw virtue in human labour and objected to usury, that is making money by charging interest for its use. The Magna Carta 1215, reflecting this moral concern, makes specific reference to the cancellation of interest debts owing to money-lenders.[9] Christian churches maintained this tradition with the writing of St Thomas Aquinas until the Reformation. The Koran is also explicitly against the concept of making money out of money and Islamic banks specifically do not resort to interest bearing loans to clients. Laws against the practice of usury were maintained in England until recent times with respect to the registration as money-lenders those wishing to lend at rates higher than 10%. Much of socialist philosophy seeks to associate wealth with the value of labour involved in its creation. However, the Labour Theory of Value is discredited in capitalist ideology, where man is viewed simply as a cost, selling his labour for as much as the market allows and is deemed to have no interest other than that identified with his employment.

The Social Consequences of Monetary Inflation
Inflation interferes with the value of money. When money circulated only in metal form and that form was either gold or silver, the intrinsic value of a unit of metal currency was equal to the quantity of metal in each unit. Hence, it was possible to debase the value of currency, by sweating out or rubbing gold or silver off coins. This reduced the exchange value of money through the reduced quantity of metal against all other goods in the market, which is the true meaning of inflation. This explains why stamping coins became a royal prerogative and an exact technique aimed at preventing such practices.[10] This early form of 'inflation' was widely practised in feudal times, when gold and silver coins circulated freely in international markets, resulting in the value of money falling against goods, when coins were weighed for their metal content.

9   Magna Carta, Article 10/11 'If one who has borrowed from the Jews any sum, great or small, dies before that loan can be repaid, his heir shall pay no interest on the debt for so long as he remains under age, irrespective from whom he holds his land. If such a debt falls into our hands, we will take nothing except the principal sum mentioned in the bond ... Let debts due to others than Jews be dealt with in similar manner.'
10 It is interesting to note that it remains a criminal offence to deface the image of the sovereign authority stamped on currency or to falsify the authenticity of currency by counterfeiting.

The rule that establishes the value of money in relation to other goods and services holds even to this day, for monetary inflation will occur when the volume of credit, which is today's expression of money supply, expands at a rate higher than the supply of goods and services.

Today's market society is one in which all human relationships share the same commercial rationale for making an infinite variety of decisions that have considerable social impact, such as agreeing on employment contracts on the basis of agreed remuneration, investing in a mortgage endowment insurance plan for the purposes of acquiring a home and paying off the debt incurred and many other decisions too numerous to catalogue. A caring society has a concern with preserving social stability, through adherence to and respect for moral values. Ensuring the stability of monetary values for market transactions, that is, preventing instability arising from the manipulation of the value of money *qua money* becomes a moral problem when questions of a social welfare nature are involved.

Despite the enormous expansion of markets since feudal and earlier times, the fundamental moral values that condition the market economy have not changed. Reflecting the Social Conscience, the market economy continues to apply moral judgements to economic conditions. This may be verified when considering government decisions with respect to monetary and fiscal policies. Monetary inflation is an evil, when considered in relation to the social problems created by devaluing, that is debasing over time, the exchange value of money for all other goods and services. Moreover, it is considerably easier today to expand the money supply through the expansion of credit, as distinct from the expansion of the supply of gold or silver in former times.

Although, the return to a gold standard,[11] or any other standard for maintaining monetary stability, has been abandoned, the need

---

[11] The 'gold standard' is, in effect, a quantum theory of money that aims at ensuring monetary stability by having the standard unit of currency expressed in terms of a fixed quantity of gold. Its last manifestation was the Rueff Plan in 1958 for monetary stability in the Common Market, through an adaptation of the gold standard. Following the devaluation of the French Franc, it sought to ensure currency stability and to prevent inflation. It provided for the free convertibility of major European currencies into gold and dollars for international settlement. The gold price is a good index of currency fears; if people believe that a currency is an overvalued currency but lack confidence in other currencies, gold is a natural reinsurance. The gold price acts as a warning signal, even though trade in general is still flourishing. Gold has now ceased to be relevant to monetary policy, but a high gold price suggests that the market 'knows' that inflation is taking place.

to avoid inflation by excessive money supply remains a major policy objective, as may be seen in the 3% limit of budget deficit over gross national income, applicable to all EU member states. Inflation is tantamount to appropriating 'money' from creditors. A young married couple buying a house with a mortgage gains financially over time in two ways: from the increase in its market value as house prices increase with inflation through time and as the real burden of the mortgage debt is eroded through time by inflation. Equally, monetary inflation helps governments to reduce the national debt in real terms over time. Theoretically, inflation could enable a government to eliminate effortlessly its national debt over time. For example, under conditions of perfect monetary inflation, a rate of inflation of 20% per annum *ceteris paribus*, that is at given constant percentage tax revenue levels and national debt repayment levels, would enable any government to wipe out the national debt in 5 years. This would be achieved by the reduction of the monetary value of the debt at the beginning of year 1 to zero in terms of its inflation-corrected value at the end of year 5! As debt interest is normally charged to current account, and as government borrowings do not generally carry the high risk that would warrant high interest rates, this element may be ignored as regards the foregoing explanation of the impact of inflation for national debt reduction. In a sense, governments, as creditors, are not worried by the presence of substantial levels of national debt, which are never repayable but simply refinanced over time.

There are two components of the national economy that may contribute to monetary inflation, seen as resulting from the excess of demand over available supply of consumer goods and services. In Anglo-Saxon countries, this distinction is seen in terms of the private sector as distinct from the public sector, which is effectively a technical difference. In Continental European countries, this is expressed as a distinction between the liberal economy and the social economy, which is a political difference that links the market economy to capitalism and the social economy to socialism. For simplicity and at the risk of seeming to fudge important features of both the private and the public sectors of the economy, it may be said that the private sector is mainly concerned with the production of goods and services, available to both segments of the national economy; whereas the social economy is mainly concerned with the redistribution of goods and services to achieve the social equity that is frustrated by the very nature of the market economy.

As regards the private sector, the market economy is philosophically conditioned towards progress as an ideal[12] and to economic growth as a natural and permanent condition. The anticipation of future financial gains, in the form of increased business income generally, increased enterprise profits, increased dividend distributions, increased asset values and increased shareholder values, drives business activity. Economic growth, as a driver, assumes two forms: real growth, where volume of activity growth occurs at a constant price, and monetary growth, where increasing prices occur with the activity volume remaining constant. Monetary growth is inflationary growth, hence it is fictitious growth as distinct from real growth.

Economic growth, whether in the form of real growth or as monetary inflation, requires additional funds to finance additional fixed and working capital that will be needed to provide additional production capacity and output volume. Both production capital and financial capital gain from real growth.

However, an industrial or commercial enterprise experiencing inflation or fictitious growth needs to finance growth in the money value of its net working capital by extra short-term borrowing. Assuming a constant activity volume level, the net working capital requirement will increase at a rate equal to the rate of monetary inflation. Higher interest costs will lead to lower profits at the same time as further credit is needed. Hence, there occurs both a profit and a cash crush on the business sector under inflation, an increased demand for credit by firms, an increase in the rate of bankruptcy. particularly in the sector of small and medium-sized businesses operating on slim profit margins, and a vicious spiral downwards that ends in an economic slump and unemployment. Where government policy acts against inflation by limiting credit supply as well as increasing interest rates, the effects on the business sector are worsened. Long-term damage to the economy results as many small and medium-sized firms are driven into bankruptcy and disappear permanently, their owners being ruined in the process. Such extensive damage may take years to repair.

By contrast, firms operating in capital markets, whose business it is to supply capital and funds to industrial and commercial enterprises, have a different experience of monetary inflation. Their business objective is to make money out of money, subject to the

---

12 For a very interesting discussion of the philosophical debate of this motivation in Western European thought, read Pollard, S., *The Idea of Progress: History and Society*, London: C.A. Watts & Co. Ltd, 1968.

overall criterion of optimising shareholder value. Trading in monetary values and financial instruments stated in money values, they do not obviously experience inflation for the simple reason that the accounting or face value of their assets and liabilities remains unchanged, $1 remaining $1.

Financial businesses gain under inflation in a number of ways. They will benefit from increases in interest rates resulting from increased demands for money. At the same time, they are well positioned to benefit from government monetary policies for dealing with inflation through increases in official interest rates. Equally, as dividends received as income will reflect increased money values, profits will tend to increase under inflation. However, their main advantage is in the possibility of increasing the shareholder value of their investments in production capital, since inflation leads to increases in the value of assets other than cash at a rate at least equal to the rate of inflation. Trading conditions become more advantageous as favourable opportunities increase for acquiring non-monetary assets with money having a diminishing exchange value.

As regards the public sector, as it is called in the United Kingdom, or the social economy, as it called in Continental Europe, there are two important pressures on public spending. The first stems from the relative influence of government in the management of the economy. Second, the financing of public spending diverts a significant proportion of the GNP to the public sector or social economy, depending on its relative size with respect to the private sector.

The commitment to 'free trade' as a political ideology that determines the role of government and the public sector in the economy, marks a lasting divide between the United Kingdom and Continental Europe. It explains the reluctance of the United Kingdom to fully support European political integration and to lose control over economic and monetary policy in adopting the Euro. There is a long tradition in European political thinking that reflects the influence of Catholicism and moral philosophy, which has conditioned thinking about the role of the State, in a direct lineage from Plato and Aristotle. The tendency to centralism in government, that existed prior to the French Revolution, was merely reinforced by the legacy of the Napoleonic period, which is important in understanding the role of the State, enshrined in France as *l'Esprit Républicain*, as restated and extended in the concept of 'Gaullism'.

The concept of centralism, associated with a bureaucratic system of administration and accompanied by extensive and detailed regulations that leave very little to individual choice, explains also the preference in France and Germany to press for a European Constitution in the form of a unified Europe, governed centrally from Brussels under a Commission, whose decisions are made in the absence of popular consultation. The separation of a political elite, that associates itself entirely with a bureaucracy allied to its interests, and that shares the same ideology and conviction, is reinforced by the setting up of such schools of *L'Ecole Nationale d'Administration* in France and also in Poland, for the education of a political and bureaucratic elite. It has resulted in a high level of agreement as to policy, defined as *la pensèe unique*, the unique thought.

The social or public sector economy in Continental Europe, backed by a political elite, is seen to be in conflict with the private sector, reflecting the market or liberal economy, and requires the objectives of the market economy to be subordinated to the social economy.

The commitment to an important public sector and to a high level of public sector spending, as in the case of France, absorbs a substantial proportion of the GNP and places the management of money supply directly into the political debate. The seeming political impossibility of limiting the growth of public spending means that there is a continuing budgetary commitment to irreducable spending requirements and to budget deficits. It explains why consistent and growing budget deficits, with their direct impact on the persistence of monetary inflation, growth in public debt and currency devaluation over time are phenomena that the European Central Bank has addressed as a priority over economic growth by imposing the famous 3% limits on budgets deficits. At the present time of high unemployment and stagnant economic activity, France, Italy and Germany find it difficult to accept that limit in the context of the political theology and the need to deal with economic recession

As already noted, monetary inflation is a positive help to the management of the national debt. The gallop into debt is often necessary to the success and popularity of elected administrations that finance increased social welfare expenditure by loans, rather than incurring market and popular hostility by increasing government revenues through increased taxation.

Provided there are no effective limits to monetary inflation, economic booms can only result in bursting bubbles when the Social Conscience is finally moved to panic and loses total confidence in the government. When that point is reached, markets collapse leading to economic ruin, such as happened during the Great Depression in the USA and in the collapse of the Mark in Germany at the time of the Weimar Republic. Hard hit by recession, the German government took to printing money so rapidly to finance government expenditure that the value the Mark fell daily at such speed that the population lost confidence in its own currency. In the end, the value of the Mark collapsed as people went round with suitcases full of money to buy simple things such as bread. The result was the financial ruin of the German people as they progressively had to sell assets for money that rapidly became valueless. It created a climate of public opinion that led the country to adopt the form of National Socialism that Hitler advocated and which led to the Second World War.

The Social Consequences of Economic Recession
Economic recession is a particular social evil by virtue of its impact upon employment. It may or may not be directly associated with episodes of monetary inflation, but it is generally associated with trade cycles and their explanations in terms of variations in business expectations and business confidence generally. The Beveridge Plan placed employment at the centre of social welfare policy and determined that government policy with respect to the management of the economy should aim at full employment, with unemployment limited at 3% of the population of working age. The figure of 3% reflects that level of unemployed that allowed for the flexibility needed by the labour market for adaptation to technological changes.

Prior to the Great Depression in the inter-war years, booms and slumps occurred as natural phenomena and were recognised as being affected by business expectations and business sentiments. The South Sea Bubble was remembered in this light. However, until relatively recent times, agriculture was the main economic activity in most European countries and remains so for much of the world. People live off the land and unemployment as such is invisible. It may be said that, where people life off the land, they are self-employed and can exist at least at subsistence level, whereas in towns, starvation may be a problem.

Poverty, as a social condition, has existed from time immemorial. It became morally insupportable as its visibility increased in the appearance of towns and cities, where deprivation was accentuated by its comparison to the social conditions of those who were better off. Almshouses, hospices and foundations for the relief of poverty, that are to be found everywhere in Europe as historical vestiges of a feudal society that cared for the poor, a duty that was insistently proclaimed in the Holy Texts and by the religious authorities.

Industrialisation in England in the 18th and 19th centuries, the concentration of work in factories and the massive urbanisation of the population in conditions of abominable squalor scarred the Social Conscience of the times and remains present in social memory to this day. There is Victor Hugo's description in 1862 of that poverty in *Les Miserables*; Charles Dickens (1812-70) told of it in moving terms in *Bleak House, Great Expectations, David Copperfield* and *OliverTwist*. Each year, *A Christmas Carol* recalls the helplessness of poverty, the ghastly selfishness of Scrooge and his pathetic and touching redemption from selfishness into generosity. Engels gave financial support to Marx in an association that produced the *Communist Manifesto* of 1848 calling for radical social changes and the conscience of England responded to Cardinal Newman's appeal to help the working classes through education.

Unemployment accentuates the poverty that is generic to industrial economies, where livelihood depends on employment and where exploitation through low wages and unfair labour conditions are features of capitalism. The 18th and 19th centuries approved the relief of unemployment and poverty through recourse to workhouses. Elsewhere, they imposed working conditions upon human beings compelling them to work in those 'dark satanic mills' that were an offence to the green and pleasant land of England. Meanwhile, hidden from view, ponies, dogs and young children lived and toiled together deep in underground darkness, where lay the heart of the energy economy, dragging carts heavy with coal away from the coalface. They lived and died young, as did many of their elders.[13]

Poverty created by unemployment continues to haunt the portals of a caring society as it struggles with the social and moral problems present in modern industrial society. Pressure for profit improvement and increased shareholder value compels large industrial conglomerates to evade the moral and sometime penal sanctions of a caring society by relocating employment to countries, where large numbers of poor will work for minimum wages and where the absence of a regulatory framework leaves them unprotected from exploitation.

---

13 My own grandfather began his working life underground as a child in a coal mine in Wallony and I heard from his lips the story of those cruel times.

Those conditions which existed in the earlier industrialisation of the 18th and 19th centuries threatened to reappear in the massive poverty that the Great Depression sparked in the USA, as shown by the appearance of soup canteens, and in the Jarrow Marchers that mobilised protest in England, when the unemployed dragged their humiliation from the North of England to the counting houses of the City of London.

Unemployment, as a cause of poverty and deprivation had become intolerable by the 1930s. Unemployment remains unacceptable to this day. Seen as resulting directly from the inability of the market economy to function so as to sustain desired levels of employment, Keynes recommended that governments injected funds into the market economy, financed by budget deficits, to raise the level of aggregate demand and financially prime a stagnant economy. Keynesian economics worked with respect to reducing unemployment caused by economic recession and was one of the important theoretical pillars of the welfare society.

The social consequences of economic recession today remain centred on unemployment, but there are new and other important problems. Acceptance of the necessity for a high level of social protection imposes upon government and on the market economy the obligation to minimise unemployment. There is general unanimity with respect to social protection in a market economy and the political obligation of governments to undertake financial and management responsibility for the provision of social services. Financing high levels of social expenditure implies high levels of taxation, much of it in the form of taxes on personal and business incomes, as well as sales taxes or value added taxes that hit consumption.

Unemployment created by recession reduces the level of government income raised through taxation and at the same time increases social expenditure on the relief of unemployment through unemployment insurance benefits. Governments are forced to finance budget deficits under recession through increased government borrowing. Unless the business community is able to revise its expectations of the future and to translate optimism into the recovery of activity, budget deficits will simply maintain aggregate consumer demand level without increasing domestic supply of goods and services, leading directly to monetary inflation.

The difficult choice decision between monetary inflation and unemployment levels associated with economic recession is seen in the policy decisions of the European Central Bank to manage monetary policy to avoid monetary inflation with the aim of maintaining the stability of the Euro as a currency. This is the preferred objective of the European Central Bank as against reducing unemployment through the removal of the 3% GNP budget restriction rule. France, Germany and Italy are all experiencing protracted recession in economic activity and persistent high levels of unemployment, which they are unable to redress by reason of the policy rule regarding budget deficits.

Furthermore, as the business sector experiences falling profitability, it becomes increasingly difficult for large European business corporations to satisfy the shareholder value expectation of financial capital investors. By exerting irresistible pressure on management financial performance through substantial and influential shareholdings, profit and shareholder value improvements have become the imperatives of foreign and invisible financial interests, which are attempting to obtain effective control of the global economy.

Profitability improvements are sought through labour cost reductions, obtained in various ways that include increasing labour productivity through reducing staffing levels and increasing labour saving technology, as well as the delocalisation of work to other countries that offer more favourable labour and tax costs conditions, as well as unregulated business environments that magnify the advantages of free trade.

From the viewpoint of a caring society, both inflation and recession are social evils. They can lead to political instability and are divisive, creating sharp distinction between the financially successful and impoverished masses. Losing one's employment today is a hydra-headed calamity. Economic growth has increased living standards and consumption and expectations of even better conditions in the future. In many European countries, families are living beyond their income and with easy access to credit through credit cards, the average level of family indebtedness is high. The cost of housing has increased beyond all reason, fuelled by self-fulfilling expectations of continuing high rates of annual percentage increase in house prices.

The financial risk to which the average family is exposed is concealed when unemployment is low. There is a potential social catastrophe concealed in this situation, for in many countries average unemployment is persistently well above the Beveridge 3% and running between 8 and 10% of the employable population. The hardest hit age groups comprise young people entering the labour market for the first time and unable to obtain employment, even with good qualifications, and middle-aged men with family financial commitments peaking made redundant at the age of 50 years or so and unable thereafter to obtain work.

The Social Consequences of Market Imperfections
It has been said that the Theory of Perfect Competition has been invented to facilitate the creation of economic models based on the hypothesis of perfect markets, such as were imagined by Adam Smith and others, and which justified the optimism of its core moral value, namely that free markets lead to the greatest well-being of the greatest numbers.

The Theory of Perfect Competition, that underpins classical economic thought, has displayed a remarkable disdain for a market reality that has consistently denied its postulates, which include free entry into markets, perfect knowledge and symmetry as between actors so that no one is capable of exerting greater influence than another. Nevertheless, it holds the position of Lesson 1 in all first-year university undergraduate courses in Economics and no one is exempted from kneeling at its shrine.

Moreover, the perfect market hypothesis has continued to dazzle by the brilliance of its simplicity the minds of leading economists and financial theorists, who have continued to venerate its profound usefulness as a tool of theoretical analysis and in the manipulation of knowledge in the form of numbers having precise contents. It provides for an initial concord between all economists, as a means of getting debate started, which rapidly dissolves into total discord, which as Churchill remarked, makes it possible to have as many divergent opinions on any problem as there are economists present in the debate.

Market imperfections in their numerous manifestations, such as distorted and misleading information often seen in advertising, corrupt business practices that are in the grey area of uncertain legality, the deliberate creation of price-rings and dominant market positions, more appropriately correspond to the truth of market conditions, namely imperfect competition.

Market imperfections stem from distortions in human behavioural patterns that are matters of the Social Conscience. Schumpeter accepted imperfect competition as being inherent in markets and thus disposed as redundant a substantial area of debate.

There is one basic rule that conditions market behaviour, the *caveat emptor* rule, let the buyer beware. The market places responsibility on the individual for decision-making. The buyer is responsible for his decision to buy: it is not for the seller to advise him in that regard. Rather, the role of the seller is to persuade the buyer to buy on the seller's conditions.

The market decision is in the form of a legal contract. The *caveat emptor* rule is stated in the Law of Contract. Legal rules that apply to market behaviour have developed in two opposed directions. Limits on the freedom to trade have been denied legality: for example, contracts in restraint of trade. For the same reasons, unfair trade practices, such as price-rings and price maintenance agreements are also prohibited. On the other hand, rules intended to protect buyers, such as rules relating to manufacturer's liability and guarantees under purchase agreements, have arisen by a general extension of product liability in the Law of Negligence. Trade descriptions are warranties with respect to fitness for intended use. The office of the Financial Ombudsman in the United Kingdom has greatly helped by intervening to protect buyers, for example, through the mis-selling of products such as endowment policies in relation to expected mortgage liabilities. This is a growing problem in the mortgage market, when home-buyers are committed over long periods to mortgage repayments using insurance products, such as endowment policies, that do not fulfil terminal value expectations. Market regulations and market practices aim to secure free markets but, even taking into account limited interventions as practised at the moment, there remain large areas open to the manipulation of demand that is a central element in dealings between buyers and sellers.

The Market Economy and its Impact on the Structure of Society
The market economy may be defined as a system that is driven by financial values involving inputs, measured as financial values, and outputs, also measured as financial values. As an economic system, the market economy is concerned with the efficient management of resources and relies on notions of scientific management to produce an optimal result. This optimal result necessarily is a surplus, which may be appreciated in accordance with different formulations of that surplus, which are always of a financial nature. It is expressed as incremental liquidity in the form of cash or near-cash, net profit for a period of activity and increased shareholder value.

The optimal result, as a surplus, may also be analysed on a time basis, for example, annual surpluses as distinguished from surpluses for longer periods of time. Finally, the scientific management of what are considered as financial values is based on the use of a consistent and logical method of reasoning in business decision-making to attain the defined, *a priori*, and sole objective.

Traditionally, and in terms of classical economic theory, this objective was stated as the maximisation of profit. In terms purely of the entity theory of the business enterprise, that is, conceiving the business enterprise as having its own peculiar interest, the question of who benefits from enterprise activity may be seen in terms of all those that are in some sense in relation with the enterprise. This has given rise to the notion of stakeholders to refer to such diverse interests as shareholders, creditors, employees, suppliers, customers, the State and the community at large. Subsuming macro and micro analyses to the same considerations with respect to the distribution of economic outputs, namely those appertaining to Gross National Income (GNI) or Gross National Product (GNP), shareholders are seen as deriving dividends, creditors as receiving interest income, employees as being paid salaries, suppliers as having the possibility of exchanging their products at selling price and customers as buying products at market price and finally the State as obtaining revenues through taxation.

Configurations, such as the GNP representation of national economic activity, are directed at considerations that are broadly social insofar as national output is considered from the viewpoint of income distribution. It ignores the classical economic theory of the firm that reflects a social theory based on capitalism[14] for considering an appropriate determination of the basis for income distribution. Statistics of GNP accept the data produced by *de facto* market principles of distribution that accept the values of the market economy, namely, the logic of market pricing with no reference to moral justifications, for example, whether wages reflect an equitable pricing of labour.

Traditionally, the family as a social unit had multifarious objectives covering the totality of human needs, including enabling the group to undertake a basic form of economic organisation through a specialisation of roles and acting in all other respects under a unifying authority that was acceptable to the Social Conscience of the group.

In effect, the traditional family was an integrated and independent social unit as regards three essential functions: acting as a

---

14 'Capitalism', as a concept, has been widely discussed and defined. Schumpeter's definition seems both concise and appropriate to this text. 'Capitalism is an economic system based on property rights, pursuit of self-interest, freedom to choose and ability to borrow. It is a method of economic change guided by individual needs and wants and financed by credit (obtained through debt and equity).' (*Capitalism, Socialism and Democracy*.)

welfare unit in a broad sense of providing protection and care; acting as an economic unit for obtaining food, clothing and shelter and the necessities of existence; and acting together under the governing authority of a *paterfamilias* or headman, whose concern for the group was his prime and only responsibility.

The traditional family has been considerably affected by the development of the market economy founded on the specialisation of labour and on the principles that determine the nature, objectives and structure of business organisation. The family, as an economic unit, has contracted out its activities to the market economy. In that sense, it has lost its independence and has become enslaved to the values of the market economy. Its members sell their services as well as their souls to the market economy. They subsequently acquire the necessities of life by buying them with the money obtained under market conditions.

In the view of many, the impact of the market economy on a caring society founded on family values has been very damaging. As long ago as 1844, opposition to a market economy acting on capitalist principles was well expressed by Marx,[15] who noted that capitalism, as a social order, created three destructive forms of alienation: the alienation of the worker from what he produces; the alienation of the worker from himself; and the alienation of people from each other.[16] According to Marx,

> no sooner is the exploitation of the labourer by the manufacturer, so far at an end, that he receives his wages in cash, than he is set upon by the other portions of the bourgeoisie, the landlord, the shopkeeper, the pawnbroker etc.'
> (*Communist Manifesto*, 1848, p.42)

Marx gave a negative answer to the enduring nature of capitalism in the celebrated statement that:

> economic production and the structure of every historical epoch necessarily arising therefrom constitute the foundation for the political and intellectual history of that epoch: that consequently the

---

15 See Marx, K., *Economic and Philosophical Manuscripts*, 1844, Moscow: Progress Publishers, 1959.
16 Marx has been subject to much criticism and opprobrium, not only from intellectuals who criticized the validity of his methods and conclusions, but also from a wider spectrum of opinion that associated his philosophy with the repressive communist dictatorships that followed in the wake of the Russian Revolution of 1917. A Channel 4 TV poll conducted in 2005 indicated Marx's return to popular esteem as the leading philosopher of all times. Although this judgement is undoubtedly excessive with regards to such names as Plato, Locke, Hume, Kant and others, it does show an appreciation of Marx's expression of the Social Conscience, its moral values, and especially the problem of destructive alienation, which has marked this generation.

whole history of mankind (since the dissolution of primitive tribal society holding land in common ownership) has been a history of class struggles, contests between exploiting and exploited, ruling and oppressed classes; that the history of these class struggles forms a series of evolutions in which, nowadays, a stage has been reached where the exploited and oppressed class – the proletariat – cannot attain its emancipation from the sway of the exploiting and ruling class – the bourgeoisie – without, at the same time, and once and for all, emancipating society at large from all exploitation, oppression, class distinctions and class struggles.

(Preface to the German edition of the *Communist Manifesto*, 1883)

Marx viewed the market economy as being in a state of permanent and necessary instability, for

the bourgeoisie cannot exist without constantly revolutionising the instruments of production, and thereby the relations of production and with them the whole relations of society ... Constant revolutionising of production, uninterrupted disturbance of all social conditions, everlasting uncertainty and agitation distinguish the bourgeois epoch from earlier ones.

(*Communist Manifesto*, 1848, p36)

As a social philosopher, Marx gave a powerful and enduring expression of the romantic attachment to the Social Conscience as to a form of society in which the individual is able to be himself. In such a society, he does so in his activities. His relationship with others may be described as a yearning for an existence in which caring and sharing is the bond that unites people and is the social cement. For most of us as individuals, this experience was our lost childhood and it does not require a deal of reflection to understand and appreciate its value.

This vision of the past and its influence on the present remains strongly entrenched in the social memory and conscience. It is highly persuasive as a model of society, as expressed in socialist philosophies and as opposed to the form of society that the market economy has created.[17] Concerned with the social ills that are attributed to the market economy and as manifested in the type of American society today, many European countries view with alarm the possibility that the European Union could move towards a 'liberal or market economy' to the detriment of a 'social economy' and the moral values that it represents. In this sense, a new European schism founded on the conflict between a 'liberal' economy,

---

17 For an interesting discussion of the emergence of a market society, see Slater, D. and Tonkiss, F., *Market Society*, Cambridge: Polity, 2001.

expressing the concept of 'free trade' and a total commitment to the principles of a market economy on the one hand and a 'social' economy, expressing the concepts of caring and sharing through socialism, as a social order on the other, fully echoes the philosophical and culture schisms that have separated the Anglo-Saxon world from Continental European countries, even before the Industrial Revolution and the French Revolution.[18] To Continental Europeans, England epitomises the socially unjust market economy that has the potential for destroying the social values of a caring society. This fundamental historic, cultural and philosophical difference that opposes and divides Europe should be recognised as a schism in identity that time will never reconcile.

Schumpeter[19] agreed with Marx that capitalism could not survive, but for quite different reasons, which he expressed as follows:

> Can capitalism survive? No, I do not think that it can. The thesis that I shall endeavour to establish is that the actual and prospective performance of the capitalist system is such as to negative the idea of its breaking down under the weight of economic failure, but that its very success undermines the social institutions which protect it, and inevitably creates conditions in which it will not be able to live and which strongly point to socialism as the heir apparent.

Schumpeter believed that the main threat to capitalism would come from intellectuals who would no longer support its value system and would revolt against it. To this end, they would foment trouble by allying themselves with the working class and also with governmental bureaucrats who would increasingly develop anti-capitalist legislative policies.

As discussed in Chapter 2, it is precisely because the market economy fails to reflect the moral values of a caring society that it offends the Social Conscience. Interpreting Schumpeter's conclusion on the survival of capitalism, it is evident – although he does not say so in so many words – that the Social Conscience holds the

---

18 These were different types of revolution, the Industrial Revolution in England being an economic revolution that shattered the existing social order, the French Revolution being a political revolution that also shattered the existing social order. However, the French Revolution maintained the same government culture in the successor French Republic and at the same time succeeded in destroying the Industrial Revolution that was in progress. France's own Industrial Revolution had to await General de Gaulle and was achieved under the doctrine of Gaullism that determined French State policy during the period that followed World War II. To this day, political parties both Left and Right maintain allegiance to this doctrine.
19 See Schumpeter, J.A., *Capitalism, Socialism and Democracy*, New York: Harper & Row Publishers, 1942.

supreme and effective authority that will determine the conditions for the survival of the market economy.

Considering the standpoints adopted by both Marx and Schumpeter, we are led into a situation that may be presented in the form of Hobson's choice. Both agree, for different reasons, that socialism will inexorably and inevitably replace capitalism. Whereas capitalism may have created a society of inequality and alienation, as Marx indicated, and through competition divided society against itself, it has had a remarkable success in raising living standards and economic well-being. Those countries that have adopted socialist economic policies have performed less well than those that have liberal or market economies. Indeed, pure socialism has been progressively abandoned by protagonist of socialism and the choice that has resulted from democratic elections has consistently been in favour of economic progress and increasing personal income to the detriment of social polices and high tax rates that reduce disposable income.

Caring and sharing are central moral values in the Social Conscience. The explanation as well as the justification for human social organisation as a collective identity that has a biological, social and economic utility is seen in the first instance in the family affiliation. The primal need for a tribal association, which is an extension of the family identity, is found in nature itself, bringing human and most animal species having an elementary social fabric, into pack structures for security and for obtaining food and other resources.

Collectivism, as an expression of socialism, has inspired various and different forms of social organisations, from a radical form in the *kibbutz* in Israel and the collective farms in Communist Russia, to industrial and commercial organisations formed on the basis of co-ownership or as co-operative and mutual societies. The market economy has made short shrift of collectivism in business organisations. Whether or not they under-perform in a business sense may be open to question in particular cases. They are disadvantaged particularly by not having a share-capital structure that gives access to financial markets and, especially to stock exchanges, which provide a market for shares. A secondary factor is that their financial performance cannot be expressed on the valuation basis that normally applies for shares, such as the price earnings ratio (PER). Hence, their management is not subjected to the same demanding performance standards that apply to companies with quoted shares and they are free to follow more conservative business policies, leading to the presence of substantial concealed undervaluation.

The real dilemma may be stated in the question, 'Is there a third way that would preserve the economic benefits derived from a market economy and yet uphold the moral values of a caring society?' That question refers immediately to the role of the Social Conscience as the sovereign authority and to the manner and the means through which it may intervene to solve this difficulty. The solution proposed by Keynes[20] was that governments should intervene through the management of the level of aggregate demand through fiscal policies to deal with the social problem of unemployment that resulted from the inability of the market economy to deal with economic depression. This proposition opened the door to the Pandora's Box of evils that Schumpeter[21] had imagined would result from the negative role that intellectuals would play in association with governmental bureaucracy precisely by hastening the demise of capitalism through anti-capitalist legislation. It brought Keynes and Schumpeter into open dispute, but it was Keynes who triumphed at the time and Keynesianism became the dominant economic doctrine.

Third-way paths essentially are means of convenience and rely on compromises that lead to unsatisfactory solutions in the longterm, because they avoid addressing the central issues and often introduce other and different problems. Democratic and piecemeal intervention in the USA under President Roosevelt through government financing of huge public works programmes, such as the Hoover Dam, made a great impression on public opinion and on intellectuals everywhere. It reinforced the existing popular notion that 'it is up to the government to do something' and, in this sense, reflected the expectations of the Social Conscience. The extent to which public expenditure, intended to pump-prime an economy in depression by channelling into it funds financed through budget deficits, is truly effective is difficult to gauge. Recessions and depressions, as well as recoveries and booms characterise business cycles that are largely influenced by market expectations as expressed by the business community. By 1937, when Keynes' *General Theory of Employment, Interest and Money* was published, the worst of the Great Depression was over and some recovery had taken place,

---

20 See Keynes, J.M, *General Theory of Employment, Interest and Money*, London: Macmillan Press, 1936.
21 Schumpeter himself made important contributions to trade cycle theory, see *History of Economic Analysis*, London: George Allen & Unwin, 1954.

stimulated also by the beginning of a process of rearmament in the expectation that a war with Germany was inevitable.

However, it was not only Keynesian economics that advocated a specific role for interventionism in economic affairs. The inter-war years were years of social hardship and strong political debate. Another towering figure at work during this period was William Beveridge, an equally powerful advocate of interventionism, whose influence led to the Beveridge Plan for a state social welfare system. As we noted in Chapter 2, it became effective through a series of landmark legislative measures in 1948, which provided for a national health service, a national insurance system and other accompanying measures. This legislation was intended to provide a complete net of social protection. It reflected a similar demand throughout Western Europe for state intervention in social welfare at a time when most intellectuals were committed to a socialist conception of society and many were committed to Marxism. Eastern Europe had passed under the control of Moscow and Communist Parties were strongly present in such countries as France and Italy.

Interventionism, as the third way that was adopted in Western Europe, brought into prominence the threat to freedom and democracy that is implicit in the nature of its actions and procedures. Popper[22] declared,

> It is undoubtedly the greatest threat of interventionism – especially of any direct interventionism – that it leads to an increase in state power and in bureaucracy ... We must plan for freedom, and not only for security, if for no other reason than that only freedom can make security secure.

According to Popper,[23] Marx believed that socialism would diminish the economic and political influence of the State, whereas interventionism used to make a social economy effective has increased the power of the State everywhere. In Europe, the alliance of political elites, irrespective of party political associations, with bureaucracy has succeeded in obtaining effective control of the apparatus of government. This may be seen in the current debate concerning the European Union, and in particular the attempt to impose on member nations a European Constitution in 2005 that would result in a unified nation state. France and the Netherlands, two countries that were allowed to vote by referendum on the

---

22 See Popper, K.R., *The Open Society and Its Enemies*, London: Routledge & Kegan Paul, 1945, Vol. II, pp.193-4.
23 *Ibid.*

proposed European Constitution, rejected by a substantial majority the proposal, which had been strongly backed by their governments and the broad spectrum of the political elite. The result indicated a schism between the people and their political leaders. It revealed the democratic deficit between a ruling bureaucracy in Brussels, allied to the political classes throughout member states, pursuing its own interests in defiance of the democratic will, insofar as this will is allowed to express itself.

Popper was eminently aware of the menace to freedom and to democracy that existed in the concept of interventionism. The presence and action of a bureaucracy that is not subject to democratic control, results in the transfer of effective political power to a ruling bureaucracy with its own leaders and supported by politicians adhering, supporting and seeing their own personal interests in its strategy and policies.

Conclusion

The market economy, as it now functions, is a successful economic system that has a significant deficit in moral values with respect to the distribution of income and the influence on society that it maintains. The reform of the market economy may be seen as involving the same basic problem implied in the reform of education, namely rendering effective the Social Conscience by integrating the action of the market economy within that of a caring society. The preservation of freedom through democracy is one of the most important moral values to which modern society is committed. Recognising the Social Conscience as the sovereign authority reconciles Marx's view of socialism as freedom from oppression and obviates the need for state interventionism that relies on an independent bureaucracy. The delegation of authority on a democratic basis, through popular elections to a state administration, implies that the Social Conscience should provide the moral values that underpin bureaucratic action. Hence, it may be postulated that the reform of the market economy does not necessarily imply state interventionism, if the moral values of a caring society can be incorporated in the market economy, rendering the reform of the nature of society itself redundant.

—6—
Accounting, Accountability and Shareholder Value

The separation of ownership and control, which has led to the appearance of a class of professional managers, is at the root of some significant problems of accountability and control, in respect of which the role of the accounting profession is subject to criticism. This criticism ranges from the relevance and adequacy of its methods and measurements to the questioning of its social role.

The distinction that has been drawn between financial capital and production capital, the influence of the control paradigm on the evolution of the global economy, as well as the reinforcement of the economic and social supremacy of capital is expressed in the concept of 'shareholder value' as the ultimate objective of business activity.

WEALTH, POMP and circumstance and vulgar displays of riches are an important part of social history. Whereas wealth was acquired historically through the socially justified exercise of military power, its acquisition today is more often attributed to the socially questionable manner in which it is realised. Sombart[1] and Veblen[2] have amply discussed the causal factors of the vulgarisation of wealth in the display of luxurious lifestyles and conspicuous consumption, as well as the necessity for such social symbols to the very rich.

The desire to be successful in a competitive economy and to be seen as being very rich as the measure of that success can only be made explicit in conspicuous spending much appreciated in the eyes of the mediatised world of the chattering classes. The desire to be rich, which is the benchmark of social and business success, is also the primary incentive to dishonesty and one of the major factors in financial criminality. It leaves open the moral judgement, 'Can one acquire great wealth or even simply become rich, through honest labour?'

1 Sombart, R.A., *Luxury and Capitalism* (English translation), Ann Arbor: University of Michigan Press, 1921.
2 Veblen, T.B., *The Theory of the Luxury Class*.

The Distribution of Income in a Market Economy

The theory of capitalism does not see the distribution of income as implying a moral judgement. Capital is seen as accumulated wealth held as private property, which is invested in business activity so that it may be profitably employed. Seen in the context of the Law of Property, the capital invested in business activity remains in the ownership of the investor. Legal ownership of business capital confers the right of control and the right to the profits realised.

The expected return on capital invested in business activity was a problem debated in Antiquity, along with the notion of the just price and the prohibition against usury. Capitalism already existed in Roman times, with early forms of manufacture and the famed *latifundias*, which were large agrarian estates managed on capitalist lines. Roman authors, such as Cato, Varro and Columella,[3] who wrote treaties on farm management, even contemplated the necessity of incorporating a return on capital in the calculation of profit.

It is amusing to note that although the Romans were uncertain of the appropriate rate of interest for this purpose, which is in effect a key element of the calculation of shareholder value, they realised its importance and fixed it arbitrarily at 6%! It is not generally appreciated that in this way, the Romans were already in advance of the thinking of our own times with respect to the notion of the return on capital, for they included the return on capital (6%) in the calculus of profit and in this way arrived at a measure of business efficiency that was based on pure profit.

Roman accounting predates modern accounting and anticipated the needs of modern capitalism with respect to the management of business capital, using concepts of stewardship accounting and management auditing through the verification of records of business transactions. It extended further into the audit of public administration, as may be seen from Cicero's *Letters*.[4] Writing to the Emperor Trajan, Pliny[5] echoes an audit problem that is common to professional auditing today in the words,

> I am now examining the finances of the town of Prusa, expenditure, revenues and sums owing, and finding the inspection increasingly

---

3 See Cato, *De Agri Cultura* (trans. Hooper, W.D. and Ash, H.B.), London: Heinemann, Loeb Classical Library, 1934, Bk I, 1.7; Columella, *Rei Rusticae* (trans. Ash, H.B), London: Loeb Classical Library, 1941, Introduction; Varro, M.T., *Rerum Rusticarum* (trans. Hooper, W.D. and Ash, H.B), London: Loeb Classical Library, 1934, Bk 1.22.1.
4 Cicero, *Letters*.
5 Pliny, *Letters and Panegyricus*, Loeb Classical Library, Vol. II, Bk X,. xvii, p.189.

necessary the more I look into their accounts; large sums of money are detained in the hands of private individuals for various reasons, and further sums are paid out for quite illegal purposes.

Roman Private Law imposed on the *paterfamilias*, as head of the family and as trustee of the family wealth, the legal responsibility for its safekeeping and good management and an obligation to maintain proper accounts. The notion of accounting, and in particular the concept of accountability, was enshrined in the legal obligations imposed upon those responsible towards others for the management of private property and public affairs. The *Jus Civile* provided a system of law, known as Roman Law, which many would argue is Rome's most significant legacy and which, together with English Common Law, constitutes the legal framework for ordering and validating relationships of all forms in most countries.

The market economy, that has succeeded earlier societies and replaced the feudal system, has not altered the legal and social structure of former times, insofar as wealth under capitalism diverts to the wealthy all the fruits of man's labour. It was an awakening Social Conscience that began to perceive that the creation of wealth might be due to man's labour and ingenuity. The Labour Theory of Value, developed by Marx and popularised by socialist writers such as Rosa Luxemburg, argued that capital as such is inert and all value is created by man's efforts. It fuelled the Communist Revolution of 1917 in Russia and inspired socialism elsewhere in Europe.

Western capitalism successfully resisted the demand for social changes implied in the popular movement, which the Social Conscience was evidently willing to support. It did not recognise the contribution of labour to the creation of wealth in the manner in which profits are distributed. Neither did it accept the need for a more equitable sharing between capital and labour of the value created by the enterprise. Instead, Western capitalism succeeded in transforming a society of workers into a society of consumers and in this way, providing for participation in the market economy. Capitalism recognises the consumer as an important person in the celebrated dictum 'the customer is king' and hence that 'the customer is always right'. His right is not only a legal right defended in law, but an effective right in the market economy. Capitalism offers the customer the freedom of choice and markets that are capable of providing improved living standards through the increased volume of output of goods and services. The successful integration of labour in the market economy, in which labour is treated as a cost and is paid in accordance with market value exchangeable for goods and services, and in which labour provides revenues to the market economy, has created a social equilibrium in which there exists a relative indifference as regards the need for changes in the social structure.

Evolutionary Capitalism: The Social Influence
of the Managerial Class
By the 2nd century BC, early forms of capitalist activities were in evidence and the stewardship of assets, the management of agricultural estates and industrial and commercial activities were entrusted by wealthy Romans to servants, who were generally freedmen. They accounted to their Roman masters in a formal manner by producing accounting statements of their stewardship. The Middle Ages, a society comprised of nobles, holding land from the sovereign, freedmen and serfs, witnessed the growing importance of stewards, as responsible and accountable managers. Stewards reported periodically to their masters under a charge and discharge accounting system, being charged with a stewardship responsibility for defined assets at the beginning of an activity period and discharged from that responsibility upon audit of satisfactory performance at the end of the activity period.

Ultimately, the advent of the Industrial Revolution called for radical changes that would open the way to the mobilisation of capital in the expansion of industrial and commercial activities that heralded modern capitalistic organisation. As noted earlier, the key to the rapid and successful development of modern capitalism was the flexibility of English law and its adaptability to new circumstances in enacting the Joint Stock Companies Act 1844. This was a revolutionary change in that it allowed wealthy persons to venture capital by speculating in business without being implicated in the business activity itself and sharing the entire profit realised in accordance with their proportionate shareholding.

A second revolutionary legal development was the enactment of the Limited Liability Act 1855, which limited the personal liability of shareholders for corporate debts to the amount paid or payable on shares. Thus, a $1 share issued at face/nominal value of $1 limits the liability of a shareholder and represents the top limit to his investment risk. When that amount is paid, no further sums may be claimed from him. The Limited Liability Act 1855 provided a critical stimulus to the expansion of capitalism by providing investors with the possibility of participating in business profits under conditions of known and limited risk. The Joint Stock Companies Act 1856 completed this cycle of revolutionary legal developments essential to a market economy based on capitalism by transforming the legal status established by the Joint Stock Companies Act 1844 from a partnership type relationship and giving it a separate legal status. Thus, a Joint Stock Company acquired the legal status of a separate legal person from that of its members. The Deed of Settlement that represented the agreement of members to trade together under the Joint Stock Companies Act 1844 was replaced by statutory documents in the form of the Memorandum of Association, that defines the terms, conditions and objects of the corporation and the Articles of Association, that define the terms and conditions and procedures for the conduct of its affairs. In particular, the Articles of Association determined the rights, duties and responsibilities of the directors as officers entrusted by appointment by shareholders with corporate management.

The Joint Stock Companies Act 1856 conferred a new status on business managers that marked the beginning of a new era in the management of capitalistic activity, namely the separation of ownership from that of control as regards the activities of businesses set up as statutory corporations.[6]

It is no exaggeration to say that the legacy of this spate of legislation was the creation of a new social order that neither Adam Smith, Bentham, Durkheim, Marx nor Schumpeter could have perceived or adequately appreciated. It is only now that the social consequences of the corporate economy are fully established and are being more widely recognised. These social consequences have a dynamic character that is geopolitical and fraught with the menace of global economic and military conflict.

The first consequence is the consecration of a managerial class with defined and extensive powers of control over assets that they do not own and with limited reporting obligations to shareholders with their ownership rights of control reduced. The considerable dilution of ownership rights reflects the spirit of the age in the freedom accorded to a managerial class that has succeeded in significantly usurping the rights of shareholders and at the same time limiting the protection afforded to creditors. Legislators were the first to recognise the implicit dangers of the granting of freedom

---

6 For a detailed study of the emergence of this new class of managers read *The Genesis of Modern Management* by Sidney Pollard, London: Penguin Books, 1965.

to control the assets and business of statutory corporations to directors and officers without providing some protection for shareholders and creditors. For this reason, the *ultra vires* rule was extended to corporations in the Joint Stock Companies Act 1856. It was a regulatory device that sought to prevent a registered corporation from entering into any type of transaction which exceeded the scope of its contractual capacity, as defined in its object clause in the Memorandum of Association. The Companies Act 1862 raised an ambiguity with respect to the *ultra vires* rule that fell to be decided in a celebrated case taken to the House of Lords in 1875,[7] where the House of Lords ruled that 'any matter which is not authorised expressly or by necessary implication within a company's objects clause must be taken to have been forbidden'.

The Ashbury case did not provide the needed protection to shareholders and creditors, for a variety of reasons, but mainly through the legal subterfuge of extending the object clause to cover almost every conceivable type of business contract that managers could conclude on behalf of corporations. The Companies Act 1989 finally abolished the *ultra vires* rule,[8] the reasons being the outdated nature of this rule in relation to present circumstances and the protection afforded elsewhere to shareholders and creditors. Nonetheless, numerous financial scandals relating to fraudulent practices by top management of large corporations continue to create misgivings with regards to the adequacy of transparency and the protection of shareholders and creditors. With shareholding in large quoted corporations being highly diffused, the reality of control is in the hands of top management. Ownership control persists only for small and medium-sized companies, where the effective link between ownership and control has not been severed by incorporation.

Having redefined that status and the role of stewards as managers and created a new social class with considerable economic and management powers over private wealth, the second consequence of the new legislation was similarly to separate the stewardship management function from its traditional stewardship reporting function and the manner in which the management function should be audited. Legislation had restricted considerably the power of shareholders to intervene to only a few areas of

---

7 Ashbury Railway Carriage and Iron Co. v Richie (1875), LR 7 HL.
8 For an interesting and full discussion of this problem see Griffin, S., 'The Rise and Fall of the Ultra Vires Rule in Corporate Law', *Mountbatten Journal of Legal Studies*, Vol. 2, No. 1, June 1998.

decision-making, namely, the appointment of directors, the appointment of auditors, the approval of annual accounts, the approval of the final dividend for the year and those areas affecting changes in capital structure. Moreover, these powers may only be exercised in formalised shareholders' meeting, notably, the Annual General Meeting. Effectively, shareholders may only pass judgement on management performance using the Annual Report, comprising the annual accounts, the directors' report and the auditors' report. The information basis on which such judgement may be made is restricted to that contained in those statements.

The third consequence of the widespread use of the statutory form of business structure that limited liability encouraged was the substitution of the role of the ownership in the audit of the stewardship reports by professional auditors, having legal authority to act as such. The accounting profession began to organise itself on a formal basis as early as the mid-19th century, namely the period during which the rules relating to joint stock corporations were established. The first body to be established under royal charter was the Institute of Chartered Accountants in Scotland in 1854, followed by the creation of the Institute of Chartered Accountants in England and Wales in 1880 (developed out of the merger of several separate bodies that had previously been created, such as the Institute of Accountants in London). Elsewhere, and particularly in the USA, similar developments occurred, the American Institute of Certified Public Accountants being created in 1887. The USA having inherited with the English language,[9] the Common Law and English institutions, diligently followed the development of English legislation in all spheres, and particularly those relating to business corporations.

Finally, stock exchanges emerged as organised markets, where shares of quoted companies could be bought and sold and provided a considerable boost to the investment of private capital in shares and other financial instruments, such as debt instruments in the form of bonds. Stock Exchange Regulations have expanded considerably the level of public control over corporations, not only through strict and expanding information disclosure requirements, but by being able to activate sentiment about management performance, in a broad sense, through the mechanism of share price movements.

---

9 It has been wisely said that Britain and the USA are separated only by a common language.

The vigorous nature of the market economy validates Marx's intuitive understanding of the vigorous nature of capitalism, enabling him to make a prediction that seems confirmed by the recent evolution of the global economy. According to Marx,

> the need of a constantly expanding market for its products chases the bourgeoisie over the whole surface of the globe. It must nestle everywhere, settle everywhere, establish connexions everywhere. The bourgeoisie has through its exploitation of the world market given a cosmopolitan character to production and consumption in every country. (*Communist Manifesto*, 1848, p.37)

By contrast, Schumpeter's prediction that the capitalist system would eventually fail by the desertion of intellectuals revolted by its ideals, seems to have been undermined by the evolution of a newly dominant managerial class completely committed to the central value system of the market economy, and which has established an enduring alliance with a ruling bureaucracy that shares its economic objectives. The result is seen in the expansion of the global economy, through regional political and economic associations such as the European Union, that seeks to transform itself into a distinct political entity with a European national identity.

Corporate Accountability, Accounting and Accountants
Accounting is an area of knowledge that predates the Industrial Revolution and reaches far back into Antiquity. Accounting records are known to have existed as early as the 15th century BC in Mycenaean and Minoan times and Homer writing in the 9th century BC refers to their existence in the *Iliad*. Accounting records predate the appearance of money in the 6th century BC. Accounting, in Roman times, reached its golden age between the 2nd century BC and 2nd century AD. The general principle of accounting responsibility attached to public office, the duty to maintain accounting records and to have them verified through audit procedures were already established. The use of special funds, in particular military pensions, showed that the Romans had developed fairly advanced accounting concepts. The *Jus Civile* defined contractual capacity as appertaining to citizenship, which was a legal status reserved to Romans only. The record of transactions, which were maintained generally by trusted freedmen, were in single-entry form, that is, a single line in the accounting records testifying to the existence and nature of a transaction, for example, 'I owe Gaius 100 *sesterces* for honey'. These accounting records had legal validity and could

be produced as sworn evidence of formal contractual transactions without further proof. The accounting legacy of Roman times, like many other aspects of Roman culture and experience, is enormously enriching to modern accounting and is thought provoking in some significant areas of current concern. In particular, it confirms the everlasting nature of the duty of care and the commitment to caring that is an overriding concern in the Social Conscience and the human experience.

The transition from the world of Antiquity to the modern world as regards social accountability may be examined by reference to some epoch-marking events. The Renaissance in Italy was such a period and it is especially important to the subsequent emergence of a market economy in several significant respects. It was during this period that the institutions, structures and procedures required for the functioning of a market economy were developed. It witnessed the appearance of partnerships as trading associations, commercial banking, multinational branches and the wide use of rigorous accounting controls. To many authorities, it was the invention of double-entry bookkeeping that was the most significant accounting development. Luca Pacioli publicised it in his *Summa de Arithmetica, Geometrica, Propportioni et Proportionalita* in 1494 and it became known in subsequent centuries as the Italian Method of bookkeeping. Pacioli is referred to as the father of modern accounting and according to some authorities, such as Professor Norton Bedford, the historical origins of modern accounting lie in the development of double-entry bookkeeping. Furthermore, it had been claimed by Sombart that

> it is double-entry bookkeeping which endows the economic world with accuracy, knowledge and system. It provided the idea of quantification, of maximising income instead of providing a living, of increasing the value of a capital sum.[10]

This view could be contested by reference to accounting developments in earlier periods, and as Yamey indicated

> the claim that this method of accounting was critical to the expansion of trade, because it afforded a systematic and rational means of profit calculation, is denied by the successful development of the wool trade in England, which did not enjoy the benefit of this method.[11]

---

10 Pollard, S., 'Capital Accounting in the Industrial Revolution', *Yorkshire Bulletin of Economic and Social Research*, Vol. 15, No. 2, November 1963, p.75.
11 See Yamey, B.S., 'Accounting and the Rise of Capitalism: Further Notes on a Theme by Sombart', *Journal of Accounting Research*, Vol. 2-2, 1964, p.64 and pp.117-36, reproduced from *Studi in Onore di Amintore Fanfani*, Milano: 1962, Vol. VI, p.833.

Indeed, single-entry bookkeeping, known as the English Method, was in general use until the beginning of the 19th century, when the Italian Method was finally accepted. The interesting aspect of the Italian Method was the concept of interlocking accounts for recording transactions which used two connected accounts to reflect the nature of the accounting flow involved, one account being used to reflect receiving (*debitum*, meaning I receive) and giving (*creditum*, meaning I give). The shift in connotation from Latin to English gave Anglo-Saxon accounting the terms debit and credit. The interlocking nature of this formulation is conceptually extremely simple, but its very simplicity frequently confounds intelligence. For example, whereas under single-entry bookkeeping, an accounting entry would appear on a single line as 'Paid Edward Jones the sum of £100', double-entry bookkeeping would require the use of two separate accounts, one headed 'Edwards Jones', in which would be written 'Received Cash £100', and another account headed 'Cash', in which would be written 'Paid Edward Jones £100'. Each account being divided into two halves, the first headed 'Debit' and the second headed 'Credit', the account of Edward Jones would show the act of receiving 'Cash £100' as a debit and the account 'Cash' would show the act of giving Edward Jones £100 as a credit, the terms shortened to 'Dr'. and 'Cr.'

The usefulness of the Italian Method went beyond the method of identifying and recording entries as debits or credit, for it afforded the possibility of controlling the accuracy of record keeping by means of establishing a trial balance in which an arithmetical equality between the total debits and the total credit entries had to exist. Moreover, it made possible the identification of individual accounts according to their nature. From this identification, four classes of accounts are distinguished, namely, revenues and expenses accounts, assets and liability accounts. These are used as the basis for establishing end-of-year financial reports in the form of income statements and balance sheets. These continue to provide the financial information that is verified by auditors prior to being released as published information to shareholders. The income statement for the year is used to calculate the profit or loss for the year as the simple difference between the total of the revenue accounts and the expenses accounts. The balancesheet is used to list the assets and the liabilities and to show the difference as the accounting value of the shareholders' interest in the balance, comprising the issued value of the shares plus the accumulated undistributed profits.

The relative public interest in net profit and the value of the shareholders' equity is a function of the manner in which their accounting representation is used. Clearly, there is a strong and persistent interest in profitability and in shareholder value. The developments linked with the Industrial Revolution and in particular, the Joint Stock Company provided an explanation of the manner in which accounting developments occurred in this period. The historical stewardship function, which had been a social necessity to ownership of wealth in prior periods, involved record keeping by individuals acting as bookkeepers. English society has always had special gifts, which may explain why, over a long period of history, its social and intellectual contributions have been unique and influential. Generally recognised as pragmatic and nonconformist, English society has other marked characteristics that are particularly noticeable in Anglo-Saxon accounting, in which pragmatism and nonconformity have created an English penchant for associative structures (its notorious clubability), the preference for compromise as distinct from conflict and the need for ambiguity[12] to provide adequate space for conflict resolution by making meaning a matter of interpretation and choice.

The 19th-century companies legislation led to the development of a formally established accounting profession under royal assent. It gave bookkeepers an official status that they had not enjoyed previously and empowered them with a distinct social responsibility. The right of entry into the profession, the regulations applicable to membership, the rules regarding the manner in which work should be carried out, and in particular, the monopoly right to carry out an audit function on behalf of ownership, have a similarity to earlier London guild associations. A significant consequence of the restriction of rights, through their delegation to recognised and formally approved associations, namely the 'club principle', is the freedom reserved to the profession for the making of accounting and professional rules under the state-delegated authority.

It may be argued that, had the accounting profession been able to develop a broader conception of its social responsibility as arbiters between the different and conflicting interests that have given rise to the fundamental problems of a caring society in a

---

12 See Empson, W., *Seven Types of Ambiguity*, London: Chatto & Windus, 1949 edn. Poet and Literary Critic, Professor of English Literature at the University of Sheffield, Empson legitimised ambiguity as a positive quality, arguing that 'the moral is that a developing society decides practical questions more by the way it interprets words it thinks obvious and traditional than by its official statement of current dogma'.

market economy, its present problem of defining its role would have been obviated. In particular, an evident impartiality with respect to conflicting interests involved would have positioned the accounting profession as legal arbiters acting for the Social Conscience, for the essential social problem that has emerged today lies in the loss of social control over the managerial class. Many of the most spectacular corporate scandals, such as Enron, Worldcom and the Maxwell case, illustrate this failure of control over criminal behaviour by top management. It is not a simple coincidence that the role of accountants as auditors in these cases has affected public confidence in the accounting profession. The dictum that auditors should act as guard dogs with respect to the interests of their constituency and not as bloodhounds in the search for deviant managerial behaviour, is an example of that use of ambiguity in Anglo-Saxon society that conveniently shelves a problem by fudging the real issue involved in a potentially conflicting situation. The principle underlying stewardship accounting is to provide effective control over management behaviour, as defined in the limits of law. Prior to the Joint Stock Company legislation, that gave relative freedom of action to management, stewards were simply agents acting for owners. The latter demanded complete explanations of the business conducted under the authority entrusted to stewards and that subservience of the control function to the ownership function dictated the nature of stewardship responsibility.

There are two areas in which the accounting profession has been unable to act for the Social Conscience and in the interests of a caring society. First, in adequately determining and obtaining from the State the delegated authority needed effectively to fulfil the audit function for the purpose of control. Although auditors are formally appointed by shareholders by resolution at an Annual General Meeting of shareholders, which also decides their remuneration, their candidature is determined by the board of directors. Effectively, this creates a conflict of interest, which explains the reticence of auditors to act forcibly in the detection of managerial irregularities, which could be indicative of criminal behaviour. As criminals generally seek to confound truth and conceal crime, the pressure on auditors not to act as bloodhounds in actively detecting corporate crime, is significant and may be understood by reference to the potential loss of substantial earnings that would be entailed. This does not imply the accounting profession condones this situation. On the contrary, it is very aware of it and has sought to tighten the discipline imposed on its membership.

However, there is sufficient ambiguity present in proclaimed dogma to weaken the effectiveness of deontology. The need for the State to intervene on behalf of shareholders and other members of society in complaints against business corporations by the creation of agencies as such the Financial Ombudsman and the Financial Standards Agency, indicates where and how the accounting profession has not responded to a situation, and where and how its experience would have made it an obvious social agent.

Second, the tendency in recent years has been for top management to award itself substantial 'financial rewards packages' in the form of salaries, bonuses, share options, pension schemes and severance pay in the form of golden handshakes. In these various ways, it has arrogated to itself a claim to sharing profits with shareholders and deciding for themselves what that share should be. Some of these arrangements do not require approval by shareholders, and when approval is needed, it has been easily obtained. This results from the lack of sufficient shareholder presence at meetings called for such purposes. Such schemes as management buy-outs leveraged out of corporate assets, the demutualisation of mutual insurance companies and other forms of non-quoted organisations, have all been devices that have enabled top management to enrich themselves by diverting to themselves, through legalised expropriation, the property of shareholders. There is now a growing outcry about the unfairness in the relative distribution of income in society that is evidenced in the exaggerated salaries and emoluments paid to corporate executives.

It is noteworthy that, at a time when the Social Conscience is becoming aware of a festering social problem, the objective of management has been refined as increasing shareholder value. This concept is at once the enunciation of a principle for corporate decision-making and suggestive of an alternative measurement base in financial reporting.

The relationship between a caring society and the market economy is fatally flawed in the reasoning underlying the manner in which shareholder value may be increased, with detrimental effect on other social groups, such as employees and consumers. One component of shareholder value is the profits arising on a periodic basis. Profits may be increased by increasing revenues and reducing costs. Much attention is given by corporate executives to increasing profits by reducing labour costs, by measures seeking to improve productivity. There are several ways in which profits may be improved to the detriment of employees. Profit improvements may be secured through redundancy, when employees are deprived of the means of livelihood and thrown on the mercy of the community. Corporate mergers and acquisitions result in corporate reorganisations in which profit improvement are sought in synergy gains from eliminating duplication leading to widely proclaimed substantial labour cost saving. This throws all classes of employees on the streets. Profit improvements are also obtained from relocating business to countries where lower labour costs may be obtained again by throwing people out of work. This is creating a paradox for the market economy of reducing the standard of living and the buying power of the constituency in which its best customers exist. In this sense, there is an obvious disconnection between what the proverbial right hand is doing as distinct from the left hand, or, in accounting language, of the social relationship between debited labour expenses and credited sales revenues. Daily, the public has to listen to media icons on so-called business shows commenting with craven felicity that such-and-such a company has reported a 25% increase in quarterly profits over the previous period, and, in the same breath, sharing the consternation of government officials and of the business community that released employment statistics have revealed that, in the same period, average pay-packets have shown an inflationary rise of 1.5%.

Finally, profit improvements are also obtained by exploiting legal loopholes and avoiding the social responsibilities imposed by a caring society. Given that laws in civilised countries reflect the Social Conscience, recent years have seen multinational corporations shifting production to areas where the exploitation of human misery in the form of child labour, long working hours, abominable working and sanitary conditions and total deregulation have permitted the worst excesses.

The accounting profession is not unaware of the moral problems implied in its mission and has taken a position insofar as it has seen itself able to act through the making of recommendations, for example, in the publication by the Accounting Standards Committee in 1975 of the Corporate Report. Over the last 30 years, it has encouraged and maintained an animated discussion of corporate social responsibility reporting. By and large, however, it has seen its function as derived from the concept of stewardship accounting, namely the keeping of accounting reports and reporting to shareholders periodically, as required by legislation. In this regard, much of its effort was directed towards the problems of periodic income measurement and particularly in developing reference standards for improving the quality of income measurement.

There is in the very nature of accounting, an intellectual bias towards procedures and techniques, rather than a wider vision of the world or *weltanschauung*. In this respect, it should be remembered that double-entry bookkeeping based on the orderly recording of business transactions derived from invoices and the verification of the information recorded through the process of audit, remains the core activity area for accountants, from which all else originates. The usefulness and the relevance of the information provided to shareholders were never in question: this was a problem that was to be discovered much later and only in recent times. Likewise, the accounting profession based its rules on the principle enunciated by Paciolo, who praised regular accounting as a social virtue. Truth was and remains one of the virtues implicit in stewardship and establishing truth in financial reports would be argued by many to be a strict and necessary professional condition. Taunted by this difficulty in the face of a known tendency to untruth in business practice, Anglo-Saxon accounting found a solution in a compromise certification of accounting reports formulated as a true and fair view of the income and of the financial position, in conformity with accounting records declared to have been properly kept. Given the strict conditions attaching to truth, the accounting profession proceeded undeterred to qualify the strict nature of truth by the relaxing condition of fairness. The resulting ambiguity pleased and satisfied all parties and no objections to this form of audit qualification were admitted, until the EEC Commission engaged on the standardisation of accounting practices in Europe with the release of the Fourth Directive on Company Accounts in 1978. Other EEC member countries and accounting bodies were and remain totally perplexed by the English audit certification, confirming their suspicious of the perfidious nature of Albion. In particular, French accountants trained in Cartesian logic could not and cannot bring themselves to reconcile truth with fairness and much preferred a direct reference of the idea of sincerity associated with regularity.

The intellectual isolation in which the Anglo-Saxon accounting profession was to develop from its inception left important gaps in its ability to meet social needs other than its own. In this regard, the Industrial Revolution in the 18th and 19th centuries was essentially an industrial revolution that made England a world industrial and economic power. The influence of the two-culture syndrome was to segregate the industrial Midlands and the North from the financial South.[13] It restricted the interest of an accounting profession that grew out of the London Institute of Accountants to financial accounting leading to the neglect of industrial and management accounting. The real crisis for the success of the Industrial Revolution lay in the need for reliable cost information for pricing. Many industrial firms went bankrupt for this reason. According to McKendrick,[14] 'the survival of the Wedgwood Company in the Potteries lay in the fact that it was able to develop a system of cost accounting that fulfilled this need'. The development of cost accounting as a distinct discipline dates only from the beginning of the 20th century, the Institute of Cost and Works Accountants having been founded in 1919.

Another and serious consequence of the intellectual isolation of the accounting profession was its complete ignorance of the needs of the investment community for information relevant to making investment decisions. Locked into the philosophy of stewardship accounting and reporting, the accounting profession focused on recorded and past transactions for producing what were effectively historical summaries of the results of business activities. Since it is accepted that the past cannot be used as a crystal ball to forecast the future, historical accounting could not be reliably used to develop forecasts needed for investment decision-making concerned with future prospects. Dominated by its audit function and the certification of published financial reports, the accounting profession could not free itself from a concern with the past to an orientation towards a clientele having different needs. Moreover, it would have implied a significant shift away from the certitude and verifiability of its information base, established in the recording of transactions, toward developing estimates and forecasts relating to future events and placing a value on them, which it did not consider as being its mission. Accountants maintained the view that they were concerned with cost allocation and not with valuation.

The growing influence of financial capital, as distinct from production capital, is seen in the expanding role of stock exchanges and of financial markets that expect and need information going beyond traditional published financial reports issued out of conventional financial accounting practices. Stock exchanges have

---

13 F.R. Leavis was much concerned with the significance of this divide, that was influential in the development of English society generally.
14 McKendrick, N., 'Josiah Wedgwood and Cost Accounting in the Industrial Revolution', *Economic History Review*, 2 Ser., Vol. 23, 1970, p.65.

taken over responsibility for developing rules relating to the information to be supplied by quoted companies, that is additional to that supplied through published financial statements. The accounting profession has been influenced by the advocacy of shareholder value as the standard for business performance, although this approach does not fit with accounting traditions and its approach to risk.

The Control Paradigm and the Social Role of Accounting Information

The dominant paradigm that explains the social role of accounting lies in the concept of control. This paradigm is implicit whenever any form of authority is delegated. It implies that there is an authority from which delegated powers are derived. It implies that records be kept as evidence to be used in the control process. Implicit, also, is the notion that effective control relies on periodical reviews of events, during which these are analysed, explanations are obtained and consequential decisions are made. This paradigm not only explains the origins of accounting, but it remains its *raison d'être* to this day and in this sense, defines the social role of accounting. The failure to perceive and to appreciate the determining signification of this paradigm by the intellectual leaders of the accounting profession explains the problematic situation that exists today with respect to the future of the profession and its social role in a market economy. The desire to maintain a social role in the market economy, which the historical experience has validated, and to seek an expanded influence in a market economy, which has created new opportunities, explains the temptation to engage in new areas of professional activities. It requires a different intellectual orientation and an appropriate competence. The wish to be all things to all men reflects an inability to understand the limits of one's own possibilities. In other words, defining a social mission is largely a matter of what it is possible to do and what is the required field and level of competence. This may be taken as being the problematic facing the accounting profession in the context of social change.

The accounting inheritance is a long experience of recording business experience as it happens, in the memory form in which it is produced. It has consisted of interpreting that experience in terms of the facts that are identified as data, analysing that data to produce summarised information useful to review and understand that experience and appreciate its meaning for making an evaluation both as regards performance and weaknesses or failures that need to be explained and corrected.

Modern information technology has reduced the social role of accountants in the area of data collection and analysis, the maintenance of accounting records and the extrapolation of information, as defined and required by users. Computer programmes created by information specialists and used in day-to-day operational activities under the responsibility of other management departments, such as sales, purchasing, personnel, etc., create, as automatically generated by-products, accounting data relevant to operational control. The management-by-exception principle also has removed the chore from accounting practice.

Legislation has conferred on the accounting profession the social responsibility for controlling business corporations with respect to the keeping of accounting records of business events and reporting to shareholders on the financial performance and financial position of business corporations. As a result, the accounting profession has been assured of a long-term future and a monopoly position in its audit function that it can exploit to advantage.

The accounting profession occupies, with the Stock Exchange, a central and pivotal position in the market economy. As a major supplier of financial information that is used by several and different user groups, it is understandable that it should be exposed to criticism from all quarters with respect to the nature and the adequacy of the information provided. Traditionally, the accounting profession has taken the position that, although financial reports are addressed primarily to shareholders, they may be understood as having a general usefulness to all user groups. In that context, the responsibility for the interpretation of accounting information published in financial statements is left to the discretion of particular user groups.

When criticism has implied culpability, the accounting profession has adopted a defensive and explanatory stance. The most strident criticisms have emanated from the financial capital community, especially analysts and theorists in that particular field of knowledge. The substantial difference that exists in the orientation between accountants and the financial capital community is that the former, locked into the tradition of *ex post* control cannot switch into an *ex ante* orientation relying on an ability to develop forecasts, which is against its nature and beyond its competence. The response of the accounting profession to the insistent call of the financial capital community for shareholder value reporting reflects an enthusiasm for the concept, but a reluctance to abandon the use of historical cost accounting for financial reporting purposes. There is also a substantial point of difference in the time profile of these two different stances: *ex post* control implies a specified and fixed period over which performance is evaluated, *ex ante* forecasts have no obvious and necessary time restrictions and usually extend to infinity, as is the case when establishing present values by discounting future cash-flows to infinity. In essence, the control paradigm is based on a control model having specific characteristics, objectives and methods; the valuation paradigm used for developing forecasts is a valuation model aimed at establishing a reference point for decision. Thus, the present value model seeks to determine the present value of a company for the purpose of a keep/sell investment decision based on indifference as to holding the investment or switching into cash.

The control paradigm reflects long-established traditions and current law with respect to the time-basis for evaluation. As much as there has been criticism of the unsuitability of the yearly period, it is enshrined in legislation concerning financial reporting to shareholders and to government authorities in the form of the annual return, and for the purposes of submitting annual tax declarations.

The legal obligation to prepare and submit financial statements to shareholders on an annual basis in most Western industrialised countries has had the logical consequence that the evaluation of corporate financial performance is focused on year-based results. As a consequence, the evaluation of management performance is conducted on the basis of the experience of only 12 months, which most feel is inadequate as a basis for judgment. Nonetheless, the behavioural influence of using this time period of evaluations has led to a tendency to focus on the short-term in corporate decision-making to the detriment of longer-term considerations. The current argument in favour of using a longer reference period for performance reports and evaluations runs counter to the urgency that is attached by the market to the detection, at the earliest possible moment, of possible failures to meet performance expectations and thus take such remedial activities as is necessary, including replacing the chief executive officer. It is for this reason that the Stock Exchange has insisted on having from quoted companies quarterly budget forecasts and the release of profit warnings at the earliest possible time. It is noteworthy that such is the impact of profit warnings on investor sentiment of what are relatively small shortfalls in profit expectations tend to lead to magnified falls in share values. Given the hypothesis that the market incorporates all future expectations in current share prices, the impact of profit warnings on share prices does show how much market expectations with respect to the future are influenced by short term considerations. This reinforces the relevance of short term performance evaluation for control purposes.

The Control Paradigm and Evaluation of Business Performance
The measurements or benchmarks used for control purposes, address two fundamental issues:

(a) establishing the result of business activities during the year;
(b) determining the value of the business at the end of the year.

Establishing the measurement base for calculating the annual result implies a clarification of the objectives for which the information is needed. The concept of income is generally used for measuring annual performance. Its meaning is derived from economic theory, and as stated by Hicks,[15] 'the purpose of income calculations in practical affairs is to give people an indication of the amount that they can consume without impoverishing themselves'. This definition has been extended by Alexander[16] to defining corporate dividend policy in terms of 'the amount that the corporation can distribute to the owners of equity in the corporation and be as well off at the end of the year as it was in the beginning'. This definition introduces the notion of capital maintenance as the benchmark for deciding the maximum amount available for distribution to shareholders as dividend in respect of a year's operations. Safeguarding capital may be taken as a prime decision objective for management, in which limiting dividend distribution is merely one aspect of the problem, which in actual practice is far more complicated and outside the scope of this text.

Two further objectives for income calculations may also be derived from the foregoing explanations. First, if the amount that may be distributed is referred to a bottom line that is the maintenance of capital, it may be assumed that that amount is also a measure of business efficiency expressed as a return on capital. For example, if the annual income is measured as 100 and the capital

---

15 Hicks, J.R., *Income and Capital*, Oxford University Press, 2nd edn, 1946.
16 Alexander, S.S., 'Income Measurement in a Dynamic Economy', in Baxter, W.T. and Davidson, S., *Studies in Accounting Theory*, London: Sweet & Maxwell, 1962.

is maintained at an accounting value of 1,000, the accounting return on capital is 10%. The reference base for this evaluation of financial performance is the capital invested, including accumulated undistributed profit, shown on the balance sheet. This approach to evaluation is useful for comparative analyses with the performance of other companies, but this supposes that their experience is similar. Second, using the same assumptions, if the distributable dividend is 10 and the market rate of return expected for investors in that company is 10%, it follows that the value of that company is 1,000, from the simple logic that a sum of 1,000 invested at 10% will produce an income of 100. It may be supposed, therefore, all things remaining constant, there is a correspondence between the accounting results and the accounting value of the company that meets market performance and shareholder value expectations, derived from the simple valuation model used by the market for valuing shares on the basis of dividend yields.

The problem facing shareholders in the company, whether to keep or sell their shares, will be affected by events taking place in the market, which are neither part of, nor foreseen, in the accounting results and valuations. Thus, if business profitability generally is on the decline and as a result, the sentiment of the market moves to accepting 5% as a reasonable rate of return for investors, their expectations will be adjusted down from 10% to 5%. If the company's rate of profitability remains constant, the shareholder value will increase from 1,000 to 2,000 and that will be the value at which they will be indifferent as to keeping their shares or selling them.

From the above, it may be appreciated that there could be a connection between accounting measurements and the process by which share values are established by stock exchanges and as between the measurement of annual income and the valuation of shares. But the periodic nature of the accounting measurement of income, which occurs at one point in time, the end of the year, and is available only after it has been calculated, makes it a historical measurement that is already outdated when released to investors. This explains the interest of the Stock Exchange in obtaining quarterly profit forecasts from quoted companies. Using these forecasts, together with other available data, the market seeks to develop valuations that are relevant to its own purposes, which are directed to buy/sell or keep decisions in share trading. Financial markets analyse profitability and make valuations using their own reference base, which is orientated towards the future and attempts in this way to use accounting information adjusted to market indices of performance and value. The first question of concern stated above, namely what is the profitability of an investment in a given company, is discussed in terms of earnings per share (EPS), which is the net profit of the year calculated on the basis of issued share capital. Another market concept of profitability is the price earnings ratio (PER), which compares the earnings per share to the current share price. The market estimates the value of a corporation by using the PER in that context. Thus, a PER of 4 means that the market share price is four times yearly earnings per share. A PER of 4 is generally considered as low and indicative of a sluggish performance. In highly speculative conditions, where growth expectations are high, in some markets PERs of 30 to 80 have been witnessed. Finally, the market also refers to the dividend yield, which interprets dividend distributions to the share price

These different approaches to determining profitability and corporate values produce radically different conclusions, since they are conceptually radically different. As explained earlier, the method used in accounting to calculate the income for the year is to await the end of the year, to terminate the recording of business transactions for the year at that date and then to extract from the records all transactions identified as comprising revenues and all transaction comprising expenses and to calculate the annual income as the arithmetical difference between the two lists. Published financial statements that have been submitted to audit carry an audit certification that the profit/loss shown is a true and fair view of the profit/loss of the year, and that the balance sheet is a true and fair view of the financial position, implying what it is worth to shareholders. This is indicated in the statement of the shareholders' net equity, comprising the accounting value of issued shares plus reserves in the form of undistributed profits and other reserves created out of profit.

Whether or not the accounting or stock exchange approach to the problem of providing relevant information as to financial performance is better, may be questioned. Take the following example.

Corporation A runs a supermarket business with stores throughout the country. It is quoted on the Stock Exchange and its shares are traded daily. Occasionally, corporate raiders have shown interest in acquiring control of Corporation A and made aggressive takeover attempts that were successfully repelled. Corporation A is viewed by the market as a very successful operation. Its policy is to sell for cash only and to have competitive prices and high sales volume. Suppliers are selected with a view to guaranteeing product quality and supply reliability. Invoices are paid subject to a 90 days interest free credit period. Average stocks are at 10 days. As a result of driving selling prices down, the mark-up on cost is reduced to a minimum and, taking into account overheads, the accounting net profit is low, and this is reflected in its dividend distribution policy. Investment in assets is low. The policy being to lease stores, fixed equipment is written off as depreciation within 5 years from acquisition and is of negligible value within a short period. Business being on a cash basis, there are no trade debtors; stocks at any time are as given, that is 10 days, at cost value.

The three facts that stand out are low profits and high cash inflows from sales, and a high level of short-term debts in the form of outstanding trade creditors

In brief, Corporation A is not making money out of its trading activity, since the gross margin on sales (the difference between selling price and cost of sales) is pitched just to cover overhead costs, leaving a small difference as net profit. It may be deduced that Corporation A will pay very little tax, since the taxable profit is low. Moreover, since dividends are declared normally out of profits, Corporation A would be justified in restricting dividend pay-out to shareholders, although at any time it holds substantial cash balances.

Neither the accounting nor the market approach to financial performance analysis based on profitability appear to be relevant to the business context and to the appraisal of Corporation A's business strategy and policy. Nor can these approaches help in estimating the worth or value of its shares in terms of earnings and a net asset approach to determining value is likewise not useful.

The conundrum is that Corporation A is making a lot of money, which it is extracting from its suppliers, each unit supplied creating 80 days of net credit at cost of sales, that is, 10 days cost of sales tied up in average stock and the balance of the 90 days appearing in 80 days of cash at selling price, this figure being inclusive of profit on sales.

In strict accounting terms, and in formal economic theory, Corporation A is not producing income, but is in the business of borrowing money! Can this activity be interpreted as being the production of income, since it defies all definitions of income, but it is creating an asset in the form of cash? It is obliged to do something with that cash, so it expands its sales infrastructure and continually increases sales by investing in available sales capacity. But keeping up this rhythm of business expansion takes on the appearance of an endless nightmare of self-generating expansion, for each added unit of sales, made possible by successive increases in capacity, is leading to constant and additional unit days of cash from sales.

How can this situation be interpreted in response to the two questions asked above:

(a) What is the result of business activity during the year, since it is not really producing income?
(b) What is the value of the business, in the face of a huge and expanding volume of short-term debt and little available cash at any time, since cash surpluses must continually be committed to expanding selling capacity?

Corporation A is clearly not an unreal situation, for it reflects exactly the market environment facing a typical supermarket. Its value is found in its ability to generate cash-flow through short-term borrowing and in its increasing effective command over goods and services.

This suggests that evaluating business performance has to be judged from an entirely different base than conventional accounting or financial theory. First, it supports the view that cash-flow measurements are more relevant to understanding the events and the experience of business enterprises. In this interpretation, accruals accounting is directed at analysing business events in a legal context, by taking into account contractual rights and obligations rather than cash management: that is the bottom line in successfully running such a business. Second, it implies that the control paradigm, discussed earlier, is more influential in evaluating performance and translating such evaluation in the process of share pricing. In terms of the control paradigm, the value of a business is its effective command over goods and services. Looking naively at the manner in which it established that control through its own efforts, *ex post*, ignores entirely the control over goods and services that may also be derived from the ability to borrow, which may be judged from an *ex ante* perspective.

Hernando de Soto[17] made a most significant contribution to the understanding of capitalism and the market economy using the

---

17 De Soto, Hernando, *The Mystery of Capital: Why Capitalism Triumphs in the West and Fails Everywhere Else*, London: Bantam Press, 2000.

insight that it is the ability to obtain credit *a priori* that makes possible engaging in business. It is the inability to obtain credit that frustrates economic development in underdeveloped countries, due to the absence of titles to property usable as loan guarantees. In the case of Corporation A, it is clearly its access and control of short-term credit, obtained from suppliers and the expanding exploitation of its credit policy and management that more accurately measures its business performance and value. Neither accounting nor financial theory is able to comprehend and express its performance and its value in conventional practice, though the market clearly does establish a share price.

Creating Shareholder Value as a Corporate Objective
As mentioned above, there are different ways in which business performance could be evaluated. The notion of efficiency is an all-pervasive intellectual influence on the modern world, which belongs to the Age of Science and whose thinking is dominated by scientific rationality. The evaluation of business performance reflects also the idea of progress.[18] A side effect of this is that the expectation of continued progress condemns stability as inadequate. The absence of progress, or the failure to maintain progress, marks the limits of tolerance and provokes change. Accordingly, progress, which is synonymous with growth, is a concept that is built into expectations regarding business performance.

These twin concepts of efficiency and progress characterise thought and action to such an extent that they overshadow other aspects of life and of the humane experience. They carry extensive and considerable implications for humanity, not only with respect to the criteria that should provide meaning to the humane experience, but to the ultimate consequences of endless progress that lie in the question, 'Where are we going?'

Business organisations are primarily structures enabling the exploitation of economic resources in a rational and systematic manner towards the attainment of desired social objectives. The entire problem of the evaluation of the efficiency of business performance is contained in the exploration and clarification of the foregoing meaning. The social structure created by the existence of private property and a market economy based on capitalism determines the context for the evaluation of business performance.

---

18 See Pollard, S., *The Idea of Progress: History and Society*, London: C.A. Watts & Co. Ltd, 1968, for a fascinating discussion of this concept.

According to the Institute of Chartered Accountants in England and Wales,[19] shareholder value is commonly measured as the growth in a company's share price over a period, together with dividends received from it, giving the total shareholder return (TSR). The logic that is incorporated in this definition is that, since share prices reflect the market's expectations of future cash-flows, it provides a value focus for management to achieve since shareholder value reflects the return required by shareholders. For this reason, it represents for management the cost of equity capital as a bottom line of management performance. Consequently, management can only create value for shareholders if, over the long term, it generates a return on capital which is greater that the cost of capital.

Creating shareholder value as the unique corporate objective restates the ambition of classical economic theory in a more pragmatic manner in which the cost of capital is the bottom line. It does not do away with the measurement problems that are inherent in the postulates of the theory of finance, which supports the shareholder value approach and which seeks to give it effectiveness in management decision-making.

A critical view is currently developing with respect to the relevance and usefulness of the shareholder value concept. According to Dr Patrick Dixon, Chairman of Global Change Ltd, the current obsession with bottom-line profit and shareholder value is looking tired: having failed to help leadership, motivation, marketing, product innovation, change in management or customer loyalty, it is in danger of destroying the value that people sought to gain.

Financial Capital and Production Capital:
Different Approaches, Different Objectives
A market economy necessarily expresses meaning by the translation of all facts and events into money values, thereby providing a common standard or benchmark as a reference base for an evaluation process leading to a judgement. The evaluation of business performance focuses on making two classes of judgements: *ex post* evaluations of past performance and *ex ante* forecasts of future performance. Both are relevant to the central problem concerning investors and managers of business enterprises, namely decision-making.

19 *Inside Out: Reporting on Shareholder Value*, London: The Institute of Chartered Accountants in England and Wales, 1999, p.6.

The major difference between these two classes of judgement is that *ex post* evaluations are based on results of past performance that fulfil requisite objectivity. This requisite objectivity lies in the fact that the numbers used result from an accounting experience based on records of past transactions. This allows reliable judgements to be made with respect to matters of concern, for example, the level of activity achieved, the efforts made and the results obtained. By contrast, the necessity of addressing decisions towards the future and to making action plans that incorporate expectations of progress and improvement are necessarily fraught with the risk implicit in making forecasts. Hence, success in the making of investment and business decisions is a function of the evaluation of risk, making the quality of risk management in the face of uncertainty the critical test of success.

Investors deal in financial markets and are concerned with financial capital, the evaluation of its performance and its deployment in the increase of their wealth. The strategies involved are entirely different from corporate managers, who are concerned with capital invested in the production of goods and services and the efficiency of the use of capital invested in that context. Schumpeter[75] refers to the necessity of making a distinction between financial capital and production capital in establishing an understanding of modern capitalism. Financial capital represents funds made available to an enterprise by a financial company, however described, which seeks to make money out of money. Production capital represents funds invested in the activities of enterprise concerned with producing goods and services and selling them in such as way as to make a profit on sale. This profit is the return on capital.

Financial capital focuses on wealth and the acquisition of control over the means of access to wealth. Capital markets provide that access through investment strategies directed at obtaining control over quoted corporations, where the creation of shareholder value may be optimised by management able to squeeze additional value out of assets, and the manner in which resources are deployed and successfully utilised to that end. Large pension funds and financial institutions control large cash-flows available as investment capital. By taking pivotal shareholding in a wide spread of different types of activity, which nowadays have global ramifications, these organisations have acquired significant control over world economic resources and in particular, natural

---

20 Schumpeter, A., *History of Economic Analysis.*

resources which are essential for economic growth and wealth creation.

In addition, financial capital is fed as venture capital into supporting new growth areas and green fields. Through the careful appraisal of risk attaching to new ventures, financial capital gains control over the shape of the future, and especially over the new wealth created. Through the process of merger and acquisition, the control that financial capital exercises over global economic activity is being concentrated in the hands of a fewer number of financial groups, now estimated in a global perspective at only six, of which five are located in the USA.

It is in this understanding that it is possible to appreciate the importance of shareholder value as the corporate objective expected of the management of production capital. The subordination of corporate management to this objective and its use in the evaluation of managerial performance is leading to the submission of the global market economy to the wealth-seeking objective of an ever smaller group of persons, whose political influence and effective financial power is coalescing into an ultimate form of dictatorship. This situation is bound to lead to a world in which conflict will characterise relations between emergent countries and the established order.

Conclusion
Mindful of the benefits that the market economy has brought to modern society, particular care has to be taken not to 'throw the baby out with the bathwater' in developing a balanced answer to the two questions postulated for discussion in this chapter, namely: 'Can a caring society exist in a market economy?' and, further, 'Is a market economy sustainable that denies man's fundamental nature and needs for caring and sharing?'

These two questions tantalised the intellects of two of the most influential thinkers of modern times. Marx and Schumpeter were both clearly equally sensitive to the concerns that are examined in this book. Sharing the same sentiments and reaching the same conclusion as to the fate of capitalism, they differed only as to the process that would bring about its destruction. The evolution of modern industrial society has shown the resilience of capitalism and its enduring capacity to extend its influence and capture the imagination of most of the world's population, even though there are in this population important religious and value differences, which indicate a schismatic tendency that is becoming a seemingly unbridgeable gulf between people. Do the social consequences of this schism portend horrendous conflict or is this conflict avoidable by the peaceful resolution of conflicting paths and the emergence of a caring society in which conciliation through sharing is the gateway to social harmony?

Caring is a sentiment whose effective influence is a function of proximity. It is difficult to care when distance hides from view and renders caring ineffective. As stated in the Prologue, sharing is a principle that is a consequence of caring, but it has a reach that is effective beyond those that are within the ambit of care. It is by focusing on the principle of sharing that the social consequences of the market economy may be perceived and their cause understood.

Capitalism cannot be stigmatised simply by reference to the excesses that are ascribed to the market economy. The market economy has proved its unique capability to inspire economic growth and improve living standards and it is this knowledge that opens the possibility of reconciliation between capitalism and socialism, which is the third way that is suggested. The shareholder value concept used in the formal structures employed by the market economy for managing economic and human resources with the aim of adding to wealth rather than to welfare, acts against the Social Conscience. The controlling influence that financial capital is able to impose upon the market economy and the concentration of power over the global economy exerted by a financial caucus located in the USA will inevitably bring conflict with the Social Conscience.

Sharing is an unavoidable obligation imposed by the Social Conscience on the market economy and, like the action of water on stone, it will permeate through the market economy with the inevitability of time.

—7—

The State, Society and Government

The process of empowering a caring society implies reforming those three principal areas that are critical to social change, namely, education, the market economy and government. Empowering a caring society means giving effect to the Social Conscience, as the embodiment of moral values. In this interpretation, government, as the representative authority in a democracy is subject to the Social Conscience, as the sovereign authority. It is this interpretation of the role of representative government elected under democratic principles that meets the criterion of government by consent. The evolution of political philosophy offers a rich discussion of ideas and reflects an enduring concern with moral values.

THE HISTORY of Western civilisation is a history of different forms of society, of evolving social structures, of political ambition and of changing social conditions. In particular, philosophers have had a special interest in political theory and with the duties and the responsibilities of rulers. Their thoughts, opinions and recommendations are embodied in a philosophical literature that brings many centuries of co-existence in a world of ideas manifesting a unity of understanding with respect to the supreme importance of moral values. From the standpoint of different social environments, speaking in different ages and in different languages, philosophers by and large share the same sentiments and have a common understanding. The Ancient World is brought into instant proximity with the Modern World in a community of shared experience of the same dilemmas and the same end-objectives. These are found in shared moral values and in the Social Conscience seen as unchanging through time.

Many eminent philosophers have left their mark on the thinking of their generation and left in memory their contributions to political theory. A few have not only marked their own generation: they lived at times of schismatic changes that marked the beginning of new eras in history. It is useful to refer the discussion of the idea of government to the thoughts of those few thinkers and establish in this way an historical sequence and a rationalised understanding of the community of beliefs which remain rooted in political theory.

Beginning with Plato and with the principles of government that he enunciated, most of political history through to the Renaissance tells of the actions of rulers, or sovereigns. Until recently, the doctrine of the Divine Right of Kings attributed their authority to divine providence. Charlemagne (742-814) was crowned King of the Franks in 768 and anointed Emperor of the Holy Roman Empire in 800 in Rome. Machiavelli (1469-1527) gives advice in *The Prince* (written 1513, published 1532); Hobbes (1588-1679) continued to subscribe to the divine right doctrine in his *Leviathan* (1651).

It is John Locke (1632-1704) whose thinking marks that most significant watershed that is the period of the Enlightenment. The doctrine of the Divine Right of Kings is refuted. The Bill of Rights (1689) transfers substantial government powers to an elected Parliament. Adam Smith (1723-90), Jeremy Bentham (1748-1832) and John Stuart Mill (1806-73) proclaim the right to freedom and a new society is born with the political ambition to promote the happiness of its people in the largest measure possible. It was finally Marx (1818-83), who recognised that caring was not possible without sharing. Marx remains inescapably the moral philosopher of modern times.

In line with this linear approach, the literature of political thought begins with Socrates, Plato and Aristotle. Aristotle (384-322BC) was the student of Plato, Plato (427-347BC) was the student of Socrates. Socrates (c.470-399BC) is the founder of Western philosophy: he left no written evidence of his thought, but they are recorded by Plato in the *Dialogues*. As mentioned in the Introduction to this text, Plato was concerned with genuine reality composed of ideal forms such as goodness, truth, beauty and justice that exist in the mind. These normative values have been incorporated throughout this text in the notion of absolute values from which moral values are derived by deduction. By contrast, Aristotle looked to the human form as the condition from which knowledge is gained. The concepts of a caring society based on the moral values that are the substance of the Social Conscience give special importance to Plato.

Plato: Moral Values and Political Philosophy
The significance and the importance of Plato's contribution to moral and political philosophy cannot be understated. According to Professor A.N. Whitehead, 'the safest general characterisation

of the European philosophical tradition is that is consists of a series of footnotes to Plato'.[1]

Plato's philosophical standpoint is that true knowledge, as distinct from that obtained by the senses, is acquired by the contemplative soul that turns away from the world. True knowledge represents the real essence of things and as such may be defined as 'real forms' or 'realities'. They are normative and, as such, are idealistic. To Plato, they consisted of truth, intelligence, beauty, harmony and goodness and are unchangeable and invisible, and therefore akin to the divine elements in us, that is, the soul. They constitute the moral values that Plato declared as being 'outside and beyond us' and at the same time, within us. Life, Truth and Love are used in this text to describe those absolute values that are outside and beyond us and at the same time within us. They may be understood as model forms and their expanded interpretations were used to provide normative values that define a caring society. Durkheim refers to them as having the function of a central value system for compelling behaviour. We have referred to this central value system as being the Social Conscience and as embedding moral values that act in instructing behaviour towards doing what is right.

Plato's conceptualisation of two worlds, the intelligible world of forms and the perceptual world, or world of the senses, provides the credo for religious thinking regarding the existence of a spiritual, eternal world and a human, temporal, material world. It also directs thinking towards the essential nature of existence and the mysterious nature of our consciousness of the eternal or spiritual world of real forms or moral values. It was in this sense that we referred to the Social Conscience as being part of the mystery of human experience and of a humane condition that may be brought under the influence of moral values that are beyond the self-instinct.

Turning the mind (or soul) to the contemplation of moral values led Plato to deduce criteria for such different considerations as the ideal nature of government, principles for the selection of leaders, principles of education and the treatment of criminal behaviour.

Principles of Government: The Athenian Democracy
The city state of Athens and its surrounding lands in Attica was a direct democracy. The term democracy was coined by the Athenians to define their system of government (*demos*, people and *cracy*, power). It is thought to have lasted from the late 6th to the

---

1 Whitehead, A.N., *Process and Reality*, 1929.

late 4th century BC and was the first democracy that responded to the notion of true democracy, which was later to be declared by Abraham Lincoln in the Gettysburg Address on 19th November, 1863 as being 'government of the people, by the people, and for the people'.

According to Plato,

> our aim in founding the [ideal] State was not the disproportionate happiness of any one class, but the greatest happiness of the whole; we thought that in a State which is ordered with a view to the good of the whole we should be most likely to find justice, and in the ill-ordered State injustice. (*Republic*, Bk IV, 420)

Plato defines the nature of an ideal State and the virtues (moral values) with which it would be endowed. These virtues are found both in the citizen and in the State for 'in each of us there are the same principles and habits which there are in the State; and that from the individual they pass into the State' (*Republic*, Bk IV, 436).

These common virtues are stated by Plato to be wisdom, courage, temperance and justice. The State is perfect in Plato's ideal form, because it is composed of individuals who embody and are governed by these same virtues. Wisdom refers to good counsel and the knowledge of what is in the best interest of the parts and of the whole. The wise is he who has in him that little part which rules and which proclaims these commands and is supposed to have the knowledge of what is the interest of each of the parts and of the whole. Courage is the virtue of standing for the truth in conformity with law. The courageous is he whose spirit retains in pleasure and pain the commands of reason about what he ought or not to fear. Temperance is bringing under control certain pleasures and desires through the rule of reason and maintaining harmony. The temperate person is a person in whom the principle of reason and spirit or desire are balanced, and in whom it is agreed that reason should rule. Justice lies in attributing to each citizen that which is his own and belongs properly to him. It includes the use of his talents and the respect of his place in society. The just person is one who is his true self and does not permit the several elements within him to interfere with one another, or any of them to do the work of others. He sets in order his own inner life, and is his own master and his own law, and at peace with himself (*Republic*, Bk IV, 442-4 summarised).

These common virtues are clearly moral values and when understood as being identified with the innate Social Conscience, provide the means of addressing the moral choice determined as being what is right. They are ideal conditions and constitute those principles of government that would ensure the optimal state of happiness of all persons.[2]

Plato points out that 'in the human soul there is a better and a worse principle; and when the better has the worse under control, the man is said to be master of himself' (*Republic*, Bk IV, 431). This applies to the State as well as to the individual. It follows that the ideal form of government may be difficult to attain and that a less virtuous State will ensue. Accordingly,

> we maintain, then that a State which would be safe and happy, as far as the nature of man allows, must and ought to distribute honour and dishonour in the right way. And the right way is to place the goods of the soul first and highest in the scale, always assuming temperance to be the condition of them; and to assign the second place to the goods of the body; and the third place to money and property.
> (*Laws*, Bk III, 697)

Plato determined the three objectives of legislation to be freedom, harmony and good sense, 'maintaining that the lawgiver ought to have three things in view: first, that the city for which he legislates should be free; secondly, be at unity with herself; and thirdly, should have understanding' (*Laws*, Bk III, 701). It is noteworthy that politics as understood by Plato was a process in the interests of the entire people, where private interests had no place. The term 'idiot' in ancient Greek meant a private person who was not actively engaged in politics and who was referred to with contempt.

Forms of Government According to Plato
Plato used the four virtues stated above, namely, wisdom, courage, temperance and justice, to consider ideal forms of government by reference to the manner and extent to which these virtues are reflected.

The highest form of government, that is, the ideal State, is one that is governed by wisdom under the leadership of a Philosopher

---

2 This contrasts with the Utilitarian ambition of ensuring the greatest happiness of the greatest numbers. Adam Smith had a more Platonic view of the objects of political economy: 'First, to provide a plentiful revenue or subsistence for the people, or more properly to enable them to provide such revenue or subsistence for themselves; and secondly, to supply the state or commonwealth with a revenue sufficient for the public services. It proposes to enrich both the people and the sovereign'. See Smith, A., *An Enquiry Into the Nature and Causes of The Wealth of Nations*, Bk IV, Introduction, Of Systems of Political Economy.

King, its citizens being courageous, temperate and just. Plato called this highest form of government aristocracy (or monarchy) – (*aristo* meaning best, *cracy* meaning power). It is government under the power of the best of the virtues, the 'best' being wisdom itself and with wisdom governing, the other three virtues of courage, temperance and justice will be apparent and provide for the greatest happiness of all citizens.

In this text, it has been assumed that the Social Conscience is the sovereign authority and that it acts according to embedded moral values to discriminate 'what is right' from 'what is wrong'. In terms of Plato's analysis, the virtues of wisdom and justice may be taken as the moral values that are embedded in the Social Conscience, wisdom meaning having the ability to perceive what is best for all and justice meaning the knowledge of right and wrong.

It is appropriate to ask if there is a useful purpose in defining the ideal or perfect State and if such an ideal is attainable. Plato gives an interesting reply to this question:

> In heaven there is laid up a pattern of it, methinks, which he who desires may behold, and beholding, may set his own house in order. But whether such a one exists, or ever will exist in fact, is no matter; for he will live after the manner of that city, having nothing to do with any other ...   (*Republic*, Bk IX, 592)

Hence, a man of understanding will employ his energies in freeing and harmonising the nobler elements of his nature and the ideal pattern of this perfect State will be the law of his life.

Plato acknowledged that the ideal State, that is aristocracy, may not be achievable, for 'in the human soul there is a better and a worse principle' (*Republic*, Bk IV, 431). In other words, humans are imperfect. Plato discusses how human vices in the form of ignorance, idleness, selfishness and greed are causal factors that shape the forms of government that are found in practice. It is these vices which explain the degeneration from the ideal State. He describes four steps in the process of degeneration from aristocracy, which is government absolutely under the virtue of wisdom. When wisdom fails to rule absolutely over other virtues, its power diminishes accordingly. As ignorance appears, the State is no longer single-minded towards wisdom and is timorous with regard to following true values. This form of government is timocracy, where men honour their rulers but are reluctant to admit philosophers and to honour wisdom itself. One of its aspects is the coveting of wealth. When a State prizes wealth over all other virtues and greed replaces wisdom and honour, it gives way to oligarchy. This is government based on wealth and property, in which the rich have power and the poor are powerless. Democracy is the inevitable progression from oligarchy, when the poor revolt against their condition and overthrow the oligarchs. In modern terms, democracy is defined as government by the people, for the people and with the people. It results from a demand for freedom and for all the freedom that the wealthy appeared to have had before being overthrown. According to Plato, democracy fails from its own insatiable greed for freedom, as wealth causes the ruin of oligarchy,

> ... the same disease magnified and intensified by liberty overmasters democracy – the truth being that the excessive increase in anything often causes a reaction in the opposite direction; and this is the case not only in the season and in the animal life but above all in forms of government. The excess in liberty, whether in States and individually seems only to pass into excess slavery, so ... tyranny naturally arises out of democracy, and the most aggravated form of tyranny and slavery out of the most extreme form of liberty.
> (*Republic*, Bk VIII, 564)

This gives way to the final state of tyranny, which is solely the government of people by a tyrant.

Beginning with the definition of the ideal form of government, Plato explains the degenerative process in some detail that ends with tyranny, as a transformational progression declining from maximum happiness to ultimate misery, from aristocracy to tyranny.

According to Plato, timocracy will partly follow the government of aristocracy and partly that of oligarchy. It will also have some peculiarities of its own. It is fitted for war rather than peace, covetous of money and longing for gold and silver. Timocrats value wealth and are miserly. They will spend that which is another man's on the gratification of their desires and are lovers of power and honour.

> The accumulation of gold in the treasury of private individuals is the ruin of timocracy; they invent illegal modes of expenditure; for what do they or their wives care about the law? The more they think of making a fortune, the less they think of virtue; as riches and rich men are honoured in the State, virtue and the virtuous are dishonoured.
> (*Republic*, Bk VIII, 551)

Timocracy gives way to oligarchy: '... as men become lovers of trade and money ... they honour and look up to the rich man, and make a ruler of him, and dishonour the poor man' (*Republic*, Bk VIII, 551).

Under a government of oligarchy there is inevitably division, for the State is not one but two – the poor and the rich. They continue living within the same territory, but are always conspiring against one another. Oligarchy exhibits both the extremes of great wealth and utter poverty. When wealth holds sway, it is a breeding ground for money makers, spendthrifts, misers and criminals. Plato describes a situation that so resembles the social conditions that exist today '... men of business stooping as they walk, and pretending not to see those whom they have already ruined, insert their sting – that is, their money – into somebody else who is not on guard against them and recover the parent sum many times over' (*Republic*, Bk VIII, 556). Thereby parasites (drones) and paupers abound in the State. Governors (oligarchs) treat their subjects badly, whilst they lead a life of luxury, in idleness of body and mind, only caring for making money and indifferent to paupers and virtue. The State has an insatiable desire to become as rich as possible.

> The rulers, being aware that their power rests on their wealth, refuse to curtail by law the extravagance of the spendthrift youth, because they gain by their ruin; they take interest and buy up their estates to increase their own wealth and importance ... in oligarchic states, from the general spread of carelessness and extravagance, men of good family have often been reduced to beggary. They remain in the city – some owe money, some have forfeited citizenship, some both – they hate and conspire against those who have their property and against everybody else and are eager for revolution.
>
> (*Republic*, Bk VIII, 555)

'Democracy comes into being after the poor have conquered their opponents, slaughtering some and banishing some while the remainder they give an equal share of freedom and power; and this is the form of government in which the magistrates are elected by lot' (*Republic*, Bk VIII, 557).

Democracy is an inevitable progression from the abuse of the power of wealth, This transformation from a wise and just State to one governed by an insatiable thirst for wealth and then to a democracy is given causality by Plato in these words: 'The good which oligarchy proposed to itself and was the means by which it was maintained was excess wealth. The insatiable desire for wealth and the neglect of all other things for the sake of money-getting was also the ruin of oligarchy' (*Republic*, Bk VIII, 562).

Democracy has the spurious attraction of offering the people all that they could wish and ask in terms of social conditions. Plato tells us that it

> ... seems to be the fairest of states. They are free; the city is full of freedom and frankness – a man may say and do what he likes and where freedom is, the individual is clearly able to order for himself his own life as he pleases. In this State, there will be the greatest varieties of human natures. For the moment, it is extremely delightful. There is no need to govern, take office, go to war unless you like to; forgiving spirit, careless regarding trifles, disregard for fine principles. Never giving thought to the pursuits that make a Statesman, they promote to honour any one who professes to be the people's friend. It is a charming form of government, full of variety and disorder, and dispensing a sort of equality to equal and unequal alike.
> (*Republic*, Bk VIII, 557-8)

Excessive freedom is the downfall of democracy. In terms others might use to describe modern democratic states, Plato declares:

> When a democracy, which is thirsting for freedom, has evil cupbearers presiding over the feast, and has drunk too deeply of strong wine of freedom, then unless her rulers are very amenable and give plentiful draught, she calls them to account and punishes them, and says that they are cursed oligarchs. Loyal citizens are termed slaves. She would have subjects who are like rulers and rulers who are like subjects. In such a State liberty can have no limit ... father grows accustomed to descend to the level of sons and to fear them; master fears and flatters his scholars; scholars despise their masters and tutors; young and old are alike, the young man competes on a level with the old in word or deed; old condescend to the young and are full of pleasantry and gaiety; they are loath to be thought morose and authoritative and they adopt the manners of the young; the slave is as free as the purchaser and there is liberty and equality of the sexes in relation to each other. The citizens chafe impatiently at the least touch of authority and at length they cease to care even for the laws, written or unwritten; they will have no one over them.
> (Selected from *Republic*, Bk VIII, 563)

Plato considers democracy as divided into three classes:

(a) The leaders or drones. They are almost the entire ruling power and while the keener sort speak and act, the rest keep buzzing about the beam and do not suffer a word to be said on the other side; hence in democracies almost everything is managed by the drone.

(b) The wealthy who are an orderly class and always being severed from the mass; which in a nation of traders is sure to be the richest. They are the most squeezable persons and yield the largest amount of honey to the drones.

(c) Those who work with their own hands; 'they are not politicians and have not much to live upon. The largest and most powerful class in a democracy. Their leaders deprive the rich of their estates and distribute them among the people; at the same time taking care to reserve the larger part for themselves.' (*Republic*, Bk VIII, 565)

Plato attributes the fall of oligarchies and democracies to the same 'disorder', namely, the lack of virtue or wisdom in the rulers. Unwise rulers he likens to drones in a hive who feed on the honey without work. These drones display different degrees of criminality. He refers to

> ... the idle spendthrifts, of whom the more courageous are the leaders and the more timid the followers, the same whom we were comparing to drones, some stingless, and others having stings. These two classes are the plagues of every city in which they are generated, being what phlegm and bile are to the body. And the good physician and law giver of the State ought, like the wise beekeeper, to keep them at a distance and prevent, if possible, their ever coming in; and if they have anyhow found a way in, then he should have them and their cells cut out as speedily as possible.
> (*Republic*, Bk VIII, 564)

The fate of democracies is to fall ultimately under the rule of a tyrant.

> The persons whose property is taken from them are compelled to defend themselves before the people as best they can and, although they may have no desire for change, the others charge them with plotting against the people and being friends of oligarchy. When they see the people, not of their own accord, but through ignorance, and because they are deceived by informers seeking to do them wrong, then at last they are forced to become oligarchs in reality; they do not wish to be, but the sting of the drones torments them and breeds revolution in them. Then come impeachments and judgments and trials of one another. The people always have some champion whom they set over them and nurse into greatness. This and no other is the root from which a tyrant springs; when he first appears above ground he is a protector.
> (Summarised from *Republic*, Bk VIII, 556)

The tyrant himself is in need of the wealth which he has stolen from the wealthy in order to pay for the loyalty and protection of those keeping him in power.

The descriptions given by Plato echo remarkably the forms of governments that exist here and there in this century, over 2,000 years removed from Plato's days. He details even further the mechanisms by which tyranny inevitably arises from uncontrolled freedom. His description of a democratic State in decline mirrors closely some aspects of society of the 21st century. In particular, the manner in which dictators come to power, following the collapse of an existing government in the face of popular revolt and then seize to themselves the reins of power, installing cruel and repressive regimes that result in the complete disappearance of democracy. Acting out of fear of the people, the repression of the people becomes the major objective of government.

Faced with recommending the most appropriate form of government for society, given that the ideal form, namely aristocracy, may not be possible, Plato states that a combination of aristocracy and democracy will likely prove to be the best form. Drawing on the experience of other States, he discusses the type of government needed for a city to be well governed in the following terms:

> there are two mother forms of states from which the rest may truly said to be derived; and one of them may be called monarchy and the other democracy: the Persians have the highest form of one and we have the other; almost all the rest, as I was saying, are variations on these. Now, if you are to have liberty and the combination of friendship with wisdom, you must have both these forms of government in a measure; the argument emphatically declares that no city can be well governed which is not made up of both.
>
> (*Laws*, Bk III, 693)

In accordance with the postulates stated in this text, the moral values that are embedded in the Social Conscience enable it to discriminate right from wrong and act as the authority to regulate behaviour. Therefore, under ideal conditions, if society were totally governed according to moral values, it would be governed only by wisdom and be in the Platonic form of aristocracy. But freedom is also a strict and necessary condition for happiness, enabling individuals to express themselves freely and organise their lives as they would wish. We discuss in Chapter 9 the concepts of authority and freedom in a caring society. Authority represents wisdom in the Platonic sense with freedom representing liberty. There is a right balance between authority and freedom, as there is between aristocracy and democracy. It is establishing the appropriate limits to freedom that is becoming a major problem for democratic governments. Excessive freedom is destructive of a well-ordered society: disrespect for law is impeding chaos.

Plato on Selecting and Educating Leaders as Statesmen
The ideal State envisaged by Plato was ruled by a Philosopher King, guided by wisdom and composed of citizens having the virtues of courage, temperance and justice. These attributes are particularly important for political leadership and the training and selection of future statesmen. He argued that

> a State led by men of wisdom ... will be administered in a spirit unlike that of other States, in which men fight with one another about shadows only and are distracted in the struggle for power which in their eyes is a great good. Whereas the truth is that the State in which rulers are most reluctant to govern is always the best and most quietly governed, and the State in which they are most eager, the worst. (*Republic*, Bk VII, 520)

Criticising the political process through which citizens seek to become statesmen, he proposed that

> ... when the best minds have attained knowledge of the good ... they should partake in the life of the State because ... the intention of the legislator, who did not aim at making any one class in the State happy above the rest; the happiness was to be in the whole State ... held the citizens together by persuasion and necessity, making them benefactors of the State, and therefore benefactors of one another, not to please themselves, but to be his instruments in binding the State together ...

Accordingly,

> ... only in the State which offers this, will they rule who are truly rich, not in silver and gold, but in virtue and wisdom, which are true blessings of life. Whereas if they go to the administration of public affairs, poor and hungering after their own private advantage, thinking that hence they are to snatch the chief good, order there can never be; for they will be fighting about office, and the civil and domestic broils which thus arise will be the ruin of the rulers themselves and of the whole State. (*Republic*, Bk VII, 520)

Clearly, Plato was concerned about the quality of political life and the way in which the world of politics is corrupted by the personal ambitions of individuals entering politics. Corrupted leaders and the corruption of political life are persistent phenomena and continue to plague the life of nations. Whereas, in the Platonic sense, the pursuit of the happiness of all and the good of the State, should be the career objectives of politicians, in practice those who find their way into politics generally are those who manifestly do not have the intelligence, the education, the knowledge nor the moral values, which are required for the highest of all social responsibilities, namely, the government of the nation. Political leaders who emerge from their ranks are considered generally as deceitful, untrustworthy, corruptible if not corrupted, open to influence, motivated by selfish interests and seeking power as their ultimate aim. They have panache and give the appearance of exceptional talent. Having glib tongues, engaging manners and the gift of persuasion, twisting lies through spinning into appearances of truth, they survive criticism and rarely achieve those goals that are their avowed pretensions. Public opinion polls consistently place politicians at the lowest end of public esteem of professional people. Yet, having no other choice, the public consistently elect such people, in whom manifestly they should have no confidence, as their representatives, and by implication of the Social Conscience, to the highest levels of public and social responsibility.

Plato's contribution to political theory and to politics has set standards down the centuries and, though rarely achieved, remain as a guide in our times. They reflect the moral values that are found in the Social Conscience. In that sense, as Whitehead declared, there is nothing more to add, than footnotes, to Plato's thoughts on good government.

The Enlightenment and the Popularisation of Freedom
The changes that are associated with the Renaissance in Italy, considered to have begun in the 14th century in the city state of Florence, percolated into Northern Europe by the 16th century, affecting all aspects of social and economic activity and heralded the New World that came into being with the Reformation and the Industrial Revolution in England. Men of immense intellectual stature and talented over a broad area of knowledge, such as Ficino, Leonardo da Vinci, Michelangelo, Galileo, Erasmus, Copernicus and Machiavelli, for the greater part Italian, led Italy into a period of creative glory and have their names written large in the History of Ideas. Their heritage is seen in many artistic and scientific forms, from music, painting and architecture to engineering designs and conceptions that foreshadowed with surprising accuracy the

resolution of the mystery of flight, enabling man at last to imitate birds, and acquire the ability to leave his natural habitat and travel in other dimensions. Fascinated by invention and new forms, mathematicians considered the art of war weaponry, invented new means of destruction as well as new means of creation. They ventured into management and information sciences, at a time when religious orthodoxy praised wealth, but viewed money with suspicion and opposed free trade, insisting on moral notions, such as the 'just price' and the prohibition of usurious interest charged by money-lenders. Business partnerships extended Italian commercial activities throughout Western Europe through local and international business partnerships and banks, which heralded the multinational corporations of recent times. The notion of financial control through financial accounting reports revealed the business acumen of an Italian society that was capable of attaining high levels of expertise in all areas of economic activity.

During this period, the Italian states were controlled by oligarchies of wealthy families, such as the Medici, the Borgias and the Orsini. The papacy, that represented the supreme temporal and spiritual authority and had assumed the mantle of the Roman Empire, passed under the political control of such families as the Medici and the Borgias. The Medici family enthroned three of its members as popes, Pope Leo X (1513-21), Pope Clement VII (1523-34) and Pope Leo XI (1605-5), and the Borgia family enthroned two of its members as popes, Pope Callixtus (1455-8) and Pope Alexander VI (1492-1503). Successive popes were actively engaged in politics and, as heads of state themselves, their authority was enshrined in three principles, namely, the infallibility of papal doctrine, the Divine Right of Kings and the absolutism of their authority as rulers. The last principle disappeared with the political changes that followed upon the Protestant Reformation and the advent of representative governments, which were to sound the death knell for most European monarchies.

The endless wars, corruption of office, political intrigue and political crimes underlined the viciousness of the struggle for political control. The moral values that Plato argued were fundamental to good government had long ceased to attract interest in an Italy that had succeeded Rome in the practice of politics and the corruptive use of political control. Lucrezia Borgia (1480-1519) and Catherine de Medici (1519-89) remain bywords in the history of political intrigue and political crime. The moral values of the time are illustrated in Machiavelli's *The Prince*, in which he stated that it is primarily the character or vitality and skill of the individual leader that determines the success of any state. Concern with practical success above all other considerations and by any means, even at the expense of traditional moral values, Machiavelli established a reputation for ruthlessness, deception and cruelty. In this sense, his legacy remains present in the modern times and in the actions of repressive and cruel dictators and such infamous leaders as Hitler, Stalin and, in recent times, Mugabe. Moral turpitude in politics remains widespread, even today in countries committed to democracy and freedom. It debases the action of many political leaders, who driven by personal ambition will resort without scruple to any means to achieve their personal objectives.

The corruption of political office and of the political power that was enshrined in the papacy during the Renaissance was a causal factor that shifted political influence away from Rome from the 16th century. It originated from within the ranks of the Roman Catholic Church and was aimed at its reform in Western Europe. It was launched by Martin Luther, an Augustinian monk and Professor at the University of Wittenberg, in 1517 with the publication of the 95 Theses concerning the sale of indulgences. It marked the separation of the Protestant Church from the Church of Rome. Initially opposed in England in 1521 by King Henry VIII, who at the time adhered to papal authority, the Protestant Reformation gained support following a conflict between a king, desirous of being freed from a marriage that had become inconvenient, with the spiritual and temporal authority of a pope, unwilling to grant him a divorce. With unprincipled effrontery, Henry VIII usurped the papal authority, using the Act of Supremacy in 1534 to make himself head of the Church in England, and between 1535 and 1540 he dissolved the monasteries and seized their property. The political influence of the Roman Catholic Church was ended by 1536. The 'Church in England', as established by Henry VIII, eventually became the established Church of England with the sovereign as its titular head. Queen Elizabeth II, the current reigning monarch, still has the title of Defender of the Faith (*fidei defensor*).

The English Reformation epitomised the first serious conflict of consequence with the concept of authority since King John was compelled to sign Magna Carta in 1215 in the field of Runnymede. It manifested itself in a nation that, in many ways, differed from their European cousins. Nonconformism and a love of independence were strong sentiments in a country that was already anticlerical. Yet, a strong attachment to traditions and traditional values tended to produce workable compromises between older traditions and newer forces that were the drivers of the Protestant ethic. These compromises led to reforms that have moved the *status quo* gently and almost imperceptibly across time, with a resulting political stability that foreign observers have often misunderstood as resulting from the phlegmatic character of the English, rather than an embedded conservatism that favours prolonged learning experiences rather than revolutionary changes. The monarchy and the Church of England have survived as institutions by reason of their will and capacity to accept changes, whilst maintaining traditional values that have retained their popularity.

The Protestant Reformation did not alter the nature of the State nor the manner in which the authority of government was exercised. The Divine Right of Kings and monarchical absolutism remained the political credo in England until King Charles I was beheaded in 1649. Much of Europe stayed Catholic and in allegiance to Rome.

The significant political changes that occurred subsequently in England with respect to the notions of authority and freedom and political consensus in the exercise of political control are associated with the period known as the 'Enlightenment', which occurred in Western Europe. It was a movement that emphasised reason and science in philosophy and in the study of human culture and the natural world. It was marked by the rejection of traditional social, religious and political ideas and an emphasis on rationalism.

The 'English Enlightenment', as this period was experienced in England, was to mark an enduring separation between England and Continental Europe that was to dictate the nature of their relationship from the Reformation to present times. Two English philosophers of great influence stood at this historical crossroad at the same time. Hobbes (1588-1679), who was a Royalist supporter during the English Civil War[3] and Locke (1632-1704), who supported the Whigs after the Restoration, were in different camps but shared the same ideals. They are reputed never to have met.

In his major work *Leviathan*, Hobbes argued that the wish of the people to live in peace and security meant that they had to organise themselves into communities for protection. Since there will always

---

3 The term English Civil War (or Wars) refers to a series of conflicts between Royalists and Parliamentarians that took place between 1642 and 1651. It led to the trial and execution of Charles I, the exile of his son Charles II, the end of the monopoly of the Church of England on Christian worship in England and established the precedent that British monarchs could not govern without the consent of Parliament.

be people who cannot be trusted, people must set up a government with their authority to make and enforce laws necessary to protect the community. The ability to provide protection is the basis of the allegiance of the people to the State. This led Hobbes to the view that reason was the basis of moral behaviour. This view brought him into opposition with Christians who believed that God was the giver of the moral code. By taking a non-sectarian approach to the understanding of morality, or what we have described as the moral conscience, Hobbes may be considered as ahead of his time in opening the debate about moral values, thereby enabling reason to seek and provide explanation. In this sense, it may be said that Hobbes heralded the English Enlightenment. Hobbes' reference to reason as the justification of moral behaviour or, as suggested above, the moral conscience, also adds reality in the form of reason to the instinct of caring and the necessity of sharing, that are the basic postulates for a caring society. Hence, the instinct of caring and the necessity of sharing are justified by reason as moral values.

Locke's two major works *An Essay on Human Understanding* and *The Two Treatises of Government* were both published in 1690. In the first of these works, Locke argued that all knowledge comes through the senses and denied the possibility that God could have placed knowledge into individuals from birth. He was a rationalist with respect to knowledge and experience. In *The Two Treatises*, Locke refuted the theory of the Divine Right of Kings, the related doctrines of the absolutism of the king's authority and the doctrine of patriarchism that defined the nature of the relationship of the king to his people. In the *Second Treatise on Government*, Locke draws explicitly on the works of Hobbes, arguing, as had Hobbes, that the reason for a political state lay in the need of people to join together in a community sense to protect their natural rights. Such a political state is in the form of a social contract, a concept largely discussed by Rousseau, in which the government, acting as an adjudicator and protector of social rights, does so with the consent of the people. The consequence of transfer to the government of a portion of their rights results in a constructive trust which, if infringed by the government, justifies the people in rebelling and choosing another government. Essentially, both Hobbes and Locke defined in this manner the concept of democracy in the notion of representative government. The basis for such a state was being forged as a consequence of the Civil War, that occurred during Hobbes' lifetime and when Locke himself was a child, his father having been a captain of cavalry in the Parliamentary army.

One of the first warning shots of the resistance of Parliament as a body to the absolute authority claimed by the king, was the response given by William Lenthall, Speaker of the House of Commons, on 4th January, 1642 to the demand of Charles I, as he strode into Parliament to claim the surrender of the five members that he sought to seize for treason, was both pithy and extraordinarily courageous, *'May it please your Majesty, I have neither eyes to see nor tongue to speak in this place but as the House [of Commons] is pleased to direct me, whose servant I am here.'* This open and public rejection of the authority of the king within Parliament itself, and the proclamation by Speaker Lenthall of its proper authority, were later to be integrated in the Bill of Rights 1689.

The substantial political changes on the road to parliamentary democracy were effectively being fashioned in England, as a consequence of the Civil War and the evolution of parliamentary authority. Such legislation as the Habeas Corpus Act 1679 and the Bill of Rights 1689[4] marked the progression of freedom under authority and a return towards the Platonic ideal of an appropriate balance between them expressed as 'freedom under law'.[5] The notion of good law considered as that combination of ideal forms leading to the best form of State, is described by Plato as conjoining aristocracy (the authority of wisdom) with democracy (the will of the people). Following the Declaration of Independence in 1776 and the American War of Independence, the USA, which declared itself a Republic, passed the American Bill of Rights in 1791 that adopted both the Habeas Corpus Act 1679 and the Bill of Rights 1689 in their Constitution, thus maintaining a close contact with the evolution of government principles with the former colonial power. This unity of sentiment between England and the USA with respect to democracy and freedom has special and global significance in dealing with the political problems that beset the extension of the global economy.

The English Enlightenment may be seen as a stem development in which moral values are again given their proper importance and the human condition becomes a major political concern. The passing of two thousand and more years sees the rekindling of thoughts that had found their expression in Plato's search for ideal

---

4 These milestones in the march to democracy and freedom are replicated and more fully discussed in Chapter 10, 'Persisting Tyranny and the Persistent Struggle for Freedom'.
5 This appropriate balance may be considered as constituting the central problem of this age and for this reason it is extensively discussed in Chapter 9, 'Authority and Freedom in a Caring Society'.

forms or conditions. Plato directs attention to moral values in government: the Enlightenment restates moral values of freedom and human happiness as political ideals. The philosophical concern during this period with the individual and with individual rights, the notion of equality between individuals, the law of nature and the social contract were to germinate later in the writings of Adam Smith[6], embodying moral values, in Jeremy Bentham and Utilitarianism[7] as a political doctrine, setting the happiness of the greatest number as the policy objective, and, finally, in the concept of representative government developed by John Stuart Mill.[8] It should be noted, however, that representative government did not imply democracy, or indeed universal suffrage, defined as the right of all people to vote. Electors to Parliament were representatives of shires and counties and, in that sense, were members of what we would call today an establishment of landed gentry, who had the property qualifications to vote. Liberal thinkers saw democracy and universal suffrage as a threat to freedom by imposing the tyranny of a majority. The Reform Acts of 1832, 1867 and 1884 extended the right to vote, but it was not until the Representation of the People Act 1918 that men over the age of 21 and women over the age of 30 had the right to vote. The Equal Franchise Act 1928 removed the voting age discrimination against women and established voting parity between the sexes. The Family Law Reform Act 1969 reduced the age of majority from 21 years to 18 years and in so doing lowered the voting age to 18 years.

Freedom, Free Trade and Representative Government
Hobbes, Locke, Smith, Bentham and Mill had all been influenced by Plato and Aristotle and their writings show the importance attached to moral values. The Age of Reason, which is another name given to the Enlightenment, consecrated reason as the supreme good, much as did Plato in raising wisdom to the rank of the supreme virtue. Government was seen as the problem of authority and responsibility and the duty of care in the context that was implied in the relationship between the ruler and the people. The Habeas Corpus Act 1679 and the Bill of Rights 1689

---

6 See Smith, A., *The Theory of Moral Sentiments*, 1759, which provided Smith with the philosophical arguments which he incorporated in his theory of perfect markets in *An Enquiry into the Nature and Causes of the Wealth of Nations*, 1776.
7 See Bentham, J., *Introduction to the Principles of Morals and Legislation*, 1789
8 See Mill, J.S., *On Liberty*, 1859, *Considerations on Representative Government*, 1860 and *Utilitarianism*, 1861.

changed the power relationship between the sovereign, as a hereditary ruler, and Parliament, representing the people in accordance with the social structure of the times, namely, landed wealth. In that sense, the 17th-century struggle between King and Parliament was a continuation of the dispute over power that King John had managed to negotiate with his nobles at Runnymede in 1215 through Magna Carta, but which was lost to the Crown by the political naivety of a less compromising King Charles I, who lost his head in the process. His successor had to accept the constitutional constraints imposed by the Habeas Corpus Act and the Bill of Rights and, in accordance with a deep attachment to tradition that marks English society, subsequent constitutional reforms were negotiated with a monarchy that was able to retain its honorific titles, including the titular head of the Church of England and the principle of hereditary succession. As a constitutional monarch, the sovereign is the head of state and from a legislative standpoint is part of Parliament, being sovereign-in-parliament. The sovereign has prerogative powers to act without the consent of Parliament and in the exercise of those powers has the right to interfere in political affairs, as was the case in 1975 when the Governor-General of Australia, acting as the Queen's representative, dismissed the Australian Prime Minister and dissolved Parliament.

The English Enlightenment and its impact on constitutional reforms, transformed economic and social policy in the 18th century with the notions of free market economics, the doctrine of free trade in economic policy, Utilitarianism as a social policy objective and representative government as a political doctrine, and heralded the social changes that were to transform Western European society in the 20th century.

If freedom was a fundamental issue for philosophers at the time, it was a special notion of freedom that was being promoted. It was not political freedom in the sense in which Plato envisaged democracy as a form of government. Political theory in the 18th century was concerned with the concept of representative government and the limitations of the powers of the monarchy. Basically, those who were made to pay for the expenses of government insisted on their consent being obtained in such matters as taxation and on certain aspects of government policy. There was no call for universal suffrage, or indeed for democracy. When Mill wrote about liberty, he meant freedom as a concept. The prospect that universal suffrage might create a democracy was anathema to him and to the ruling class at the time.

In particular, freedom, transformed into free trade and free markets, was the major preoccupation of an England that was shortly to embark on a massive trade expansion. The Empire was built on the notion that England was to be the industrial heart of a commercial empire of overseas markets that would buy English manufactured goods in exchange for English purchases of raw materials. The attachment to free trade within the Empire continued well into the 20th century, when the Empire was transformed into the Commonwealth, the term being composed significantly of the two concepts that it inspired, namely wealth commonly shared. It meant that commercial privileges were to be limited to countries who were members of the Commonwealth, hence maintaining the principle of imperial preference and protective tariffs against non-Commonwealth countries.

In the same way that free trade was really concerned with creating trading conditions that were favourable to those involved in market activities and in so doing with protecting their interests, so too, representative government was a means of protecting the interests of the ruling oligarchy of wealth with respect to government policy carried out in the name of the sovereign. democracy was the very last thing that this oligarchy wished to see happen.

During the 19th century, the sinews of imperial power were further strengthened by the success of free trade and the global commercial expansion that saw Britain the last of the great empires. Free trade also resulted in establishing a market economy that was independent of government authority. During this period of commercial expansion, the market economy was virtually deregulated. The sovereign delegated authority to commercial interests by granting royal charters, which created commercial monopolies over huge areas of the Empire, for example the East India Company, the Hudson Bay Company and the British South Africa Company.

In effect, a market economy that served the interests of capital was not an area of government responsibility. Moreover, Members of Parliament were themselves intimately involved with the market economy, hence their own interest in securing its prosperity and expansion.

The working population, which was totally unrepresented in Parliament, had no influence in policy making with respect to their own social and economic conditions. Government policies that were to the advantage of the oligarchy of wealth represented in Parliament, generally operated to the disadvantage of the mass of the population, who were the poor and the workers. Both the poor and the workers shared the same problems.

The oligarchy of wealth represented in Parliament refused to countenance the right of the working classes to create representative organisations. In an earlier period, the unity of owners, managers and workers had been substantiated in the medieval guilds, or *métiers* in France. This form of industrial organisation was structured in a hierarchy headed by a master, under whose authority journeymen worked and apprentices acquired their training on the job. This structure created a form of social unity, vestiges of which remain today in the London guild societies, for example, the Merchant Tailors Guild. They are honorific societies with social and charitable objectives.

The factory organisation that provided the structure for industrial activities was regulated by the Factory Acts along capitalistic lines. It brought factory owners and managers into conflict with the workers with respect to wages and working conditions. It transformed the mutuality of interest that was fostered by the earlier guild system into one in which labour was exploited by capital in a system that sought to maximise the wealth of owners (or capitalists). Factories were locations in which conflict was centred. Often, conflict between owners and workers degenerated into riots and violent repression.

Attempts by the masses of workers to act to improve their conditions and organise themselves into representative unions outside Parliament were treated in law as seditious activities, and thus as threats to the security of the State. The two General Combination Acts of 1799 and 1800 outlawed combinations and strikes in England and Wales. These were repealed in 1824, but new restrictive measures were introduced in 1825 that made it an offence to intimidate and molest other workers. The sentencing of five agricultural workers, known as the Tolpuddle Martyrs, to transportation for the mere taking of an illegal oath created an outcry. It reflected the widespread intimidation both by State and employers of workers' organisations that lasted until 1875, when legislation permitted peaceful picketing in the furtherance of a trade dispute. Even as late as 1901, the Taff Vale judgment ruled that trade unions could be held liable for wrongful acts committed by their officials.

The social reforms of the 19th century were addressed to the relief of poverty in its many forms. The Industrial Revolution had reduced the mass of the population to extreme poverty and distress. Much of this resulted from the enclosure movement, for deprived of their land and impoverished, they moved to towns seeking work and their vulnerability was exploited. The Corn Laws, first introduced by statute in 1815 following the end of the Napoleonic Wars, were intended to maintain high prices for corn, by forbidding the import of corn until the price of domestic corn had reached 80 shillings a quarter. It protected the landed rich, who controlled Parliament, at the expense of the poor and deprived masses, imposing starvation on many of the poor. The Reform Act 1832 gave the vote to merchants and changed the balance of power in Parliament towards traders, who saw their advantage in the repeal of the Corn Laws in 1846.

The treatment of poverty in England is a history of shame. The Poor Law Amendment Act 1834 prescribed the treatment of poverty as follows:

(a) no able-bodied person is to receive money or other help from the Poor Law authorities, except in a workhouse;
(b) conditions in workhouses are to be made very harsh to discourage people from wanting to receive help;
(c) workhouses are to be built in every parish, or, if parishes are too small, in unions of parishes;
(d) ratepayers in each parish, or union of parishes, are to elect a Board of Guardians to supervise the workhouse, to collect the Poor Rate and to send reports to the Poor Law Commission.

Charles Dickens amply demonstrated the social evils of the poor laws in England, which were maintained until they were replaced by the Welfare State after World War II.[9] Other social reformers, such as Cardinal Newman, were much concerned about the education of the working class. The Education Act 1870 was another milestone of social legislation, which extended the provision of basic education throughout the country. However, although Wilberforce was able to secure legislation abolishing the slave trade in British ships through the Abolition of Slave Trading Act 1807, working conditions in England remained appalling – long hours, low wages, child labour, the employment of both men and women in unhealthy and dangerous conditions. The expanding awareness of poverty

9 In an article on Votes for Women in 1909, Elizabeth Robins noted that the State kept 22,483 children in workhouses. Poverty relief remained a matter of the Poor Law. Following the abolition of the Means Tests in 1941, Ernest Bevin, Minister of Labour, declared in the House of Commons that 'the Poor Law is buried'.

and its exposure by social reformers compelled government eventually to accept a political responsibility for social welfare.

Government and Social Welfare
No improvement in the conditions of the masses of the working population could be expected from a Parliament that did not represent their interests. England's industrial and commercial empire was based on the enormous wealth created during the 19th century. Rule Britannia was reflected in its economic, military and political supremacy over other nations: Pax Britannia was the manner in which order and control were maintained in accordance with English law. The working classes were harnessed to this gigantic effort. Extant Master and Servant legislation made it a criminal offence for a worker to break his contract. Social welfare was not a concern of the market economy and that remains true to this day. Compassion for the poor and unfortunate and caring about them were sentiments manifested by some of the more sensitive individuals in the ruling parliamentary cabal, wealthy philanthropists and religious organisations.

Social reformers were in a minority and ineffective in forcing through the social and political reforms that were needed. The substantial political changes that the second half of the 19th century heralded were imported into England from the Continent and in particular Germany. The clarion call came from Marx (1818-83) and Engels (1820-95) in the form of the *Communist Manifesto* in 1848 in Berlin and called for 'the workers of the world to unite'. Both Marx and Engels were Jewish and of German origins. They shared the same philosophical interests. Persecuted for his political activities in Germany, Marx fled to England in 1849. Much in line with Jewish tradition, Engels used the wealth derived from textile manufacturing in Manchester to financially support an idealist philosopher Marx in Dulwich, giving the latter the opportunity to write *Das Kapital,* the first volume of which appeared in 1867.

As immigrant Jews, the success of Marx and Engels in promoting the interests of the working classes was due in no small measure to the fact that they were not beholden, nor were expected to hold allegiance to the ruling oligarchy. Their ideas spread like wildfire in Europe, but neither appeared to have made an impact in England, despite their publications and their renown. Marx spent his time reading in the British Museum and complaining to Engels of the unbearable poverty that his family endured. Yet, in philosophical terms, Marx was sentimentally close to both Bentham and Mill with respect to the basic notions that were enshrined in Utilitarianism, namely an ideal state based on the happiness of the largest number of its people.

Much as Utilitarianism was vaunted by Bentham and Mill as a political philosophy, 19th-century society appeared blind to its implications for the masses, for otherwise there would have been an active campaign to extend its principles to the working classes. It was Marx who took the Utilitarian argument further, arguing in effect that the largest number of the people was the proletariat and called for a state which would be governed by the proletariat and in the interest of the proletariat. This was the essence of the revolution: the struggle for control between a commercial and industrial bourgeoisie of wealth and the masses of the workers that it exploited.

For the first time, Marx and Engels added to the notion of caring, the political objective of sharing. But the notion of sharing was and remains anathema to oligarchies based on wealth. Despite the social and economic changes that have occurred to this day, oligarchies of wealth, that have effective control over the economies of both developed and underdeveloped nations, have successfully resisted the concept of sharing in any significant and effective sense. The struggle by the working classes for a better share of the wealth that they regarded as created by their labour was argued in term of a Labour Theory of Value, propounded by socialist thinkers, in opposition to classical economic theory and the neo-classical school.

The Impact of Universal Suffrage and Representative Democracy
Socialism, as a political credo with a strong Christian influence, developed in England with the growth of the trade union movement. It did not have a formal presence as a political party. While Marxism played an important part in the social unrest that rumbled continuously across Europe during the latter part of the 19th century, neither contemporary thinkers nor leaders of the nascent trade unions in England took an interest in its message. The point of no return between the controlling oligarchy of wealth and the workers, who finally were uniting as a political force, was contrived by the revolutionary activities of men such as Lenin. This movement, which claimed to be Marxist, called for the creation of a revolutionary working class that would overthrow capitalism and

bring about a new society under the control of the working classes, which Marx had referred to as the proletariat.

The Great War that ended in 1918 saw a devastated and exhausted Europe reeling politically under the impact of the release into civilian life of millions of soldiers, revolted by the war and by those who had led them into a conflict that had had as its flashpoint the assassination of Archduke Francis Ferdinand of Austria and his wife, the Duchess of Hohenberg, in Sarajevo, Bosnia in 1914.

Meantime, revolutionary fervour had gained an unstoppable momentum in Russia that ended in the October 1917 Communist Revolution, putting the Bolsheviks in power for the next seventy years. The murder of the Tsar of Russia and his family and the abdication and the flight of Kaiser Wilhelm to Holland, severely depleted the ranks of the family of King George V and those royal cousins who had been the crowned heads of the European states. It has been said that George V feared also for his own throne, as the returning soldiers claimed the right to live in a land fit for heroes. It was against this background that the Representation of the People Act 1918 enfranchised an army of the discontented. Despite the economic crisis of 1919 and massive post-war unemployment, there was surprisingly no communist revolution in Britain and Ramsay MacDonald became the first Labour Prime Minister as early as 1924.

The enlargement of the representation within the House of Commons that followed upon the introduction of universal suffrage clearly altered the balance of power, with the election of a large number of new members, who were of working class origin. The relative smoothness of the transition to a new representative order was due in some degree to the political astuteness of Ramsay MacDonald, who was seen as both a man of compromise and a man compromised by the oligarchy of wealth by which he was surrounded in London. As a socialist politician, he was to herald that new breed of parliamentarian, the artful dodger with a silken tongue, the smooth operator, the man who was all things to all men and true only to his personal interests and advancement. Such is the memory that he has left. But he has had many emulators to this very day as the father of modern politics who redefined the nature, scope and method of political theory.

Conclusion

As Crick has so well explained,[10] politics is a matter of political tactics that appertain to game theory, rather than a concern with a conception of society that has to do with the happiness of its members. From the position declared by Plato (that placed wisdom as the supreme virtue in government), to reason (seen by Locke as the supreme moral value), to expediency (that was seen as a necessary tactic maintaining the oligarchy of wealth by making concessions to enfranchised workers), spin finally enthroned deceit as the essential art of politics. It is now exceptional to identify a politician or a political leader who is not primarily a careerist, obsessed with his own advancement by whatever means, rather than the interests of those who have pledged their faith and trust in him as their representative. Spin has marked the final descent into ignominy and abolished moral values as an inconvenience to government, relying on Machiavelli's resuscitated doctrine that 'the end justifies the means'.

---

10 Crick, B., *In Defence of Politics*, University of Chicago Press, 2nd edn, 1972.

—8—

Citizenship and the Democratic Deficit; Governance and Accountability

The general acceptance of democracy as the best form of government is based upon the concept of freedom, which was at the heart of the political and social changes inspired by the Enlightenment. The continuing effect of the Enlightenment in this regard is seen in the immense attachment to freedom that characterises our times. Freedom has lent strength to the Social Conscience that holds the belief that democracy is a state of government based on moral values. Social cohesion relies on the understanding that moral values should guide the actions of government and that political leadership should be judged on that basis.

Democracy lends particular meaning to citizenship as its key concept. The democratic deficit may be interpreted in the different ways that will be discussed in this chapter. Recent times have witnessed a substantial erosion of public confidence in government and a considerable credibility gap that has dangerously damaged the trust that is crucial to good government. This is one aspect of the democratic deficit. Politicians as a group in society are widely seen as untrustworthy, unreliable and susceptible to corruption and to all forms of dishonesty. Public opinion polls rank politicians at the lowest end of professional classes with respect to the criterion of confidence. The notion of governance associates citizenship with the action of government. Although this notion is susceptible to different meanings, it may be taken to address the problem of the 'quality of government'.

Finally, there is the democratic deficit that is attributable to limited and imperfect accountability. Those in whom a mandate to govern for an allotted period of time has been vested by universal suffrage are in effect trustees. The election process creates an implied trust, under which government is made responsible for its actions. Accountability is formalised in the supremacy of Parliament. The Social Conscience, as the sovereign authority, is ultimately the sole arbiter of the actions of those to whom the responsibility for government has been entrusted. It is in this larger dimension of responsibility and accountability that the Social Conscience is made manifest.

HISTORICALLY, the subject matter of politics has been rule and government. Plato's writings on the subject are undoubtedly his most important legacy with respect to the understanding of the role of the State in society. He saw the combination of the wisdom of aristocracy with the consent of democracy as the best formula for attaining social happiness. Neither condition now appears to be a significant political influence in an age torn apart by conflicting interests that have eroded social cohesion.

In effect, it may be argued that social cohesion should be one of the main political objectives of democratic government. History has provided many examples where devastating revolution has destroyed regimes that have failed to recognise social cohesion as a basic pillar of social stability and failed to understand the role of government in ensuring social cohesion.

Defining democracy as 'government by the people, for the people and with the people' enshrines social cohesion as its essential objective.[1] According to this definition, democracy makes impossible the exclusion of the people from each of these three essential aspects of the government process. Democratic deficit may be defined as being present whenever there is insufficient or ineffective participation of the people in government. As practised in the city state of Athens, Athenian democracy provided its perfect example. The strict and necessary condition for democratic participation was citizenship, that is, the status of being a citizen. Citizenship defines identity as nationality and imposes on that status citizenship rights and duties. They include freedom under law, the right to vote and participate in this way in the democratic process. Various duties are attached to citizenship, such as military service and certain civil obligations as required. To this day, a non-citizen cannot vote, may not be able to claim residence as of right, may not be called up for military service or for jury service and may be excluded from some areas of government employment.

Hence, the concepts of democracy and citizenship are totally interdependent. A democratic deficit will occur whenever citizens are excluded from full participation in democratic government. Given that most modern states have their historical origins in non-democratic regimes and that there is an important carry-over of non-democratic conditions into their constitutions, it is not surprising that a substantial democratic deficit is normal in what are claimed to be democratic states. In theory, the role of citizenship in democratic government would imply that the notion 'government by the people' be expressed by reserving legislative power to

---

1 Democracy is defined variously in terms of a rule of three. Lincoln stated these three rules as 'government of the people, by the people and for the people'. Dictionary definitions of democracy generally state that it is 'government by the people' as the first rule. The author includes 'government with the people' as the third rule to stress the consensual nature of this form of government, particularly with respect to direct democracy as used currently in Switzerland.

democratic approval by popular vote; the notion 'government for the people' is expressed by the concept of caring, as defined in this text; and the notion 'with the people' is understood as being with the consent of the people, and consequently implying full accountability to the people. The only modern European state that comes anywhere near meeting these conditions is Switzerland, whose Federal Constitution is founded on the concept of direct democracy.

Swiss democracy is participative democracy, that is full democracy in the Platonic sense, and must be distinguished from representative democracy in which the legislative power lies in the hands of the National Parliamentary Assembly. As provided under the Swiss Federal Constitution, proposed legislation must be submitted to popular approval by referendum. Legislation may emanate from the federal government, composed of seven Sages representing the total spectrum of political opinion in the Federal Assembly. The federal government does not have the monopoly of legislative power: legislation may be submitted by any group of individuals that has collected at least 100,000 signatures in support of any particular legislative proposal. The failure of the government to obtain approval for legislation that it has submitted to popular referendum does not constitute a vote of no confidence, requiring the resignation of the federal government or any minister. It simply means that there is insufficient public support for the proposed law. For example, the federal government has twice failed to obtain the consent of the citizens to adherence to the European Union. Switzerland is probably the only country in the world in which citizens voting by referendum have approved increases in taxation!

A concordat between the parties governs the proportional representation of political opinion in the federal government. There is no formal opposition to the federal government itself, although its administrative decisions may and often are criticised. The President of the Federation is nominated on the basis of annual rotation and each of the seven Sages becomes President of the Federation during his or her period of office. Each Sage heads a ministry and has total delegated authority for decision-making. The President of the Federation is not a prime minister and has no effective powers in that sense. His functions are more akin to that of a monarch, as representative of the Swiss nation. Once a Sage has served as President of the Federation and his period of office in the federal government has ended, that person effectively retires from politics and will have no further function of a political nature.

The comparison between representative democracy and direct democracy highlights the nature of the democratic deficit, its constituent elements and the manner in which it could be reduced by extending the role of citizenship. As discussed in Chapter 4, citizenship has been recognised as important in consolidating the foundations of democracy and social cohesion under democracy. To this end, educational reform has led to 'citizenship education' through changes in the school curriculum to include citizenship education. It has been argued that significant problems of society could be remedied by a greater awareness of citizenship among the population and particularly among the younger generations. In this chapter, it will be argued that it is not sufficient to instruct the young in the 'principles of citizenship'. It will be argued that citizenship is the effective integration between government under democracy and the people, the quality of which is an indicator of social cohesion. A concept of citizenship limited to an extension of the school syllabus may be considered as perfectly sterile, unless it leads to a reduction of the democratic deficit through the concept of 'effective citizenship'. Indeed, in the context in which advocates of citizenship education have formulated their proposals, it may be said that citizenship education is as likely to be functionally relevant as sex education is to *castrati*.

The concept of a direct democracy is not just a Platonic ideal: it has remained an ambition,[2] and the Swiss model has established it in current practice. Developments in computer technology and communication, in particular such as the internet, have removed the obstacles to the implementation of direct democracy presented by population size and geography. The relevant machinery and communication technology is already available and is widely used by large commercial firms and organisations. Access to and by designated or registered users is immediate and confidentially is secured through the use of passwords. The frequent use of public opinion polls to test popular reaction to various aspects of political and governmental action confirms that the testing of opinion through democratic referendum is an established custom though an informal practice. Consideration could easily be given to the manner in which informal popular consultation could become

---

2 Paine, T., *Common Sense*, 1776, explained how an independent government could be established and controlled by the people, and how rich and poor could share equally in privileges and duties.

democratically effective in reducing the democratic deficit. Internet banking, for example, demonstrates how individuals are identified by account numbers, accessed using a confidential code and containing confidential information, which is instantaneously transmitted and can be rapidly analysed and summarised, regardless of the mass of detail or complexity. One could envisage the implementation of direct democracy through a specific electoral site, under the control of the head of the judiciary (in the USA, the President of the Supreme Court, and in England, the Lord Chief Justice), thereby guaranteeing its legal and constitutional independence. Each citizen, qualified to vote at elections, would be given an electoral registration number and a secret access code. Direct democracy would mean that legislative approval is conditional upon a majority of votes across the entire nation. This would remove distortions due to current voting practices in which a constituency result is often a minority vote and in which national imbalance in voting opinions results from demographic concentration that reinforces such factors as wealth or poverty, employment and unemployment, racial or religious influences. The role of Parliament reassumes one of its earliest and principal functions, that of a meeting place that is much in the tradition of a market, where views, opinions and information are exchanged in continued debate, allowing the voters to understand the meaning of proposed legislation. Parliamentary debates are televised and audience participation is commonplace, as may be seen from the example of the entertainment business.

The current crisis of government, the reduced importance of the role of Parliament and the move towards tyranny as the direction of change widely perceived as a prospect, stress the necessity for a new political vision. Given the strength and the manner in which vested interests depend on the maintenance of existing political structures that have been substantially corrupted to the use of political oligarchies, any expectation that the democratic deficit might be reduced by consent is doubtless far-fetched. Social cohesion where citizenship is distanced from government through lack of participation and lack of trust is an uncertain foundation for political stability. As social cohesion gradually weakens and as government feels increasingly threatened, tyranny replaces consensus and in such circumstances revolutionary change becomes ever more likely, as historical experience has shown. The collapse of public confidence in political leaders, political parties and policies, is an early harbinger of a catastrophic end to the democratic experiment in the form of representative government and universal suffrage.

Political Change and Universal Suffrage
The advent of universal suffrage in 1918 marked a schism in the evolution of the State and in political doctrine in a number of ways. The concept of representative government created a voting majority among parliamentary electors, whose participation in the market economy was limited to selling their labour in a deregulated economy that operated under conditions of free trade. The emancipation of the working classes was to create an essential dichotomy in 'politics' that remains to be resolved to this day, namely, the reconciliation of the financial interests of a market economy with the social interests of an electoral majority, which looks to government for protection and welfare.

The first manifestation of this problem occurred with the Great Depression of the inter-war years that followed the Wall Street Crash of 1929. The market economy experienced a collapse of confidence that led to massive business failures and to mass unemployment. It was the first time that mass poverty was caused directly by the market economy. The Soup Kitchens in the USA and the Hunger Marches in England had a political significance that was to create a new dilemma for government, namely, the nature and extent of government responsibility in a deregulated market economy. This responsibility was clearly two-fold: a responsibility for addressing the cause and a responsibility for dealing with the effects.

The market economy revealed its inability to deal with economic depression and to activate the process of recovery. Whereas it is able to profit from economic prosperity, it is incapable of acting creatively as an agent of social welfare. In other words, it can provide employment in periods of prosperity; it cannot provide social support to the unemployed in periods of poverty. This appreciation led to a revolution in economic theory, known as Keynesian economics,[3] which argued that the market economy required government intervention to foster the recovery of activity by the stimulation of the level of aggregate demand. This required a new vision of fiscal policy, that of making huge injections of public funds into the market economy using budget deficits for the purpose and resorting to government borrowing for financing.

---

3 See Kenyes, J.M., *General Theory of Employment, Interest and Money.*

Keynesian economics acted as an important breach in the doctrine of free trade, both in England and in the USA, homes of unrestrained capitalism.

The social problems created by the market economy during the years of the Great Depression also had to be addressed as a government responsibility, since the market economy had ruled itself out as social agent. The social response to the Great Depression was formulated by Beveridge, working within the Government, by providing a welfare security net to provide for unemployment insurance, poverty relief, retirement pensions and health insurance for all the population. The Great Depression saw the emergence of the Welfare State, as a concept of government that was entirely new in political theory. The Welfare State marked the birth of a caring society, in which the principles of caring and sharing became official Government policy through necessity and reason.

Achieving Democracy through Universal Suffrage
The advent of universal suffrage was to provide a new understanding in political theory by associating the right of each individual, qualified to vote, to exercise his vote freely on periodic occasions. Universal suffrage, expressed as 'one man, one vote', freely cast during parliamentary elections, was seen as instituting a democratic system of government based on individual freedom and equality of voting influence.

In effect, universal suffrage provided a restricted popular meaning to the concept of democracy, as expressed by Plato, namely the right to vote periodically in free elections. Such elections attest the existence of democracy and they are seen today as evidence of the fact by international observers acting on behalf of international organisations.

Universal suffrage was also to provide a restricted popular meaning to freedom. The right to vote at an election has become the universal symbol. Democracy and freedom are joined together as a common symbol of the highest political virtue and the criteria that characterise the ideal State. The delusion that freedom can exist unconditionally and that individual freedom should be unconstrained flies in the face of self-evident truth. As it will be argued in Chapter 10, freedom can only exist under authority and is a social fact that is subject to law. The delusion is fabricated that democracy can exist as a single and unique expression of that freedom, ignoring that it exists in the ability to make a range of social choices, which include the right to work and the right to full social integration. Both democracy and freedom are meaningless to those who are excluded from or rejected by the market economy and have no other choice but scavenging for food on Skid Row. They are also meaningless to those innumerable human beings, living in primitive conditions in poor and undeveloped nations, to whom that impossible choice is offered as the *summum bonum* of political, economic and social progress. The conversion of heathens to Christian religious beliefs by the sending of missionaries in the wake of soldiers and traders, when Europe created its empires through colonization, has now been replaced by dispatching politicians to preach the gospel of democracy and freedom and installing political stooges as local dictators. Where deemed necessary to obtaining allegiance to that credo, it is imposed, as was the attempt in Iraq, by the force of arms and the rigour of brutal military rule.

The advent of universal suffrage led to another significant development in political theory, in which political parties subverted the will of the people, as expressed in free parliamentary elections, to the will of doctrinaire political parties. The inability of a functioning democracy to take account of the will of the people in every decision of government has made the expression of the will of the people a matter of party political debate. The result is that the will of the people is shaped by propaganda in which choice is simplified in terms of alternative policies, which are generic with respect to political beliefs, expressed doctrinally in such broad terms of socialist or capitalist, republican or democrat, radical or Christian, labour or conservative, liberal or independent, and which are specific in terms of policy declarations on particular matters.

Periodic plebiscites offer electors a choice between parties presenting an agreed agenda in the form of a manifesto or an action plan. An election is a competitive situation in which the attractiveness of particular agendas is a mixture of a known past experience and a set of 'electoral promises', which are conditional, not only upon party success at the ballot box, but also on the possibility of realising those promises. In effect, elections have become a form of 'auction' in which, in the frenzied desire for electoral success, parties outbid each other with promises that they have no hope, or even intention, of keeping.

Elections are the first stage in a process that all participants know to be based on deception. The electorate little realise that they are effectively being bribed, as taxpayers, by their own money. Once elected, there is no obligation to carry out promises made. Nevertheless, a relationship of trust is implied through which electors are able to express a preference based on electoral promises. Moreover, the failure to give effect to such promises and carry out the conditions of the implied trust would in any other situation be deemed, in a court of law, a breach of trust and the electoral promises treated as misrepresentations that could conceivably void the election result.

Thereafter, the communication between political parties and the electorate at large has become managed or, as the process is known, is fixed through spinning a different but desired meaning and effect. The net result is that the relationship between politicians, as a professional class of legislators voted into paid employment as Members of Parliament, and citizens at large is contaminated by distrust. Opinions polls, as a rule, generally place politicians in the lowest segment of public approval. The poor opinion in which politicians are held is often confirmed by their involvement in corruption and various forms of dishonesty. Democratic elections do not produce the type of guardian that Plato mentions, persons of the highest virtues to whom political responsibility should be entrusted.

The State, Democracy and the Market Economy
Marxist political theory gave rise to the notion of a society divided by a class struggle between an oligarchy of wealth, known variously as bourgeois or capitalists and those whose sole economic contribution was their labour, known variously as the workers or the proletariat. This class struggle produced two alternative theories of government: one representing a state in which the interests of an oligarchy of wealth are uppermost, the other representing a state in which the interests of the citizens at large, without wealth distinction, are dominant. In this latter version, the notion of caring and sharing is the guiding principle, but in practice a privileged bureaucratic class emerges.

Finding terms that adequately describe these opposing views depends very much on the historical experience of different countries. In the USA, the distinction is drawn between Republicans and Democrats, which conveniently ignores the obvious confusion that the USA is constitutionally defined as a democratic republic. In Britain, the distinction is drawn between Conservative and Labour, which distinction is quixotic in that it implies that 'conservatism' is a political choice, rather than a frame of mind, and ignores that labour is an activity in which all participate without distinction! In France, the distinction reflects the dominant

Cartesian logic of a people who are eternally seeking direction, as well as instruction, and 'right' and 'left' are used to define political positions. In effect, these definitions of political standpoint have little to do with day-to-day political policies that have administrative imperatives. Keeping the country in relative stability and avoiding social turbulence are constant policy objectives, irrespective of the regime in force.

The substantial difference between these different definitions and the concept of the State as a unified social entity stems from the concept of private property, as a social phenomenon. It is also at the root of the distinction between capitalism and socialism. It segregates the market economy as a distinct phenomenon from the State as a social entity. In the model case that we have defined as the family unit, economic and social unity is present in a shared sense of community acting under the authority of an elder, or *paterfamilias*, who is trustee for the welfare of the family. In this model, property is owned by the community and its use is shared. It is a model that continues to work well and maintain social harmony in communities that enjoy close relationships, as is the case with Asian families. As a social experiment on a wider basis, the experience of the *kibbutz* is Israel appears also to have been successful.

The significance of the 20th century, in relation to the earlier period of the Enlightenment, may be argued as residing in the importance of Marx's social theory that gave rise to communism in Eastern Europe and in the different outcomes of that model of society, as opposed to the evolution of the market economy based on individual freedom in Western Europe and in the USA.

The Enlightenment and the Age of Reason, which manifested itself so strongly in the notion of rationality and its expression in logic and mathematics, saw its full application in the scientific and industrial revolution that is a continuing experience, in what became the information revolution and the use of machinery, in the form of computers, in everyday life. It made little effective contribution to dealing with the major problem of society, namely, the concept of life as a community experience based on family values, which we have defined as the moral values of caring and sharing. Indeed, the Industrial Revolution optimised the use of individual freedom as expressed in the market economy, which blossomed and grew vigorously during this period. But the very success that created enormous fortunes also drove the mass of the people into abject misery and poverty. It is noteworthy that the collapse of communism in Eastern Europe in recent times and the rapid switch over to a market economy, under pressure from the USA and the World Bank, almost instantly threw the mass of the population into dire poverty and enabled a very small minority to become enormously wealthy. This was the case in Poland and later in Russia. The current fear in Western Europe at the moment is that the process of enlargement of the European Union and its open door economic policy with respect to the global economy may well create great wealth for those who control that evolution, but the social costs will be borne by the mass of the population who will lose their jobs and see their living standards brought down to a much lower level. In this sense, the experience of the expansion of the market economy has been a learning experience of social distress. To argue that the market economy improves living standards generally is not seen in the USA either, where a substantial proportion of the population lives below the poverty level. Nor is it seen in the United Kingdom at this time, where such is the level of household indebtedness that the mass of the population is at the mercy of instant bankruptcy, should there be an uncontrollable recession.

Socialism, Communism and the Tyranny of Bureaucracy
In social terms and in the learning experience that it provided with respect to political theory and the prospects of a reformed society based on moral values, the Communist Revolution of 1917 in Russia was, in retrospect, nearly as significant as the Enlightenment in bringing to light the differences and consequences of two opposed concepts of government, namely, socialism and capitalism. Hobbes and Locke, among others, preached freedom as the supreme virtue, in much the same way as Plato exalted wisdom. In consequence, freedom from arbitrary government as a political and economic virtue implies a reduction in the influence of authority. In other words, a free market economy insists on the minimum of government intervention and the maximum of deregulation.

The initial reaction to the Communist Revolution was one of horror at the murder of the Tsar and his family and the brutality that followed. It horrified aristocratic and bourgeois Europe in much the same way as had the earlier French Revolution, when the execution of the King and his wife and the bloodshed that persisted until the Revolution was taken over by Napoleon, who crowned himself Emperor. After the initial shock, the Communist Revolution made little impact with respect to the social, economic and political concerns of Western Europe during the inter-war years. The major concerns were closer to home and the atrocities imposed on Russian society by the tyrant Stalin received little attention. Socialism grew in influence, but offered a democratic choice as a political party. Communism, as a state concept, was distasteful to the majority of people and attracted only the interest of fringe groups and certain intellectuals.

The end of World War II presented a different scenario. The triumphant allies found themselves bedfellows with the ignoble Stalin and a Communist empire that had become a major political and military influence on a global scale. Berlin was now part of Communist Europe, Rome and Athens had barely avoided the same fate, Paris had to listen to messages from Moscow relayed by an all powerful French Communist Party that controlled France at the factory level. Many intellectuals throughout Western Europe were pro-communist and the USA panicked itself into a state of neurosis in the form of McCarthyism so that even an ageing Charlie Chaplin had to seek refuge in Vevey, Switzerland.

The social model offered by communism had three significant features. First, it led to the abolition of private property with all property being owned by the State for the common use of all citizens. Second, the market economy was abolished and all the means of production and distribution were brought under the control of the workers in a state that gave effect to the dictatorship of the proletariat. Third, with the virtual disappearance of an economy of exchange, the regulation of demand and supply, that had formerly been under the control of the price mechanism, was replaced by a system of rationing and fixed pricing regulated through bureaucratic control. Its ideology was that the abolition of private property and the shared community of existence would bring about true equality between people. The causes of social conflict, seen as competition between people, being thus removed, social harmony would result and the need for a state, as such, would eventually become redundant, leading to freedom as the natural human condition. These ideas, crystallised by Marx, found their expression in the opportunity that the post-Industrial Revolution circumstances offered.

The consequences of communism was the emergence of a state based on the tyranny of bureaucracy, characterised by the manner in which the administrative execution and enforcement of legal rules are socially organised by regularised procedure, formal division of responsibility, hierarchy and impersonal relationships.

Bureaucracy is present in administration, for it is formalised control, an essential ingredient of management in a broad sense. The general rule is that the larger the extent of administration, the greater is the degree of bureaucracy. The most repugnant aspect of bureaucracy in a social sense and in the context of a social ideal represented by the family unit and family values, is that bureaucracy dehumanises society and removes the personal relationship that is the substance of the humane condition. Bureaucracy is demonised as representing the perversion of means and ends, so that means become ends in themselves and in the process the general interest is substituted by bureaucratic self-interest. Most importantly it is seen as being at best inert with respect to moral value judgments, and at worst, void of moral values. Bureaucracy as a form of social organisation is considered generally as placing emphasis on control through restricting freedom and in so doing frustrates creativity.

The experience of socialism, and of communism as its extreme manifestation, lasted for most of the 20th century and virtually ended with its collapse. Its failure was seen as total. As a form of social organisation, the importance that it gives to bureaucracy became intolerable: as a form of industrial organisation, its reliance of bureaucratic control frustrated initiative, creativity and economic development and lowered rather than improved living standards in comparison with other nations that seemed to benefit from a thriving market economy. For example, the rational management of production through a price mechanism that regulated demand and supply was replaced by bureaucratic control that could only measure quantities and not utility as expressed in a demand price. Likewise, product costing could not take account of some factors of production, notably the depreciation of fixed assets as a cost element, since assets were owned and financed by the State and industrial managers took no account of such assets.

The Failure of the Socialist Experiment
Paradoxically, the prediction made by Schumpeter, that capitalism would fail by reason of the revolt of its own intellectuals and would be substituted by socialism, did not materialise. Instead, the Communist empire collapsed internally and communism was rejected by the leaders of the Communist Party in Russia, beginning with Gorbachev.

The socialist experience ended in Europe with a sense of disappointment among intellectuals and social reformers and triumphalism in the USA, where it was seen as a vice and a threat to the American way of life. In Western Europe, the commitment to the concept of a Welfare State, as defined by Beveridge, was decently buried, leaving social problems as residual areas for government activity. A deregulated market economy thus freed of government intervention, assumed global proportions.

The failure of socialist paradigm to achieve the economic objectives that make improvements in living standards possible, has radically altered the perspectives open to Western society. The consequence of that failure was to destroy socialism as a political alternative to capitalism and the Welfare State as a social alternative to a market economy. The appeal of the market economy to the broad spectrum of the electorate lay in its ability to sustain high levels of personal consumption by encouraging consumerism and extensive consumer choice. As a political doctrine, Marxism could not sustain its justification in terms of the oppression of the working classes by the bourgeoisie, nor could it maintain the concept of the class struggle as its *raison d'être*, when the market economy proclaimed that the consumer was king. The market economy gave the worker a dual status as a producer and as a consumer and the prosperity of the market economy was based on maintaining high levels of aggregate demand and employment. So much for the oppression of the working classes. Moreover, the freedom to trade, that the market economy proclaimed as a fundamental right, was also extended to the individual in the freedom to seek better conditions for his family through hard work. This message had an undisputable appeal.

The tyranny of bureaucracy, the constraints on freedom and creativity resulting from extensive controls through government regulations, the nationalisation of major sectors of the economy, the power and influence that it lent to politicians with respect to policy and decision-making, created and maintained strong bonds between the community of politicians and the bureaucratic community and a mutuality of self-serving interest. Effective decision-making lay with the bureaucracy that acted as arbitrator between all claims and passed judgment on all matters. Bureaucracy established a state-within-a-state with its own constituency of employees and its own growth objectives. Within the bureaucracy there co-existed a pluralism of quasi-autonomous colonies with their own establishments and traditions, for example the Treasury, and the education, health and defence services. All these colonies competed for funds and were jealous of their independence.

The end of the tyranny of bureaucracy had effects that were akin to the collapse of empire. The market economy, which was the enemy that it had long contested, reflected a totally opposite concept of government. The market economy thrives on freedom and deregulation of all the activities that fall within its ambit. It has its rules, its own objectives, its own policies and its own agents. The harmony that exists in the market economy is created by money, for the market economy is essentially a money economy. As an organism, the market economy may be defined as a closed system. It has an all-pervading ethos, which defines knowledge as that which has meaning in money terms and rationalises decisions in terms of the logic of money. Contrary to Kant's logic of reason, as the basis of rationality, the logic of money does not attempt to reason on the basis of moral judgments, for it has no morality.

The Tyranny of Bureaucracy and the Tyranny of Money
In effect, the end of the tyranny of bureaucracy, which was the self-destructive vice with which socialism was infected, marked the installation of another and different tyranny, namely the tyranny of money. As the supreme arbiter in the market economy, money ensured liberty, equality and fraternity and established an open society that was accessible to all, without distinction of race, sex or religion. All men and women being equal before money, the sole manner in which money manifested itself as a tyranny was the strict and necessary condition that money constituted the unique basis for access to the market economy and indeed, to the society that it created. In this regards, it was noted earlier that the market economy had created a new form of society, namely the market society,[4] in which all relationships and activities are conducted on the exchange principle.

However, whereas the tyranny of bureaucracy encompassed all individuals under its aegis, the tyranny of money regulates the relationships and activities only of those who have access and are part of the market economy, and has no influence outside the market economy.

The tyranny of money especially confronts the Social Conscience with respect to moral values. Protagonists of the market economy often argue that its virtue is that it encourages individuals to

4 See Slater, D. and Tonkiss, F., *Market Society*, 'a theory of markets always implies a larger theory of social integration and regulations ... and in this sense offers a broad set of responses to the problem of whether and how social processes can be co-ordinated' (p.2).

assume personal responsibility for their well-being. They consider that poverty is either a vice or a self-induced condition.

Rousseau argued that we are all born equal and that it is society that creates inequality. This understanding would lead to the postulate that the aim of social reform is to reduce inequalities, where possible, or otherwise mitigate their effects. There is a strong belief among protagonists of the market economy that competition, which brings to the fore the inequality between people, is necessary for improving the human condition. This echoes the views of Malthus, and also Darwin, who considered that natural law would eliminate the weakest individuals from the population in the process of natural selection. According to Cowling, as a High Priest of modern Conservatism in England,

> If there is a class war – and there is – it is important that it should be handled with subtlety and skill ... it is not freedom that Conservatives want; what they want is the sort of freedom that will maintain existing inequalities or restore lost ones.[5]

Even if it is admitted that a large part of the inequality between individuals is socially contrived and that, taking the correction of this form of inequality should be the form of discipline and punishment through comparative deprivation, there is an inequality that is non-negligible and that cannot be ignored. It is the poverty of illness, of physical and mental misfortune; it is the absence of help when help is needed to deal with the misfortune that is the effect of adverse chance. To paraphrase Sartre, all human certitude hangs by a delicate thread!

The Meaning of Governance
In dealing with the problems newly brought into perspective by the success of the market economy, the tyranny of money and of its agents, the Social Conscience has developed a new doctrine, namely the Doctrine of Governance. This doctrine is of recent origin and has provoked considerable public and political interest as representing a new dimension or, indeed, an alternative conception of government. An extensive ventilation of the concept among politicians, the business community and an intellectual debate among academics has resulted in a large literature on the subject. The intensity of interest in the far-reaching implications of the subject and its relevance has failed so far to produce a sufficient clarity about its meaning and its rules of application.

---

5 Cowling, M., *Conservative Essays*, London: Cassell, 1978.

According to the European Commission's White Paper on 'Governance in the EU' (July 2001), the issue has arisen from the need of economics (as regards corporate governance) and political science (as regards state governance) for an all-embracing concept capable of conveying diverse meanings not covered by the traditional term government. European governance is stated as referring to the rules, processes and behaviour that affect the way in which powers are exercised at the European level, particularly as regards openness, participation, accountability, effectiveness and coherence. These five 'principles of good governance' reinforce those of being subsidiary and proportionate. This raises the question of the sense in which this definition conveys a different meaning to what could be understood as good government.

Undeterred by its own internal problem of successfully leading 26 countries into a new vision of Europe, the European Commission's White Paper makes recommendations for strengthening its contribution to global governance as follows: the European Union '... should seek to apply the principles of good governance to its global responsibilities and endeavour to boost the effectiveness and enforcement powers of the international institutions ...' Again, it is difficult to hear the meaning amidst the thunder of the message.

According to Rhodes,[6]

> ... the concept of governance is currently used in contemporary social sciences with at least six different meanings: the minimal State, corporate governance, new public management, good governance, social cybernetic systems and self-organised networks ...

There is more than a hint in this definition that governance may indeed mean no government!

Almost accidentally, the European Union White Paper stumbled upon a definition of governance that has a semblance of meaning by referring to its essential focus on problems of society. The White Paper declared that:

> ... the structures and the quality of governance are critical determinants of social cohesion or social conflict, the success or failure of economic development, the preservation or deterioration of the natural environment, as well as the respecting or violation of human rights and fundamental freedom ...

6 Rhodes, R., 'The New Governance: Governing Without Government, *Political Studies*, Vol. 44, 1996, p.652.

Corporate governance is given a specific and unique meaning that refers to the role of business corporations in the market economy, as distinct from the wider society that we have been discussing as 'a caring society'. In the sense currently employed, corporate governance as relating to the 'government' of business corporations really means 'corporate management'. There is an extensive literature on corporate management that began a long time before 'corporate governance' took on a separate meaning in management literature. Within that literature, the essential role of corporate management is the optimisation of shareholder value. In orthodox economic theory, the shareholder value determinant for management decision-making is the overriding corporate objective, and creating shareholder value is a financial outcome that is significantly influenced by actions that reduce financial costs. Investors and stock markets judge corporate performance in that single and unique dimension. It is the price determinant for acquiring shares in business corporations. In this logic, a good company is judged solely in terms of its value to shareholders. Hence, the first difficulty in speaking about corporate governance is the relevance of that concept.

Corporate governance may be discussed as an outgrowth of an earlier concern with the relationship between business corporations and society and, in particular, the negative by-products of industrial activities, such as the social costs of environmental pollution. This concern eventually broadened out to a discussion of a wider context in which their social contributions might be examined. As early as 1971, the Economic Development Committee in New York led a study in the social responsibilities of business corporations. By 1975, the Accounting Standards Steering Committee in the UK issued *The Corporate Report* that contained major recommendations for widening the scope of financial statements and soon afterwards the *Sudreau Report* 1975 in France required corporations to publish a Social Report along with their Annual Financial Statement. The theoretical interest taken in social responsibility accounting has already been discussed extensively in Glautier and Underdown,[7] and a recent article in *The Economist*[8] commented:

> ... it would be a challenge to find a recent annual report of any big international company that justifies the firm's existence merely in

---

7 Glautier, M.W.E. and Underdown, B., *Accounting Theory and Practice*, London: Pitman Publishing, 1st edn, 1976.
8 'A Survey of Corporate Social Responsibility', *The Economist*, 22nd January, 2005, pp.3-18.

terms of profits, rather than service to the community ... Today corporate social responsibility, if it is nothing else, is the tribute that capitalism everywhere pays to virtue ...

In line with this view, the declared concern of the OECD with respect to corporate governance is with '... good practice in corporate behaviour with a view to rebuilding and maintaining public trust in companies and stock markets ...'[9]

Governance: The Legacies of Plato and Marx
The concern with governance viewed as a meaning or understanding that considers social problems in the light of moral value judgements, may be explained uniquely in the context of a caring society. The substantial reason why governance has been and continues to be so extensively discussed, both in broad political terms, involving principles of good government and in the narrower terms of the management of the market economy, is the observed breakdown of social cohesion and loss of trust in those who are deemed to have responsibilities for government in an overall context in which society is seen as a unified State. In essence, therefore, governance is an extension of the discussion of government. Its significance is that it refers that discussion to moral values in the postulate that governance reflects a general expectation of 'good' government.

Plato's vision of society was a State that was socially unified: Marx's vision of society was a State split asunder by a class struggle in which one group exploited the other and in which the State maintained that dichotomy. Plato's legacy was the statement of the virtues that should characterise the ideal government and ensure the happiness of the people. Marx's legacy was the recognition that social cohesion is the core objective of a caring society and that government should restore social cohesion by addressing systematised inequalities that are the root cause of oppression. In this view, Plato and Marx have much in common to contribute to an understanding of governance as constituting moral dimensions as benchmarks for the behaviour of those entrusted with government in both its macro and micro aspects.

It is worth recalling the four virtues on which Plato insisted as ideals for the best State. The virtue that Plato judged as supreme is wisdom. Three other supporting virtues are courage, temperance and justice. Interpreting these virtues in terms of an expectation

---

9 OECD, *Principles of Corporate Governance*, Paris, 2004.

of a State, expressed as any government structure for the regulation of society of whatever dimension, national, international or global, or of a business corporation, it is evident that, whether as citizens, shareholders, investors, employees or clients, wisdom made manifest in decisions and actions is the universal and most imperative expectation. It is the action of intelligence that finds the path to that situation which secures the highest common good. It is so easily understandable why Plato should rank wisdom as the supreme virtue. Courage is the will to seek and adhere to wisdom, whatever the circumstances, while temperance and justice are the ways in which wisdom manifests its action. Insecurity, doubt and conflict are stilled in the presence of wisdom and the social cohesion that it secures results in the greatest happiness of all. One interesting definition given of corporate governance refers to its role in conflict resolution and corporate cohesion as being '... concerned with the resolution of collective action problems among dispersed investors and the reconciliation of conflicts of interests between various corporate claimholders ...'[10] However, it is evident that governance cannot be defined in terms of sectarian or limited interpretations of social responsibilities and can only be adequately judged in term of a broader and indeed global context in which wisdom is seen as manifest.

It is convenient to discuss governance as applicable to the manner in which the State exercises its authority over society in general and over the market economy in particular, these being the two large sectors for which it has legislative and sovereign powers. Reference has been made earlier to the absence of trust, or the mistrust, in the actions of politicians and in politics as an area of public responsibility. Numerous scandals in most countries show the corruption that is present in the abuse of power or misuse of influence by political leaders in the pursuit of policies and in actions in which their personal interests determine political objectives. The very close association between the political process and the business community is an important factor in creating mistrust between government and citizens at large. The market economy is controlled by capitalist financiers: politicians are frequently suborned to business interest through the process known as political lobbying. In a recent survey, *L'Hebdo*,[11] a leading Swiss weekly, reported that 72% of Swiss parliamentarians had obtained business

10 Becht, M., Bolton, P and Röell, A., *Corporate Governance and Control*, European Corporate Governance Institute, Finance Working Paper, October 2002, No. 2/2002.
11 *L'Hebdo*, No. 10, week of 10th March, 2005, pp.16-26.

mandates after their election; 55% of them defined themselves as 'lobbyists' earning substantial revenues from business firms. This financial dependence of parliamentarians is deemed to make it impossible for Parliament to pass legislation that is against the interests of the business community. The President of the Swiss Society for Public Affairs is reported to have had the effrontery to assert that lobbyists are necessary to the good functioning of democracy! Elsewhere and in all countries, political leaders are often paid lackeys of big business and financial interests. The problem of governance at State level is essentially a problem of political corruption, in which the tyranny of money dictates the ends and provides the means.

Governance: Discretionary Managerial Behaviour and Agency Theory
A seminal work by Williamson in 1967[12] contradicted orthodox economic theory, which stated that the objective of business corporations is to optimise shareholder value and that corporate managers act in accordance with this principle. He argued that the existence of managerial discretion in corporate decision-making made it possible for their own personal interests to influence such decisions. An important literature developed out of this postulate that refers to agency theory and is largely relied upon to explain human behaviour in organisations. This theory extends the traditional theory of the firm based on the theory of finance to include psychological, sociological as well as political considerations. In particular, it assumes that, as a result of the principal/agent relationship represented in the ownership/management structure of business corporations, the delegation of management control by shareholders to professional managers, who are effectively employees, creates through that relationship, a special interest group with considerable powers. We have mentioned earlier in Chapter 5 that the separation of ownership and control, through the use of the Joint Stock Company structure, has limited the effective control that shareholders can exert over corporate directors. This is particularly so where shareholding is highly diffused and no single group of shareholders are able to dislodge or counter the decisions made by boards of directors. In a sense, in these situations boards of directors enjoy most of the legal rights that would properly belong to the owners, without themselves having a significant financial

12 Williamson, O.E., *The Economics of Discretionary Managerial Behaviour: Managerial Objectives in a Theory of the Firm*, Markham Publishing Co., 1967.

interest in the capital of the firm. Company legislation limits matters that have to be referred for decision to formal shareholder meetings, and even with respect to such decisions, boards of directors are able to push through the decisions that they are recommending to shareholders.

The extensive discretionary powers that boards of directors enjoy effectively transfer to them most of the legal rights that properly belong to ownership, except for a few critical decisions. Those decisions that are reserved by law to shareholders, such as the approval of annual accounts, dividend declarations and the appointment of auditors, are presented to shareholders by boards of directors as formal propositions and are seldom contested at the Annual General Meeting of shareholders, which is the only occasion at which shareholders are able to question directors. The Annual General Meeting of shareholders has become a routine that is usually poorly attended by shareholders.

So extensive is the effective control of boards of directors on all aspects of corporate business that they have virtually a free hand to do as they wish, within the law. This includes deciding upon their own remuneration. In recent years, payouts to directors in the form of salaries, fees, bonuses and share options have attained such a proportion as to cause massive public protest that has been of no avail, for the procedures of approval that are employed for the purpose generally were perfectly within the law. On the few occasions where shareholders have taken legal action against boards of directors with respect to grossly excessive remuneration tantamount to siphoning off profits properly due to shareholders, the courts have upheld the directors.

Such is the tyranny of money that corporate directors have on notable occasions gone beyond the legal limits of their discretionary powers and conspired to embezzle corporate funds on massive scales. Robert Maxwell, as Chief Executive of the Mirror Group, not only ran the business as though it were his own property, but misappropriated money even from the Group's pension fund for employees, leaving retired employees without adequate pension. In the USA, a string of massive frauds led to the bankruptcy of large corporations, such as Enron, Worldcom, Tyco and others. In Italy, the Chairman of the Parmalat Group was prosecuted for the largest corporate fraud ever committed in Italian history, running to over $14 billion. As a result of these frauds, many investors lost their money and other firms also went into bankruptcy. In other cases, embezzlement has taken other forms that have not caused business failure and so escaped attention, for example, setting up private family companies into which to siphon off business contracts, thereby creating parallel business activities. Cases of improper use of business assets are legion as are luxurious living styles financed as business expenses.

Two troubling features in all these cases have been the absence of legislation capable of preventing such frauds and the failure of audit firms to discover or report on corporate fraud. The consequences of the Enron case were twofold: the enactment of compliance requirements for public companies, and the liquidation of Arthur Andersen as auditors responsible for the audit of the Enron Group. The implication of Arthur Andersen staff in concealing and destroying vital information relating to the discovery of fraud revived misgivings concerning the role of auditors and, in particular, their responsibilities towards shareholders.

Democratic Government and Accountability
Until the advent of democracy, through universal suffrage, the people had no part in the activities of State and government, save as servants to the monarch and subject to the law under his will and person. This was the understood meaning of the obligation of allegiance that imposed on the subject unquestioning obedience to an absolute monarch. The monarch, under Common Law, was accountable to no one save to God and The Law, by whom he was recognised as having been empowered by divine right to be king.

The relationship between the monarch and his subjects was dictated by the law of the land. Such concessions as the monarch was willing to grant became law for that reason and he was held to those concessions, which were to form the basis of constitutional law. In this context, the sovereign is subject to law. The growing influence of Parliament acted as the path to democracy, but it was not until 1918 that it could be said that the people became involved in the activities of State and of government and acquired some constitutional rights with respect to electing representatives to Parliament. However, Britain is not a democracy as generally defined and cannot be compared to other countries in that respect. It is a constitutional monarchy with a Parliament elected by universal suffrage and has a representative assembly, with rights that have been granted to it over time by the monarch. However, the Prime Minister is appointed by the monarch and, as such, reports to the monarch in respect of his responsibilities and duties as

Prime Minister, or as he is officially known, as First Lord of the Treasury.

The meaning of democracy and the nature of the relationship between the executive, as the governing body, the parliamentary assembly on the one hand and the electorate on the other, differs as between countries. The constitution, which formalises constitutional rights and duties, is generally in a written form and has absolute legal authority. England does not have a written constitution and its constitutional law is found in various statutes, legal precedents and accepted custom. There is a considerable difference between the notion of representative government or parliamentary democracy, as practised in Britain and direct democracy, as practised in Switzerland. In the former case, the people only have the constitutional right to elect Members of Parliament and have no constitutional right to participate in the decisions of the executive: in the latter case, it is the people from whom the executive must seek approval for decisions that it wishes to make. In Britain, popular consultations occur once every four years or so at elections: in Switzerland, the participation of the people in government is realised through referendums, or *votation*, as these are known, that occur at frequent intervals, when the decisions of the people are required. Hence, if democracy is to be taken to mean 'government by the people, for the people and with the people', the freedom to participate in the election of a parliament on a very occasional basis hardly qualifies Britain as a democratic state. Hence, the much-vaunted association of freedom with democracy is as much pretence as it is a fiction.

For many countries having a long history of nationhood, the transition from absolute monarchy or tyranny to democracy was not a clear severance with the past. The concessionary nature of parliamentary rights by the monarch in England has left untouched important areas of government within the prerogative of the monarch, exercised by the Prime Minister, for example, the right to wage war as was seen in the decision to invade Iraq that was made by the Prime Minister and did not even require parliamentary approval. The French Revolution, which brought the French monarchy to a drastic end and replaced it with a Republic, having a written constitution, left to the Republic many of the rights that were previously within the prerogative of the monarch. In a celebrated instance when two French secret service agents blew up a boat belonging to Greenpeace in a New Zealand harbour and were arrested by the New Zealand police, this matter was declared to be an 'affair of state' in France and therefore a state secret. This example reflected the continuity of absolutism with respect to the use of the *Cachet*, the secret Royal Command, which was sufficient authority for all actions.

It follows that discussion of accountability is governed by constitutional law and is understood differently in different countries. In the USA, the Constitution reflects a concordat between the Executive, the Legislature and the Judiciary, as three distinct organs of state with specific rights and duties. Just as democracy may be judged to be an imperfect form of government with respect to Platonic principles, so too the notion of accountability lacks substantial effectiveness.

There is an increasing awareness today that government is in crisis.[13] This concern inspired the extensive discussion of the notion of governance, which has confronted the idea of government with the requirement of quality of government. Similarly, there is a growing awareness that quality of government implies improved transparency through extended accountability. Hence, it may be postulated that, beyond the evidence that there is a crisis in government, the underlying crisis is a democratic deficit in the limited access of the people to the activities of state, and participation in government. Improved and extended public accountability could well provide the way to reducing this democratic deficit.

The Democratic Deficit and the Parliamentary Mandate
It has been argued that democratic deficit arises whenever the application of the principles of democracy, understood as 'government by the people, for the people, with the people', is imperfect. We have seen that a significant democratic deficit results from the general failure of most so-called democratic nations to meet the first criterion, namely, 'government by the people'. We now turn to examining that part of democratic deficit attributable to the general failure to meet the other two criteria, namely, 'government for the people' and 'government with the people'. It is through the concept of government accountability that the presence and extent of democratic deficit may be examined.

The existence of a caring society depends to a large extent on the will of the nation as a whole that social relationships should be

---

13 See Foster, C., *British Government in Crisis*, London: Hart Publishing, 2005, for a full analysis of perceived defects that have undermined the effectiveness of government.

established on that basis, and that the economic and social policies adopted by government should reflect the values of a caring society. This is the concern to which the second criterion for democratic government is directed, namely, 'government for the people'. In view of the many and varied interest groups whose needs have to be addressed, meeting this criterion in a manner that is considered as satisfactory and acceptable to the entire nation places considerable demands on government managerial competence. In effect, democratic deficit may be considered as resulting in part from schisms in society itself, that are prime factors in weakening social cohesion.

Where government policies and actions manifestly favour particular groups, the resulting democratic deficit will undermine government and create conflict between government and sections of society. It is in the context of class or group conflict that the democratic deficit appears. Governments that favour big business and wealthy sections of the population cause divisive social conflicts. Bias in fiscal policies, that results in fiscal inequality by reducing the tax burden on the rich, policies restricting the rights of some in favour of others, thus creating social inequality (for example the favouring of special-interest groups), provoke resentment. In effect, 'government for the people' is a requirement of the concept of equality of attention to the needs of all, which is enshrined in the expectations of a caring society.

'Government with the people' as a criterion of democracy refers especially to the consensual nature of the relationship that should exist between government and people. An important element in ensuring and maintaining consensus, as the vital link between government and people, is the quality, relevance and sincerity of the information that flows from government to the people. Trust in the government is so fundamental to the concept of 'government with the people' that it deserves endless repetition and emphasis. It is the absence of honesty in the information provided by government and the presence within it of endless and gross lies, often appearing as ill-fabricated distortions of evident truths, which have brought governments generally into disrepute. The frequency with which political leaders are involved in business and financial scandals, the endless judicial enquiries into alleged abuses of office and the publicity that is given to the conviction of high profile and close associates in criminal proceedings, has brought political life in many countries into disrepute. Truth has now become such a parody in government statements that formal official statements asserting or denying certain facts or circumstance are immediately reversed to derive a meaning that is used as confirming the untruth of an assertion or the truth of what is being denied.

'Government with the people' may also be considered by reference to the manner in which this criterion is rendered effective in practice and relates to the nature of the authority or mandate that gives effect to this principle. A mandate is a legal authority given by one party to another party that entitles the latter to act on behalf of the former. In a strict sense, a mandate implies the existence of an agency agreement. It defines the nature and the limits of the authority of the agent to act on behalf of the other, who is known as the principal.

There can be no question that democracy, as defined by Plato, enshrines all rights in the people and that government is a delegation by mandate of the authority to govern. The mandate is given as the result of the process of election designating those in whom the authority to govern is granted. It is universally accepted by custom and constitutional law that governments have a general mandate to govern. This means that it is within the discretion of government in using its mandate to make such decisions as it considers necessary to achieve the purposes of government. All countries refer the extent of the mandate of government to constitutional law. In those countries having written constitutions, the powers of the executive are formally stated and, where there is a constitutional separation of powers as between the Executive, the Legislature and the Judiciary, their distinct and separate powers are also stated. In the case of England, that has an unwritten constitution, constitutional law consists of custom, precedent and those powers that have remained in the royal prerogative. The history of England reflects the traditions that have characterised English society as it adapted to changing social forms, and in particular from feudalism, brought over from Normandy by William the Conqueror and consolidated under the reign of Henry II, to a modern society based on parliamentary democracy or representative government that has evolved since the Bill of Rights 1689, which effectively redistributed the balance of power between sovereign and Parliament.

The nature of parliamentary democracy, as it evolved in Britain, transferred effective political power to Parliament without disturbing the structure of government or organs of administration. The leader of the parliamentary majority, which emerges as the result of general elections, seeks audience with the

Sovereign at the conclusion of the elections, presents himself to the Sovereign as such and is nominated by the Sovereign as First Lord of the Treasury. Thereupon he is entrusted by the Sovereign with the task of forming a government. Names are subsequently proposed by him to the Sovereign. As a sign of symbolic allegiance to the Sovereign, they are invited to kiss hands at an official ceremony, upon being conferred with the seals of office that mark their official appointment. The government that has been appointed in this manner acts on behalf of the Sovereign and not on behalf of the people, for the people or with the people. It is the government of the people, on behalf of the Sovereign and under the Sovereign's authority.

Historically, Parliament has acted as the kernel of the relationship between government and people in England. If there is a democratic mandate in Britain, it can only be one that arises out of periodic general elections, when candidates offer themselves for election as parliamentary representatives to citizens registered as electors in designated electoral areas, known as constituencies. When elected, they become automatically Members of Parliament. Hence, becoming a Member of Parliament is in the gift of the people.

The Role of Political Parties
In all democracies, political opinion is developed and organised in terms of differing political visions and agendas, formulated and presented by different political parties. Often they reflect political beliefs and traditions that may be specific to different countries. Broad categorisations are formed on a doctrinal basis that sees different roles for government. 'Socialism', described as a political credo, is highly influential in European countries that expect government to assume the task of installing a caring society and imposing the duty of sharing its financial cost through taxation. They include parties of the left and centre left calling themselves variously Democrat, Socialist, Labour, Social Democrat or other appellations indicating commitments to social welfare. Other parties, having orientations towards the centre or right of the political spectrum, set more store by economic growth and a strong and healthy market economy as conducive to improved living standards and hence social welfare. They call themselves Republican, Liberal, Conservative, Christian Democrat or other appellations concerned with minimising the role of government and favouring free markets and individual freedom. The need to appeal

to public opinion, which tends to reflect the Social Conscience when considering political issues, modulates extreme political positions towards the larger consensus that is found in the political centre. Nowadays, it is exceptional to find a political party that does not declare a significant concern with social welfare in its political agenda.

The role of political parties is to clarify options for government action and seek popular support for their particular agenda. The essence of parliamentary democracy may be stated as obtaining democratic approval of the agenda of political parties, as platforms for government action. Although nothing precludes anyone from presenting him or herself as a parliamentary candidate, success depends very much on being associated with a political party, whose platform attracts greater popular appeal. Given that the choice between parties is made on the basis of a political differentiation that is narrowly situated about the centre of the political spectrum, there is often little to distinguish their agenda. Long-term government policies are determined only in part in response to the views of electors. Often, they reflect national and international considerations over which political parties tend to find agreement. Thus, the results of parliamentary elections have little possibility of changing long-term government policies.

Viewed in terms of these various considerations, the nature and extent of the mandate to govern in a parliamentary democracy seems to be extremely unclear and uncertain. It is unclear because political declarations made during elections and with the objective of obtaining public support are presented as election promises. In fact, elections are more like auctions, in which the parties strive to outbid each other, offering improved benefits for whatever group or whichever circumstance is likely to win over popular support, at taxpayers' expense. Promising the moon during the period of electoral courtship and facing the consequences of unrealisable ambitions produce a short post-electoral honeymoon period, which hastens the sense of deception that is the general sentiment of the public with all governments.

Hence, the nature of the mandate to govern is, at best, obtained on the basis of false promises. Governments challenged in Parliament as to their actions defiantly assert their validity in terms of the mandate obtained from the people. Electoral promises are conveniently forgotten with time and through the confusion of meaning and distortions that confound truth, whenever honesty is in issue. The most vociferous assertion as to the truth of a lie is made by the liar himself. Politicians have remarkable talents for self-preservation and for escaping responsibility whenever it should become a threat. Faced with proof of the making of an offending or false statement, they ingeniously protest that the statement was never intended to have the meaning given, or that the meaning of the statement was twisted in its interpretation.

The foregoing explains the most serious cause for loss of faith in politicians and loss of trust in governments. It explains that part of the democratic deficit, which is due to a general low level of public interest in politics, poor attendance at political meetings and relatively low levels of participation in elections. Supremely confident in their own convictions and declarations, the perception gap between governments and their citizens is sometimes revealed as quite considerable. This was the case when electors both in France and in the Netherlands voted against the proposed new European Constitution to the immense surprise and chagrin of the entire European Commission and the governments of those countries. The President of the European Commission at the time was so appalled by this unexpected result which he, together with other members of the Commission, considered to be inopportune to the extent of possibly being invalid. He was reported as suggesting that it should be overlooked and that the election process should be repeated. Within a short time, he evidently realised the enormity of his recommendation. Reluctantly, and within days, it dawned upon the European political community that public opinion, given the opportunity to express itself – which opportunity had not previously been granted – had voted against the tyranny of bureaucracy that is reflected in the actions of the European Commission and which it widely detested.

Clearly, the matter of mandate in its democratic expression is problematic. At the constituency level, there is no law that defines the legal implications of a supposed agency relationship between a Member of Parliament and his constituents. Echoing the idealism of the Enlightenment, Edmund Burke enunciated the credo that has remained to this day the generally accepted view, as follows:

> Parliament is not a congress of ambassadors from different and hostile interests; which interests each must maintain, as an agent and advocate, against other agents and advocates; but parliament is a deliberative assembly of one nation, with one interest, that of the whole; where, not local purposes, not local prejudices ought to guide, but the general good, resulting from the general reason of the whole. You choose a member indeed; but when you have chosen him,

he is not a member of Bristol, but he is a member of parliament. And further: Your representative owes you, not his industry only, but his judgment; and he betrays instead of serving you if he sacrifices it to your opinion.

(Speech to the Electors of Bristol, 3rd November, 1774)

The role of political parties in creating their own constituencies within Parliament has changed significantly the role of Members of Parliament as enunciated by Burke. Affiliation to a political party is vital to the career of a politician. He depends on national and local party headquarters for his selection as candidate representing his party and for obtaining all needed support and help in securing his election as Member of Parliament. In effect, far from representing his constituency in Parliament, or serving as a Member in the national interest, as Burke stated, a Member is bound by allegiance to his own party within Parliament. The two-party system, that considers Parliament as divided into government supporters and opposition supporters, requires that Members of Parliament toe the party line on all essential matters and vote, as the party wishes, on legislation before Parliament. The failure to adhere to party discipline carries the threat of exclusion by the withdrawal of the party Whip. Very few members of the party will attempt rebellion to that extent, even though they may disagree in conscience with the policy or actions of the party leadership. There is too much at stake from a career and financial viewpoint. The ambition to achieve high political office, the enjoyment of influence, the social status of Member of Parliament, the facilities available for carrying out the duties involved, the financial support in the form of travelling and official expenses, not forgetting the substantial salary that the average Member of Parliament would have difficulty in earning in any other capacity, are all determinant factors that bend the will and conscience of a Member of Parliament to the overriding imperative of obedience to the will of the party. His most important duty is to vote according to the party line and to temper comments implying criticism. As member of the party in power, his absolute duty is to maintain the Government in office by guaranteeing its voting majority in Parliament.

The docile obedience of Members of Parliament to the party Whip has substantially devalued the role of Parliament, for Parliament is not longer the place where the sovereign's ministers may effectively be called to answer for policy or administrative decisions or be censured by vote of confidence. Such a procedure would force Members of Parliament to face the risk of a general election, that none of them would wish to contemplate. The invasion of Iraq, for example, met with substantial opposition within the population, as well as from military and industrial leaders, but the Labour Party in office maintained solid support for a Prime Minister who was widely disapproved of, despite strong private opposition within its ranks to his war policy. On the other hand, the authority of the Prime Minister was ultimately weakened by the revolt of Labour Members of Parliament over his insistence on 90 days as the maximum for detention of terrorists without charge, indicating in this way the inherent strength of Parliament.

The Concept of Accountability
From the foregoing discussion, it would be very difficult to apply the concept of agency, implying representation and accountability, in considering representative government as democratic by reference to its expression as 'government with the people'. Indeed, the much-argued notion of the 'mandate', that assumes an agency relationship between the people, as principals, and elected representatives and Government, as agents for the people, is not sustainable. The only test of a mandate, if such mandate exists, occurs at very long intervals through general elections.

Public opinion polls that might show disagreement with government policies carry such weight as is willingly given to them by political leaders, such weight being mainly conditioned by prospect of forthcoming elections. Supported by a strong majority in Parliament, with time in hand before the next general elections, a government in office is effectively accountable to no one, and certainly not Parliament.

The concept of accountability as a duty to report and explain the objectives and results of government actions, such as would be the rule for other bodies such as corporate enterprises, is irrelevant to the need of exposing government behaviour to the Social Conscience. Unpopularity as an index of disapproval has little influence, most of the time, on a government in office.

However, the concept of accountability is susceptible to two interpretations that are relevant to the doctrine of accountability. The first refers to individual or group responsibility under law in respect of the harmful consequences of actions deemed to have been committed. These actions may be criminal offences and punishable as such or they may be infringements of the rights of others and give rise to damages or compensation for loss suffered as a result. For simplicity, we shall call this concept of accountability legal responsibility.

With respect to the executive function, governments in most countries are placed on the same footing as ordinary citizens with respect to full legal responsibility for wrongful or harmful acts. As a result of the legal fiction carried over from feudal times, the monarch in England remains as the fountain of justice and, for this reason cannot be cited in a court of law. It is for this reason that acts of government are conducted in the monarch's name. This preserves the impunity of the monarch and leaves those acting on the monarch's behalf fully legally responsible.[14] Hence, acting on behalf of the monarch in carrying out the adminis-trative responsibilities of government, the executive has a representative responsibility and is accountable for its actions in a court of law.

In some countries, the practice of national assemblies and of governments to legislate immunity for their members from prosecution for criminal offences committed during office, or even simply whilst in office, is a perversion of the rule of law. It gives criminals the freedom to commit crimes relying on the holding of public office, as a simple and incontestable defence and given blanket exemption from the rule of law.

The second interpretation of accountability is under international law. International agreements of many and diverse nature impose obligations on signatories to respect the terms and conditions of such agreements and are made enforceable by designated international bodies created for the purpose. This is one form of accountability that cannot be avoided. Many current international disputes are of this nature, for example, disputes between the EU and the USA with respect to tariffs and trade.

Accountability for heinous crimes carried out under the authority of a government has now been made the subject of penal procedures before an international tribunal. The Geneva Convention, the international convention relating to human rights, the European Court of Civil Rights and the International Criminal Court have their origin in the wish to stamp out heinous crimes committed by governments.

The Nuremberg tribunal that condemned the surviving political leaders of Nazi Germany to death by hanging or to life and

---

14 It is interesting to note that Government mail carried the symbolic description 'On Her Majesty's Service'.

long-term imprisonment for war crimes and crimes against humanity inaugurated a new chapter in international law.

The principle that no one is beyond the law has been recently restated with vigour by the prosecutor of the International Tribunal for War Crimes in The Hague. The immunity from prosecution for war crimes and crimes against humanity, as well as all forms of crimes, committed by the coalition forces that invaded Iraq, which was imposed on the puppet Iraqi administration that was installed, is an intolerable perversion of the rule of law.

The refusal of the USA to submit to the rule of law, as expressed in the Charter of the International Court of Justice, and the pretext of its non-applicability to war crimes and crime against humanity committed by US forces simply by reason of the refusal to be signatory to the Charter establishing such courts, should not be allowed to stand as a defence to the crimes alleged to have been committed.

It is inevitable that the time will come when the US Government and the British Government will be brought before the International Criminal Court and will have to answer for war crimes committed in Iraq, including the illegal invasion of that country. This will be a new departure in abolishing war as a political option for governments.

Adapting the biblical statement that 'the fear of the Lord is the beginning of wisdom' into 'the fear of the law is the beginning of wisdom' underlines the importance of the supremacy of the rule of law in implementing wisdom, which together with democracy, makes for the ideal form of State.

Conclusion
Ensuring and improving social cohesion is viewed as the first responsibility of government. This obligation determines that government policies and actions should reflect the Social Conscience and the expectations of the people. It requires a unity of agreement between the political leadership and all sections of society as to policy essentials, which should have the support of a broad consensus. The presence of a significant democratic deficit that fails to give effect to democracy, defined as 'government by the people, for the people and with the people' frustrates the effective participation of people in government and emasculates the functional role of citizenship. Lack of confidence in government, loss of trust in political leaders, corruption and abuse of office and

the practice of spinning when truth is needed in information provided to the public, have undermined democratic ideals that are at the heart of the Social Conscience. This awareness has prompted the call for greater transparency and improvements in government through the concepts of governance and accountability.

PART III

THE GREAT DEBATE

—9—

Authority and Freedom in a Caring Society

The discussion focuses on the notion of freedom as originating in authority. Freedom does exist, but is subject to the authority of moral values. The realisation of self, through the reality of freedom as identification with others in a humane society may be understood as the gateway to ultimate freedom.

THE CONTEXT WITHIN which it seems relevant to debate the nature of authority and freedom as co-existing realities, directs us to consider authority as being the source of freedom and freedom also as having its source in moral values. For freedom is delegated to individuals or social groups in accordance with an understanding that freedom may only be used justifiably in accordance with law, expressed either in terms of legislation or custom having the authority of socially accepted usage.

It has been argued that the social glue that acts to regulate relationships between individuals and social groups is derived from culture and that culture is the basis of identity and social cohesion. This does not explain the manner in which the notions of caring and sharing act on individuals or group relationships. Another postulate, derived from market theory and extended to the analysis of the sociology of individual and group behaviour, would suggest that market theory explains how social relationships are formed and motivated in what is argued to be a market society.[1]

The Meaning of Authority and Freedom
Authority and freedom have been and remain eternally twinned in the debate about society in all its forms, from the family unit to the larger unit that is the nation. Whatever situation brings the individual into a relationship with others, there arises the question of freedom that determines the existence as well as the quality of the

[1] Slater, D. and Tonkiss, F., *Market Society*, Cambridge: Polity Press, 2001.

relationship. In many cases, relationships with others, explicitly or implicitly, juxtapose the desire for freedom and the acceptance of the authority of another or others, as part of a contractual arrangement or a consensual accord. From simple obligations implied in a friendship to a marriage contract, to accepting a position, to undertaking a mission and to all relationships of whatever kind, individual freedom is in some sense traded against another advantage.

Perfect freedom, in the form of absolute individual rights, cannot exist as reality. Authority reflects the extent to which the rights of others are recognised as limits to individual freedom that have to be accepted. Thus, authority has its existence in law as a compromise that acts to bind individuals together in different forms of social relationships. Without authority, there is chaos: where there is chaos, there is no freedom since there are no rights that are recognised.

Whereas freedom is most often discussed as appertaining to the individual, it is also discussed in social terms and in that sense of being experienced collectively. Freedom of speech and freedom of assembly are examples of freedom that are experienced collectively. The market economy is founded on the freedom of association, through corporations established under the authority of specific laws. The latter determine the rights and obligations of members and officers in the context of activities having a commercial nature and profit-making objectives. Freedom may also be a matter of national independence, for example, when a nation enjoys freedom in the form of self-determination and is not subjected to the authority of another nation. It is evident that at that level, nations are only as free as circumstances allow and that national freedom is constrained by diplomatic relationships or international agreements of different sorts.

Freedom may also be seen as a matter of belief, or even of sentiment. Whether it has a justification *per se*, whether it is a reasonable claim, is a matter of rationality that does involve moral values. In any event, freedom as a social concept can be pleaded only as a concession from authority. To wrest freedom from unwilling authority destroys authority and leaves an impossible vacuum in its place.

It follows that freedom properly belongs to the realm of rationality, as does the notion of authority. The demand for freedom must be negotiated and justified in terms of the resulting good, that is, in terms of moral values. Authority also is justified whenever it acts for the common good. Hence, both freedom and authority have their essential justification in terms of moral values and are conjoined on that unique basis.

Nowhere has the debate about authority and freedom been more controversial in recent years than in the debate about family values. Long recognised by religious authorities, supported by law and realised in personal relationships between men and women, which are vital to the survival of the human species, the family as a social unit has appeared to some as a situation involving loss of freedom in the presence of unreasonable authority. The authority that religion and law entrusted to the husband, as *paterfamilias* and the undisputable authority that husbands have exercised over their wife and children in the traditional family, have provoked a demand for freedom by feminist groups, expressed as a demand for women's rights.

In truth, men possessed of their own natural authority have never questioned the authority attached to the status of their wife and their innate knowledge and talents in so many aspects of family and civil life. The role that women have played at the highest level of state testifies to the importance of their contribution to society. The rejection of the notion of authority and the demand for individual freedom is a process that threatens the fabric of society through permissiveness, which denies any form of discipline or constraint. The disaffection with religious authorities and conventional views of marriage as a legal institution reflects a demand for personal freedom that is not compatible with the objectives that are proper to marriage itself. Modification to the rights created under marriage, the concessionary rights created or demanded in favour of informal unions, weaken family values and limit the potential of a caring society undermined by the loss of authority within the family structure. Women claim the right to bring up children without fathers; children reject all forms of authority and permissiveness passes as freedom. The resulting social chaos presents society with problems to which solutions will have to be found.

The demand for freedom is also to be seen within the market economy. It is in the very nature of the market economy to require a large measure of freedom from authority, expressed in the doctrine of *laissez-faire*. In order to prevent abuse, to protect the rights of other participants in the market economy, such as employees, creditors and customers, States enact regulatory frameworks that place limits on what business corporations may do in the pursuit of business objectives. Such regulations also impose obligations on corporations, which are often viewed as restrictive of freedom and limiting profit opportunities. It has been a feature of recent years for business corporations to demand greater freedom in the form of deregulation and the withdrawal of the State from private sector activities. The market economy is accumulating moral criticisms as the result of the social consequences of its activities. There is a latent social crisis of authority versus corporate freedom, which bodes ill for the future of Western industrial society.

Finally, the need for transparency and accountability regarding the exercise of power at State level has become evident in recent years. There has been a tendency towards a form of despotism confined to a narrow group within the Cabinet that seeks to bypass or reduce the influence of Parliament.

In terms of Platonic ideals, the authority of the State secures the common good. This innate conviction has perpetuated itself through time and maintained the hopes of successive generations that the common good could be established only through the authority of the State. The State should act in the interest of the nation as a whole. Much of the historical experience has shown the opposite to be true. Despotic monarchs and totalitarian governments have followed one another in the oppression of the people and the enslavement of individuals to autocratic rule. It is the historical absence of individual freedom and the excessive abuse of authority that has made the demand for freedom such an obsessive objective in the popular mind.

The concessions made in favour of authority are considered as reducing freedom. As in all things, *prima facie* assumptions may be deceptive, for absolute freedom does not exist in a world of social relationships. Indeed, freedom may only exist when protected by authority. In this sense, authority may be a superior value. But, authority also has the power of destroying freedom, as Plato explained, by installing tyranny.

An intelligent discussion of authority and freedom must be open-ended with respect to the relative importance of these notions to social welfare and human happiness. The humane condition, that is a caring society, sees both freedom and authority as necessary twins joined in a mutuality of interest.

The Social Conscience and the Reality of Freedom
Concepts such as authority and freedom, as well as the beliefs that they inspire and the emotions that they arouse, combine in

forming judgements which are normative and qualitative. They result from the extension of reason to uphold the aim that good should be the outcome desired of all human activity.

'What is the Social Conscience?' is only the first of a series of questions that may be asked in the quest for the origin of good and the explanation of the humane desire to see the realisation of all its attributes. The first observation is that reason, that is rationality, is a process of thinking that constrains emotions and directs action. Dawkins[2] has postulated that there is in the psychology of human nature, a genetic cause and effect that explains instinctive behaviour, of which an emotive situational response would be characteristic. Hence, rationality in humane behaviour is a form of natural jurisprudence that instructs belief and alters a predisposition to an alternative response or reaction based solely on emotion.

A secondary observation that may be supposed is that rationality is a process of thinking in which logic is justified by reference to experience. For example, primitive man on seeing a bird enjoying the freedom of movement through flight, might well have had the desire to enjoy the same imagined freedom and attempted to copy the bird in the experience of flight. Greek mythology tells of Icarus's dreadful mishap, when he tried to fly. Leonardo da Vinci, on the other hand, anticipated the solution to the problem by studying the mechanics of flight based on wing movement. By the end of the 19th century, after failed attempts, man successfully managed to lift himself mechanically from the ground and within a few decades, he relied on air transport as the most useful way of travelling both short and long distances. The reliance on rationality to realise a most astonishing dream is fascinating and instructive for understanding the meaning and reality of freedom. How often have we not all had the experience of flight in our dreams and suddenly been awakened by the sensation of falling! Deep down in transmitted genetic memory, has *Homo sapiens* inherited an earlier stimulation to fly by emulating birds and kept in instinctive memory the failure to succeed in the sensation of falling? And finally, is the desire for freedom in all its manifestations so strong that man never ceased to dream of the freedom that flying inspires and that he applied rationality to the objective of overcoming the logical impossibility by inventing a surrogate to natural flight by mechanical flight?

2 Dawkins, R. *The Selfish Gene.*

In other words, freedom may be simply a meaning that exists in imagination. What inspires imagination is that miracle that occurred at some distant time when *Homo sapiens* became a rational animal and began to develop knowledge through experimentation and experience. Through developing tools and emulating naturally occurring phenomena, he was able to light a fire and enjoy its various uses in the preservation of life.

However, it is not sufficient that the meaning of freedom should exist only in imagination, it needs to be confirmed as a reality. Rationality requires that freedom should be justified and sought on the basis of reason. This leads into the third observation, that freedom is a concept that has its reality as a moral value. Once more, rationality integrates the concept of good as its driving argument. Seeking after good is the rationale of a caring society. A caring society based upon this moral principle identifies itself completely and naturally with rationality and does not really depend on other justification.

Thus, we are led into an understanding of the meaning and reality of freedom through the concept of 'good' as a moral justification. Why is the Social Conscience so strongly aware of what is conceived as good and so opposed to what it identifies as its contrary? Given that the Social Conscience is the strongest influence in rationality, directing reason towards establishing the difference between 'good' and 'bad' and influencing reasoned behaviour towards what is good, the Social Conscience becomes the supreme authority. This conclusion corresponds well with the concept of jurisprudence, which explains law as having its source in custom.

Finally, we arrive at the heart and soul of meaningful freedom as expressed in the Social Conscience. Given that rationality results from putting imagination to the test through experience to arrive at a reasoned conclusion, it follows that the distinction between good and bad in the Social Conscience is the outcome of experience. What is good conditions social improvement; what is bad is harmful to what is experienced as good. Good and bad are circumstantial consequences that do not have the characteristics of being absolute truth, for as consequences, they are susceptible to alteration. The concept of freedom, therefore, is vital to a caring society in that it is a strict and necessary condition for reforming behaviour towards social improvement.

The Social Conscience and Reality of Authority
The juxtaposition of authority and freedom reveals even more clearly the reality of freedom as existing subject to authority. Authority creates freedom, staunchly protects it and jealousy defends it. As the mother of freedom, authority intends that freedom should be applied to the good of society. It condemns the misuses of freedom, as well as all forms of conduct for which freedom has not been accorded. Authority creates a framework within which ordered freedom may be enjoyed and provides a set of rules within which freedom is defined and may be exercised as a collection of individual rights. Although authority is the source of freedom, that freedom is established through order, requiring discipline, justification in law and susceptibility of being enforced. For freedom to be enjoyed by all, the freedom of each individual must be limited so as not to infringe the equal right of everyone to enjoy freedom.

Generally speaking, freedom is considered as properly residing in individual duties. Although extendible to nations, such as the concept of free nations consisting of freedom loving people, freedom is essentially related to the manner in which life may be enjoyed by individuals. Since society is made up of individuals sharing life together, freedom is a social concept relating to individual freedom. It is completely opposed to anarchy, defined as the absolute right of any person to total freedom and is the denial of authority with respect to that right.

Authority may also be considered as the logic of reason with respect to freedom. Authority is a natural condition present wherever any form of society exists. This expands the notion of order, implying a social structure that defines individual rights in the context of a willingness to submit to the logic of its reason, which is the notion of discipline. Plato, Hobbes, Locke, Rousseau, Kant and Durkheim shared this sentiment, insisting particularly on the notions of authority, reason and order. Hence, it is not surprising to find that the concept of authority is implicit in all social relationships of whatever kind. Whether imposed by force, by absolute rulers or dictators or consensually agreed in democracies, authority determines the conditions under which individuals or groups of individuals relate to each other in the context of specified social structures, for example, national government, employment, marriage, sporting and social clubs, etc.

The popular attitude to authority is deeply conditioned by the particular meaning ascribed to it in each society. Common Law countries, such as the United Kingdom and the USA more readily accept authority, expressed in the law as a set of social rules. This may be explained by the manner in which the Common Law, which is the foundation of law in these countries, was created out of custom by the judges on assize representing the sovereign, as the authority. Hence, the law in these countries incorporates the moral values considered as necessary for the good of society. Far from contesting or disobeying the law, Anglo-Saxons respect the law, observe the rules that are prescribed and appeal to the protection of the law when necessary. It is interesting that, to this day, the sovereign in Great Britain is still, in terms of Constitutional Law, the the fountain of justice, confirming in this way the proposition, advanced earlier, that authority is the source of freedom.

Continental European countries, which have had a different historical experience, have a different popular attitude to authority as represented by the law. In England, the sovereign acknowledged the Common Law that was common to the people and also enshrined a measure of freedom in Magna Carta and later the Bill of Rights. The sovereign came to recognise Parliament as an assembly of the people, in which the House of Commons represented the interests of the common people and eventually was able to accept the transformation of an absolute monarchy into a constitutional monarchy. The English did not experience despotic authority in the same manner as did their French cousins.

Absolutism did not die with the French Revolution and in many ways remains alive in the manner in which the Republic wields authority. This authority is centralised in the presidency and in the manner in which laws are decreed. In sharp contrast with the English experience of authority and its relation to freedom, the French experience is the reverse, in that authority only concedes freedom and is jealous of it. This explains why it is considered that only authorised conduct is lawful and that which is not authorised is forbidden. This sentiment is expressed in a well-known French saying *tout ce qui est autorisé est permit: tout ce qui n'est pas authorisé est interdit* (all that is authorised is permitted, all that is not authorised in forbidden). Whereas the English have a comfortable relationship with the law, their French cousins finds themselves constantly on the defensive in all situations in which a legal rule is invoked. The law is used to define authorised conduct and as a result it is very extensive as well as very repressive. For example, under French law, personal visiting cards have to be in an authorised size. Such is not the case in England. It is a matter of both pride and good sense for each French citizen to maintain that he knows the law, since he is required to observe it. This leads to endless amusing situations where on a point of disagreement, each person will maintain that since he knows the law, the point is not worth discussing! The general uneasiness with respect to authority and the personal sense of freedom in France, which is the country that proclaimed as its motto, 'Liberty, Equality and Fraternity'. is summarised in another common French saying, *'le citoyen est un repris de justice en liberté provisoire'* (the citizen is a convicted felon on parole).

Such is the difference in the relationship of authority to freedom in Continental Europe and so profound are the consequences of this relationship on the Social Conscience, that it behoves well for citizens of Common Law countries to be aware and consider how foreign are other countries with regard to their personal and unique sense and experience of law, authority and freedom.

Authority and Freedom under Law
Authority is the source of freedom. The exercise of authority and the enjoyment of freedom are both constrained and regulated by law. The arbitrary exercise of authority by the sovereign power has been at the centre of the relationship between the sovereign and the people over a very long period. The process that brought the modern state from government by an absolute and hereditary monarch to an elected democratic government has been a continuing struggle between authority and freedom under law. The evolution of this struggle is marked by three outstanding legal landmarks, Magna Carta 1215, the Habeas Corpus Act 1679 and the Bill of Rights 1689, which remain as the very foundations of constitutional law in England and later, by adoption, in the Constitution of the United States of America of 1787.

At a time when the concern for freedom has come to dominate the Social Conscience, it is well to recall that the process through which authority granted freedom under law also imposed duties and obligations. In a caring society, those duties and obligations are as significant as the freedom or rights that are recognised under law. The relationship between authority and freedom is an ordered relationship that aims not at denying or limiting freedom, but is intended to result in improvements in the humane condition. Jurisprudence, defined as the science of law, belongs properly to moral philosophy by its constant reference to the vital question, 'What is right?' It is this search that explains the manner, or the *ratio decidendi*, by which judicial decisions are reached. First, the facts are elucidated with respect to truth, next the rules of law applicable to those facts are identified and provide the legal reasoning for the decision.

The rule of law that conditions the exercise of authority and the use of freedom is the hallmark of democracy. It acts in three distinct ways:

(a) to regulate the exercise of authority and the use of freedom as regards the relationship between the State and the citizen. The landmark legislation referred to above deals with this relationship. Subsequently, further laws were developed to deal with a variety of situations involving the State and individual rights, for example, laws relating to treason, sedition, unlawful assemblies and recently the controversial rules relating to the detention of individuals under laws aimed at the prevention of terrorism;

(b) to regulate the use of freedom (or rather, the abuse of freedom) by individuals through behaviour, which is forbidden and proscribed by the State under its own authority. This is the field of Criminal Law. Murder, assault and battery, theft, bigamy, sedition, forgery etc. are acts that are expressly condemned in law as constituting offences against the State, which is the reason why the criminal prosecution for such offences is the sole prerogative of the State. Some criminal offences are also infringements of the freedom or rights of innocent parties, for example, a person whose property has been stolen by a thief, or an individual who has been physically harmed as the result of an assault. In these cases, the State has the right of precedence in prosecuting offences under the Criminal Law and thereafter an individual may sue under Civil Law for damages suffered. However, it is illegal under English law for a member of the family of a murdered person to kill the murderer in reprisal.[3] Lawful killing, through the administration of a death sentence pronounced by a court having jurisdiction in such matters, is a punishment that has now been abandoned in many countries. However, there is much concern at the moment with the

---

3 The offer by the IRA to kill those of its members involved in the murder of a Catholic man in Belfast in 2005 was quite illegal and would have constituted murder.

practice of abortion and euthanasia, reflected in the debates on the right to life and the right of individuals to end the life of their unborn child or their freedom to end their own life;

(c) to regulate the use of the freedom or rights that individuals enjoy as individuals and having regard to rights enjoyed by other individuals. The law administered in the civil courts dealing with the Law of Contract, the Law of Property, Company Law, Insurance Law, Banking Law, Matrimonial Law originated in the Common Law and has been considerably extended by legislation, as the need for new laws appeared. Much of it has now been codified in statutes, for example the Law of Property 1925. In each case, the law itself is defined in terms of the rights, the duties and the obligations which apply to the parties involved and also the liabilities or penalties that may be incurred for breaches that the parties may have committed, or rules that they may have failed to obey. Laws dealing with civil matters strongly reflect the ideals of a caring society, not only in its concern for the rights of individuals and their freedom to exercise their legal rights, but also in the context of the duty of care towards the other parties involved and the respect for their legal rights. This duty of care exists whenever the parties may suffer loss or damage as the consequence of the failure of one or other of the parties to exercise care. This failure may be in the form of a wrongdoing, negligence in doing or an omission to do, as a result of which a party is exposed to loss or damage. For example, under the law of contract, the failure to disclose or the act of falsifying or misrepresenting information that is vital to the contract itself, may render the contract void giving the injured party the right to claim damages. Offering for sale a horse, described in the act of sale as being free from vice when in fact the horse has a dangerous temperament, would normally void the contract of sale.

The Law of Tort is an aspect of Civil Law which is particularly relevant to the concept of a caring society, for it provides clear definitions of circumstances under which a citizen is required to conform to a standard of behaviour with respect to others and has an obligation under civil law in that regard. The Law of Negligence has expanded considerably in the last fifty year in extending liability for negligence. Professional liability and third party liability are particular areas in which the Law of Tort has made significant contributions in rendering moral values effective under legal doctrine. The landmark case in this regard was the High Trees House case of 1947. Lord Justice Denning, the Master of the Rolls as he then was, ruled that, whenever a person relying on a statement made by another person, and in circumstances under which he might be expected to rely and upon which he did rely, and as a result of that reliance suffered financial loss, that person had a right to claim damages against the person making the statement. The judgement in the High Tree House case created a new and considerable area of legal duties and obligations with respect to the principle of care. For example, if a solicitor or an accountant or a banker, or any other professional person acting as such, gives negligent advice to a client, upon which the client relies and suffers loss, then that client has a claim in negligence against his advisor. Today, the rights of persons suffering any form of loss as the results of negligence in circumstances are extensive, whenever a duty of care is deemed to exist. Moreover, whenever a duty of care is stated in terms of a statute, for example under the Road Traffic Acts, under which a driver is expected to drive with reasonable care, the failure so to do will expose such a driver to Criminal Law penalties for what is defined as criminal negligence, which may result in imprisonment.

Freedom as Individual Rights
Given that freedom is delegated to individuals or groups of individuals that exist and co-exist within a structure determined by authority, for example, the sovereign authority at national level, it follows that freedom may usefully be discussed in terms of individual rights. The historical experience explains how such rights have been obtained in different nations, whether through an evolutionary process in which they were negotiated (for example, Magna Carta 1215 and the Bill of Rights 1689), or through a revolutionary accident in which the historical process is brutally interrupted through popular violence (as in the case of the French Revolution of 1789 and the Communist Revolution in Russia in 1917). Regardless of the manner in which these rights have been obtained, they exist under law at national level and in this sense, they are

correctly described as constitutional rights. The term constitutional itself defines them as existing under authority.

The set of individual rights that are classified as 'constitutional' in the foregoing sense, are those that generally are attributes of citizenship, namely the rules of law that are available to citizens. This is an ancient notion for law as a privilege of citizenship goes back to Roman times, when only Romans citizens as distinct from others, could claim the right of access to Roman courts of law. The rights to vote in elections, to reside in a country, to travel abroad under the protection of a passport, are constitutional rights in all countries. In countries having written constitutions, for example the USA, constitutional rights may be more specifically defined, for example the right to the 5th Amendment. This is the right of a person not to make a declaration in a court of law that may adversely affect him.

Constitutional rights, as defined above, which are not available to non-citizens, may be quite extensive. Non-citizens may be barred from entry under immigration laws, may be denied social benefits, may be denied the right to work, the right to own property, access to public education etc. Although citizens of another state and enjoying constitutional rights therein, such individuals may not similarly exercise those rights in the country in which they have been granted residence. For example, under the rules of Islam a man may have more than one wife, but, if he were to attempt to enjoy this right while residing in the USA or in the UK, he would be committing the criminal offence of bigamy. Freedom, expressed as individual rights, may be limited to the jurisdiction of particular states. They are not universal rights.

Freedom expressed as individual rights also bear obligations. In this sense, freedom as a right that is acquired under law is consensual as well as contractual. For example, a US citizen is obliged to pay income tax on worldwide income to the Internal Revenue Service, whether or not he is resident in the USA. If he is resident outside the USA and earns his income in the country of his residence of choice, he remains liable to US Income Tax on that foreign income. Hence, he is liable to double taxation on the same income – in the country of residence and in the country of citizenship. Likewise, a citizen under the obligation of military service cannot avoid that obligation by residing in another country. The concept of freedom does not preclude obligations or liabilities.

Individual Rights and Human Rights
Those freedoms that are discussed as constitutional rights available to citizens and not to others under state law, nonetheless may be basic rights. The concept of basic rights underlines the special characteristics of some essential freedoms, such as the freedom from arbitrary arrest and imprisonment. As freedom is indivisible, the freedom from arbitrary arrest and imprisonment has been abused by members of terrorist organisations, posing as freedom fighters, to cover activities of a criminal nature. In countries such as the USA and the United Kingdom, these basic rights exist as constitutional rights under such general laws as the Bill of Rights. They define the relationship with the sovereign authority in defined areas, such as the freedom from arbitrary arrest and the principle 'No taxation without representation.'

The recognition of the importance of basic rights that should be freely available without distinction of citizenship, race, colour or religion, is an expression of the universal insistence among people for equality of treatment under law without discrimination. As such, it reflects an international concern for better conditions for all and made explicit under international law. It is in this context that the term human rights is now used when referring to basic rights. The Universal Declaration of Human Right 1948 was followed in Europe by the European Convention for the Protection of Human Rights and Fundamental Freedom 1950, effective 1953, and the setting up of the European Court of Human Rights. They include the following:

Article 2: The right to life
Article 3: Prohibition of torture
Article 4: Prohibition of slavery and forced labour
Article 5: Liberty and security
Article 6: Right to a fair trial
Article 7: No punishment without legal process
Article 8: Respect for private and family life
Article 9: Freedom of thought, conscience and religion
Article 10: Freedom of expression
Article 11: Freedom of assembly and association
Article 12: Right to marry.

Succeeding protocols extended these rights to the protection of property, the right to education and the right to free elections.

The recognition of human rights, as defined above, is essential to a caring society concerned with the well-being of each and every member. They restate and widen the scope of basic principles to their international acceptance and, as such, provide the legal framework necessary for ensuring the interests of a caring society in an expanding market economy, which is assuming global proportions. In this sense also, the recognition of stated international human rights extends a protection against abuse and exploitation of less-developed people by international firms seeking commercial and cost advantages through practices that are illegal in developed countries.

Freedom as Consisting of Rights and Duties

From the foregoing, it is seen that freedom is constrained in a number of ways. It is constrained by law in the case of individual freedom, by the extent of the particular right that is granted under law, and in the manner in which that right may be exercised. For example, the right to participate in democratic elections is limited to those having that right, normally by being citizens through nationality and not to foreign nationals who are residents. Moreover, qualified voters are required to register as such in the constituency in which they are resident, residence being the primary qualification for voting in a constituency. Exceptions to these rules are citizens who are temporarily absent on a voting day and military personnel absent on service, both categories being entitled to claim the right to vote by post. The large number of people living as residents in a country, as immigrants, have no right to vote, but do have the duty to pay tax on income. In these cases, it is the right to work that has been granted and which carries the obligation to pay taxes. It should be noted that clandestine workers are liable to pay tax on income, even though they have no formal authorisation to work. Whereas most countries accept immigration under conditions, they are unwilling to extend citizen rights to immigrants, save under the strict conditions imposed through naturalisation procedures. Some countries are moving towards removing this form of discrimination, particularly as regards local elections.

Where law creates discrimination as between citizens and residents who are non-citizens with regard to legal rights, it is evident that such legal discrimination will act adversely on social cohesion by conferring a different legal status.

The right to freedom of expression has been acknowledged by

society at large as having a potential for harm. Activities and actions that threaten society, that are formally recognised by law as having that potential, are proscribed. In particular, those likely to disturb public peace, such as seditious statements at public meetings, meetings banned under Public Order Acts. Statements that are denials of truth are punished under the Defamation Acts, insofar as they are harmful to the good reputation of individuals or organisations. Recently, these forms of proscription have been extended to statements or behaviour that are susceptible or result in racial, sexual or religious discrimination. The foregoing restrictions on the freedom of expression are intended to protect and maintain moral values and therefore reflect the concerns of a caring society.

It is evident that where freedom is defined as a right, it imposes on others the duty to respect that right. The right to use the highway is a general freedom and no one is entitled to deny the use of that right by blocking its use in any way. The act of marrying or cohabiting with another person carries a duty of care, expressed as an obligation of maintenance. That obligation may crystallise in a formal court order of financial maintenance against one of the parties and in favour of the other party in the event of a rupture in the relationship.

The duties or obligations that arise from the exercise of freedom or rights may be classified into two categories. First, there are duties that are attached to particular rights, which may be towards the public at large, or they may be specific towards an individual or a group of individuals. The two examples given above illustrate this distinction. In terms of formal legal classifications, the failure to respect a duty owing to the public at large when exercising a general freedom, such as the use of the highway, is a criminal offence subject to prosecution in a court of Criminal Law. The failure to respect a duty owing to a particular individual in the context of a contractual obligation is considered as a personal claim for redress and/or damages to be claimed in a Court of Civil Law.

There are also duties or obligations towards both the public at large and to classes of individuals as well. A good example is product liability. An industrial enterprise, which exercises its freedom to manufacture and sell to the public at large any product, has a duty of care towards intended users of that product, defined both as involving a public liability as well as a civil responsibility. There are particular areas of activity in which product risk is high, for example, in the manufacture of pharmaceutical products that cause serious and unexpected harm from the intended use. There is a considerable concern about the responsibilities and the duties of care of industrial enterprises for the adverse effects on the environment of air, water and land pollution as well as the health effects of poisonous substances released as waste.

A commercial or service enterprise has similar duties and responsibilities. An audit firm that certifies the annual accounts of a publicly quoted company as representing a true and fair view of its financial position and financial result, which subsequently appears not to be the case, may be liable to criminal prosecution for the making of false statements, if they were known or suspected not to be true at the time they were made. Shareholders and investors acting on the information contained in such financial reports may also sue for damages in civil suits against the auditors.

Second, the general and specific duties of care that society imposes on all its members reflect an overriding principle that is central to a caring society. More difficult situations are those that involve a measure of personal risk in providing assistance, such as helping a person being attacked by a gang of knife-wielding youths, or a person being held at gunpoint by a bandit. The duty of care is a reasonable expectation in given circumstances. Society admires heroes. It recognises and rewards heroism, but does not expect it from its members.

The Authority of Custom and Freedom
In a general sense, custom may be defined as the habits or uses that are accepted and observed by mutual consent in society with respect to any particular circumstance. Custom defines accepted, and in that sense, expected behaviour. It does not have the force of law and its authority resides only in the Social Conscience.

Given that much of custom has been integrated into law, through precedent or through legislation, pleading custom at the present time is limited to a freedom purported to constitute a legal right in a particular circumstance. Such a custom is defined as a legal custom. It is created as a consequence of accepted and consented use over a determined period of time, after which it cannot be contested and appears as a customary right. Examples are the customary use of public or personal rights of way over property, or the customary use of public land for grazing cattle.

Beyond legal custom, much of social behaviour is subject to and justified by custom, which is basically the respect for tradition.

It is the influence of the past that is carried into the present. Its continuing influence has a significant resemblance to established law itself in that it consists of both rights and duties. The continued observance of particular customs reflects a majority support in society for recognised and hence approved conduct. The failure to observe custom has no enforceable consequences, but it impacts directly on business, professional and personal relationships in which custom, as *modus operandi*, has considerable and even determining influence. The observance of custom in this sense reflects both the respect for others and the desire to get along with others.

Custom, as an inheritance from the past that is accepted and continuously validated in daily observance, should be distinguished from fashion. Fashion, which is usually associated with personal adornment in the form of clothing for men, women and children, has the characteristic of constantly changing. However, in popular terms, it includes all ideas, art forms, ways of expression and manners of behaviour that are of recent origin and usually are in conflict with established custom. All realities or expressions that appear as fashion have the characteristic of being transient.

Both custom and fashion act to impose uniformity on behaviour and in that sense to constrain freedom. Authority expressed either as law that is formally stated, or as custom and fashion that may be described as the informal regulation of conduct, may both be considered as reflecting moral values. The major difference is in the manner by which their observance is enforced. The authority of custom and fashion is asserted discreetly and privately in the social disapproval and discrimination that attends those who insist on their right to be nonconformist. The penalties are subtle and varied and range from tolerated and amused acceptance of eccentricity to revulsion and social rejection.

Custom has much to do with the notion of not giving offence to others. Given that there are so many ways in which offence may be given and that the susceptibility to taking offence may vary as between individuals, the notion of reasonable behaviour dictates how relationships should be conducted. For an American to walk into a superior's office and interrupt a conversation without invitation would not be seen as offensive; for a French person to do likewise would be an unacceptable behaviour. For a Frenchman to respond to the call of nature on the public highway would offend no one: for an Englishman to do likewise would amount to indecent exposure constituting a criminal offence.

Accordingly, customs are uses that may be specific to different countries and civilisations as well as to different groups or classes within society. Social conventions, as manners, often take the form of social rituals, for example, shaking or kissing hands, bowing and even ritual hissing. They inhibit considerably the notion of personal freedom and are especially important in more traditional societies.

Social conventions or manners are transmitted through generations in informal ways and form part of the process of education. We referred earlier in Chapter 4 to Kant's declaration that 'a man is nothing more than what education has made him'. This is echoed in the statement that 'manners maketh man'. Indeed, the term educated person is often used to designate a well-mannered person. The argument in favour of including civics in the school curriculum is founded on the notion that education is also a matter of learning how to behave.

Authority and Freedom in a Market Economy

The relative significance of authority and freedom to a market economy may be argued to be almost inverse to that existing in a caring society. A market economy thrives on freedom and the absence of regulation. The market economy insists on free trade as the guarantee of its success. Freedom for the individual entrepreneur or enterprise is the right to carry on trade unimpeded by regulations of any kind. Hence, government interventionist policies in favour of a caring society will bring the State into conflict with a market economy. Moreover, any form of intervention that acts against the freedom of business to organise and manage factors of production, as the logic of profit and shareholder value insist, is also viewed as unwarrantable interference. The market economy staunchly argues for a reduced role for government, limited to those spheres of action which are agreed to be outside its competence, namely the administration of the State itself, justice and defence.

The empowerment of a caring society through government intervention significantly raises costs that are incorporated in final product and service costs. Profitability is adversely affected by social costs absorbed in labour costs, as well as other environmental costs that are reflected in structural costs. Last, but not least, a caring society is expensive to maintain and directly affects enterprise profits through taxes on business and corporate revenues that provide the financing required.

The market economy is also adversely affected by state intervention in the regulation of working and trading conditions. Factory legislation relating to physical working conditions, maximum working hours, paid holidays as well as the prohibition of price fixing arrangements and business monopolies are anathema to the profit objective. It is for these reasons that the market economy and the profit motive favour deregulation, where regulations exist.

In the pursuit of continuous profit improvement, enterprise will relocate activities that are most adversely affected by intervention to countries where such regulations do not exist. Illustrations of such policies are the registration of ships in countries such as Liberia, Panama, Malta and Cyprus, where shipping companies are not subject to regulation concerning working conditions or safety regulations. Sending ships to Bangladesh to be demolished by hand by cheap labour and even child labour in the most deplorable and dangerous conditions is a current practice among ship owners in Western industrial states.

The profit motive that drives business affronts the progress of civilisation and the improvement of living conditions. The removal of barriers to trade and especially to profit is another expression of the demand for freedom by the market economy. The creators of the European Common Market, and those who are the current standard-bearers of a European Union, are unable to hide from public opinion in the more advanced member States the negative effects that these developments will have on employment and on personal incomes, as business is transferred to lower cost zones

The market economy accepts custom with difficulty. Custom reflects the authority of the Social Conscience in all aspects of life and also with regard to the relations between a caring society and the market economy. Custom rejects injustice, particularly as regards the manner in which employees are sometimes treated, such as unfair dismissal, harassment and discrimination. The authority of custom is also made evident in the refusal of employees to accept the surrender of acquired rights with respect to working conditions, working hours, schedules and remuneration.

Thus, the demand for freedom seems to be a prior concern for business in a market economy. However, business is also dependent on authority to defend the freedom on which its existence depends. Authority protects patents, trademarks, designs and all forms of intellectual property on which profits and shareholder value depend. The authority of the law provides a framework of rules and a judiciary necessary to the enforcement of such rights as contractual rights and rights against third parties. Authority protects business from unlawful expropriation by foreign powers: it will also act on behalf of business in negotiating agreements with foreign nations.

Freedom and authority in a market economy require to be equitably balanced with respect to the benefits that they confer. Both the market economy and a caring society have mutual interests in capitalism and the economic advantages that it brings in its wake. The issues that provoke conflict are related to the manner in which profits are calculated and distributed.

Authority, Freedom, Tolerance and Political Correctness
Finally, it is necessary to mention tolerance in the context of freedom. Tolerance may take two distinct forms. The first is the formal recognition of freedom through the delegation of rights to individuals to enjoy freedom to act in a defined area, but still subject to the authority of laws. This is the principle of freedom under law. The second is the acceptance of behaviour, which forms part of the variety which is not within the law, but which is tolerated as being non-threatening to the authority of the law and eccentric in the sense of being very much outside the mainstream of conformity. This is a sentimental tolerance expressed in the notion of a free country. The saying that the English love an eccentric reflects that sentimental notion of individual freedom that is so much the vital sense of freedom that is peculiar to England. In both senses, tolerance is a concessionary freedom that exists under the authority of the law. It is that flexibility that is needed in a democracy that believes in freedom, but insists that tolerance is a necessary understanding of freedom. In the sense in which reason is a measured appreciation that is rational in defining the limits to understanding, then freedom is measured tolerance. Both authority and freedom are intolerant towards anarchy, since anarchy is destructive of authority and of freedom, as we have already discussed.

Tolerance represents that open space that is the essence of freedom. Whilst it is admitted in a limited manner by authority, which favours formal expression of rules, it belongs more appropriately to that part of the Social Conscience that is expressed in custom. Custom is a consensus that is authoritative as regards acceptable or expected conduct, but is much more flexible and tolerant than is the law in the enforcement of rules of conduct. Made up largely of traditions, it follows that custom may reflect historical viewpoints or values that may have lost their relevance or significance in changed circumstances. Time being the solvent in which all difficulties are resolved as solutions are ultimately perceived, custom is a melting pot in which traditions adapt to change.

Custom fosters inclusion, rather than exclusion, for it integrates various opinions in the Social Conscience as time goes on. Whilst accepting differences in identity, beliefs and habits imported through immigration, custom seeks to smooth out differences in an accepted conformity. Tolerance, in this sense, is two-edged. Since caring and respecting others is in the nature of a caring society, tolerance is the acceptance of differences and of their justification. On the other hand, since caring is a function of identity, if significant and enduring differences in identity persist and threaten social cohesion, this may well result in custom, as the Social Conscience of the host population, being a source of intolerance. Hence, tolerance also means bringing understanding to situations that are potentially conflicting and altering those situations by integration and the abandonment of customs that would otherwise be permanent causes of social conflict.

Intolerance is a denial of freedom. At national level, it is expressed in autocratic, despotic, absolutist and dictatorial forms of government. At an individual or social level, it is expressed in bigotry, which is the refusal to seek a consensus in the presence of conflicting viewpoints. Traditionally, intolerance is found in the inflexibility of opposing religious or political beliefs. Intolerance and bigotry may assume extreme forms. Extreme bigotry is the suppression of the freedom that is the right to hold other viewpoints. Its most violent forms have occurred in religious persecution, such as the persecution of the Cathars in France in the mid-13th century, the burning of Joan of Arc at the stake as a witch in Rouen in 1431, the persecution of Catholics in England in the 16th and 17th centuries, the horrors of the Spanish Inquisition during the same period, frequent pogroms over centuries against the Jews of Eastern Europe, as well as the holocaust in recent times. Bigotry is a persistent evil and a hydra-headed monster. It was prominent during the Prohibition Years and in the McCarthy period in the USA.

Even though the Social Conscience, which is shared by a majority of citizens, rejects bigotry and seeks the reasonable path of tolerance in all things, bigots are strongly committed to their beliefs and generally determined to impose these beliefs on others.

The significance of this intolerance is the persistent harassment of those who maintain alternative views.

Bigotry is constantly motivated by intolerance and seeks indefatigably to justify itself by capturing the moral high ground. Generally, bigots are very much a minority in society, but are tolerated by the majority, though viewed as persistent nuisances. Their views, being generally exceptional or extreme, are often in the form of carping criticism with regards to the Social Conscience and to custom, provoking an instinctive antagonism to what is seen as ridiculous.

The concept of political correctness is a recent development that had its origins in that section of the American population that historically has been its most bigoted. It has gained a foothold in England, through the resignation and vassalage of English culture and tradition to modern American trends. Political correctness attempts to gain a wider audience in the non-Anglo-Saxon world.

Political correctness begins with the plausible justification of the need for tolerance of others, which is completely in line with the Social Conscience. It seeks to establish its political justification and viability by finding in custom the logic of its argument. In effect, it attempts to limit freedom of expression by establishing conventions of political correctness under which statements or behaviour may be criticised.

By and large, political correctness is an obligation to respect others. To the extent to which this obligation is already naturally present in the Social Conscience, political correctness is a superfluous diversion in the political debate. It assumes different forms and often expresses itself as eccentric intolerance of all situations that it declares as morally offensive. By arrogantly assuming the moral high ground, it provides ammunition to anyone engaging in criticisms of custom. However, to the degree that political correctness re-emphasises and renews the need to respect others, it is a moral value that may be appreciated as such.

Conclusion
The effectiveness with which a caring society attains its social objectives requires the existence of a sovereign authority capable of realising those objectives. It may be argued that the role, purpose and duty of the sovereign authority is to act as trustee and agent of a caring society and it is in this sense that it has a mandate to govern.

Notions of what is right and what is good that are embodied as drivers in the Social Conscience of a caring society are given real and constructive authority in jurisprudence and in custom. The Social Conscience provides that unity of thought and action between a caring society and its sovereign authority. It embodies those shared moral values by which it justifies its existence. Hence, it is the influence of the Social Conscience as the soul of a caring society and as the embodiments of its moral values, as seen in its jurisprudence and custom, that acts as the ultimate authority in a caring society.

The Social Conscience is not an obstacle to freedom. Both freedom and authority exist, but both are made subject to law, thereby protecting a caring society from excessive authority in the form of despotism and tyranny and irresponsible freedom in the form of anarchy.

—10—
Conflict Resolution and Crime Control

For our purposes, there are three main types of conflicts that are the concern of a caring society. The first affects the individual, which may be seen as the conflict that impedes an individual from the full realisation of the self, which is the notion of the whole person. The individual, in this perspective and as such, is as important as the family itself. The second conflict is one that affects the family unit, with which individuals are identified and in which they have their closest and most valuable relationships. The third conflict is one that affects society as a whole and which may be discussed at the level of a nation, or at an international level. In a caring society, the resolution of conflicts is achieved through a sympathetic understanding of human needs and the awareness that it is in sharing that harmonious relationships are restored.

A caring society is a just society and expects that freedom will be exercised in a lawful manner. The rule of law is a strict and necessary condition of a caring society. Behaviour that denies and defies the rule of law is considered as a transgression of moral values and harmful to the well-being of society. In a caring society, criminal justice seeks to deal with the problem of unlawful behaviour that is unacceptable to the Social Conscience, through crime control.

THIS CHAPTER examines the nature of social conflict and crime control and their enduring nature in society. Social conflict *per se* is not necessarily wrong and inadmissible, when viewed as a process in which different views and convictions are distinguished and contrasted in a social context seeking to determine what is right as the basis for conflict resolution. However, where there is a general and unconditional understanding of what is wrong, and a determination in the Social Conscience that proscribes it, the debate moves from conflict resolution to crime control.

Conflict Resolution

The debate about freedom and authority is an ongoing discussion between individuals and throughout society, in which justification for freedom, as rights, and for behaviour under freedom, has to conform to the Social Conscience. It is through conflict resolution that this justification is established.

The Origin and Nature of Conflict
Freedom, expressed as rights, has two facets. They are general in their applicability and specific to individuals or groups. The difficulty that sometimes appears in reconciling universal rights and individual or group rights is sometimes referred to a judgement in which the 'public interest' is the point of reference. What is the public interest, who defines its meaning and who applies the judgement are all questions of great significance to the Social Conscience, particularly with respect to those who have control or attempt to gain control over public opinion.

The conflict to establish freedom as rights is wide ranging, covering all aspects of society. It begins with the demand for a particular right, as part of the process of obtaining that right, for example, the long campaign for women's rights as a series of demands ranging from the right to vote associated with the emancipation of women, to the right to abortion, which is a continuation of the women's liberation, or women's rights, movement.

The conflict regarding freedom also appears as one in which different groups claim rights that are incompatible. Thus, the right to life in the case of an unborn child is evidently contested by the mother's right to abortion. This conflict is creating an enormous schism in society that has as much to do with the nature of motherhood, as with a woman's right to separate motherhood from her personal being as an individual and to have the right of choice. The right of choice is the most fundamental personal freedom and it is difficult to deny. However, motherhood is the most important symbol of life and has always been promoted and defended by the public interest. There is universal agreement that all women should have the right to bear a child. This is recognised in the right to artificial insemination. The termination of pregnancy is the wilful termination of life that raises the question of justification. The Social Conscience has recognised its necessity in certain cases, and always when the mother's own life is threatened. Equally, the prevention of life, by the use of contraceptive methods, is generally unopposed, though it remains a core dogma in the Catholic Church. The Social Conscience is so strongly in favour of the principle of life and of the motherhood of woman, as its symbol, that the question has never been raised of the right of an individual woman to bear a child. In this regard, the right of the unborn child to have, as a mother, a person possessing all the talents for care and well-being for her child that nature has conferred only on women, is assumed as a natural condition in all cases. Yet, there is much evidence of the inability of some women to fully bear the responsibilities of motherhood for a variety of reasons, some that have to do with personality, some that are the result of illness, some that are the consequences of poverty or deprivation. It was Bertrand Russell who put his finger on this problem when explaining his longevity by reference to his careful selection of his parents! This great unspoken problem that raises the entire question of the morality of selection by bringing the action of nature under the influence of science, that has so marked the improvement in the human condition, carries such a potential for social conflict that its discussion is too contentious to contemplate. Clearly, genetic therapy, which opens the door to immense progress in medical knowledge, implies an interference with the forces of nature and pre-empting possible harmful effects, through removing genetic deficiencies.

The conflict regarding freedom resulting from the pursuit of incompatible goals is generally also an expression of freedom and cannot be penalised in that respect. However, there is a huge grey area in which the division between conflict in the sense given above and crime, as an objectionable act punishable in law, is not clear. There is a moral dilemma present in conflict resolution when a decision regarding what is right has to take into account an element of wrongdoing.

Conflict and Conflict Resolution
Conflicts are found at all levels of human activity and may be present wherever freedom as rights exists. They may range from simple differences of opinion to outright war. Conflicts are divisive and impair social relationships and should be considered as short-term episodes requiring solutions. If opposing viewpoints or positions are intractable, conflicts may endure and may not be susceptible to being resolved. Permanent and deep-rooted conflicts bar the way to peace within society and to the co-existence that

depends on social cohesion. There are many examples of the permanence of deep-rooted conflicts stemming from religious, cultural and racial differences that have made lasting social peace seemingly impossible of achievement. Memories of wars and violent conflict may also leave scars that never completely heal and resurface to revive antagonisms.

In all situations and in every case, conflicts have their origin in the conviction or sentiment that rights or freedom are being or have been denied or transgressed, or are being threatened. Hence, conflict resolution implies identifying the grievance, elucidating its consequences and removing the grievance by negotiating an agreed solution. The first step in identifying a grievance is establishing its reality. Thereafter, its justification may be examined and referred to the same legal rules or moral values as the conflict is referred. Only thereafter may the discussion of possible solutions be initiated.

Freedom and social progress may be born out of conflict and from battles that have been fought, often by individuals moved by a concern for others to fight what they have perceived and understood as injustices. The history of social progress is particularly marked by courage in standing out against those exercising the power of control over society. Such efforts are characterised by selflessness and often the sacrifice of self. Jesus Christ opposed the Roman and the Jewish authorities of his day, Wilberforce stood against slavery, Schweitzer gave his medicine to the poor, Gandhi opposed violence by non-violence as a doctrine, Mother Teresa shared the humility of poverty in caring for the excluded from society. The list of outstanding individuals, showing selfless concern for others, is a monument to greatness in tracing an exemplary path of obedience to the instinct of caring for others.

Grievances as root causes of conflict may be real or imagined. Generally, they are fired by emotions indicating sentimental demarcations between right and wrong. These commit the Social Conscience to resolving the issues involved by a coalescence of views about what is right. This process may provoke a rejection of established law or custom and rules that may themselves be the reason for conflict. It is the strength of the public emotion that is stirred by a sense of injustice that has resulted in social progress. This is true, for example, with respect to the rejection of child labour and the discriminatory treatment of women in work situations.

The eternal contrast between good and evil, generosity and selfishness, pride and shame results in unavoidable comparisons being made in discussion of grievances. Some conflicts are deliberately provoked by groups within society who have their own agendas. Grievances are invented and promoted by agitators, disseminated through media channels that rely on sensationalism to maintain audience attention and promote their interests. They surface at public meetings and in open disputes in which personal ambitions strongly motivate agitators, who present themselves as politicians, social reformers and committed do-gooders, whenever a cause is revealed which offers an occasion for self-promotion. They aim to create a power base for themselves through the influence that they are able to acquire within targeted audiences. They strive to become leaders of a public opinion that has been manipulated by misinformation in the form of spinning and downright lies, which are projected as self-evident truths. Generally, such individuals are outstanding verbal manipulators and have a gift for convincing their audience through the persuasive clarity of lies and deceptions, which are paraded as instant truths. Dismissing intelligence and knowledge as obstacles to their personal success, they harness support and magnify their influence over others by perversity, undermining in this way the moral value of democracy that underpins a caring society.

Imaginary grievances are often exploited by political parties and political activists for arousing a sense of grievance as a way of deflecting attention away from a genuine grievance which is difficult to solve. Equally, there are a number of causes that are born out of a will to impair cohesion and create divisiveness in society.

Conflict Resolution: Major Issues for a Caring Society
The previous chapters examined the major issues for a caring society under three distinct heads: social problems seen as problems of society, social problems seen in the context of the coexistence of a caring society in a market economy, and social problems attributable to the role and responsibility of the State in maintaining and adhering to the policy objectives of a caring society. The aim of empowering a caring society was discussed as motivating changes in behaviour within these three areas of concern.

In each of the foregoing, the action of a caring society is manifested in a sympathetic awareness of human needs. This leads to an understanding of the nature of conflicts as originating in situations where effective relationships do not exist and human needs are ignored. Conflict resolution implies addressing the problem of social cohesion and of recognising human needs in a social context.

According to Burton,[1] human needs theory asserts that conflict resolution cannot result from the imposition of a solution by one party, as would follow from a political process that has win-win objectives. In line with this view, conflict resolution has been defined as a comprehensive approach based on mutual problem-sharing, implying that deep-rooted sources of conflict are addressed, behaviour is changed so that it is no longer violent, attitudes no longer hostile and structures no longer exploitative. It has a general relevance to conflict resolution.

Family Values and the Resolution of Social Conflicts
The history of civilisation illustrates the importance of family values. They are central to religious teachings and to moral philosophy. They give meaning to life and within that meaning, they justify a purpose that is understandable and which reconciles emotion with intelligence.

The realisation of the self, the ability to express oneself and the possibility of realising one's talents are concepts that are associated with the notion of individual freedom. The realisation of self, as implied in the notion of the whole person, has a particular meaning in that its effects are seen in an individual's personality. However, as a unique experience limited to an individual's personality, it may be judged as sterile unless it is also expressed in a social sense. Individual freedom implies an extended range of freedoms that includes freedom of expression, freedom of choice, freedom of association and freedom of movement. These are legal concepts. The market economy offers another freedom that may be described as economic freedom, without which many would say that all other freedoms would be meaningless. This basic freedom is the ability to obtain the wherewithal to life, of keeping body and soul together

From the viewpoint of self, as well as from that of society as an organisational structure, two other notions oppose the concept of individual freedom. The first such notion refers to discipline, which implies a compelling force constraining freedom in two different ways, acting either by coercing or by repressing individual behaviour. Discipline may be self-discipline, through which an individual submits behaviour to the dictate of his conscience, which we have postulated as his embedded Social Conscience. In the absence of self-discipline, for example in unruly behaviour, discipline may be

---

1 See Burton, John W. (ed.), *Conflict: Human Needs Theory*, London: Macmillan Press, 1990.

imposed by society. Persuasion and punishment are alternative means of disciplining behaviour.

The second notion refers to order implying that behaviour may be organised or structured in accordance with objectives and procedures susceptible of ensuring the attainment of desired results. Both discipline and order aim to control behaviour. They assume that unconstrained freedom is not an absolute moral value and that the prevention of chaos that would result from uncontrolled freedom would be destructive of self and of society. As we have already seen, both Kant and Durkheim represent this line of thinking, with Durkheim insisting on the functionality of moral values for controlling behaviour

The need for discipline and order lies in the logic of reason that justifies and commends thought and action. Self-discipline is viewed as an important functional influence on personal behaviour in providing the instrument through which the individual is able to develop his personality and realise his talents. The criteria that are used in evaluating the whole person constitute a benchmark of embedded moral values. These criteria are seen in family as well as in educational values. Social order is the variant of self-discipline applicable to society as a whole. Hence, social order relies on the same instructed and embedded moral values as those applicable to the individual.

Looking at nature and the wonderful harmony that exists in creation, many would argue that discipline and order are necessary to harmony, which implicitly means the absence of conflicting factors. Nature in its perfect expression is conflict-free. Personality and social organisations, such as the family, are social constructs. It is through the process of control that personal and social harmony is achievable. From the viewpoint of organisational theory, control is essential not only to the realisation of objectives, but in ensuring that all forms of systems function as intended and that deviations appear as abnormality and may be corrected.

It follows that control is more than just defining parameters for constraining behaviour: its functional value lies in correcting deviations or variances from standards. From a social perspective, such standards may be taken as criteria of tolerance that we have defined as moral values.

Foucault[2] established an association between discipline and social

---

2 Foucault, M., *Discipline and Punish: The Birth of the Prison* (trans. Sheridan, A.), London: Penguin Books, 1979.

control to develop a social theory in which a disciplinary society enforces control through punishment. Justifying this thesis through the history of violent corporal punishment applied to the body and later to mental punishment applied to the soul, Foucault presents a view of society as a prison in which discipline and punishment are handmaidens of social control. Foucault made a profound impression on current social theory, which is not limited to prison reform but to the use of punishment generally in enforcing obedience to rules of behaviour, however defined.

The Social Conscience now views punishment as undesirable as a corrective instrument. Discipline, as a result of its association with punishment, is questioned as a social value and contrasted with freedom, as the *desideratum* of prime importance.

In a general sense, it may be argued that the denial of discipline, as well as the reluctance to repress or coerce deviant behaviour has undermined authority in society. This sentiment is now becoming evident in the public concern over unruly behaviour, increasing public violence and the general disrespect for authority. The freedom movement, that has inspired an extended panoply of individual freedoms, together with rising living standards which have greatly enlarged economic freedom and fostered the phenomenon of consumerism, has created new forms of conflict.

Conflicts Within the Family Itself
The first concern of a caring society is with its children, their physical and emotional well-being and the possibility for them to fully develop their talents and eventually assume the responsibility of adulthood as parents and as citizens. There is unanimity throughout society with respect to the love and care that is the entitlement of each child. Accordingly, this generation of adults has made a considerable investment in the welfare and education of children.

Nature defines and determines the relationship of parents and offspring. The freedom of the young is constrained by the rules that are imposed by adults. These rules are intended to teach the young how to deal with the various problems that they will face as they grow to maturity. In this way, Nature transfers the experience of life from adult to offspring and the learning lessons that adults have made their own. Likewise, the role of adults is determined by natural instruction: male and female coexisting in the freedom of their being and in harmony with their natural instincts. Few people would see in Nature a prison that is conditioned by punishment and the nightmare of an inferno as imaged by Dante, which seemingly has influenced Foucault. Rather, optimism refutes pessimism, as light repels darkness. Looking to the good, most people wonder at the coexistence of freedom in harmony, for what is harmony but controlled existence!

Conflicts may arise within the family structure. Human needs theory has made an important contribution in identifying such conflicts in terms of the failure to take human needs into account, pointing to a sense of deprivation as explaining dysfunctional behaviour and the origins of family disputes. In this context, human needs may be defined as individual needs in a social group, in which individual members share common interests and a shared experience of life.

Many family conflicts have problems of self, that place the reconciliation with oneself as the beginning of a healing process. It has been said that loving oneself is a precondition to being able to love another person. Feeling unloved is a reactive emotional condition, in which an individual feels unappreciated and hence undervalued. It is the most common contentious statement that is made during family disputes. Adults and children are as easily hurt by the sense of being unloved. Husbands or wives blurt out in anger, 'You don't love me,' or, 'If you loved me, you would behave differently.' A child will say, 'Mummy doesn't love me.' It is clear that love is the basis of the family relationship and that, within families, the human need for love to be expressed in speech and action is the most urgent and constant need in daily experience.

By definition, family conflicts are conflicts of self interests that have two distinct origins. They originate from lack of affection towards others in the failure adequately to meet human needs and expectations in that regard. They originate also in perceptions that individual members develop, that may be justifiable or imagined. Personality problems are often due to lack of self-esteem that stem from an insecure emotional environment in which harm is inflicted on all members of the family. Correcting a vision of oneself as being inadequate by comparison to others and less worthy in consequence is an internal conflict that can only be resolved by an ample dose of self-love and a generous view of oneself.

Conflict between Generations: The Generation Gap
The generation gap is more than an age gap between young persons and an older generation consisting of parents and adults in general: it refers to a cultural difference in which interests, ideas,

tastes and even values are seen as differentiating the young as a separate and identifiable sub-culture within society. Identification is seen in conformity with popular forms of dress, behaviour, tastes, music. It is also seen in the rejection of the preferences, notions and cultural values that have been the life experience of parents and teachers, and in the standards of those institutions that have formalised them in rules of conduct and criteria of appreciation. The generation gap in that sense reflects the aspiration to freedom from parental control and the right to express their own identity that is a step of major importance in the passage to adulthood and self-realisation.

The generation gap is not a conflict inspired only by a new generation seeking its own freedom and newness of vision: it is also inspired by the protective instinct that has motivated parents towards children that cannot easily surrender to the inevitability of fundamental changes in the parent/child relationship

The generation gap is also expressed in the denigration of existing cultural forms and ideas that popular culture contradicts in many ways. This also is normal in the evolution of ideas. However, the generation gap may also express the rejection of conditions that young people deem intolerant and which their parents have been forced to accept. This form of generation gap is schismatic and threatens social cohesion. It is aggressively reactive and is described as the revolt of the young. There are many social trends and economic tendencies that augur a future fraught with difficulties and heighten insecurity.

Recent concern with children's rights has led to the development of a legal doctrine that has enlarged children's rights and placed them at the same level as those of adults, without the possibility of imposing the same obligations or responsibilities. It has created an environment in which children feel free to act with impunity. It has created a state of permissiveness and undermined the necessary authority of parents, of teachers and of police officers. Faced with the impossibility of imposing order and discipline within the family and society at large, adults have resigned from their duties and obligations towards children. Public authorities have tended to abdicate from the responsibility of safeguarding society from disorder and protecting adults from the incivilities of rampant juvenile offenders. However, there are now signs that adult society is unwilling to accept disruptive and unruly behaviour of children and adolescents, either at home, at school or on the streets and in several countries, restraining measures are being taken under the recent legislation against anti-social behaviour.

The resolution of the generational conflict between children and adolescents and adults at home and at school does involve questioning the legal environment that the freedom movement has created. In this respect, it is time that public authorities and the legal system intervened to redress the balance of rights and duties. It is also time for social reformers and educationalists to take a renewed interest in the lessons of past experience. Discipline is a strict and necessary condition to social progress and social harmony. Control is a strict and necessary requirement for effective discipline. Effective discipline is consensual: it recognises moral rules and limits the expression of inappropriate behaviour. Where persuasion, reason or love cannot achieve consensus as to appropriate behaviour, indiscipline invites alternative corrective measures. Behavioural disorders that have their origins in problems of personality should be treated as such, pure wickedness should be opposed by repressive measures, if necessary, as the lesser evil.

Gender Differences: Substantial or Engendered Conflicts
The love and the community of interests that male and female have shared traditionally and which find expression in the unity of family life, has been affected by the economic and social changes that have been the hallmarks of a successful market economy. In the context of family values, the women's rights movement has made much of the distinctiveness of male and female attributes and needs. In stressing gender preoccupations over a wide range of social issues, feminists have focused on gender differences for the purposes of identifying social areas, where women are exposed to discrimination and where their rights and human needs are inadequately recognised.

Burton's human needs theory is criticized by feminists for being gender neutral and thus ignoring specific female gender needs.[3] In seeming to give emphasis to differences between male and female characteristics and explicitly different human needs, gender theory has encouraged the belief that gender differences are at the root of many social issues that should be addressed urgently and should be understood as of worldwide importance.

The human condition of both women and men has been

---

3 For a full critique of Burton's Human Needs Theory from a feminist viewpoint, see Reimann, C., *All You Need is Love ... and What about Gender? Engendering Burton's Human Needs Theory*, University of Bradford, Department of Peace Studies, 2002.

improved considerably by the social and economic changes resulting from rising living standards, particularly since the end of World War II. However, globally the same trend has not been observed. Each society has its own vision of things and its own cultural specificity. These are visible in family life and in the different roles of male and female. What is fair or unfair must be judged in the context of a specific social and cultural environment. In this sense, the awareness of gender differences as a significant social factor in the form of gender conflicts is of relatively recent origin.

Nature has endowed gender differences between male and female as the needed complement for family life and for a society based on family values. It is the essence of a caring society that explains the family relationship as one in which the human needs of all its members are fully met. To declare that the human needs of men and women are different is not a cause for conflict, for the love that draws men and women together creates a permanent bond of mutual concern for each other's needs. It is the *summum bonum* of family life and it is what men and women expect from each other in the persistence of the desire to live together in shared happiness. This ambition may be rendered fragile by circumstances but it is not redundant in its relevance to human needs.

Social Fractures within Society
Social cohesion is present whenever tolerance, understanding and unity are found. A sense of national identity secures a high level of social cohesion. Nations are created through the process of integration that establishes a community having a clear sense of identity. The national character is one such recognisable identity. It is forged through time, expressed in traditions, culture and language. It lends substance to beliefs. It often explains positions and policies that are taken at national level. It follows that social fractures may be seen as events that subsequently appear and threaten an established sense of national identity. A humane approach to healing conflicts that have left their residual effects in bitterness relies on forgiveness through understanding, such as that used by the Truth and Reconciliation Commission in post-Apartheid South Africa.

Social fractures are damaging to national unity for they create divisions within society. They may be considered in different ways. In recent years, massive immigration into countries having clearly defined national characters based on a high level of identification in terms of race, language, history, culture and beliefs has resulted in the appearance of pluralist societies. This term is a politically convenient way of presenting a fundamental social fracture in the form of a society composed of several different identities. Pluralism creates social conflict through the presence within one nation of several identities that are in potential conflict. The problem of a pluralist society is finding a path to reconciliation between different sub-cultures having marked identity differences that could lead to open hostility and social disorder.

Another social fracture stems from the tendency for groups to regard themselves as distinct within an established social structure. It is seen in the notion of class distinctions. This phenomenon is widespread and is particularly significant in European and Asian countries, where history or religion has been influential in creating stratified societies. Old Europe, in particular, was socially stratified into three levels. The first level comprised ruling nobility that surrounded and supported a sovereign nobleman. Entry into this group was and remains through congenital descent, commonly referred to as blood. The second level, referred to as the middle classes or the bourgeois, also known as 'burghers', comprising merchants and professional groups that were and are the managers of the market economy. The third level, which Marx referred to as the proletariat, is the workers, those who depend on employment for their livelihood. They are often the least considered in society and the most in numbers. Among the proletariat are found those who are the most oppressed ... In India, the most oppressed are stigmatised as the 'untouchables'.

Yet another social fracture stems from the poverty gap. This distinction between the haves and the have-nots is worldwide and pernicious. It is found in all societies. Poverty may be created by oppression. Poverty results also from misfortune. The poor are identified as a social group and poverty as a condition of life. Its symbols are poor nutritional standards, poor housing, inadequate health care, lack of education. Oppression of the people into poverty leads to rebellion and to destruction. The despair of poverty is a breeding ground for depravity leading to crime, for many forms of crime are now attributable to an environment of poverty.

Seeing social conflicts at the national level as fractures in society underlines not only their true significance as deep and long-lasting divisions, but also their intractable nature. Class distinctions remain deeply embedded in modern society. In particular, wealth manifested in excessive consumption is symbolic of class distinctions, the rich and hyper-rich gilding their lifestyles in such a way as to incite envy and satisfy the need for public admiration. To become rich in today's society is the ultimate mark of success in the market economy.

Class distinction is a social fracture that is endemic and may never be resolved. Allied today with the market economy, luxurious spending is a feature of just one extreme class in a society that has formed a deep attachment to consumerism.

The poverty gap is a social fracture that is also endemic and long-lasting. It is a major policy concern for a caring society. It is difficult to imagine that the root causes of poverty could ever be eliminated or that the division between the haves and the have-nots could be suppressed: but it is totally realistic to commit society to alleviating the effects of poverty and reducing its extent. It may be less expensive to have to care for a minority than to have a huge welfare state that is costly to run, inefficient, creates welfare dependence and drags more and more people into its net.

The social fracture that pluralist societies present causes deep and widespread concern across the world. Conflict resolution in a pluralist society is generally discussed in terms of a need for distinct racial or religious groups to find common causes through conciliation and mediation within a national political framework relying on government policies and instruments of state. A comprehensive examination of conflict in pluralist societies conducted by the Bertlesmann Foundation[4] focused on the normative character of conflict in pluralist societies and on the presence of intermediary institutions able to mediate between different cultures. It may be supposed that the sense in which conflicts relate to central value systems, resolution of such conflicts, which are in effect conflicts of civilisations or cultures, are unlikely to be resolved through mediation towards acceptance of a common central value system. It cannot be expected that communities adhering to different religions will go beyond a simple and non-violent acknowledgement of their differences. Hence, it may be feared that the social fracture in pluralist societies is unlikely to be reconciled through conciliation, even if intermediary institutions are present in the process. However much it may be regretted, it is quite likely that a tendency towards segregation may be reinforced, with different communities

---

4 *The Limits of Social Cohesion: Conflict and Mediation in Pluralist Societies*, ed. Berger, P.L., Report of the Bertlesmann Foundation to the Club of Rome, Oxford: Westview Press, 1998.

located in different areas. This trend is already noticeable in certain areas of the United Kingdom, where immigrant groups concentrate according to religion or origin. Earlier immigrations in such countries as the USA showed the same pattern; for example, Poles tended to locate in Chicago and Detroit, Scandinavians in Minnesota and Wisconsin. However, this concentration did not produce conflict, but allowed different cultures to maintain themselves and to provide social cohesion through the preservation of identity.

Federal structures of government are attempts at coping with cultural diversity, as is shown in the case of Switzerland, Belgium and Canada. The desire for some measure of autonomy that recognises normative differences is seen in other countries where strong group identities exist, either on a racial or religious basis. Belgium is an interesting example of a country born out of a conflict between two communities, the Flemish and the Walloon; it was finally recognised as a separate state by the Treaty of London in 1839. The Flemish are cousins of the Dutch and speak Flemish, which is, as is Dutch, a Germanic language. The Walloon are cousins of the French and speak French. Both communities share the national capital Brussels. Conflict between the two communities is pronounced and violence is frequent. The antipathy between Flemish and Walloon has persisted ever since the country's creation.

In the United Kingdom, the Grand Rabbi of Britain and the Muslim Council of Britain represent the religious and community interests of the Jewish and Muslim populations. Whilst maintaining a traditional strategy of having influence over government policies, Jewish communities have never had formal community representation in Parliament and have focused their national ambition in the state of Israel, their Promised Land. Muslims have left their homeland when settling in the United Kingdom. For most Muslims, the homeland remains in Asia or North Africa. The possibility cannot be excluded that, should the regional concentration of Muslims transform original English communities into minority racial groups, the law of large numbers could create a demand for a Muslim state within a federal Britain. Such a deepening fracture would make inter-community conflict unavoidable. Antipathy between English and Muslim already exists and is exacerbated by a pronounced normative conflict. The association of Muslims with radical Islamic groups and the bombing outrages committed by English-born Muslims in July 2005 has increased tension between the two communities. It has led to the Government taking urgent steps to try to forestall a conflict situation that is likely to worsen with the radicalisation of Islam on a global basis. The devolution of governmental authority to separate regions, as is now the case for Scotland and Wales, would complete the transformation of the United Kingdom into a multiracial state with a federal structure.

Conflict Resolution at an International Level:
War Studies and Peace Studies
War has been permanently and deeply engrained in human experience and in the history of conflict. Indeed, the history of nations is very substantially a history of warfare between nations engaged in violent conflict aimed at the realisation of the personal ambitions of leaders. Many of the outstanding people who have stamped their name in the annals of history have been violent men and their success is recorded in the glorification of the destruction of their enemies. They mastered the art of warfare and saw the achievement of victory as the only way to the resolution of conflict. Peace as a long term objective never appeared as a permanent ambition, rather the permanent ambition was expressed as the maintenance of control over vassals and conquered nations. Alexander the Great, Genghis Khan, Charlemagne were followed by many others, whose memory have had lasting impacts, such as Napoleon and Hitler. Intellectuals brought their skills to fashion war theories, for example, Machiavelli[5] and von Clausewitz.[6]

War studies feature prominently in the ranking of necessary knowledge and all countries maintain institutions for the education and training of elites responsible for successfully carrying out government war policies, for example, St Cyr in France, West Point in the USA and Sandhurst in the United Kingdom. *A contrario*, peace studies are of relatively recent origin and appear to have been motivated by private interests and fringe groups, which manifested their opposition to war, following the disaffection with the concept

---

5 See Machiavelli, N. (1469-1527), *The Prince* (1513) and *The Art of War* (1520). Focusing on the importance of the skill of the individual leader in the success of the State, Machiavelli argued that achieving practical success was justified by any means, even at the expense of traditional moral values. The adjective 'machiavellian' has passed into common language to qualify the presence of ruthlessness, deception and cruelty as mental attitudes. In *The Art of War* he expounded a war theory for using military force.
6 See von Clausewitz, C. (1780-1831), *Vom Kriege (On War)* (1832), the classical text for the teaching of war studies in military academies throughout the world.

of war that invaded the Social Conscience with the end of the Second World War. The horrors of the Holocaust and of Hiroshima, the infamous use of indiscriminate chemical warfare in Vietnam and, above all, the retaliatory implication of nuclear warfare at last swung the pendulum against war and in favour of peace. Universities created Peace Departments, with Chairs in Peace Studies.

War studies were maintained, but peace studies took the centre stage of an international concern with the avoidance of armed conflict and the elimination of war by permanent international institutions, such as the United Nations that are committed to the maintenance of peace, through such procedures as those of the Security Council. The resolution of international conflicts of every sort, ranging from violent warfare to the use of sanctions in the form of trade embargos, as well as the extension of fundamental human rights to all citizens of the world, has been the focus of much of the attention given to conflict resolution.

Crime Control

A structured and meaningful discussion of the problem of criminal behaviour, which is relevant to the moral issues that are the concern of a caring society, raises a series of related problems, which should be clarified before policies and strategies for the control of crime may be considered.

Criminal Liability
Criminal liability is the strongest formal condemnation of behaviour considered as reprehensible by society and is punished by deprivation of the ordinary liberties of the offender. Restrictions on ordinary liberties are common features of most laws, for example, the amputation of a portion of one's income under tax laws. The distinguishing feature of criminal liability is the normative injunction expressed as 'ought not to do' or, more forcibly as 'thou shalt not'. Criminal liability, as a formal censure, has a special social significance and requires clear social justification.

The definition of criminal liability is often a matter of intent, legally defined as guilt. Whereas it is a principle of law in most cases that ignorance of the law is no excuse, the lack of intent, the absence of a mental ability to develop intent, as well as a legal incapacity to formulate an adequate quality of intent, are all factors that are taken into account when assessing guilt.

The determination of guilt, as full and undiminished responsibility in law for criminal behaviour, marks the beginning of one of the most controversial problems of our time, namely, how to deal with criminals when they have been found guilty. Hence, beyond the problems associated with the nature of crime and the social policy objectives involved in confronting criminal behaviour, there remains to deal with the manner in which the criminal should be treated. Punishment, vengeance, retribution, suppression, prevention and protection suggest different approaches to dealing with criminals. Foucault has made much of the historical importance attached to the body of the criminal as the object of punishment

Criminal liability may be considered under three headings: the range of offences, the scope of criminal liability and the conditions of criminal liability. The range of criminal liability is extensive and has increased considerably in recent years. It covers five types of criminal behaviour:

(a) violations of the person, that include all offences against the person, such as murder, wounding, sexual offences, certain public order offences, safety standards at work and public places, firearms and traffic offences;
(b) violations of general public interests, that include state security, public decency and tax offences;
(c) violations of the environment, that include pollution, health and purity standards and public nuisances;
(d) violations of property, that include wilful damage, theft, unlawful entry, fraud and deception;
(e) violations of the regulatory framework, that include offences of a financial, industrial or business nature.

Whilst Criminal Law targets mostly seriously anti-social behaviour, there is liability to criminal prosecution for a large variety of acts that do not carry a substantial social stigma, for example, parking offences and dropping litter. There was a time when spitting was considered as a Continental habit that was particularly offensive to English custom and the command 'No Spitting' was signposted in most public spaces. This made it perfectly clear to foreigners that 'we English do not spit' and indicated a firm resolve to have that rule respected. Likewise, the custom in France for males to answer the calls of nature whenever felt and wherever given expression, is viewed in that country with understanding sympathy and is treated as inoffensive under French law. By contrast, English law is unbending and qualifies such behaviour as the serious sexual offence of indecent exposure and punishable accordingly.

In effect, criminal liability is often used as a means of controlling behaviour, without necessarily implying social condemnation. For this reason, as Simester and Sullivan[7] explain, 'there is no general dividing line between criminal and non-criminal conduct which corresponds to a distinction between immoral and moral conduct, or between seriously anti-social and other conduct.'

In general terms, a crime is infringement of a rule of law imposed by the State. As such, a crime is an offence against the State as distinct from an offence against the person affected by wrongdoing. By contrast, a wrongful act against a person is a civil offence. Some crimes are also civil wrongs, for example, a pedestrian who has been injured by a motorist found guilty of dangerous driving is also entitled to sue him in a civil court for damage suffered as a result.

A wrongful act against a person may be made the subject of criminal prosecution where it implies a public interest in prohibiting such acts. This is illustrated with regards to domestic violence, which generally occurs in the privacy of homes. As stated by Duff,[8]

> whatever else is unclear about the rights and wrongs of a domestic dispute ... violence should surely not be seen as a matter for negotiation or compromise. It should be condemned by the whole community as an unqualified wrong and this is done by defining and prosecuting it as a crime.

Criminal liability in the form of domestic violence, such as wife-beating that is more prevalent than one cares to admit, raises other social considerations, in particular the extent to which private lives should be brought within the scope of the law. Domestic violence expressed as persistent gross cruelty is one thing: a furious wife who strikes her husband with a rolling pin on his return from an excessively happy reunion with old friends is an example of domestic violence that is seen differently the next day. A habitual drunkard who has no other way of coping with alcohol than hitting his wife and children deserves to be severely punished. But in both

---

7 Simester, A. and Sullivan, R., *Criminal Law: Theory and Practice*, 2000.
8 Duff, R.A., *Punishment, Communication and Community*, 2001, p.62.

cases, a decision to prosecute by officers of the law will depend on the consent of the injured party.

Correcting children, as a response to violent and unacceptable behaviour, both at home and at school, has been made the subject of Criminal Law, if it involves physical or other treatment deemed as infringing children's rights legislation. Whether replacing the authority of parents and teachers by the authority of the law has been a good thing is questionable, taking into account the current extent of juvenile anti-social behaviour that many ascribe to the inability of parents and teachers to discipline the young.

The reform of criminal liability has reflected changing views of morality and anti-social behaviour. Some aspects of homosexuality and of abortion, which were criminal offences prior to 1967, are no longer deemed as criminal, whereas the possession of indecent photographs and insider-trading are now criminal offences.

The appearance of new threats to society, such as international terrorism, criminal networks engaged in the trafficking of human beings and organised paedophile networks using the Web, not to mention illicit drug trafficking, has expanded the definition of criminal behaviour enormously.

Social Policy and Crime Control

The objective of crime control raises important matters of social policy. Historically, the punishment of crime has taken precedence over all other considerations. Punishment also responds to the emotional demand for vengeance by those upon whom a crime has been perpetrated. The cry, 'Let the punishment fit the crime,' or the Biblical dogma 'An eye for an eye, a tooth for a tooth', define that particular social expectation. Likewise, the notion of retribution in respect of a crime was also extended to the concept of compensation. The right of an injured person to compensation is as old as crime itself.

Retribution and compensation are two different notions: retribution is a returned act that, in some sense, reflects the crime itself, whereas compensation is an offering of amends. Foucault[9] has vividly described the ghastly extent to which the criminal Damiens, found guilty of patricide, made the *amende honorable*, or honourable amend, in 1757 before the main door of the Church of Paris, by exposing himself publicly to incredible torture that terminated in his body being pulled apart by four horses, and

---

9 Foucault, M., *Discipline and Punish: The Birth of the Prison*.

eventually by six horses, as four horses were insufficient for the purpose.

Another important aspect of social policy with respect to crime control is the notion of suppression of criminal behaviour. Here again, two notions are involved: that of suppression, as distinct from repression. Suppression implies making criminal behaviour impossible: repression implies taking action to stifle crime. For example, the suppression of a rebellion or a mutiny against the authority of the State involves that degree of organised physical force sufficient to destroy the rebellious elements. By contrast, sedition, which is a less violent revolt against state authority, is repressed through laws that render seditious declarations and seditious meetings illegal.

The correction of criminals has long been considered as an important social policy objective and was realised through the concept of houses of correction, as prisons were once known. Correction, as our forbears understood the term, implied punishment through discipline. Houses of corrections were institutions of incarceration that applied a rigorous discipline. Rigorous discipline has remained in the public imagination as a value having a remedial potential and hence a remedial virtue. Houses of correction were Spartan establishments in which beneficial correction restored the criminal through corrected behaviour to moral health.

Correction also fitted conveniently with the dominant religious ethic that accepted sin as a rupture between God and man and preached reconciliation through the recognition of sin, as a prior condition to its correction. 'Go and sin no more,' reflected the command in which forgiveness and redemption are associated in a loving care that effaced the memory of crime. This is surely also the sentiment of a prison warden when seeing a released criminal leaving the prison, and the belief of the released convict that, having done his time, the crime is effaced by redemption. Correction implies that criminal behaviour may be brought under control through systematic procedures that have a redeeming intention. It reflects the belief that a released criminal may be fit to return to open society as a permanently reformed character. The success of prison policy is still measured in terms of the level of recidivism.

The prevention of crime is of relatively recent prominence in social policy. It may reflect the limited means available to deal with crime, as against such other objectives of state policy, notably the commitment of the sovereign's effort to the pursuit of war.

Although the existence of guardians of the peace, night watchmen and others concerned with protecting innocents against violence to body and property, is recorded in the annals of history, an organised attempt at crime prevention that targeted criminals is recent. From about 1750, for example, Bow Street Magistrates' Court in London established a uniformed band of runners, known as Bow Street Runners, to catch criminals. It was left to Robert Peel, as Home Secretary, to use this model of crime control in establishing the Metropolitan Police Force in 1829, since when a member of this force has been affectionately known as a bobby, in remembrance of Sir Robert Peel.[10]

Finally, whereas the protection of the innocent must be viewed as the most socially important objective of crime control, no satisfactory solution has been found that adequately meets this objective. Increasing criminality and violent behaviour have served to increase the sense of public insecurity, compounded with a sense of helplessness and resignation in the face of crime. This is exacerbated by the relative impunity of criminals with respect to the gravity of offences and the leniency that seems to characterise the attitude of authorities and the justice system towards particular classes of offenders, notably violent juveniles and adolescents. In this regard, it is not unusual to find adults, defined as persons over the age of 18 years and thereby possessed of full legal capacity and assumed intent, described as adolescents or young persons, although they are in their early and even middle twenties.

Compassion and Limits to the Tolerance of Crime
Criminal behaviour provokes two emotional responses that oppose each other and make difficult identifying the appropriate solution to the social problems commonly perceived as the main causal factors. Criminal behaviour is shocking and incomprehensible for two main and indisputable reasons. First, it is exceptional in nature among a population that is humane, peaceful, law abiding and in which the Social Conscience is a strong determinant of individual behaviour. Second, the visibility of criminal behaviour magnifies a threat against which there appears to be inadequate protection.

In essence, criminal behaviour is cowardly and often targets the weaker and more defenceless members of society, such as children, old and infirm people. Often too, the visibility of criminal behaviour

---

10 As Home Secretary from 1822 to 1830, Peel made significant reforms to the penal system, which included the repeal of more than 250 statutes and a big reduction in the number of offences that carried the death penalty.

is due to its concentration among the poorer members of society, where also the most defenceless are found in greater number. Historical reasons lend support to the belief that criminal behaviour through its apparent association with poverty has its roots in the social deprivation that is found in the poorer sections of the population. Unemployment, poor educational standards, poor housing and health conditions, broken homes and the range of social vices that are seen as attributable to hopelessness, such as drug addiction, drunkenness, prostitution and vagrancy. Condemned to live as rats and surviving by wit rather than work, criminals sometimes benefit from the sympathy of people who regard crime as an enforced alternative for surviving under conditions of poverty. The cruel punishment inflicted for theft that ranged from hanging and flogging to deportation, is echoed in the popular saying 'might as well be hanged for a sheep as for a lamb'. Notorious highwaymen, such as Dick Turpin whose house is still to be found in the village of Thaxted, not far from London, were viewed as popular heroes. The legend of Robin Hood is founded on his reputation for taking from the rich to give to the poor. In times not so long ago, the poor in the East End of London customarily survived from the casual theft of food and some other necessities of life, described as 'what fell off the back of a lorry'. So strong was the Social Conscience that these spoils were shared with the immediate community.

The tolerance of criminal behaviour is also reinforced by its punishment after the fact, when time has moderated anger and compassion has taken its place. On the day of judgement, crime in all its forms is seen as a failing and as a tragedy both for the criminal and for society. It is a loss of the potential for good that is recognised by the Social Conscience as the rightful heritage of all individuals. So strong is compassion on the day of judgement that forgiveness by the victim is often part of the reaction to crime that accompanies the judge's sentence.

The tolerance of criminal behaviour that is manifested by compassion results from the awareness of the fundamental goodness of human nature, which was the credo of the Enlightenment. This awareness attempts to distinguish the essential goodness of the individual from the reprehensible nature of his criminal behaviour and seeks to deal with them separately by restoring the individual on the one hand and exorcising his criminal behaviour on the other. In effect, there is no tolerance of criminal behaviour, even though there is compassion for the criminal. This is shown in the view of many that criminal behaviour is in the nature of a defect or illness for which a cure is never beyond the bounds of possibility. In effect, given that there is no tolerance of criminal behaviour as such, the need for its repression cannot be avoided. Herein lies the essential dilemma when dealing with crime control. It opens the mind to the contemplation of the possibility that compassion blurs and falsifies the reality of the problem, which is the very preservation of society and the integrity of the Social Conscience and its values.

Views and opinions dealing with the problems of crime control range from those who argue that crime is far more prevalent than is admitted by statistical evidence and insist on the need for severity in expunging its existence, to those who take a more casual view of the extent of criminal behaviour and are more open to methods for dealing with offenders. From whichever standpoint, the saying 'Let the punishment fit the crime' is essentially still the only relevant criterion to finding appropriate ways for dealing with criminal behaviour in an open-minded context. The rationalisation, through the rule of 'the lesser of two or more evils' as the better choice, is ineluctable. Taking an extreme example, locking up a persistent sexual offender in prison as against neutralising his deviant propensities through legalised castration poses such a choice. It offers a different form of restriction of freedom that criminal behaviour has rendered necessary. It is a freedom regained against a freedom lost. It is a matter of choice.

Law Enforcement: Wisdom and Political Courage

The Social Conscience delegates to government the obligation for maintaining social cohesion. Criminality is one of the most destructive threats to social cohesion and, if unchecked, will bring to nought all that previous generations have contributed to modern civilisation. Consequently, there is need for some measure of unanimity in popular support for government policies for dealing with criminal behaviour. It may be assumed that the quantum of courage that governments will display on any particular matter is a function of likely popular approval for any proposed policy.

Vacillating endlessly between the thunderous right and the shrieking left, governments give priority to political survival and tend to navigate according to wind and noise. They respond according to the direction of the wind and the volume of accompanying noise in dealing with tendentious issues. Rarely will political leaders stake their future on any issue. Yet, as Plato clearly indicated, courage is one of the most important virtues of government.

Much of existing law, as it affects criminal behaviour, is in the form of rules enacted as legislation. It results from government action that expresses policy which is often associated with political objectives. In a very broad sense, the objective purpose of legislation is to provide either a rule requiring or allowing a specified action or behaviour, or imposing a rule prohibiting a specified action or behaviour. Such legislation requires their observance and contains penalties for non-observance. The originating reason for any piece of legislation is to clarify what must or may be done and what is not permitted. Clearly, much of extant legislation reflects the will of successive governments with respect to social behaviour.

Public attitudes to law is often a matter of culture and nations are law-abiding in varying degrees. Law enforcement reflects culture in the manner and extent to which legal rules are seen as indicative of desired behaviour. Hence, policy with respect to law enforcement has to take cultural factors into consideration, if law enforcement is to be socially relevant. For example, in a country such as England where motorists generally are law-abiding and respectful of others, the rigorous enforcement of speed limits, by severely punishing the slightest excess speed, would certainly be dysfunctional in creating a negative attitude to law by motorists.

An important limit to law enforcement resides in the ability of policing authorities, whether as civil servants or as officers of the law, to obtain compliance with the many laws in force. Repressive or tyrannical governments divert considerable resources to law enforcement and spend much of the national income to that end. The percentage of the population engaged in police activities becomes a function of the degree of repression.

Wisdom in the selection and enforcement of law is a matter of taking a balanced view of where existing laws should be enforced, taking into account public policy concerns that reflect public opinion and optimising the use of police resources. Political courage is the will to face up to the need to deal with criminality that must be suppressed at all costs, where it represents serious and unacceptable threats to society. Wisdom and political courage are both needed in holding back those elements in society favouring stronger law enforcement, even at the cost of those civil liberties on which freedom is founded, as well as holding back those forces that weigh the cost of law enforcement solely in terms of loss of civil liberties.

Much of petty criminality is banal. Larceny, deceit, small-time organised crime, blue-collar crime and incidental violence reflect the eternal presence in society of a minority of misfits and, in some instances, the culture of sub-groups that have always opposed authority. The errors of youth often mark the passage of adolescence – stealing apples, throwing a stone at a lamppost, hurling abuse and other mild forms of uncivilised behaviour – are treated generally with relative clemency by magistrates who have seen it all before. However, a passage before the courts does leave a stain in the form of a police record that can carry social consequences. The aim of criminal justice should be to grant maximum freedom (balanced by duties) to law-abiding citizens. Breaches of the law should be punished by varying degrees of loss of freedom, the degree depending on the severity of the breach.

Up to now, England has been extremely wise in treating mild criminality. The practice in some European countries is to open a criminal offences file for each individual at the moment of birth. In France, it is known as a *casier judiciaire* (criminal record). A person who has never committed an offence will be asked to produce his *casier judiciaire* in certain circumstances, for example, when applying for a job. The *casier judiciaire* is a formal state document and is issued upon request. A person without a criminal record will receive a copy of his *casier judiciaire* with the remark '*néant*', i.e. nil. If England were to adopt such practices, as a consequence of membership of the European Union, as the formal identity card and the criminal record certificate, it would diminish every English person who has had the experience of freedom.

Serious crimes pose different problems. Broadly speaking, serious crimes are all crimes that threaten society and citizens generally. The Social Conscience requires government to act forcefully and successfully in eradicating serious crimes. Dealing with serious crimes brings into considerations a number of issues, some of which are argued in mitigation of sentences. The traditional sentence for murder was the death sentence, reflecting the heinousness of the crime. Public sentiment in Europe has rejected the death sentence. It has been substituted by lengthy prison sentences that include life imprisonment. Underlying this reasoning is the need to protect society and to this end, to remove the murderer from its midst. In effect, the essential problem that serious crime poses is the protection of society. Few would consider the social redemption of the criminal as the immediate objective of sentencing. There are two forms of serious crimes that may be considered as the most menacing threats to society, namely criminal violence and drug abuse.

The Nature and Extent of Criminal Behaviour

Statistics show that the percentage of the population imprisoned for criminal behaviour in England and Wales is insignificant in relation to the total population. According to *Home Office Crime Statistics* for 2002, there were 137 persons in custody for every 100,000 members of the general population. It is the highest rate for European countries, possibly reflecting a historical tradition of severity in sentencing criminals. By comparison, the USA has 702 persons in custody for every 100,000 members of the general population, the highest rate in any country in the world. As the richest and most powerful nation in the world and in the forefront of the struggle for freedom and democracy, the USA suffers from the highest level of crime. According to statistical information for 2001, the prison population in the USA numbered 2.3 million inmates out of a total population of 296 million. In percentage terms, this is not quite 1% of the total population. Again, in percentage terms, this figure is more than 40% higher than anywhere else in the world. The general view of the USA is that of a country where violence is commonplace and where gratuitous violence is embedded in its culture. Hollywood has done much to promote such an unfavourable view. The Republic of China, which is known for the repressive nature of its political system and its disregard for human rights, has a prison population of only 1.5 million inmates out of a total population of 1.3 billion inhabitants, which is just over 0.1% of the total.

Statistical evidence for England and Wales shows that the volume of recorded crimes is much higher than the prison population, since imprisonment is considered as the severest form of punishment. Also, the extent of unrecorded crime is not known and could be quite high. The tendency is to adapt sentences to take account of the nature of the crime, any previous record, the character of the convicted person, mitigating circumstances and the usefulness of a particular form of sentence. Fines and suspended prison sentences, as well as community service orders, are used generally for all but the most serious offences. Home Office crime statistics for England and Wales are interesting as illustrating the nature of criminality in those countries.[11]

---

11 *Home Office Crime Statistics for England and Wales,* April 2003-March 2004.

All crime for England & Wales April 2003-March 2004
The total population was 52,570,245

All crimes	5,927,514
Burglary	818,597
Criminal damage (dwellings, other building, vehicles)	1,205,456
Drug offences	140,971
Fraud & forgery	317,130
Robbery	101,187
Sexual offences	51,143
Vehicle & other theft	2,263,990
Violence against the person	955,407
Other offences (including violent disorder offences)	73,633
	5,927,514

From the foregoing, vehicle theft represents the single most important form of criminality, accounting for 38% of all crimes. However, taking all forms of violent crime together (criminal damage, robbery, sexual offences and violence against the person) violence accounts for 41% of all crimes. Drug offences recorded as crime are quite low. However, as will be noted later, drugs are involved in many forms of crime, particularly theft and fraud.

Home Office Prison Statistics for England and Wales for 2002[12] show that the prison population totalled 70,860, an increase of 7% on the previous year, an increase of 16% compared to 1997 (5 years earlier) and 55% compared to 1992 (10 years earlier). This worrisome trend is accompanied by an increasing proportion of long sentences, rising from 42% in 1992 to 48% in 2002, with the proportion of drug offences and violent crimes increasing at above average rates.

The analysis of long-term trends over the ten years from 1992 to 2002 shows alarming increases for both male and female components of the prison population: the male sentenced prison population increasing by 57% in this period, with a threefold increase in drug offenders; the female sentenced prison population increasing by 184%, with a 453% increase for robbery and a 414% increase for drugs offences. The substantial increase in the male prison population were those persons sentenced for violence against the person, burglary, robbery and drugs offences. Drugs offences account for much of female criminality.

The conclusion that may be drawn from the foregoing statistical evidence is that criminal violence and drug offences are the two

---

12 *Home Office Prison Statistics for England and Wales*, 2002, CMD5996.

most serious threats to society, showing rapid rates of increase in both cases. The rigour of current law enforcement has increased substantially the prison population in respect of these offences, but does not appear to have been overly effective in bringing these types of crime under control.

Criminal Violence
Violence is endemic in society. It is, however, ephemeral in its manifestations. It is generally emotional and often provoked by anger. It tends to be reactive and spontaneous. It aims at hurting another or others. It is a denial of the instinct to care that is at the heart of the Social Conscience.

Violence may take different forms. It may be physical, it may be verbal and it may be psychological. It may be directed towards all forms of life, against property, against authority, institutions, other nations, as well as other faiths and cultures. Frequently, it assumes a sexual expression in which women are made the object of sexual abuse and sexual violence. Gang rape of adolescent females by juveniles of school age is one of the most horrifying consequences of the degradation of women for entertainment purposes.

Violence may be used as a strategy and planned as part of a premeditated act. It may be an integral part of an intention to instil fear and to terrorise others. In this sense, violence is used as a winning strategy.

Violence is regardless of the likely harm that may be inflicted on others. It cares not whether children or the innocents suffer. It places no limits on cruelty.

Violence is a culture in itself. It is the culture of war: establishing supremacy over others, seizing their goods, depriving them of their rights. It is justified by those who, having no moral values by which to reason, simply reason that the ends justify the means.

Violence is limitless as to its extent, for it grows upon itself. It recognises no law, but is a law unto itself.

Violence inspires awe and often also admiration. It is a way of behaving that is considered as most expressive in communicating messages or impressions. It is so much part of entertainment that violence is a recognised art form. It is part of music, theatre, painting and advertising. The film industry uses violence as one of its main forms of expression.

Violence may enter into sport. From pugilism to more physical group sports, such as rugby, play is transformed into violence when the rules of play are broken. The well-known Marquess of

Queensberry Rules define rules for boxing, making it a managed activity with strategies and objectives. Hunting, shooting, and fishing target other species, but rely on the same principles.

In effect, the civilising influence of Western culture that looks to moral values for creating a society worthy of human kind is now under the threat of generalised violence. Shockingly violent images brought into homes and before guileless children by television producers and inspired by the perverted minds of creative artists, writers and playwrights, whose vision of life corresponds more to Dante's *Inferno* than the happiness that should be the aim of life. Defined as art, it defines its own moral values and claims the absolute freedom of expression, which is so grossly abused.

The outward manifestation of the perversion that has been undermining society over many years, since censorship was abolished and unbridled freedom granted to all forms of expression, has heralded the victory of insanity over good sense. Violent children assault teachers in schools and anyone who happens to be in their way outside schools: young hooligans, without gainful employment or activity, hunt down fathers, mothers, children, old people, in gangs; and criminals let out of gaols by lenient authorities make the streets unsafe for all. Drunken crowds invade football stadiums, using a Saturday fixture as an occasion for fighting and wrecking. Meanwhile, on the football pitch, popular heroes show little respect for the rules of the game and resort to exchanging blows at the slightest pretext. Criminal violence is everywhere a present threat and no one is safe.

Accepting that all violence is criminal and that violence has so extensively permeated the social fabric, Government needs to show wisdom and political courage in setting limits to violence, to determine a strategy for subduing violence, to define priority objectives for legislation and to commit adequate resources to restoring order.

In many cases, violent behaviour shows up in the behaviour of individuals perpetrating such crimes as robbery with violence, common assault, domestic violence and violence at school. The inability of parents and school authorities to impose discipline on children and young adults is one of the major concerns today. A general climate of permissiveness, of violence and disrespect for others, the fear that undermines adults when dealing with aggressive and demanding children are all part of the problem. Child psychologists and moralists of every ilk have persuaded society at large that previous generations did not know how to bring up children and that discipline could not be other than an unforgivable constraint on the child's right to freedom of expression, necessitating the unquestioning acceptance of an infantile diktat. It will take political courage to see the wisdom of recognising that this type of progress leads only to a return to the jungle and to the collapse of order.[13] There is no other way but to restore parental authority and the teachers' authority in the classroom, by backing their judgement in all cases with sufficient legal authority. A recent step in this direction by stigmatising particularly obstreperous young adults and making them subject to Anti-Social Behaviour Orders[14] (ASBO) is a step in the right direction. However, ASBOs only apply to an individual whose behaviour affects one or more persons who are not in the same household as himself.

Gang and group violence is particularly rampant requiring a different treatment. The responsibility for dealing with these forms of insurrection rests with the police authorities. There is sufficient legislation, developed out of the experience of earlier generations, for dealing with the breakdown of law and order. Armed with adequate powers and backed by the courts, the police have been successful in dealing with gang violence, football hooliganism and binge drinking, showing that political courage and wisdom can be effective, when brought to bear on the treatment of criminal violence.

Drug Use and Abuse

Nature supplies in a bountiful manner all that mankind could possibly need for survival. Plant life is an ample source of food as well as having a proved usefulness for medicinal purposes – the earliest discoveries of the uses of plants for medicinal purposes belonged to those societies that existed at the dawn of civilisation. Chinese traditional medicine practised advanced forms of medical care using plants as well as other forms of treatment such as acupuncture, requiring a detailed and special knowledge of the functioning of the body itself. In fact, the Chinese first documented the use of cannabis as a medicine as far back as 2800 BC. Its use spread and by the 19th century, it was popular throughout Western Europe for pain relief and as a sedative. By this time, it was

---

13 Golding, W., *Lord of the Flies*, London: Faber & Faber, 1954, depicts with remarkable force and insight how children left to their devices gradually descend into savagery.
14 See Home Office, *A Guide to Anti-Social Behaviour Orders and Acceptable Behaviour Contracts*, November 2002. Anti-social behaviour is given a wide legal definition and covers any behaviour that is likely to cause harassment, alarm or distress. It includes graffiti, abusive language, excessive noise, fouling the street with litter, drunken behaviour and drug-dealing.

being used increasingly as an intoxicant and it was finally made illegal in the United Kingdom in 1928. Over recent years, cannabis has been under research for the relief of some of the symptoms of multiple sclerosis and the first pharmaceutical products based on cannabis could be approved for use in the future. Pharmaceutical companies are intensively researching the possible use of other plants to develop new drugs and Chinese traditional medicine continues to attract attention.

Along with the curative powers of drugs obtained from plants, plant derivatives have been used traditionally for the purpose of pleasure. Wine, beer, tobacco and various opiates, such as cocaine, opium and heroin, have been in common use for as long as can be remembered. From earliest times, many of these drugs were considered as pleasing in their use and harmless with respect to their effects. Under French fiscal law applying to alcohol, wine is not taxed as alcohol and no self-respecting French person will accept that wine is alcohol. Tobacco was considered by the Incas and early Indian civilisations as beneficial to long life. The opium dens in the Far East allowed people to enjoy a pipe, thereby inducing the hallucination of both peaceful and erotic pleasure. Opium smoking that had been brought into England from the East was considered as an unexceptional habit among the wealthy classes in the 19th century. According to Conan Doyle, Sherlock Holmes himself was not averse to the occasional 'pipe'. Visitors to the Sherlock Holmes public house, just off Northumberland Avenue in central London, will see an opium pipe among the different memorabilia associated with the late Sherlock Holmes.

Wine, beer, and other drugs have their effects magnified through the quantity absorbed. Those effects can go from simple exhilaration to death, through drug overdose or poisoning. It is only in recent times that the harmful effects arising out of abuse have also been identified as connected with the casual use of drugs. It is now an established fact that the health hazards of smoking are not limited to cancer; more significantly, it can damage the cardiovascular system. Tobacco is such a powerful poison that passive smoking is as noxious as smoking itself.

The harmful effects of drug abuse from such substances as tobacco and alcohol go beyond the damage to physical health to their effects on the mind and on behaviour. Herein lies the greatest threat from drug abuse: brain damage and its consequent behavioural effects. Furthermore, drugs are habit forming and lead to drug dependence. Once hooked on drugs, it is extremely difficult to shake off the habit and recover one's freedom.[15] An individual enslaved to drugs also becomes the slave of the dealer who controls supply and dictates his activities.

The dividing line between drug use and drug abuse is established in law. In England, the law categorises illicit drugs into three classes, A, B and C, according to their degree of harmfulness. Class A drugs, which include cocaine, crack, ecstasy, heroin and LSD are considered the most harmful. Class B drugs include amphetamines and Class C drugs include anabolic steroids, tranquilisers and cannabis (from January 2004).

In all cases, possession of drugs is illegal, but the law regards drug-dealing, including possession with intent to supply, as being a more serious offence than possession for personal use. This is reflected in sentencing policy. The penalties for dealing and supplying Class A, B and C drugs are life imprisonment for Class A and 14 years imprisonment respectively for Class B and C drug offences, whereas the penalties for possession are much lower, being 7 years imprisonment for possession of Class A drugs, 5 years for possession of Class B and 2 years for possession of Class C drugs. This distinction indicates an interpretation of government responsibility that places emphasis on the protection of the community and hesitates to interfere with individual freedom in imposing the same penalties for both possession and personal use. The presence of a strident rights lobby is an inhibiting factor to any government action that might be construed as imposing restrictions on individual freedom. This lobby has been arguing for years in favour of the de-penalisation of mild drugs and is responsible in large measure for the climate of general permissiveness existing today.

There are grave doubts about the wisdom of re-classifying cannabis from a Class B to a Class C drug. As a consequence of re-classification, penalties for first offenders have been reduced. For persons over 18 years of age, it results in a warning and confiscation; for persons under 18 years of age, there is usually arrest and warning. The downgrading of the offence, accompanied by greater leniency, has created an easier climate of relationship between the police and the drug community and saved on efforts of policing. Dealers are able to persuade children and young adults that cannabis is both legal and harmless. There is ample evidence

---

15 There is a curious exemption to this rule when morphine, which is a derivative of heroin, is used medicinally in the treatment of pain. It has been observed that, in such cases, the use of morphine does not lead to addiction, whereas heroin used for pleasure has a strong and immediate addictive effect.

that the use of cannabis is escalating among children and some are arriving at school in the morning already high on drugs and unable to learn. Cannabis is known to be a 'gateway drug' to Class A addiction and its adverse effects are being seen in increased mental illness, heart and respiratory damage and in various forms of cancers. The use of Class A drugs is also increasing as dealers reduce street prices. Dinner parties at which cocaine and cannabis are offered on the menu are commonplace.

There are other forms of drug addiction to which no reference is made in the above list, for example, the addictive use of aspirin, of tranquillisers routinely prescribed for anxiety problems such as Librium and Valium and sleeping pills. The use of drugs to improve performance in competitive sports also appears to be widespread. Routine testing for drug use by athletes in international competitions leads to disqualification and sometimes exclusion. It has not stopped the search for drugs that are capable of escaping detection. In this respect the medical teams involved in the supervision of training and performance improvement have a moral duty to prevent the use of drugs for this purpose.

Among the very poor, drinking methylated spirits is the last stage to total destruction. Glue-sniffing among some young people is also a terrifying threat to mental health and appears to be widely practised.

Prohibition and Tolerance
It is commonly accepted and there is no doubt that substance abuse is harmful to health. The disparity of treatment applied to users and dealers is intended to stamp out drug trading, which is extremely profitable and is operated by very powerful crime syndicates. The criminal proceeds from this business goes through a money laundering process through banking networks to be reinvested in 'clean' businesses.

There is a huge and concerted effort by authorities on a worldwide scale to attack the drug trade at the production level, by crop destruction; at the distribution level by closing down networks; at the management level, by arresting and imprisoning drug barons and at the financial level, by seizing funds from illegal drug operations. However, the suppression of the use of drugs does not show the same rigour, as may be judged by disparity in penalties.

The reluctance to prohibit the use of illicit drugs and enforce the law rigorously in that regard may be considered as paradoxical. There is little difference from a culpability viewpoint between a dealer accosting a client and a friend at a party sharing drugs with others, let alone those wealthy individuals who provide cocaine on tables for all to share. Moreover, social consumption of illicit drugs may be considered as a more significant way of expanding drug abuse. For these reasons, there is no logical or moral reason for imposing lesser penalties on users than on dealers.

The reluctance to stamp out drug use may be understood from the practical difficulties in achieving success in suppressing drug abuse at the entry point of consumption, because of widespread use. This also explains the recent declassification of cannabis use, whilst imposing prohibition on the supply side. The farcical nature of this change in the law, which has the effect of decriminalising use and saving costs on law enforcement, is evident to all. Why penalise supply, if use is authorised? Moreover, it has created a sense of outrage, for research evidence has indicated that cannabis is as dangerous to health as crack.

The reluctance to condemn the social use of drugs may also be the sympathy extended to those caught in the act. Going into rehabilitation is almost symbolic of a genuine effort towards redemption. Hence, it is laudable! So many celebrity figures and icons do it regularly. Hence, it is normal!

The paradoxical attitude of the authorities towards tobacco is worthy of comment. The health hazards associated with the use of tobacco are now so well known and documented in terms of social health costs that smoking is being banned in public places and in workplaces. The effects of passive smoking being as toxic as smoking itself, the smoker has been forbidden to poison his neighbour. Smoking in public places is forbidden and penalised. Tobacco is recognised as being addictive and creating dependence. It is probably as difficult to shake off the smoking habit as the dependence on cocaine. Moreover, it has been alleged that tobacco companies reinforce the addictive property of tobacco by adding further addictive substances during production.

The challenge to government is to set a limit to tolerance. This requires political courage. The responsibility of government is to act to protect society and to prohibit the propagation and use of harmful products. This also requires political courage. The decision point for government is when the moral case is the overriding consideration. Political courage was seen in the abolition of the slave trade by the English Government following the campaign that was led by Wilberforce and others in the later 18th and early 19th centuries. It was a difficult decision that needed political courage. The slave trade was vital to the expansion of the colonies and the development of business, for it supplied cheap labour that was the major source of energy. It was also the lifeblood of such English cities as Bristol, Liverpool and Birkenhead. Vast supplies of slaves were needed for the cotton fields of the Commonwealth of Virginia and for the sugar and tobacco plantations in the West Indies. Yet, the moral case was of such overriding consideration as to lead the English Government to proclaim the prohibition of slavery throughout the colonies. This was achieved in two stages beginning with the Abolition of the Slave Trading Act 1807, which was followed by the Abolition of Slavery Act 1833.

The production of tobacco is a similar case today: its prohibition is a hard financial decision, but an unavoidable moral commitment. Tobacco companies are huge businesses, making enormous profits. They make significant contributions to state budgets through corporate taxes. However, it is the tax on consumption of tobacco, in the form of the excise duty that is one of the most important sources of state income. Tobacco production and consumption both contribute to state revenues, whereas drug production and consumption do not have that merit. Nonetheless, if the total social costs of tobacco use, as seen in health care costs, shortened lives and invalidity, could be compiled, it is probable that total social costs are higher than the financial revenue derived by the State.

The prohibition of the use of tobacco is clearly a policy objective. At the moment, the only restriction imposed by law on tobacco companies is to indicate on their products that the consumption of their products is harmful to health. In line with this reasoning, they are forbidden to advertise tobacco products as such, but they are not prevented from advertising themselves, rather than their products, through the sponsoring of social activities, such as sporting venues and the arts.

Likewise, the suppression of drug abuse is the only possible policy objective, given that tolerance is not an option. Prohibition has failed in the objective of preventing the spread of drug abuse. But the havoc that drug abuse is creating throughout society requires determined action. Given that legislation and law enforcement are the only means available for dealing with a social problem that has reached crisis dimensions, what action is needed to attain the objective of eradicating drug abuse?

Malaysia features as the state that has been most successful in eradicating drug abuse by prohibition and the ruthless application of the penalties. Possession or intent to supply prohibited drugs, even in minute quantities, carries a mandatory death sentence. Numerous executions have taken place and have raised international protest, when the condemned persons have been of European extraction. English law imposes life imprisonment, which is a very severe sentence. But the death sentence is a particularly difficult matter. It has proved effective in Malaysia and, for that reason, might also be successful in England. However, it is hardly conceivable that the death sentence could be restored in England in view of the public sentiment against the death sentence, as well as the widespread consensual use of prohibited drugs. Yet, there are renewed calls for a mandatory death sentence for the murder of police officers acting in the course of duty. This indicates the high level of public support for the police force in dealing with criminality. The drug threat to society as a whole is at the same level of urgency. It consists of allowing drug dealers to bring young people into drug dependence and, as a consequence, destroy their lives as effectively as does the crime of murder. This parallel is recognised in those countries that have decided to impose the death sentence on dealers. It could be associated with the murder of police officers as totally unacceptable and punished accordingly by the severest of penalties.

The Extent of Drug Abuse in England and Wales
Drug-taking may begin at any stage of life, but is most common in the late teens or early twenties. Official information in England and Wales suggests that 3 in 5 of all schoolchildren would have been offered drugs and 2 in 5 have taken drugs by the time they leave school. A survey carried out by Channel 4 TV in 2003 confirmed that more than two thirds of teenagers smoked cannabis regularly.

According to the *British Crime Survey* 2002/2003, 4 million persons between the ages of 16 to 59 (12% of the population of England and Wales) had taken an illicit drug during the year; 1 million persons (3% of the population) had taken a Class A drug; 3 million persons (11% of the population) had used cannabis during the year. On a global basis, it is estimated that 200 million persons, or 5% of the world's population between the ages of 15-64, had used drugs during the year 2003/2004.

Another index of the extent of Class A drug abuse was a report in August 2005 by the BBC World Service that 99% of banknotes in circulation in London bore traces of cocaine.

Drug Abuse and Criminality
There is a strong correlation between drug abuse and criminality in all its aspects. The need to fund illegal drug habits in the United Kingdom was estimated to amount to £6.6 billion in 2001 and doubtless has since increased. Home Office figures put the number of households in that year at 21 million, from which it was deduced that the average wealth squandered to fund illegal drug habits in the United Kingdom ranged between £785-£1,050 per household.

It has been estimated that the main source of the £6.6 billion spent on illegal drugs in 2001 came from the proceeds of crime. The main crimes were illegal trading in stolen goods, theft by shoplifting, burglary, robbery or mugging, fraud and in particular fraudulent claims on the National Insurance Fund. Prostitution, blackmail and corruption were also found to be significantly drug related. A substantial proportion of the £6.6 billion referred to above was estimated to result from trading in stolen goods. It is thought that 80% of all thefts are drug-related and it is also estimated that there is a drug related crime in London every few minutes. The cost to society of drug related criminality is huge. The National Audit Office revealed that for the year 2002/2003, £2 billion was paid out on fraudulent social security claims; an estimated £500 million was lost in housing benefit fraud and £1 billion in social security overpayments.

Conclusion
The presence of social conflicts and criminality is destructive of social cohesion. Conflicts within society may emerge for a variety of reasons, some of which may be more difficult to resolve than others. Typically, where group identification is more powerful than national identity, by reason of differences of race or religion, the effort needed for conflict resolution will be much greater. Today, the generation gap represents an important differentiation in which different cultures appear to conflict. Criminality is also an expression of social conflict, where individuals or groups of individuals, do not accept the moral values that are the foundations of society. Two forms of criminality are particularly destructive, namely criminal violence and drug abuse. The point of no return seems to have been reached. Criminality has overwhelmed decent and law-abiding society. Burglar alarms, car security systems, CCTV cameras and paper shredders have become as necessary as kettles in kitchens. Security gates and neighbourhood watch have become

absolute necessities. Violent louts and drug addicts have usurped civil authority.

Fear and suspicions reign. It is the time for courage and the moment of decision for the vast and silent majority to act. It is high time for the rule of law to exorcise the fear of the criminal.

PART IV

GLOBAL TRENDS AND PERSPECTIVES

—11—

Towards the Future: The Dynamics of Change

This chapter brings together and interprets those problems of society most significant to the humane conditioning of happiness and well-being. Opposing the perceived contradictions between a caring society and the market economy, the moral values that characterise the family as a social unit, and which may be called family values, form the basis of social cohesion through the principles of caring and sharing. It was suggested that there are three areas where reform aimed at empowering a caring society should be given attention, namely education, the market economy and government.

The dynamics of change are identified and discussed as those elements which may be deemed to carry the greatest potential for change. For this reason, they warrant sincere, unbiased and dispassionate discussion, which charged emotion generally precludes. The Thinking Mind has the greatest potential for change, for its perceptions and understandings are in constant evolution. The market economy hurtling along at gathering pace, driven by the need constantly to re-create, destroys all in its path. Moral values are sacrificed at the altar of financial values. Opposing ideologies, genetic manipulation, disparities in access to economic resources and well-being, environmental protection, the need for world order and effective world justice are some of the many problems that face this generation.

THE ENTIRE DISCUSSION in this text has been directed to attempting an answer to the two questions postulated at the outset in the following form:

Can a caring society exist in a market economy?

Is a market economy sustainable that denies man's fundamental nature and needs for caring and for sharing?

These questions confront two different concepts of society; a caring society that is instinctive and founded on moral values and a market society that rationality has constructed. The justification for the concept of a society having a primarily social orientation is found in the instinct to care and the necessity to share that is an integral aspect of caring. These instinctive drives create, maintain and justify the social relationships that characterise humanity. The market economy has its justification in the efficient management of economic resources and the rationalisation of decisions in terms of profit-making.

Economic progress and improved material well-being have created social chaos consequent upon the destruction of those structures and institutions that had been fashioned to the needs of prior generations living under different conditions. A changing world has broken from the bonds of the past with the violent destruction of all that impeded its march to another vision and other ambitions. Marching under the banner of freedom and democracy, enlightened by science and guided by rationality, scientific knowledge has revealed the extensive possibility that intelligence can achieve in overcoming limits. Equally, the scientific management of economic resources through the market economy has transformed the human condition beyond recognition.

In the midst of all these miracles, when materialism has become the substance of the Promised Land, there persists another sense of being that reaches beyond the material. It insists in believing in moral values and the experience of life as shared happiness and well-being. This belief in another sense of existence is certainly based on sentiment and without doubt utopian. It has always been present in consciousness. It is the permanent hope to which humanity attaches its destiny.

The foregoing considerations have motivated the discussion that has been conducted in previous chapters. The expansion of the market economy on a global basis, its rules and its imperatives are not unconditional and are subject to acceptance. It is the Social Conscience that is the reference point for acceptability. The driver that justifies action in the market economy is shareholder value, which is an expression of the profit motive. That motive is exclusive, divisive and oppressive. This is unacceptable to the Social Conscience and there is much in public opinion to support that view. The market economy has yet to test the limits to its expansion. The resistance points are already manifest in the conflicts that are emerging where it meets different interests, cultures and beliefs. This chapter attempts an examination of the dynamics of change.

Consciousness and Existence
In a philosophical sense, discussion has been about consciousness examined in a social context as the Social Conscience and about existence, as a limited and distorted experience of living under

conditions that are dictated by a phenomenon described as the market economy.

Consciousness and existence are subjects of infinite significance and of unquestionable relevance to reflection. As the world becomes more complex and problems seemingly more intractable, the mind seeks a greater measure of understanding through an enlarged and more profound perception of existence.

The acknowledgement that consciousness and existence could be joined in a unity of thought, was expressed in a simple but startling declaration of immense profundity. Descartes[1] declared, 'I think, therefore I am.' In this logic, since thinking is the act of existence, consciousness acquires a further dimension for it acquires a meaning as an activity. Hence, consciousness, in the act of thinking, is not a passive awareness: it is the condition of mind that defines the state of existence. This provides a key to understanding Plato's classification of the two worlds, defined as the visible and physical world and the invisible world having its own specific realities. Plato's distinction of these two different realities was used to develop an understanding of the Social Conscience, based on moral values, applied to an existence constrained by the imperatives of a market economy, in which behaviour conflicts with those moral values.

Tawney[2] chose the subject heading *Religion and the Rise of Capitalism* to discuss the relationship, as he saw it, between religion that acted as a constraint on change and the new social force of capitalism, that was going to revolutionise the human condition through the market economy. He was not alone in this quest for understanding, as Marx and Schumpeter were equally concerned with the question. However, both Marx and Schumpeter were unhappy with the dominance of a sense of existence that was so much in conflict with the moral values that were embedded in consciousness.

Religion, that places existence in the invisible world, was unable to hold the high ground as an influence on behaviour in the face of materialism that found its justification in the new vision revealed by the Enlightenment. Religion could offer no resistance to science. Scientific knowledge, through wondrous inventions, established Man as a Creator. God, the Creator of the universe, who had given the Law to His People, was seen as redundant to the market

---

1 Descartes, R., *Le Discours sur la Méthode*.
2 Tawney, R.H., *Religion and the Rise of Capitalism*.

economy and unhelpful in promoting progress through successive scientific revolutions. Rationality, which spurred science towards perfectibility through materiality, also gave to science the exclusivity of reason and logic.

Science and theology remain substantially opposed and situate consciousness in distinctive senses of existence. Their conclusions are mutually incompatible. However, science and theology find common ground in that they are both concerned with the same and unique question, which may be referred to as the 'fundamental question'. The fundamental question is the root question for all activities of mind. It lies in the relationship between cause and effect that is summarised in the question 'Why?', in which cause and effect are understood as having and sharing an inseparable co-existence and co-dependence. It may be said that there is no reality that lies beyond the fundamental question, which defines the boundless nature and infinite dimensions of the mind's quest for understanding. The postulate that there can be no cause without effect and no effect without cause is the unique explanation or *raison d'être* of the reason 'why'. It places the reason 'why' as the initial point in the process of thinking. Thinking as a reality is inconceivable without that postulate. The question 'Why?' precedes and outranks all other questions, however formulated. In particular, it places the question 'How?' as a subsidiary question.

The question 'Why?' is fundamental to religion in establishing the relationship between God and his Creation as one of cause and effect. The invisible God is manifested in his Creation: cause and effect give substance and credibility to theology. All religious explanations are expressed as dogmas that establish the undeniable nature of life as resulting from the act of creation. Life is the effect of Creation, which is its cause. The question 'Why?' as perceived from a religious standpoint, has been espoused in much the same manner in science. Life is an effect that must have had a cause, which to this day remains speculative in the absence of proof, though current explanations of its physical nature, which is the sole concern of science, are more persuasive than earlier attempts. Whereas Darwin provided a persuasive explanation of the origins of man through a process of evolution, DNA has provided a functional explanation based on the harmony of genetic relationships that are the basis of life forms.

As science is driven by the logic of reason to identifying with certainty the original cause of life, rather than its effects, science and religion remain companions in speculation as to the concept of existence in an absolute sense. Religion is not subject to the necessity of proof and relies on faith as the needed evidence. Hebrews 11.1 proclaims that, '... faith is the substance of things hoped for, the evidence of things not seen'. It is reinforced through the cause/effect relationship in its justification through the affirmation that 'faith leads to understanding'.

More significantly than an apparent identification in the reality of existence through thinking, religion and science share in an intimate manner a common consciousness that is based on moral values. Shared moral values add credibility to both religion and science in relation to existence. As stated earlier, whether God created Man in His image and likeness, or whether Man needed to create God in his image and likeness, it is the divinity of moral values which, overriding all other considerations, finally determines the nature and purpose of the Social Conscience. From whichever viewpoint, the quite exceptional presence of moral values drives thinking to an ultimate explanation of life, through which both religion and science might reach consensus.

In this reasoning, there is considerable incompatibility between a caring society and the market economy as to commonly shared values. A caring society places moral values at the centre of importance in its reasoning and a concern for humanity as the objective of policy. It is the awareness of others that motivates action and the spirit of sharing that defines its identity. The market economy is driven by self-interest and the awareness of others is strictly conditioned to exploiting others to one's own advantage. The market economy is motivated by financial gain, but is obliged to heed those moral values that lend legality to its action in the observance of the rule of law. It is identified with an oligarchy of wealth, which is able to exert control over society to its own advantage. Accordingly, the market economy is extremely limited in its awareness of others and, driven by self-interest, is unable either to care for others or to admit the moral obligation of sharing in an equitable manner the undoubted material benefits that flow from its action.

The only condition under which a caring society may exist in a market economy is through the intervention of the rule of law exerting its influence in favour of social justice and, as the embodiment of the Social Conscience, acting by defining rights and duties in the broader context of a humane society.

The market economy is daily confronted by the Social Conscience through an unceasing questioning of its impact on society. Its influence on society is not entirely negative. It encourages individuals to assume the natural duty of taking responsibility for personal and family well-being. It commits social effort to creatively imagining ways of improving living conditions through scientific and technological innovation. Relying on the principles of industry, initiative and sacrifice, it shows the way forward out of misery into ever-improving living conditions. Embracing the idea of progress, it stimulates ambition and exerts a constant pressure on effort directed to achievement. However, the nature of greed, seen in wanting ever more, creates perpetual dissatisfaction. It is also part of the distinctive identity of the market economy, driven by the necessity for endless profitable growth through increasing demand-stimulated production. It has invented an exclusive justification for man's endeavour in the impossible dream of an endless expansion to consumption. The earth's resources are unable to sustain that dream, let alone feed its rapidly increasing population.

The sustainability of the market economy again must be conditioned by the Rule of Law which, recognising the moral value of freedom as the right of each individual to self-realisation, sees that right as having its true value and social purpose in relation to others. In this sense, the sustainability of the market economy resides in its social importance. The future of the market economy in its global dimension is, in fact, the future of Planet Earth. There is now a general consensus that it is the Rule of Law that stands as guardian over life on earth, in all its manifestations. This explains the justification perceived in the need for the creation of a world order, the authority of which is not the military might of the strongest nation, but the wisdom of recognised international law.

The Thinking Mind is on a Voyage of Endless Discovery
The consideration of the potential for change and the dynamics of change are matters of the intellect and of the influence of thought on action. The history of Man's voyage across time is one of endless discovery and of boundless changes inspired by the Thinking Mind.

Sometimes, casual observation of a physical fact has sufficed to bring about significant changes in his circumstances resulting from the discovery and subsequent acceptance of a law of nature or natural truth. This was the shared experience of Archimedes and Newton, both inseparable companions on that voyage in which time is merely a measure of distance; both sharing an eternal existence in the Thinking Mind that is a commonly owned public good.

Sometimes, the Thinking Mind releases itself from the observation of what is visible to the contemplation of what is invisible and projects itself into dreams and speculation. There is nothing substantial or insubstantial, visible or invisible, which constitutes boundaries to thought or barriers to imagination. In this sense, Plato and Einstein shared the same experience in creating reality out of the invisible and structuring into substance what their intellect perceived.

Often the Thinking Mind has been opposed by the rigidity of dogma and has been persecuted for claiming the right to freedom of thought and expression. Knowledge founded on observation often conflicts with imagination that sees another reality. The imagined possibility that the earth could be round, when visual observation confirmed with certainty that the earth was flat, was denied by all authorities until Columbus persuaded the King of Spain in 1492 to finance a sea journey that established the truth that the earth is round.

Sometimes, the Thinking Mind relies on experience to develop awareness. Occasionally, such prudence is warranted and acts as a safeguard against error. But prudence restricts the imagination, for risk is that step into the unknown which is encouraged by the possibility of discovery.

Kuhn argued that progress in knowledge results from a revolution in thinking, requiring a willingness to reject what is known in seeking the unknown. Heretical disbelief is most propitious to the Thinking Mind, but it generally leads to that peculiar solitude that exclusion inflicts. Its justification resides in that defiant and adventurous declaration: 'I think, therefore I am.'

Jesus of Nazareth shared with Mohamed, and with Isaiah and many other prophets, a conception of another existence and shared a vision of another world, unrestricted by time or physical being and subjected to the moral laws dictated by a supreme and unseen authority, whose diktat determines all conditions of life. This vision is also an aspect of the activity of the Thinking Mind. It defies the logic of existence, as derived from science, and the logic of reason, which determines our own enlightenment.

The greatest threat that the Thinking Mind poses to the established order based on accepted wisdom is its ability to formulate an alternative vision and to demonstrate its validity. This explains the strong resistance, which is provoked by the freedom of thought and expression, often stigmatised as sedition that justifies condemnation and suppression. The history of man is replete with instances of this form of persecution that has always accompanied progress.

The question 'Why?' applied to the fundamental question, which is the logic of the cause and effect relationship, can only be considered under conditions of unconstrained freedom of thought and expression, leaving the Thinking Mind to create its own world of consciousness and existence. Rationality, belief and imagination provide the required environment in which infinite variety is the kaleidoscope through which vision shapes understanding.

Rationality demands a process of reasoning in which the result is predictability as its exclusive quality. Given the same set of facts and the same circumstances, rationality creates knowledge in the form of tested experience. Its usefulness lies in the confidence that the stability of the experience will be confirmed in its repetition.

Belief also follows a process of reasoning, but is free from the restriction imposed by the requirement of predictability under conditions of repetition or replication. It leaves the relationship of cause and effect to faith, which is a state of relative conviction about predictability. Faith is as persuasive as rationality. If it is influence that is the operating criterion, then reason and belief are of equal force. In this view, therefore, the use of science and religion is simply a matter of evaluating that influence on behaviour which resides in rationality as against belief.

Imagination is the third way in which the Thinking Mind contemplates the relationship of cause and effect. It allows the Thinking Mind to construct a totally unrestricted view of that relationship, since all the conditions can be created. Freed from the limits of reason or belief, imagination is the way through all constraints on the mind. Imagination breaks all barriers to thinking, removes obstacles that result from experience or blockages that are due to belief. Imagination is the most creative activity of the Thinking Mind.

The Thinking Mind is able to traverse from the physical or visible to the invisible world using reason, belief and imagination as vehicles. Immortality in that sense becomes a conceptual reality and is as persuasive an influence as any other view of existence.

The Reality of the Social Conscience and its Influence
The Social Conscience is the most significant driver in the dynamic of change. It has its reality in the invisible world, its meaning in mind and its expression in action. It is a reflection of an awareness that is substantial only in terms of moral values. To attempt to discover the origin of that awareness is beyond rationality, for rationality is founded on justification and justification requires the complete understanding of a phenomenon. Rationality is the basis

of scientific thinking in which all the knowledge necessary to a particular understanding finds its usefulness in predictability and becomes scientific knowledge as a consequence. The quality of scientific predictability is no less than its certainty. Such is the quality required of good theory. Should that criterion not hold, the theory itself cannot be sustained and must be discarded.

The invisible world is beyond rationality, since there are no phenomena of that world susceptible to proof of existence and hence of scientific reality. For scientific reality is the only inference of existence in rationality.

The activities of mind may be exposed to rationality and that is a different proposition. The activities of mind that may be discussed in terms of rationality have been the subject of intensive scientific research in many areas, ranging from medical illness to the psychology of normal and abnormal behaviour, to the understanding of emotions and their impact on thinking, through to understanding how behaviour may be conditioned.

The mind is surprisingly free and no limits have been discovered to the range of the potential experiences that it can convert into a meaningful reality, provided that rationality is not imposed as a barrier to thought. Once freed from the constraint of rationality, imagination opens up a boundless world of invisible reality. Freed also from the strait-jacket that limits the vision of reality to its scientific proof, the need to justify or to prove no longer limits the mind's exploration of the invisible world. There are many recorded instances where rationality has been exposed to an alternative perception of an established scientific reality, leading to the reformulation of scientific knowledge. Kuhn used this phenomenon to explain the nature of scientific revolution through the necessary destruction of existing knowledge. Destruction theory is now firmly established in the idea of progress.

There is a real sense in which extant knowledge may stultify imagination and provide opposition to progress. Imagination is the only plausible pathway to revelation. There has been much speculation on the manner in which the mind itself speculates and constructs reality out of imagination. Berkeley suggested that the eye saw what it saw and communicated it to the mind and, in the process, what the eye saw became reality. In effect, the eye intervenes in the activity of mind in the way in which it formulates what it sees. But the eye is necessary to a perception of physical reality. It has no useful purpose in apprehending the invisible world. The expression 'I see' is the revelation of an understanding. It follows that disturbances in the functioning of the brain could provide not only a different vision in the Berkeleyan sense, but also a different understanding by way of a different revelation. The Museum of Art Brut in Lausanne, Switzerland, is devoted to extraordinary paintings by mentally ill artists, proving that mental illness itself, defined in accordance with criteria of scientific reality, is not an impediment to a different understanding and to a different revelation. Moreover, in the same way as the physical eye is irrelevant to understanding, and may be misleading of reality, so too mental normality and mental abnormality are not strictly necessary to revelation. This line of approach has been developed in recent years by testing alternative methods of reasoning. Rationality that found its expression in the scientific method relies on either induction or deduction to derive hypotheses from observations and submit them to the test of proof for validating the conclusion as theories. The linear method of reasoning was contested by de Bono for its exclusion of all other speculations that fell on either side of a linear path. By forcibly removing the linear barriers to thinking, he advocated the usefulness of 'lateral thinking' for developing alternative perceptions and expanding knowledge.

There exists a long tradition of inducing hallucinations and trances, in which the mind abandons the constraints of conditioned behaviour and seeks out a different state of experience that becomes a different existence. The mind that is lodged in an identified body is induced, through drugs or other emotions, to depart from its host body. Under hallucination, the mind voyages along totally unexplored paths and it is revelation that produces understanding. Under trance, the mind may lodge itself in another body. Speech may assume its expression in the voice of another person; the body itself may assume a different expression.

Visionaries and prophets are worshipped because the revelations to which they bear witness are beyond conventional understanding. By like token, heretics have been burnt at the stake for denying the conventional understanding of a reality belonging to the invisible world and offering a different revelation.

Beliefs and rationality may be seen as simply different forms of understanding. Beliefs are speculations about realities that may belong indifferently to the visible or the invisible world. They lack the credibility of proof. As far as the visible world is concerned, beliefs may or may not be rational: they may be transformed into knowledge and converted by rationality into scientific theory. As far as the invisible world is concerned, beliefs have their sole justification in their acceptability, for there are no paths that allow passage from the visible to the invisible world and vice-versa. The strength of beliefs lies in their persuasive ability. This effect is not necessarily innate to the belief itself and is more likely to be the influence of the authority of the person(s) expressing the belief. Where transformed into credo or dogma and accepted as such by groups of persons, they acquire the power of influencing both judgement and behaviour.

The Social Conscience is a unique phenomenon in that it transcends the limits of the visible world that are imposed by rationality, but does not have the objective of circumscribing life in the visible world to beliefs about the invisible world concerning fundamental existence. The Social Conscience does not oppose religious beliefs. It is multi-denominational and accords with religious teachings insofar as such teachings reflect the moral values upon which its own judgements are founded.

The Social Conscience is a daily presence that accompanies all activities of mind. Unlike rationality that places the search for truth as its unique driver, the Social Conscience seeks to establish what is right as the decision rule. The Social Conscience seeks what is right and attempts to achieve that objective as the desired condition. It has the humility to accept the possibility of failure, but it is marked by a persistent refusal to accept what it considers as 'not right'.

The influence of the Social Conscience resides in the support that it obtains through being a social phenomenon. It is a shared conscience in which all individuals are joined. It is the basis of social cohesion as well as being the rallying standard for identity. It does not belong to any one individual: it manifests itself only when it is shared. Its influence resides only in consensus. Its strength lies in the moral values that it claims as its own. It is the incontestable and compulsory nature of the social acceptance of these moral values that endows the Social Conscience with unique and permanent authority.

The mystery that surrounds the origin and the justification of the moral values that are enshrined in the Social Conscience are beyond comprehension. These are realities of the invisible world that transcend the rationality of egoism that sees life as a personal gift. As moral values cannot be encompassed in any tangible or rational manner, for they transcend dimensions of personality and of time, they are accepted as Absolute Realities. They are expressed as symbols: they belong to Divinity and are expressed in a

Trinity. They are Life, Truth and Love. These Absolute Realities enlighten the wondrous firmament in which mind allows imagination to expand awareness.

Reason and Religion[3]

Beliefs that oppose rationality in the rejection of both its methods and conclusions find their justification in faith. Faith becomes the evidence of things unseen and is used to develop theories with their own predictive content. Religious beliefs are founded on faith, for they assume that life is a continuing experience that knows no death and that physical death leads to resurrection into life. Accordingly, religion negates reason, as understood in rationality.

The Enlightenment provoked a historical schism that has not yet entirely arrived at its conclusion. The Enlightenment provided another view and the Age of Reason encouraged the quest for understanding that also brought into existence the Age of Tolerance. By contrast, the historical experience of religion had been characterised by intolerance and persecution. The fear of God and the threat of damnation and eternal punishment were instrumental for establishing order and maintaining the authority of the Church. The cohabitation of religion and science that followed upon the Enlightenment was conducted in a spirit of tolerance in which radicalism, as an option, was laid aside in the acceptance of speculation as to the reason 'why', both by theologians and scientists. Many theologians had the conviction that, ultimately, science would bring proof to faith.

In a historical sense, the Enlightenment may be viewed as a period that began some three centuries ago. It promoted the idea of freedom as a birthright that was individual and inseparable from personality. It considered freedom to be inalienable and rejected slavery. It rejected censure and proclaimed the right to freedom of thought and expression. It released the Thinking Mind from all constraints, but insisted on reason and tolerance as essential conditions to human happiness and well-being.

The Enlightenment progressively undermined religious beliefs by the corrosive effect of reason on their sustainability, leaving faith as their unique pillar. Faith, however, has a quality that reason does not possess and which religion proclaims, upholds and justifies. That quality is hope. The influence of hope, which lends

---

3 See Pope John Paul II, Encyclical, *Fides et Ratio (Faith and Reason)*, 14th September, 1998, for a masterly discussion of this subject.

conviction to religious beliefs, is far greater on the Thinking Mind than reason, which leaves no space or room for hope. Scientific knowledge only contains what is known and certain and leaves nothing further to add through hope.

The human need for hope lies at the root of religious fervour. Scientific progress has contributed much to the solution of many social problems, but the belief in the possibility of human omniscience is not provable or refutable According to Appleyard,[4] science is the faith, system, theory, methodology that sustains liberal democratic secularism. The faith on which science relies may be expressed as liberalism, democracy or progress. These faith concepts are embedded in the market economy. The market economy, as an endless process of destruction and re-creation, has itself re-created and reinforced the need for hope to sustain human fragility through the problems that it creates. In this sense, reason has re-created the need for religion.

Reason opens the door to the consideration of beliefs of every kind and makes their acceptability as beliefs a question of reasonableness. Hence, reason is not only a method of thinking that has rationality as its sole characteristic. It is rationality constrained by conformity to a recognised truth. Thus, it would be irrational to contemplate a belief that is manifestly false by reference to what has been attested by experience. Reasonableness goes further than rationality as a characteristic of behaviour or response to beliefs. It is an attitude of open-mindedness and tolerance in which freedom, justice, fairness are behavioural determinants. Reasonableness as a frame of mind does not feel threatened by beliefs and is not influenced in its conclusions by a sense of insecurity.

By contrast, religion consisting of dogma constructed on hope suffers from the insecurity that is the uncertainty attached to hope. Reasonableness is understood generally as a characteristic of individual behaviour. In terms of the theory of groupism, it may also be shared by several individuals, but it is not an exclusive condition to group participation. It requires neither faith nor conviction to guarantee its continuity of existence.

Since religious beliefs cannot depend on the exactitude of dogma, but only in the hope that they instil in individuals, the insecurity that is attached to hope is compensated by groupism as a necessary condition. The uncertainty that exists in the hope that

---

[4] See Appleyard, B., 'People in Glass Houses', *New Scientist*, 8th October, 2005, pp 50-1, for a very interesting discussion of fundamentalism in science.

lies in credo does not diminish the influence of hope to the extent to which hope is shared by groups of individuals of like persuasion. This phenomenon, known to zoologists as obligatory gregariousness, explains human behaviour as conditioned by the necessity to share, which we have defined as a basic instinct. The empathy for others, which drives people to share the experience of being in common, through a sympathetic awareness of others, is seen in obligatory gregariousness. According to de Waal[5]

> one of the greatest challenges of our time is to extend to others the empathy we feel for family and friends – to draw people of other countries or on other continents into our circle of reciprocity. There are plenty of clues in our primate ancestry as to how we might go about it.

The Collision with Fundamentalism

Fundamentalism has been present from time immemorial in religious beliefs. It is based on a literal interpretation of religious teachings or dogmas and a strict adherence to doctrines in daily life. Fundamentalism also developed as a rejection of mainstream religious doctrine, reflecting the spirit of nonconformism that marked the Protestant ethic. Often persecuted for their beliefs, such groups as the Plymouth Brethren and Baptists share the same commitment of fidelity to the literal interpretations of Biblical teachings.

Beliefs that seek an understanding of life based on creationism, venture fearlessly into fundamentalism in an effort to rally with the Absolute. Fundamentalism requires great courage and devotion in a resolve that dismisses the prudence that characterises the conclusions of rationality. Whereas, rationality will impose conditions on its conclusions, fundamentalism affirms without reservation.

Fundamentalists may also exist as communities sharing ways of life that conform to religious teachings. The Amish people, who settled in Ohio from Germany some two centuries ago, faithfully perpetuate to this day their original style of life and methods of work, refusing to adopt the new technologies that science has developed.

The uncompromising and hard-line positions that characterise fundamentalism may extend religious dogma to social and political standpoints. Moreover, in recent times, fundamentalism has led to the appearance of sects, holding extreme and tendentious beliefs

---

5 De Waal, Frans, 'The Emphatic Ape', *New Scientist*, 8th October, 2005, pp.52-4.

veering to fanaticism. Their faith endows them with extraordinary and fearless resolution.

In a special report on Fundamentalism, *New Scientist*[6] examines the rejection of reason, tolerance and freedom of thought by fundamentalists as a desire to turn the clock back to a golden age, when religion was untainted by secular influences. Nowhere is this tendency more evident than in the radicalisation of Islam and its growing opposition to Western traditions and values.

Religious radicalism, expressed as fundamentalism, may be arguably just an extreme point of intensity in the spectrum of religious conviction. It is not isolated to Islam. It is strongly present in the all branches of the Christian religion. Fundamental Christianity is a real force in American public life and has significant political influence through its close identification with ultra-conservatism. Consequently, it is a radical constituency within the Republican Party.

The radicalisation of Islam is a recent development, and its growing influence throughout the world appears to be attributable in large measure to widespread anti-Americanism. Fundamental Islamism and American imperialism are now locked in an intense conflict, which is immensely threatening to world peace and is likely to endure. The official declaration of the War on Terror marked the start of the Bush Presidency and followed upon the attack on 11th September, 2001 on the World Trade Centre. The subsequent invasions of Afghanistan and of Iraq, with threatened further military interventions looming over Iran and Syria, have polarised opposition to the USA across the world. It has destabilised the traditional alliance between Europe and the USA and has weakened the influence of the United Nations as a forum for maintaining world peace.

The unfolding tragedy of a conflict, in which religion and race seem to be implicated, has its flashpoint in the Middle East, where the resolution of the interminable Israeli-Palestinian conflict appears impossible. The implication of Zionism in the conflict has a significance that goes much beyond the creation of a homeland for the Jewish people. In its simple form, the objective of Zionism was met with the creation of the state of Israel in 1948. It fulfilled the promise to the Jewish people that was contained in the Balfour Declaration of 2nd November, 1917. This was contained in a letter of that date signed by Balfour, then Foreign Secretary on

---

6 'End of the Enlightenment', *New Scientist*, 8th October, 2005, pp.40-54.

behalf of the British Government and addressed to Lord Rothschild, supporting the creation of a Jewish state in the area known as Palestine. At that time, Britain held the mandate over the territory. The Balfour Declaration received the support of the USA and was recognised by Jews as a formal and unconditional promise. At the same time, the Arabs, who had supported Britain during the First World War in the campaign in Mesopotamia, believed that Palestine would be attributed to them as a reward for their loyalty. The creation of the state of Israel in 1948 was considered by the Arabs as a betrayal and that sentiment has been reinforced ever since in the failure to admit that Palestinian Arabs also have a right to their own state. The persistent refusal by Arab states to recognise the state of Israel led to several wars and the end of hostility did nothing to diminish mutual antagonism. Palestinian Arabs were dislodged, for the most part, from their homes and dispossessed of their lands and dispersed over neighbouring countries. Those that remained concentrated in the Gaza region and the West Bank area endured years of oppression. Resentment took the form of a violent insurgency known as the *intifada*.

Expressed in a fundamentalist form, Zionism associated with the wish to create a Greater Israel out of Arab land promised to Jews by God, is anathema to surrounding Arab nations, to whom that land has belonged for centuries and for whom Mohamed is the Prophet. The inclusion of Islamic and Christian holy shrines under the Israeli control of Jerusalem, denies the possibility of lasting peace. The influence of Zionist Christians in the USA, as well as the influential Jewish lobby, has made it impossible for succeeding administrations to act impartially in the resolution of the conflict. A further damaging effect is the identification of the vital interests of the USA with the state of Israel, seen in the belief among Arabs of the existence of an alliance that is against the Arab World in general and Islam in particular.

The fragility of the existence of the state of Israel, despite USA support and its overwhelming military superiority and alleged possession of weapons of mass destruction, whose use in the circumstances would be suicidal, is seen in its gradual withdrawal to within the confines of an area ultimately to be protected by a perimeter of defence in the form of a wall, the most primitive of defence strategies. Outside those walls, the enemy gathers its increasing force in the rapid expansion of a Palestinian population driven by desperation to a form of guerrilla warfare to which no effective response seems possible. The eventual forced withdrawal of the USA from Iraq may complete the isolation of the state of Israel. There is every reason for the world to view the Middle Eastern flashpoint with the greatest apprehension.

Genetic Manipulation and the Frankenstein Spectre
Scientific research has greatly expanded knowledge of the physiology of a whole spectrum of living creatures, including the human body in all its aspects, as well as detailed information explaining the mechanisms by which cells function and reproduce.

The discovery of the structure and purpose of DNA, in particular, has been revolutionary in the sense that it revealed how genes control life functions. It also led to an understanding of the natural mechanisms which produce variety in nature. In so doing, it offered a scientific basis for those practices of biological engineering that have been in common practice for centuries, that is, the deliberate selection of desirable or needed features to give variety, obvious examples being the breeding of dogs or horses for specific needs and the development of new varieties of plants. Applied biology in agriculture and farming have led to higher productivity, for example, selective breeding to give high yield grains and the conservation of useful genes such as those determining resistance to disease.

The study of cell functioning at the molecular level has had extensive influence in medicine and led to new and sophisticated forms of drug treatment for illnesses. The outcome of recent biotechnology, such as the genetic engineering of bacteria to produce drugs like human insulin, has been immensely valuable and few would question the ethics of the use of drugs produced in this way. However, the degree to which the genome of any species may be manipulated and yet remain within the boundaries of what is right is highly questionable. There is growing public concern about the possible detrimental and far reaching effects of genetic engineering. The interference with the natural boundaries between species stirs deep unease.

There is also fear of the unwelcome side effects of genetic engineering on the economy. Improved food yields have created huge farm surpluses, forced prices down and driven farmers from the land. Genetically modified seed production and the production of fertilisers have fallen under the control of large multinational corporations. To maintain their stranglehold on the farming sector, these corporations ensure the dependence of farmers by selling modified seeds permitting only one season's yield. This has particularly devastating effects on farmers in developing countries, as it prevents them from maintaining their traditional methods of farming using end of season seeds for future crops. There is also the fear of the consequences of modified genes escaping and so entering the general ecosystem; herbicide and insecticide-resistant genes from crops may be incorporated into the genome of other closely related varieties of plant and generally into food chains, the consequences of which are still unknown

Equally important moral issues arise with respect to the identification and isolation of specific sections of DNA carrying genes with known functions. These isolated genes may be used for different purposes, one being gene therapy. Understanding the causes of genetically inherited diseases has led to treatments which would ordinarily deal with symptoms, but the possible use of gene therapy for these conditions has instilled hopes of achieving cures. This is a new vision for medicine aimed at limiting the expression of genetic defects arising during life, present from the moment of birth or even pre-birth.

On the other hand, isolated genes from one species may be spliced into the genome of another to bring about designer creatures. Where will the boundary to intervention be placed and by whom? Will Nature, herself, rebel and act to prevent, or will the unrestrained imagination and inventiveness of mankind lead to disaster. The explosion in knowledge of genetic mechanisms faces society with new scientific challenges, as well as deep and daunting moral issues about whether conscious decisions about human evolution could or should be made. Should the human race enhance its biological quality? These moral issues confront the very essence of humanity.

Another area which is both useful and dangerously restrictive follows from advances in DNA fingerprinting and sequencing techniques. There are now a number of instances where it is possible to test apparently healthy and unaffected individuals and thereby determine whether or not they are carriers of certain genetically inherited conditions. These individuals may or may not give birth to either affected offspring or carriers of these diseases. Should individuals with the potential to produce such offspring be allowed to reproduce? Should this information be made available to whoever wishes to have it? Should an embryo, pronounced as having a genetic disorder, be allowed to develop to full term and be born, even though gene therapy may provide protection in the future? Should details of genetic make-up be private or public property? These are huge questions for the Social Conscience.

Imagine the restrictions on freedom that would be consequent upon genetic details becoming public property. Employment may be denied, movements restricted, special surveillance may be enforced and a person constituting thereby a public threat may be placed in confinement. Access to resources such as insurance, housing and mortgage facilities could be denied.

Stem-cell research offers the possibility of astonishing medical achievements. Both the medical profession and industry see this work as one of the most important scientific developments of recent times. Stem cells have the remarkable ability to reproduce and develop into various tissue types. There are two main sources. They are found in many adult tissues and when these cells are isolated and cloned, they will give rise to the same tissue type from which they originated and become a source of material to replenish tissues which have become damaged or malfunctioning. The other source of stem cells is from embryos and these cells may be encouraged to differentiate into a number of tissue types. It is from the concern over this source of cells that most of the ethical objections arise. Embryonic stem cells become available as a result of *in vitro* fertilisation techniques and would be used within a few days of embryonic development. Pro-life activists would argue that life starts at conception and to use these embryos as a source of tissue would be equivalent to taking a life even if used to save one.

Clearly, there is remarkable potential in the medical use of stem cells, but many consider that this comes very close to the manipulation of life and the act of growing spare parts from stem cells under controlled laboratory conditions for implanting into patients, has provoked disquiet. The possible outcome of stem-cell research combined with the skills of genetic engineering is indeed very thought provoking. Simply stated, there appears to be no limit to the possibilities open to the development of spare human parts. This has raised the spectre of creating human beings that have been cloned from basic stem cells and would be used for providing human spare part materials for therapeutic purposes. Further, the creatures that would have been created in this way could be used for many purposes and conceivably eventual substitutes for labour. Being human in a physical sense, but not human as to the rest of personality, society would be venturing into uncertain and perhaps unsafe territory in replicating a population that would exist as automatons. Experimental cloning with sheep and cows has already been undertaken and has produced alarming results in the creation of live animals with defects and short lives. Early trials of new knowledge often prove disappointing for various reasons. Generally, the appropriate technology is developed and the required performance standards may ultimately be obtained, but this cannot be guaranteed. It may well be that defects, unknown at this stage, could appear in successive generations. In the case of animals bred for human consumption in this way, there is the risk of replicating the same problems as modified crops with respect to their fitness for human consumption. Having already proceeded to cloning animals, some scientists are claiming that they are able to clone human beings. This imminence of the possibility that cloned human beings might perambulate as look-alikes to human forms poses a vast range of ethical, legal and social problems. It recalls the experience of the scientist who created Frankenstein, who discovered that he had created a monster in his laboratory. Is there a danger of producing a race of such monsters?

The Global Expansion of the Market Economy
The global expansion of the market economy has two significant effects. The first, through the expansion of multinational business corporations, is to bring the economic resources of underdeveloped countries under the control of the market economy. Although subject to domestic laws, in the same way as local enterprises, and purporting to subscribe to welfare objectives in the various ways that affect employees, consumers and the environment, the global enterprise is committed emphatically to the principle of creating shareholder value as the objective of business decisions. The second is the extension of the political control of the market economy over nations through the creation of federations, such as the European Community, having economic growth as the main objective and creating a legal environment favourable to market expansion by abolishing traditional frontiers, and further freeing trade through deregulation.

The transfer of production to developing counties secures huge labour cost savings, both in terms of low wages and by the avoidance of the need to provide social benefits to employees. Likewise, the absence of regulations applying to industrial activities, such as the control of environmental effects, allows the global enterprise to externalise what would be significant industrial production costs in developed countries. The transfer of low-cost finished goods for sale in established markets in developing countries enhances profitability as well as competitiveness leading to the elimination of local competitors, by mergers and buyouts, resulting in the global enterprise enjoying quasi-monopolistic advantages from vertical and horizontal integration.

As already stated, the changes in the moral and ethical climate brought about by the globalisation of the world economy have not only given priority to shareholder value as the cornerstone of business policy, but have lent it moral and ethical justification as most conducive to economic growth and hence to improved welfare for all. The most visible symbol of economic growth is expanding income. The translation and expression of well-being into money terms has given money and the attitudes associated with it a central place in our culture and world of ideas.

Business success is found in achieving high growth levels expressed in activity volume and in profitability. It is not unusual for companies to announce quarterly expansion of activity as high as 30% and profit growth of equally vertiginous dimensions. A relatively small fall-back in expectations in the maintenance of such targets provokes substantial falls in share price and general dismay. At the same time, wage increases of 2 to 4% per annum are viewed by business and governments as calamitous and having the effect of pushing up costs, reducing competitiveness and provoking harmful inflation.

Political leaders and the business community share the same understanding of the management of the economy, regarding sustained and increased economic growth as the panacea for all ills. The cause and remedy to social problems are linked to economic growth as the only means of improving social welfare. A closer examination of this link reveals several inconsistencies. The pressure for greater volume and profit takes its most visible form in labour productivity and management performance. The human contribution to the market economy is evaluated as a cost expressed in money terms. Increasing output through increased sales revenues and improving profit through cost reductions is the simple calculus that determines success in the market economy. It results in a completely distorted view of society and the relationship of the market economy to society as a whole.

The market economy looks to government to maintain and promote continuing economic growth. For developing countries, this takes the form of encouraging capital development and, in the absence of sufficient local demand, to aim for export-led economic growth. These countries offer low labour costs, fiscal and other financial incentives and a climate of deregulation, giving business the opportunity of avoiding the high levels of social costs that restrict profitability in developed countries, such as the provision of pensions, redundancy payments, health care, staff training, good working conditions, industrial safety standards and the prevention of environmental pollution. The relationship of the market economy to local society is based on low pay, long hours, hazardous working conditions, often child labour and always the discipline of grinding poverty. In destroying their existing social structure based on family values and sharing on a community basis, the market economy fulfils the Biblical prophecy of 'taking away even that which they have'.

For developed countries, the partnership between the market economy and government encourages economic growth through the management of aggregate demand. It was a policy that proved its worth during the Great Depression and it remains the cornerstone of government policy. However, in present circumstances, the Keynesian solution to the funding of the deficit of aggregate demand through budget deficits is no longer as relevant. It was applicable to dealing with massive unemployment as a social tragedy. The level of aggregate demand remains of critical importance, but in the context of maintaining high levels of consumption required to maintain and expand economic growth. The Great Depression was more than a hiccup in the transformation of Western society into a market society. It emphasised its total dependence on employment and its economic, social and political fragility in the face of unemployment. Cost-cutting strategies, involving staffing reductions and increased productivity targets, as well as relocating activities, and mergers have destroyed a social work ethic in which people realised an important part of self in working productively and enjoying the security of long-term employment. Employment has become a social environment of oppression often resulting in stress-related illnesses.

The dependence of economic growth in developed countries on high levels of consumption means that government policy has to hold a difficult balance between a high level of money supply and overheated aggregate demand with the objective of ensuring that consumption continues to rise. Clearly, high levels of employment and high wages would themselves encourage the levels of consumption needed by the market economy, with the condition that either employment or wages or both should continue to increase. Whereas high levels of consumption ensure activity and revenue volume, high levels of employment impact negatively on costs and on the pressure for increased profits. Squeezing out labour costs through redundancy, maintaining output potential through higher productivity, lowering wages by constantly shifting out of high wage to low wage labour, relocating work whenever possible, expanding output and sales capacity through mergers leading to significant labour cost savings, show up in the insecurity of employment and the uncertainty of income. Deregulation and the reduction in the size of government have put society at the mercy of the market economy.

As the market economy is unable of itself to deal with a deficit of consumption arising from the insufficiency of household revenues, it looks to government for the maintenance of high credit levels for gearing up household consumption. Credit card debt, mortgage levels, bank overdrafts etc., have reached such a level that it is estimated that, in the case of the United Kingdom, average household solvency, expressed as the time-lead between available funds and debt commitments, is only two weeks. In effect, if income should fail, technical bankruptcy defined as failing to meet debts due for payment is two weeks away for the average family. If the social impact of the market economy on society in developing countries is persistent family enslavement to grinding poverty, in developed countries it is persistent household enslavement to grinding debt. The enslavement to grinding debt is artificially created as a means of mopping up funds flowing through the market economy operating under full steam. Excessive credit, as it fuels price increases, is mopped up into debt that provides interest income and expanded activity for financial institutions. This is most evident in the property market, where increases in property prices have maintained the demand for credit and absorbed increases in household disposable incomes. Speculation about increases in property values has sustained a demand that has now placed house prices beyond the means of the average wage earner. It has translated grinding debt into the social distress that results from the grossly overpriced right to a roof over one's head and falsely created a housing shortage.

The necessity to maintain high levels of consumption to fuel the market economy in developed countries has two further consequences for society. High economic growth levels not only need high levels of disposable funds for consumption, but also the capacity to consume as represented in the need to consume. In terms of the theory of diminishing marginal utility, demand satisfaction would be totally achieved quite quickly once people have all that they need or could ever imagine needing. Hence, the market economy has constantly to re-create and expand demand by stimulating real or imaginary consumption needs. Production capacity that depends only on the replacement of existing goods is insufficient for the market economy to achieve its volume and profit growth objectives and would rapidly plunge the market economy into collapse. Consequently, the market economy creates waste as a means of sustaining output. This results in shortened product lives and created obsolescence. Products that would otherwise have a long life in use are designed to fail within a determined period and sustain the maintenance of a replacement demand. Created obsolescence results from the production of new products that, in terms of added usefulness, make insignificant contribution. This is the 'new model' syndrome that creates product differentiation on the sole basis of marginal obsolescence.

The nature and the volume of waste created by the market economy threaten society in a number of ways. First, it accelerates the consumption of non-renewable natural resources. Second, the increasing industrialisation of the global economy is creating such high levels of pollution as to endanger Planet Earth through its environmental effects. The USA, which accounts for only 5% of the world's population but produces 25% of worldwide carbon dioxide pollution, has not yet taken a commitment to participate in the Kyoto Agreement on Climatic Change, considering that such measures would adversely affects its economy. China and India are about to become major industrial nations and are likely to take the same view on pollution control as the USA. Third, the disposal of industrial and household waste contaminates the environment, for many products either cannot be disposed of efficiently or the process of disposal itself creates further environmental contamination.

Finally, the global market economy is creating fictitious shortages by preventing access to resources. Market logic identifies consumption needs as translated into effective demand through the ability to pay the market price. Large multinational corporations often have control over market pricing that satisfies their own profit targets and it is one of several methods used for controlling profitability. One of the more immoral aspects of the global market economy is the wilful denial of products to populations that are in urgent humanitarian need and that do not have the means to pay the established price. The deplorable failure of the pharmaceutical industry to provide adequate assistance to poor nations in dealing with the HIV crisis is a brutal example of the absence of moral values in the market economy.

For both the developing and the developed countries, the market economy destroys the substance and the realisation of happiness that lie in a sense of gratitude expressed in the contentment with what life offers presently, substituting dissatisfaction and creating envy through the speculation of what might be tomorrow, and can never be in terms of its own logic. In the momentum of the market economy, there is acceleration towards a destiny for humanity, which cannot be determined either in terms of a meaning or of a destiny.

Persistent Tyranny and the Persistent Struggle for Freedom
Tyranny usually is defined as government by a ruler or small group of people who have unlimited power over people and use it unfairly and cruelly. It also exists whenever a situation or a person or groups of persons control the lives of others in an unfair manner. Both in a national and in an individual context, tyranny has many forms and is widespread. Tyranny lurks in the presence of freedom and appears whenever there is injustice. The denial of freedom is the open door to cruelty, which is inflicted in the many ways in which pain may be experienced. There is the tyranny of poverty, the tyranny of discrimination, the tyranny of abuse and of exploitation. There may be tyranny in the home seen in the behaviour of a parent or that of children; there is often tyranny in the workplace in the manner in which employees are treated by their superiors, and in the way they are made to accept intolerable working conditions.

Tyranny and freedom represent the two furthest points in the spectrum of human relationships. Tyranny has its quintessence in selfishness and all the ambitions, desires and fears that centre on self. Freedom has its quintessence in the liberation from self through its sublimation in caring relationships with others that bring the gifts of happiness and security, for freedom exists only when understood in terms of sharing relationships. In its most simple expression, tyranny results from selfishness and freedom is found in generosity.

Tyranny is the worst form of rule. It is a counterfeit authority that falsely claims its authenticity in law. It is void of moral values and seeks to crush opposition from the Social Conscience. Proclaiming the wisdom of its decisions, it justifies the most callous and brutal behaviour. The most moving reaffirmation of the Social Conscience of recent times was the speech by Senator Edward McCain in the United States Senate in December 2005 opposing the use of torture in the war of terror, claimed as justified by the Bush administration, in which he declared, 'What matters is not what they [the terrorists] are, but what we are!'

The opposition to tyranny, as a form of rule, has existed for centuries and is maintained in the popular demand for democratic government. Important statutory declarations of freedom have signalled victories over tyranny. They represented successive steps forward in the evolution of democracy. The Magna Carta was wrested from King John by his own barons in 1215; Habeas Corpus in 1679 was another step in opposing arbitrary arrest and imprisonment, and the Bill of Rights was passed by Parliament in 1689 with the agreement of the joint monarchs, William and Mary.

Freedom's victory over tyranny is never final, for tyranny changes its face and its action, continually seeking to oppress. Its agents are often erstwhile friends. The Reform Movement of the 19th century viewed universal suffrage as threatening the tyranny of democracy and echoing Plato in the need to have wisdom combined with democracy for good government.

Today, freedom struggles under the menace of tyranny. Its existence is threatened by the market economy, which arose from the freedom to trade, and from democracy that was made possible by the grant of universal suffrage. Freedom has been usurped by the tyranny of money exercised through the market economy and the tyranny of bureaucracy, which elected governments have created and to which they have delegated the responsibility of administration.

The Dominance of Financial Capital over the Global Economy
The distinction made by Schumpeter and referred to earlier in Chapter 5 between two forms of capital made available to finance enterprise activity, namely financial capital and production capital, is critical to understanding the manner in which capitalism is extending its control over the global economy. Production capital represents the investment of funds in the production of goods and services. It is the permanent capital that is invested on a long-term basis and represents the shareholders' or capitalists' contribution of capital to the enterprise. In engaging capital in this manner, a shareholder is a permanent investor who combines his money with the efforts of management and workers in industrial or commercial activities. Management and workers are paid for their efforts from the enterprise and the remainder of the surplus realised, called the net profit, accrues entirely to the shareholders after

deduction of business taxation, and is added to the capital already supplied to the business. It is available for distribution to shareholders in the form of dividends. Shareholders acting in this manner commit themselves to the enterprise itself and are actively involved in its success.

Financial capital represents funds supplied by financial institutions or companies that are essentially in the business of making money out of money. In a very broad sense, and at the risk of oversimplification, they are in the business of money-lending and have behavioural profiles that are akin to pawnbrokers of old. Their strategy is to maximise the return obtained and at the same time to secure themselves from risk by holding shares as security. In a sense, their presence as investors in an enterprise is no different from other investors. However, they act in an entirely different manner and play an entirely different game.

First, their enterprise objectives are different. They are not interested in obtaining the average returns that are associated with production activities or in long-term commitments to a business enterprise. Second, they will provide equity financing in circumstances offering the possibility of high rates of return with correspondingly high risk, and risk-management is their speciality. It will include making funds available to start-ups, green field ventures, takeovers and acquisitions and special projects. In all these cases, venture or financial capitalists will take a shareholding position in an enterprise for the duration of their investments, price the security as low as possible with a view to making a substantial gain on disposal, limit the duration of the investment and squeeze out the maximum return that may be obtained from or imposed on the 'client' enterprise during the period of the investment. In effect, in view of the type of risk which is financed and the size of funds often needed, it is only through financial capital that the needed funds are obtainable. Generally, venture or equity capitalists control the situation and can manoeuvre at will. Third, enterprises may be seen as targets for a financial operation that may involve aggressively obtaining a controlling shareholding for the sole purpose of stripping off valuable assets and keeping only a limited segment for development, or for engaging in a rescue aimed at value-improvement on a short-term basis. The variety of operations open to financial enterprises is extensive.

The huge increase in the flow of funds associated with the expansion of the market economy has placed financial capital in a dominant role over the global economy. Generally, the funds utilised by financial enterprises are mobilised from savings institutions, pension funds, insurance companies and sometimes, wealthy private investor groups. By acquiring control over global businesses, financial institutions obtain ownership rights to income and assets and ultimate control over management strategy and policies. They energise the market economy by raising profitability expectations and increases in shareholder value by requiring more stringent approaches to asset management.

The downside is that ownership is further removed from the enterprise's social structure consisting of management, employees, retired persons and customers. In most cases, financial institutions are managed by faceless persons having no contact with the enterprise itself. Neither do they have a community of interest nor any social welfare engagements. Devoid totally of moral values or sentiments for others, exploitation aimed at financial gain is the sole motivation. The alienation of the human context of business from its financial context is complete. By sharpening the immediacy of needed action for increased profits, value creation and financial performance improvements often focus on short-term actions that have immediate impact.

In the search for significant cost reductions, the global enterprise deals in a global labour market and will easily switch production and other business activities to countries where living standards and labour costs are lower. It constitutes a serious threat to the well-being of communities living in the more advanced countries.

The Surrender of Sovereignty to Foreign Bureaucracy
The acceptance of the principle of surrender of national sovereignty implicit in the establishment of an effective international order was initiated in Europe by the signing of the Treaty of Rome on 25th March, 1957, under which six founder nations agreed to create a Common Market in the form of a European Economic Community (EEC). It was to have its own administration headed by an appointed permanent President and an executive board of appointed full-time Commissioners, having the power to issue its own regulations in the form of Directives, which once accepted were integrated in the laws of member nations.

Inspired by de Gaulle of France and Adenauer of Germany, it began as a tandem between these two nations that persists to this day and which had greater political and economic ambitions. It was said that the political ambition that drove France to a closer collaboration with its erstwhile enemy was a wish to bring Germany under French political influence and to frustrate the attempts of the United Kingdom to pursue its traditional policy of keeping Europe divided and thus spiking any possible threat to British interests. The economic ambition was to create an enlarged market capable of becoming a serious competitor to the USA. Along with the EEC were created parallel authorities in the form of the European Atomic Energy Community (Euratom) and the European Coal and Steel Community, which have become known as the Treaties of Rome.

The Treaty of Nice, which came into force on 1st February, 2001, and the attempt to agree on a European Constitution, failed to move Continental Europe into a larger measure of political integration, when the proposed European Constitution was rejected through the referendum process. The European Economic Community became the European Union through the Treaty of Maastricht on 1st November, 1993. The Treaty of Maastricht was a further step in the direction of European integration through the creation of the Euro as a common currency under the control of the European Central Bank.

The European Union, enlarged to 25 nations, with a distinct political structure in the form of an Executive and a Parliament and legislative powers, is faced with the considerable problem of nation-building out of the extensive and extremely complex diversity that exists between member states. The political ambition to create a powerful European state, based on the political union of most of the countries in Europe, is driven by politicians with at best lukewarm popular support. The real force behind the creation of a large common market is the prospect for economic growth that such a market offers to industry and business. Nationhood and social cohesion, founded on national identity, are being sacrificed to the imperative of the market economy. The loss of national identity and the subsuming of national interests in wider economic and political unions are creating political and social tension and rendering social cohesion improbable for generations. Moreover, the political objective of creating a powerful economic bloc is threatened by the impossible task of unifying cultural and institutional differences in governmental traditions, in particular with respect to budgetary policy and debt management. The stability of the Euro, as the common currency, is given critical importance by the European Central Bank, which is obliged to give precedence to monetary policy for ensuring monetary stability and preventing inflation through debt control, rather than encouraging growth by relaxing limits to government deficits during periods of stagnation and recession.

There exists a seemingly unbridgeable gulf between the divergent interests of governments and political elites and those of ordinary citizens. An arrogant, autocratic and distant bureaucracy has separated government from the people, replaced democracy by a tyranny that has arrogated to itself enormous supranational powers and fostered widespread antagonism.

The expansion of the European Union managed within the framework of a Commission, acting as a government or executive body, carries within it the seeds of almost every possible problem for member states in the future. In particular, it has failed to meet most of the essential requirements to ensure its social cohesion. It was imposed in several countries without popular consent. In the public mind, it seems that the Commission itself is the effective ruling authority. The manner by which it is appointed and in which it operates fails to meet the basic criteria needed for social cohesion.

It is especially noteworthy that the action of the Commission, as the real authority, is associated with and directed through a huge and expensive bureaucracy, that is effectively an executive acting also as law-maker, imposing its rules in the form of Directives and seemingly uncontrollable and answerable to no one. Popular dissatisfaction with the Commission is widespread and reflects how virtually non-existent is its link with the population that it governs. It demonstrates the extent to which this form of bureaucratic government frustrates social cohesion and is foreign to the tradition of those freedom-loving nations, such as England, that have struggled for centuries against despotic rulers.

The dominant interests of the market economy are undermining the commitment of governments to social welfare and to the ideals of a social economy. Most Western states have heretofore managed welfare programmes through state agencies, financed out of taxation. Budgetary constraints aimed at ensuring currency stability have made governments sensitive to the cost of social welfare programmes. Several European states that traditionally were committed to social welfare are actively seeking to cut budgets through reductions in welfare spending. In particular, the transfer of welfare costs to private sector financing is strongly advocated by some political groups. It will not be long before the global economy will have levelled all countries, in this regard, to the same standards as those found in the USA.

Today, we are not only witnessing a radical change in moral and ethical values, but a return to the creation of large empires. These empires carry the seeds of future serious political and social problems that relate to the sense of identity and social cohesion that existed in countries, where the link with the government authority was clear and unambiguous and where freedom from oppression had been a national struggle for centuries.

Born of wild dreams and ambitions, the wish of relatively few leaders to create a gigantic economic and political empire in Europe can hardly meet with durable success. Emulating the USA as a model for creating a United States of Europe is to forget the crucial differences between these two models. What makes it possible for the USA to enjoy stable and permanent social cohesion is the fact that it has a common language, legal system, religion and cultural tradition. The eventual United States of Europe, towards which political ambition is directed, does not have those essential preconditions for stability and permanence.

It is the barely unconcealed ambition of the protagonists of a United States of Europe to develop a strong military capacity and a centralised military command. Would its essential strategic objective be to ensure internal stability and permanence? If so, is the eventual social conflict implicitly inherent in its social structure seen as a policing problem addressed to social order, or as a military problem addressed to the suppression of a society in a state of insurrection? Is it conceivable that the objective would be defence against a potential enemy, in a world that in the future would be composed of only three or four potential world powers? If that were so, a war with the USA or China is hardly conceivable and would be too destructive even to contemplate. Clearly, the growth of influence of Islam in the world, as it spreads across populations representing a significant and increasing percentage of the human race and adopts a radical form, is a threat to the established world order. At the moment, its radical action is defined as being of a terrorist nature, terrorism being interpreted as unorthodox military action or revolt in a violent and unorthodox manner by groups within populations against the USA and its coalition of allies and client nations. However, the Islamic nations have the potential of forming a united group capable eventually of attaining the status of a world power, having as they do, many of the criteria required for social cohesion.

It is noteworthy that, in several significant respects, the economic, political and military empire that our EU leaders are seeking to emulate has many of the features of the recently defunct Soviet empire, which did not last a century and collapsed from its own internal dissensions and fundamental weaknesses.

The Universal Rule of Law
The Social Conscience, as the sovereign authority, relies on the Rule of Law to give effect to the formal statement of its governing principle, namely, the judgement on what is considered as right in all matters of dispute. Recourse to established legal doctrine is the conventional procedure for conflict resolution. The global expansion of the market economy and the breakdown of traditional national boundaries, within which market society identifies its activities, have resulted in the urgent problem of ensuring that the rule of law be effective on a global basis, thereby upholding the fundamental principle that no one is beyond the reach of law. The Rule of Law expressed as a universal rule, not only declares that no one is beyond the reach of law, but also that no one may be denied the benefit of law. The Social Conscience is concerned, as is the law, with upholding what is right. In so doing, it upholds the authority of the law and places freedom under that authority. The Social Conscience is not divisible. It is universal and shared by all. It constrains the enjoyment of freedom to that which conforms with what is right, which is the fundamental rule that instructs the law as well as the Social Conscience.

The rule of law is concerned with the idea of justice and ensuring that justice is made manifest in all human relationships. The law applies only to matters that have their significance in human relationships, whether these matters concern property rights, civil rights or indeed, human rights. The law seeks not only to prevent injustice as a denial of rights, but to establish rules of conduct that will ensure that justice is seen both in principle and in practice.

The law can only address injustices that result from wrongdoing. There is much injustice that occurs naturally and does not necessarily arise from wrongdoing. In addition to the harm that is self-inflicted as a consequence of wrongdoing, there is the injustice of birth, when a person is born handicapped, there is the social injustice that is a function of circumstances. The Social Conscience may act to compensate injustice that the law cannot redress by caring for those who suffer injustice and helping them in their misfortune. The development of social legislation in the form of health care, education, social security and social assistance is a relatively new extension to social responsibility at government level. Only the most developed countries have moved in this direction. Most developing countries are unable to finance social welfare programmes and international agencies, such as the World Health Organisation, Christian Aid and many others are able to deal only with emergencies.

Laws have their source in the concept of sovereignty that is attached to nationhood. The enforcement of rules of law that have international force rests on international agreements between nation states, under which they agree on the principles and the manner with which those rules shall be given effect. Although most countries share the same philosophy of law, known as jurisprudence, they differ on points of interpretation and application. The field of international law is concerned with the conflict of law between different countries. Nowhere is this more evident than in the field of income taxation and in the manner in which two countries agree to deal with double taxation when it occurs. Thus, a resident of the USA is taxed in the USA on his worldwide income and may be taxable in the United Kingdom on income that has its source in the United Kingdom, giving rise to the double taxation of the same income. This fiscal injustice is settled by the application of the Convention between the USA and the United Kingdom for the relief of double taxation on income.

Rules of law that have international force result from agreements between two or more countries, which are formally expressed in the form of an international treaty that comes into effect once the parties have signified their consent by signing. The legislative right of sovereign nations is an inalienable right. This means that the right to make law belongs exclusively to the State itself. In England, the power to make law resides in Parliament as the legislative assembly or in the declarations of judges as to the Common Law.

The signatories to international conventions incorporate the provisions of the treaties in their own legal systems. However, those international provisions take precedence over domestic law when they conflict. The enforceability of international conventions depends absolutely upon the consent of signatory states. An international convention has no effect in a country that is not a signatory to it.

By contrast, the global economy has both an international and a supranational character, for its activities are conducted across national boundaries and are supranational in character for they can only be subjected to legal regulations, if such regulations exist and can be enforced. One of the major drivers of the global economy is the quest for much greater freedom through a business environment that enjoys a large measure of deregulation. Multinational companies are able to choose where they locate their business operations, and business contracts can stipulate the jurisdiction which is to apply in interpreting the terms of the agreement.

International Tribunals and the Enforcement of Law
As distinct from bilateral treaties, multinational treaties have several or many countries as signatories and seek to create a body of rules as well as institutions to which their administration is entrusted and which generally include a regulatory framework. The manner in which these regulations may be made and enforced forms part of the founding agreement. The countries that are signatories to such treaties generally agree to honour their commitments, either by integrating such regulations within their own laws, or providing that they should have overriding authority in the event of conflict. The main difference between bilateral and multinational agreements is the effectiveness with which they may be enforced. In the event of dispute and the refusal of one or both parties to accept the conclusion of an arbitration procedure in case of a bilateral treaty, it simply becomes ineffective.

Recently, the tendency has been for multinational treaties not only to act as the legal framework of the international institutions which are created thereby, but also to establish a court of justice for the purpose of arbitration. The United Nations Charter 1945 provided that the role of the Security Council would include arbitrating on disputes between members through the issue of formal resolutions, stating the decision of the Security Council and which an offending country was expected to obey. In the event of non-compliance, there is little that the Security Council may do, except to propose sanctions. The Security Council is not a court of justice, as such, but a political body whose decisions are subject to veto by any member having the right to veto and whose procedures do not conform to generally accepted trial procedures. As a result of the deliberations of world leaders in September 2005, a fundamental step was taken by the United Nations when it was declared that a duty of care for its population rested on the sovereign power and that, if not observed, the Security Council could authorise intervention to prevent genocide.

The Treaty of Rome also established a European Court of Justice for dealing with disputes between members, as well as enforcing European legal rules, including those approved and issued as

European Union Directives. The European Court of Justice is a formal court of justice acting as such and observing conventional trial procedures. Its decisions may include fines and/or orders, which are enforceable. As yet, no member country has been willing to risk exclusion, which would be the ultimate penalty, and which is the effective sanction behind a decision of that court.

International treaties may address different legal objectives, which may be the enforcement of rules relating to civil matters – for example, GATT (General Agreement on Tariffs and Trade) – or criminal matters – INTERPOL (International Criminal Police Organisation 1923) – or the Geneva Convention that relates to the treatment of prisoners of war, or human rights that are enforced by the European Court of Human Rights.

The development of an international jurisprudence is not only essential for the expanding global economy, but also to provide protection under law for humanity at large in a world in which national boundaries allow perpetrators of injustice to escape the reach of the law. Ensuring that no one is beyond the law and no country, however powerful, is above the law, is the ultimate aim and justification for the creation of a world authority based on law.

It is interesting to note that the first step in international cooperation had a humanitarian objective. The Geneva Conventions consist of four treaties formulated in Geneva, Switzerland, that set the standards for international law for humanitarian concerns. The conventions were the results of efforts by Henri Dunant, who was motivated by the horrors of war which he witnessed at the Battle of Solferino 1859. The First Geneva Convention 'for the Amelioration of the Condition of the Wounded and Sick in Armed Forces in the Field' was adopted in 1864. It followed the foundation of the International Committee of the Red Cross in 1863. All signatory states are required to enact sufficient national law to make grave violations of the Geneva Conventions a punishable criminal offence. The recent allegations of torture committed by US military forces on Iraqi prisoners held in Iraq, or those other detainees held in Guantanamo, if proved, would constitute criminal offences under USA law by virtue of the Geneva Convention and could, in principle and on the basis of the precedent established in the Nuremberg Trials, lead to the criminal prosecution of those within the Bush administration deemed responsible for such crimes.

The European Court of Human Rights, based in Strasbourg, was created to hear human rights complaints from member states of the Council of Europe. Its purpose is to enforce the Convention for the Protection of Human Rights and Fundamental Freedoms, ratified in 1953. Its current form dates from 1st November, 1998 and replaced the previous enforcement mechanisms, which included the European Commission of Human Rights (created in 1954) and the previous limited Court of Human Rights (created in 1959). Complaints of violations by member states are filed in Strasbourg. Any decisions of the court are binding on member states. It is the role of the Committee of Ministers to supervise the execution of court judgments, though they have no formal means of forcing member countries to comply. The ultimate sanction of non-compliance is expulsion from the Council of Europe.

The European Court of Justice is the supreme court of the European Union. It is based in Luxembourg. It adjudicates on matters of interpretation of European Law, for example claims by the European Commission that a member state has not implemented a European Directive or other legal requirement, claims by member states that the European Commission has exceeded its authority, and references from national courts in the European Union member states asking the European Court of Justice questions about the meaning or validity of a particular piece of European Union law. Individuals cannot bring cases to the European Court of Justice directly. An individual who is sufficiently directly concerned by an act of one of the institutions of the European Union can challenge that act in a lower court, called the Court of First Instance.

The most reprehensible acts that are the object of universal condemnation are usually associated with the barbarism of war. There is a complete understanding that war and the cruelty and destruction associated with the savagery of war should be banned from human experience. On this point, the Social Conscience speaks loudly among all nations and everywhere. Yet, it is in the perverse nature of politics and of political leaders, and within the scope of the authority that they are able to impose upon their fellow beings, to commit a nation to war with another nation or nations. Even in so-called democratic nations, the prerogative for taking a nation into war resides in the hands of its leader or government.

Wars are barbaric in the manner in which they are conducted. The intention is to kill and destroy and to use such means as are available, regardless of humanitarian considerations or of their victims. The casualties of war are mostly innocent civilians. In the calculus of military action, their deaths and often abominable sufferings are accounted as collateral damage and in that reasoning totally dehumanised. Hiroshima and Nagasaki, Vietnam,

Afghanistan and Iraq rank high in the annals of atrocity. Likewise, the abominable treatment of prisoners, the practice of torture, genocide, and concentration camps are such denials of the moral values that lend dignity to human conduct as to warrant the severe punishment of those responsible

The Nuremberg Trials of the political, industrial and military leaders of Nazi Germany were a landmark in establishing the criminal guilt of those responsible for the crime of war and crimes against humanity. Their successful prosecution was undertaken by those who won the war, confirming another truth, namely that the punishment of crimes against humanity is a matter of *force majeure*.

The International Criminal Court was created under the Rome Statute and entered into force on 1st July, 2002. Some 99 member countries of the United Nations are parties to the International Criminal Court, but the USA and Israel have so far refused to recognise it. It extended the precedents established by the Nuremberg Tribunal 1945-6. The creation of the International Criminal Tribunal in the Hague in 1993 for the prosecution of war crimes committed in the former Yugoslavia and the Rwanda Tribunal for war crimes in Rwanda 1994, reasserted the universal condemnation of acts of war that offend the Social Conscience.

In the case of the Iraq war, the Social Conscience is present in the worldwide condemnation of the USA and its coalition allies for their conduct and for their treatment of civilians and war prisoners. The Iraq war has created a deep conflict with the Muslim world which, is likely to have untold consequences in the future.

The events connected with the Iraq invasion led by the Bush administration are considered by some as creating a legitimate demand to have the leaders of that war brought to trial before the International Criminal Court. If the prosecution of the United States Government for the crime of war and war crimes committed during the Iraq invasion in 2003 were eventually possible, the International Criminal Court would be in a position to achieve its ultimate objective of eradicating wars. The fact that the USA is not a signatory to the International Criminal Court and does not recognise its legitimacy does not prevent the International Criminal Court from trying the accused *in absentia*. The accused persons charged with war crimes at Nuremberg were charged in their own names and not in the name of the defunct German Government. Given that wars usually originate in the personal intentions of political and military leaders, they would be forced to face the consequences of their actions.

Conclusion
As the market economy extends its influence across the globe and in the process radically alters traditions and social relationships that date from the dawn of time, it augurs ill for the future of mankind. Religion has reappeared as a focal point of conflict, traditions are abandoned, value systems are changing, long-established institutions are undermined as a consequence of changing perspectives and expanding knowledge. The Social Conscience and the philosophy of the market economy have incompatible objectives that seem irreconcilable. Economic growth and increase in living standards are worthy objectives, but social justice is needed to ensure peace within nations and between nations. The hope for social justice lies in the evolution of a Unity of Conscience enforced by the rule of law.

Epilogue

THE SOCIAL CONSCIENCE is the soul of a nation that unites mind and heart in the wisdom and the moral values that justify its action. The Prologue to this book declared the ambition to tell of the past and discuss the present condition of a society, in which the Social Conscience is manifested through the instinct to care and an acceptance of the necessity to share.

The mystery that surrounds the origin and the justification of the moral values, which are enshrined in the Social Conscience, are beyond comprehension. They transcend time and personality and are expressed symbolically as Life, Truth and Love. These symbols are accepted as Absolute Realities. They represent at once the mystery which, being beyond our understanding, is yet within us, as are the moral values derived from them. They enlighten the wondrous firmament in which mind allows imagination to expand awareness.

The Social Conscience is a shared conscience which, embodied in each one, is the collective of all individuals seeking to do what is right. Its force resides in consensus. Its strength lies in the moral values that it claims as its own and that endow the Social Conscience with unique and permanent authority. Faced with endless daily choices, it is through a sympathetic awareness of others, expressed in the caring instinct that individuals are guided as to the right decision to take and best course of action to follow in any circumstance. It is this Unity of Conscience that is the significant symbol of identity and the enduring basis of social cohesion. As such, it is the irresistible force that is able to deal with all difficulties, to dispel doubt, to defeat opposition and to restore confidence in the hope that it inspires and on which humanity depends.

Science has contributed much to the solution of many problems. It is the faith, system, theory, methodology that sustains liberal democratic secularism.[1] As such, it is embedded in the market economy in such faith concepts as liberalism, democracy and progress.

---

1 See Appleyard, B., 'Special Report on Fundamentalism', *New Scientist*, 8th October, 2005, p.50.

The expanding influence of Western civilisation, through the emergence of a global economy, is placing different cultures on a collision course and bringing an awareness of problems of a magnitude that could not heretofore have been imagined. The present is a special moment in history and a time of special danger for humanity and Planet Earth, as the market economy brings the world under its control. The market economy, as an endless process of destruction and re-creation, has itself re-created and reinforced the need for hope to sustain human frailty through the ups and downs that it creates. In this sense, reason has re-created the need for religion. The conflict between wisdom and wealth is seen as a moral conflict in which the Social Conscience holds the moral high ground and wealth, through money, controls the market economy.

The past, present and the future are linked together through the influence that the Social Conscience bears on succeeding events. It acts as a prism for an understanding of the past and of the present and is visionary in the anticipation of the future. A new world dawns and reaffirms that Unity of Conscience, which is the family of man, in which each is equally deserving as to his needs and in which all share their destiny. The vision that the Social Conscience inspires and to which humanity commits its hopes and endeavours is founded in the Universal Rule of Law which, respecting differences in cultures and national identities essential to social cohesion, will promote the common interest in economic progress, social justice and maintain peace among nations.

Meditation

If I could talk to flowers and bees,
Communicate with birds and trees,
Share thoughts with cats and dogs,
How wonderful would be
Being closer to thee,
Spirit of Life.

If I could ask all living things,
Flowers and bees and birds and trees,
And ask of those closer to me,
Cats and dogs and those I also eat,
What you do think your life should be?
How would you like to share with me?

If I could ask all those I know,
And many more I do not know,
White, Black, Brown and Yellow,
From whom I steal by stealth
And plead 'shareholder wealth'
What do you think your life should be?
How would you like to share with me?

If I could ask of those inspired
By vision, goodness and desire
Declare true values and Commandments
For men who govern and betray
Those values every day.
What do you think your life should be?
How would you like to share with me?

If I could ask the sick and needy,
Of human kind and every specie,
Who suffer much in every way,
Unspeaking turn to me each day
For instant help.
What do you think your life should be?
How would you like to share with me?

If I could ask of those oppressed
By violent injustice dispossessed
And overwhelming might suppressed,
Who cruelly detonate their awful protest
Regardless.
What do you think your life should be?
How would you like to share with me?

If I could ask the Mind Divine,
Who made the Plan of Life
For each and every kind
And especially, Mankind,
Let good and kindness and sharing be
The Spirit of Life
In generosity
Free.

© Michel Glautier 2004

General Reading

Anderson, B., *Imagined Communities: Reflections on the Origin and Spread of Nationalism*, Amsterdam: Centre for Asian Studies, 1983.
— *Long Distance Nationalism: World Capitalism and the Rise of Identity Politics*, Amsterdam: Centre for Asian Studies, 1992.
Aquinas, St Thomas, *Summa Theologica* (1276-1273), Tr. Benziger Bros, 1947 edn.
Aristotle, *Politics*, Harmondsworth: Penguin Books, 1981.
Bagehot, W., *The English Constitution*, Cambridge University Press, paperback edn, 2001.
Bentham, J., *An Introduction to the Principles of Morals and Legislation*, 1789, New York: Prometheus Books, 1988.
— *A Manual of Political Economy*, 1795.
Berger, P.L. (ed.), *The Limits of Social Cohesion: Conflict and Mediation in Pluralist Societies*, Colorado: Westview Press Inc., 1999.
Besley, S., Weston, F.J. and Brigham, E., *Essentials of Managerial Finance*, Ohio: South Western College Publishing, 12th edn, 2000.
Beveridge, W., *State Provision for Social Needs: The Beveridge Committee Report on the Welfare State*, London: HMSO, 1992 edn.
Black, A, Wright, P. and Blackman, J.E., *In Search of Shareholder Value: Managing the Drivers of Performance*, Price Waterhouse Cooper, *Financial Times*/Prentice Hall, 2nd edn, 2000.
Blake, L.L, *The Royal Law: Source of Our Freedom Today*, London: Shepheard-Walwyn (Publishers) Ltd, 2000.
Bloch, M., *Feudal Society* (translation), London: Routledge & Keegan Paul Ltd, 1962.
Bloom, W., *Personal Identity, National Identity and International Relations*, Cambridge Studies in International Relations, Cambridge University Press, 1990.
Boatright, J.R., *Ethics and the Conduct of Business*, New Jersey: Prentice Hall/Pearson Educational International, 2003.
Burke, E., *Reflections on the Revolution in France*, 1790, Harmondsworth: Penguin Books, 1977.
Campbell, C. and B.G. Peters (eds), *Organizing Governance: Governing Organizations*, Pittsburgh University Press, 1981.
Churchill, W.S., *A History of the English-Speaking Peoples*, London: Cassell, 2002.
Collingwood, R.G., *The Idea of History*, Oxford University Press, 1961.
Crick, B., *In Defence of Politics*, Harmondsworth: Pelican Books, 1964.
— *The Sense of Identity of the Indigenous British*, in Parekh, B. (ed.) *British National Identity in a European Context*, *New Community* special issue, Vol. 21, No. 2, 1995, pp.167-82.
— *Education for Citizenship and the Teaching of Democracy in Schools*, Report of the Advisory Group, London, 1998.

Crick, B. (ed.), *Citizens: Towards a Citizenship Culture*, The Political Quarterly Publishing Co. Ltd, 2001.
Dawkins, R., *The Selfish Gene*, Oxford University Press, 1976.
Dearden, R.F, Hurst, P.H. and Peters, R.S., *Education and the Development of Reason*, London and Boston: Routledge & Keegan Paul Ltd, 1972.
Descartes, R., *Le Discours de la Méthode*, Pt 4, 1637 (translation), London: Routledge & Kegan Paul, 1999.
De Soto, H., *The Mystery of Capital*, London: Black Swan, 2001.
Denning, A.T., Lord, *Freedom under Law*, London: Stevens, 1949.
Dewey, J., *Democracy and Education*, New York: The Macmillan Company, 1916.
Dobb, M.H., *On Economic Theory and Socialism*, London: Routledge & Kegan Paul, 1965.
Drummond, H., *The Greatest Thing in the World*, London: Collins, 1930.
Fama, E., *The Theory of Finance*, New York: Holt, Rinehart & Winston, 1972.
Foster, C., *British Government in Crisis*, London: Hart Publishing, 2005.
Foucault, M., *Discipline and Punish*, Harmondsworth: Penguin Books, 1977.
Friedman, Milton, *Capitalism and Freedom*, University of Chicago Press, 1962.
Galbraith, J.K., *The Affluent Society*, Harmondsworth, Penguin Books, 1969.
— *The New Industrial State*, Harmondsworth, Penguin Books, 1972.
— *The Anatomy of Power*, London: Hamish Hamilton, 1987.
Glautier, M.W.E., 'The Idea of Accounting: A Historical Perspective', *The Accountants' Magazine*, Vol. 77, August 1973, pp 437-42, reprinted in Mueller, G.G. and Smith, C.H. (eds), *Accounting: A Book of Readings II*, New York: Holt Rinehart & Winston, 1976.
— 'Searching for Accounting Paradigms', *Accounting Historians Journal*, Vol. 10, No. 1, Spring 1983, pp.51-68.
— and Underdown, B., *Accounting Theory and Practice*, London: F.T. Pearson Education, 7th edn, 2000.
Hawawini, G. and Viallet, C., *Finance for Executives: Managing for Value Creation*, Ohio: South Western College Publishing, 2001.
Hayek, F.A., *The Road to Serfdom*, University of Chicago Press, 1944.
Hayek, F.A. (ed.), *Capitalism and the Historians*, University of Chicago Press, 1963.
Heilbroner, R., *The Wordly Philosophers*, Harmondsworth: Penguin Books, 7th edn, 2000.
Held, D. and Koenig-Archibugi, M. (eds). *Global Global Governance and Public Accountability*, Oxford: Blackwell Publishing Ltd, 2005.
Hobbes, T., *Leviathan*, 1651, Harmondsworth: Penguin Books, 1981.
Hodgkinson, B., *Bhagavad Gita* (verse translation), Delhi: Books for All, 2003.
Holland, S., *The Market Economy: From Micro to Mesoeconomics*, London, Weidenfeld & Nicolson, 1987.
John Paul II Encyclical, *Fides et Ratio*, Vatican: 14th September, 1998.
Keynes, J.M., 'The End of *Laissez-Faire*', in *Essays on Persuasion*, New York: Harcourt, Brace & Co., 1932.
— *General Theory of Employment, Interest and Money*, London: Macmillan, 1936.
Kuhn, T.S., *The Structure of Scientific Revolution*, University of Chicago Press, 2nd edn, 1970.
Latouche, B., *The Birth of the Western Economy* (translation), London: Methuen & Co. Ltd, 1967.

General Reading

Leibniz, G.W., *Discourse on Metaphysics*, 1686, Manchester University, 1990.
— *Essays on Human Understanding*, 1704, Cambridge University Press, 1982.
Locke, J., *Essay Concerning Human Understanding*, 1690, New York: Dutton, 1979.
Lukes, S., *Emile Durkheim, His Life and Work: A Historical and Critical Study*, London: Allen Lane, The Penguin Press, 1973.
Mandeville, B., *Fable of the Bees or Private Vices, Public Benefits*, 1732, Oxford University Press, 1924.
Marx, K., *Manifesto of the Communist Party*, 1848, Chicago: C.H. Kerr, 1947.
— *Foundations of the Critique of Political Economy*, 1858, Harmondsworth: Penguin Books, 1973.
— *Das Kapital*, 1867, Washington: Eagle Publishing Co., new edn 2000.
Mickwitz, G., 'Economic Rationalism in Graeco-Roman Agriculture', *English Historical Review*, Vol. 52, 1937.
Mill, J.S., *Principles of Political Economy with some of their Applications to Social Philosophy*, London: Longmans, Green, 1929.
More, Sir Thomas, *Utopia*, Tennessee: Neuvision Publication, 2003.
Morris, D., *The Naked Ape*, London: Cape, 1986.
Newman, J.H., *The Idea of a University*, London: Longman, Green & Co., 9th edn, 1889.
Paine, T., *Common Sense*, Philadelphia, 1776, New York: Prometheus Books, 1995.
— *The Rights of Man*, New York: Dover Publications, 1999.
— *The Age of Reason*, New York: Dover Publications, 2004.
Peters, R.S., *Ethics and Education*, London: George Allen & Unwin Ltd, 1966.
Peters, R.S. (ed.), *Education and the Education of Teachers*, London: Routledge & Kegan Paul, 1980.
— *The Concept of Education*, London: Routledge & Kegan Paul, 1987.
Plato, *The Dialogues of Plato*, Jowett, B. (trans.), New York: Random House, 20th edn, 1937.
Pirenne, H., *Economic and Social History of Medieval Europe* (translation), London: Routledge & Kegan Paul, 1965.
Polanyi, K., *The Great Transformation*, New York: Farrar & Rinehart, 1944.
— *Personal Knowledge*, London: Routledge & Kegan Paul, 1958.
Pollard, S., *The Idea of Progress*, London: C.A. Watts & Co. Ltd, 1968.
— *The Genesis of Modern Management*, Harmondsworth: Penguin Books, 1965.
Popper, K.R., *The Open Society and its Enemies*, London: Routledge & Kegan Paul, 4th edn, 1962.
— *The Poverty of Historicism*, London: Routledge & Kegan Paul, paperback edn, 1961.
— *Objective Knowledge*, Oxford: Clarendon Press, 1972.
Rappaport, A., *Creating Shareholder Value: A Guide for Managers and Investors*, New York: Simon & Schuster Inc., 1997.
Ricardo, D., *On the Principles of Political Economy and Taxation*, London: John Murray, 3rd edn, 1821.
Robbins, L., *A History of Economic Thought*, Princeton University Press, 1998.
Roberts, A. and Mountford C.P., *The Dreamtime: Australian Aboriginal Myths in Paintings with Text*, Sydney: Rigby Ltd, 1965.
Roll, E., *A History of Economic Thought*, London: Faber & Faber, 5th edn, 1992.
Rousseau, J.P., *The Social Contract* (translation), Harmondsworth: Penguin Books, 1969.
— *Emile* (translation), Charleston: Phoenix Press, 1988.

Sartre, J.-P., *Existentialism and Humanism*, London: Methuen, 1948.
— *Being and Nothingness*, London: Methuen, 1958.
Schumpeter, J.A., *Capitalism, Socialism and Democracy*, New York: Harper & Row, 1942.
— *History of Economic Analysis*, London: George Allen & Unwin, 1954.
Simester, A. and Sullivan, R., *Criminal Law: Theory and Practice*, London: Hart Publishing, 2000.
Slater, D. and Tonkiss, F., *Market Society*, Cambridge: Polity Press, 2001.
Smith, A., *An Inquiry into the Nature and Causes of the Wealth of Nations*, New York: Modern Library, 1937.
— *The Theory of Moral Sentiments*, New York: A.M. Kelly, 1966.
Strike, K.A. & Egan, K., *Ethics and Educational Policy*, London: Routledge & Kegan Paul, 1978.
Tawney, R.H., *Religion and the Rise of Capitalism: A Historical Study*, Harmondsworth: Penguin Books, 1972.
— *The Acquisitive Society*, London: G. Bell, 1926.
Tenney, F. (ed.), *An Economic Survey of Ancient Rome*, Baltimore: The Johns Hopkins Press, 1940.
Van Horne, J.C., *Fundamentals of Financial Management*, New Jersey: Prentice Hall, Englewood Cliff, 12th edn, 2004.
— *Financial Management and Policy*, New Jersey: Prentice Hall, Englewood Cliff, 12th edn, 2001.
Veblen, T., *The Theory of the Leisure Class: An Economic Study of Institutions*, New York: Macmillan, 1902.
Weber, M., *General Economic History*, Knight, F.H. (trans), London: Allen & Unwin, 1928.
— *The Protestant Ethic and the Spirit of Capitalism*, London: Allen & Unwin, 1930.
Wheen, F., *Karl Marx: A Life*, New York and London: Harper Collins, 2000.
Wittgenstein, L., *Philosophical Investigations*, Oxford: Blackwell, 2001.

Index

Abolition of Slavery Act (1833) 290
Abolition of Slave Trading Act (1807) 188, 290
absolute values xii, 17, 63, 167-8, 307-8, 335
   Life xii, xiii, 17, 27, 61-3, 168, 300, 308, 335
   Love xii, xiii, 17, 27, 46, 61, 64-5, 168, 308, 335
   Truth xii, xiii, 17, 61, 63-4, 151, 168, 218, 236, 308, 335
accountability:
   and accounting profession 137, 144-53
   and democratic deficit 193, 195, 209, 215-17, 227, 234
   concept of 139, 224-6
   corporate accountability 144-53
accountancy 137-165 *passim*
   accounting profession 97, 137, 145, 147-55
   double- and single-entry bookkeeping 145-7, 151
   the control paradigm 137, 153-61
   see also shareholder value; capital
Act of Supremacy (1534) 180
Articles of Association 141
advertising 14, 35, 95, 127, 283, 290
agrarian economies xv, 24, 30-1, 44, 49, 106, 138
Agrarian Revolution 24, 49
Alexander, S.S. 156
Ancient World xi, xii, 45, 72, 144-5, 166
   see also Greeks; Romans
Anderson, B. 9
Appleyard, B. 309, 335
Aristotle xvi, 24, 31, 46, 79, 85, 117, 121, 167, 184
Australian aboriginals xi, 72
authority:
   of custom and freedom 247-9
   social conscience and 237-9
   see also authority and freedom; sovereign authority
authority and freedom xv, 93, 113, 181, 231-54 *passim*
   and conflict 256

authority and freedom—*contd*
   and Social Conscience 234-9
   and tolerance and political correctness 251-3
   in a market economy 249-51
   meaning of 231-4
   under law 239-42

Balfour Declaration 311-12
barter 31, 108 (n.3)
Beethoven, Ludwig van xv
Belgium 269
Bentham, Jeremy 23, 31-2, 49, 52, 110, 141, 167, 184, 189-90
Berger, P.L. 13 (n.5)
Berkeley, George 305-6
Bertlesmann Foundation 268
Beveridge, W.H. 36-7, 52-3, 123, 126, 135, 199, 206
   see also Welfare State
Bill of Rights (1689) 51, 167, 183, 184, 185, 219, 238, 239, 242, 244, 322
Blair, Tony 53
Blake, L.L. 48 (n.3)
Bloom, W. 7
Bonaparte, Napoleon 50, 203, 270
Britain *see* United Kingdom
British Crime Survey 291
bureaucracy 29, 122, 134-6 *passim*, 144
   foreign bureaucracy, surrender of sovereignty to 324-8
   tyranny of 203-8, 222, 322
Burke, Edmund 222-3
Burton, John W. 260, 265
Bush, George 311, 322, 331, 333

capital 4, 23, 33-4, 35, 38, 54, 107-8, 120-1, 133, 137-40 *passim*, 143, 145, 154-8 *passim*, 162, 186, 187, 214
   dominance of financial capital 322-4
   financial capital and production capital 115-17, 162-4, 322-4
capitalism xiv-xv, 3, 4, 23-42 *passim*, 43, 44-5, 49, 52, 54, 55, 66, 106-7, 115, 119, 124, 129, 130, 132-3, 134, 138-44 *passim*, 160-1, 163-5, 187, 190, 199,

capitalism—*contd*
   202, 203, 205-6, 211, 251, 299, 322
   evolutionary capitalism 140-4
caring society:
   and conflict resolution 259-60
   and family values 57-61
   and market economy 28-30
   moral values 55-7
   nature of 26-8
caveat emptor 127-8
Charlemagne 167, 270
children 12, 14-16, 233, 284-5
   and discipline 66-8, 70-1, 91-3, 233, 264-5, 274, 284-5
   and drugs 287-8, 291
   and family 65-70, 90-1, 100, 233, 262-3, 264, 321
   child labour 24, 150, 188, 250, 258, 318
   children's rights 67, 70, 85, 257, 264, 274
   see also education
China 67, 281, 285-6, 320, 327
Churchill, Winston S. 60, 127
citizenship xvi, 10, 14, 16, 96, 144, 173, 193-227 *passim*, 243
   education 100-1, 103, 196
Civil War *see* England
class distinctions 20, 131, 132, 142, 174-5, 190, 201, 206, 208, 211, 218, 267-8
   social influence of managerial class 140-4
collectivism 73, 133
Columbus, Christopher 303
communism xvi, 29-30, 52, 53, 73, 130-1, 133, 135, 139, 144, 189, 191, 202-6 *passim*
   and bureaucracy 203-5
   collapse of 205-6
   Communist Manifesto (1848) 124, 130-1, 144
   Communist Revolution (1918) 36, 103, 139, 190-1, 203-4, 242
Companies Acts (1862, 1989) 142
computers 88-90, 94, 154, 196, 202
Comte, Auguste 49
conflict:
   social 13, 16-17, 20, 30-1, 34-5, 44, 51, 59, 65, 103, 122, 131-2, 147-8, 180, 187, 204, 209, 212, 218, 252, 266-70, 292, 298, 327, 328
   international 9, 20, 21, 24, 25, 46, 58, 141, 164-5, 270-1, 191, 311-12, 329, 330, 333

conflict resolution 19, 147, 212, 256-71, 292, 328
   and family 27, 260-3
   and gender differences 265-6
   and Love 65
   and social fractures 266-70
   at international level 270-1
   conflict and 257-9
   conflict between generations 263-5
   major issues for a caring society 259-60
   origin and nature of 256-7
consciousness and existence 298-302, 304
control paradigm 134, 153-61
Co-operative movement 24-5, 133
Corn Laws 188
corporate identity 8-9
Cowling, M. 208
Crick, Prof. Bernard 10, 16, 100, 191
Crick, Francis 73
crime control 271-93
   and criminal behaviour 281-3
   and criminal liability 271-4
   and criminal violence 283-5
   and drug abuse 281-2, 285-92
   and social policy 274-6
   law enforcement 278-81
   tolerance:
      and compassion 276-8
      and prohibition 288-91
crime statistics 40, 281-2
criminal behaviour 15, 62, 68, 113, 148, 179, 225-6, 281-3, 331, 333
custom xiv, 17, 30, 37, 40, 47, 51, 56, 66, 74, 84, 107, 113, 196, 216, 219, 231, 236, 238, 247-54 *passim*, 258, 272

Dante 263, 284
Darwin, Charles, 49, 208, 300
da Vinci, Leonardo 178, 235
Dawkins, R. xiii (n.4), 235
de Bracton, Henry 48 (n.3)
Defamation Acts 246
de Mandeville 31, 32, 113
democracy 37, 40-1, 49, 53-4, 97, 100-1, 133-6, 166, 168-9, 172-6, 180, 182-4, 185-6, 190, 193-7, 199-201, 204, 213, 215-22, 224, 226-7, 237, 239-40, 245, 251, 259, 281, 298, 309, 322, 332, 335
   and accountability 215-17
   and rule of law 240-2
   democratic deficit and parliamentary mandate 194-5, 217-20
   direct democracy 196-7
   in England 51, 53, 57, 182-5

Index

democracy—*contd*
  in Plato 172-6, 199
  in Switzerland 195-6
  representative democracy 190-1, 198-203
  the Athenian democracy 168-9, 194
  see also government; oligarchy; politics
Descartes, René 49, 98, 299
de Soto, Hernando 160
de Waal, Frans 310
Dewey, J. 85
Dickens, Charles 24, 33, 124, 188
Diderot, Denis 49
discipline xv, 26, 57, 66-7, 70-1, 91-2, 94, 208, 233, 237, 260-2, 264-5, 275, 284
Divine Right of Kings 48, 51, 167, 179, 181, 182, 215
Dixon, Dr Patrick 162
Doyle, Sir Arthur Conan 286
drug abuse 15, 67, 68, 90, 100, 274, 277, 281-2, 285-93
Duff, R.A. 273
Duke of Normandy 59
Durkheim, Emile xiv, xvi, 48, 85, 99, 100, 168
duties 14, 41, 67, 68, 70, 78, 84, 100, 141, 166, 194, 215-16, 217, 223, 237, 239, 241, 242, 245-7, 248, 264, 265, 280, 301
  rights and duties 14, 141, 194, 216, 217, 241, 245-7, 248, 265, 280, 301

Economic and Social Research Council 10
Edgeworth, F.Y. 111, 112
education xv, xvi, 38, 52, 76-105, 136, 188, 196, 249
  and citizenship xvi, 196
  and discipline 91-3, 100
  and family 68-105 *passim*
  and religion 101-4
  formal and informal 83-5, 93-5
  higher levels of 79-80, 96-7
  general 78-9, 85-90
  purpose and meaning of 80-3, 99, 104-5
  ongoing debate about 96-101
  reforming society 78-81
  societal influences 93-5
Education Acts (1870, 1871) 79-80, 188
elections 54, 97, 133, 136, 193, 197, 199-201, 219-24 *passim*, 243, 244-5
  see also universal suffrage
Empson, W. 147
enclosure 187-8

Engels 25, 124, 189, 190
England:
  accountancy in 143, 145-6, 147, 151-2, 162
  Church of England 180-1, 185
  Civil War 181, 182, 183, 185
  democracy in 51, 53, 57, 182-3, 201, 215, 216, 219, 238, 251, 326
  Empire 186, 189
  English Enlightenment 23, 49, 167, 178, 181-6, 222
  English Reformation 24, 50, 178, 180-1, 252
  free trade and capitalism 31-2, 50, 66, 107, 124-5, 132, 185-6, 188, 189, 198-9
  multiracial character 59-1, 269-70
  see also Home Office; Industrial Revolution; law; legislation; slave trade; United Kingdom
Enlightenment, the 23, 48, 49, 167, 178-86, 193, 202, 203, 222, 277, 299, 308
Enron 148, 214-15
Equal Franchise Act (1928) 184
Europe:
  Eastern xvi, 7, 25, 60, 66, 135, 202, 203, 252
  Western 49, 50, 135, 179, 180, 181, 202, 203, 204, 206, 285
European Central Bank 112, 122, 125-6, 325
European Court of Human Rights 244, 331-2
European Court of Justice 330-1, 332
European Union xvi, 7, 10, 11-12, 13, 20, 50, 119, 121-2, 131, 135-6, 144, 151, 195, 203, 209, 222, 225, 250, 280, 316, 324-8, 330-2
European Constitution 7, 135-6, 222
existentialism xiii

Factory Acts 187
family:
  and debt 126-7, 319
  and education 78, 84, 85, 90-3, 96
  as economic unit 66, 69, 130, 139
  as social unit xiv, 5-6, 12, 14, 19, 26-8, 57-8, 64, 65-8, 75, 129-30, 133, 231, 233, 297
  breakdown of 12, 14-16, 26-7, 69-70, 233, 265
  conflicts within 6, 19, 27, 255, 260-6 *passim*
  discipline and 57, 66-8, 70-1

family—*contd*
  family model 14, 19, 26, 41-2, 43-4, 51, 54-7, 75, 80, 97, 105, 202, 205
  family values 23, 43, 55-61, 62, 66, 68, 69, 71-2, 73, 78, 96, 102, 130, 202, 205, 233, 260-2, 265-6, 297, 318
  parental authority and children's rights 66-8
  responsibilities of members 68-70
  survival of 57, 64, 71-3
  women's rights 15, 19, 233
  see also children; identity
Family Law Reform Act (1969) 184
Financial Ombudsman (UK) 128, 149
Financial Standards Agency 149
Foucault, M. 261-2, 263, 272, 274
four pillars of society 3, 5-22, 28, 51, 57
  see also: identity; moral values; social cohesion; sovereign authority
Foster, C. 217 (n.13)
France xv, 10, 11, 35, 38, 40, 48, 49-50, 60-1, 70, 121-2, 126, 132 (n.18), 135, 151, 187, 201-2, 203-4, 210, 216-17, 222, 238-9, 248, 252, 270, 272-3, 280, 286, 324-5
  accountancy in 151
  and EU 324-5
  Gaullism 121, 132
  see also French Revolution; law: in France
Franklin, Rosalind 73
freedom:
  and conflict 256-65 *passim*
  and democracy 54, 135-6, 172-4, 176, 193, 199-100, 216, 240-2, 251, 281, 322
  and Social Conscience 234-9, 254, 256
  and tyranny 176, 206-8, 321-2
  as a moral value 65, 112-13, 183, 203, 231, 302
  as rights and duties 245-7
  custom and freedom 247-9
  economic freedom 30, 260, 262 (*see also* free trade)
  individual freedom 23, 27, 28, 33, 38, 39, 41, 43, 49, 50, 52, 62, 65, 66-9 *passim*, 94-5, 97, 110, 112-13, 176, 193, 199, 202, 204-6, 209, 220, 231-54 *passim*, 256-65 *passim*, 280, 315
  of expression and censorship xvi, 62, 94-5, 101, 112, 245-6, 253, 260, 284-5
  of managerial class 141-2, 147-8, 214

freedom—*contd*
  political freedom xvi, 16, 41, 139, 167, 185, 193, 203-6 *passim*, 216
  under law 39-40, 51, 170, 183, 194, 225, 231, 239, 243, 244, 251, 254, 255, 328-30
  see also authority and freedom; Enlightenment; free trade; *laissez faire*; Rousseau
free trade 3, 23, 32, 35, 39, 50, 107, 110, 112, 121, 126-8, 131-2, 139, 179, 185-6, 198-9, 203, 206-7, 220, 233-4, 249-51, 316, 322
  and representative government 184-9
  and state intervention 113-14
French Revolution xv, 40-1, 49-50, 61, 120, 132, 203, 216, 238, 242
  see also Rousseau
fundamentalism 310-13

Gandhi, Mahatma 258
General Combination Acts (1799, 1800) 187
generation gap 263-5, 292
genetic manipulation 257, 297, 313-16
Geneva Conventions 225, 331
Germany 10, 16, 49, 122-3, 189, 225-6, 324-5
Glautier, M.W.E. 210
global economy xv-xvi, 3, 4, 13, 21, 28, 35, 45, 55, 102, 114, 126, 137, 141, 144, 163-4, 165, 183, 186, 203, 206, 212, 245, 298, 302, 316-21, 322-4, 326, 328, 329-30, 331, 336
Golding, William 285 (n.13)
gold standard 118
governance xvi, 193, 217, 227
  discretionary managerial behaviour and agency theory 213-15
  meaning of 208-11
  Plato and Marx 211-13
Great Depression 36, 53, 123, 125, 134, 198, 199, 318
Greeks, Ancient xi, 31, 72, 144, 170, 235
  the Athenian democracy 168-9, 194
  see also Aristotle; Plato; Socrates
Greenpeace 216-17
Griffin, S. 142 (n.8)
Gross National Income (GNI) 119, 129
Gross National Product (GNP) 121, 122, 126, 129
groups:
  and conflict 256, 259, 263, 267-8, 270-1, 280, 285, 292, 327
  family 27, 56, 58, 73, 75, 129-30, 263

Index

groups—*contd*
  financial 154, 164, 324
  groupism 8-10, 267, 309-10
  immigrant 11, 269
  in-/out- 8, 10
  political 164, 193, 195, 204, 211, 213, 218, 221, 234, 242, 321, 326
  primitive 30
  religious 269-70, 310, 327
  social 5-14 *passim*, 17, 19-20, 21, 26, 28, 30, 40, 41, 43, 44, 75, 77, 82, 88-9, 149, 231, 237, 256, 259, 263, 267-8, 309-10
  see also identity; social cohesion

Habeas Corpus Act (1679) 183, 184-5, 239
Hicks, J.R. 156
Hippocratic Oath 62, 97
Hitler, Adolf 16, 123, 180, 270
Hobbes, Thomas 27, 167, 181-2, 184, 203, 237
Home Office:
  ASBOs 285
  Crime Statistics for England and Wales 281-2, 292
  Prison Statistics for England and Wales 282
Homo sapiens 49, 235-6
Hugo, Victor 124
humane condition xii, xiv, 1-74, 99, 168, 205, 234, 239, 297
humanism xii, xiii, xiv, 54
human rights *see* rights
Hume, David xvi, 49, 85, 130 (n.16)

identity xvi, 3, 4, 5-12, 13-14, 16, 17, 19-20, 21, 59, 60, 65, 73, 75, 95, 132, 133, 144, 194, 231, 252, 264, 266-7, 269, 280, 292, 301-2, 307, 325, 327, 335
  national 5, 7-8, 9-12, 13, 16, 19-20, 21, 144, 266, 292, 325
  see also family; groups; self
immigration 10-13, 20, 21, 58-61, 67, 103, 243, 245, 252, 266-7, 269
  see also pluralist societies
Incas 72
income, distribution of in market economy 138-40
India 60, 67, 267, 320
Industrial Revolution 24, 31, 49, 124, 132, 140, 147, 151-2, 187, 202
inflation 34, 106, 114, 117-23 *passim*, 125-6, 150, 317, 325-6
  social consequences of 117-23

Institutes of Chartered Accountants xvi, 143, 162
International Criminal Court 58, 225, 226, 333
International Criminal Tribunal 333
international tribunals 225-6, 330-3
Iraq 53, 58, 200, 216, 224, 226, 311, 313, 331, 333
Israel 46, 73, 133, 202, 269, 311-13
Italy 122, 126, 135, 214
  in Renaissance 49, 145-6, 178-80

joint stock companies 106, 107-8, 140-3 *passim*, 147, 213
Joint Stock Companies Acts (1844, 1856) 107, 140-2, 148
Judicature Acts (1875) 101
'just price' 24, 31, 138, 179

Kahneman, D. 112 (n.7)
Kant, Immanuel xvi, 49, 74, 82, 85, 93, 130 (n.16), 207, 237, 249, 261
Keynes i, 33, 35-6, 39, 52, 154, 125, 134-5, 198-9, 318
King Alfred 59
King Charles I 181, 183, 185
King George V 36, 191
King Harold II 59
King Henry II 219
King Henry VIII 180
Kuhn, T.S. 116 (n.8), 303, 305
Kyoto Agreement on Climatic Change 320

Labour Theory of Value 34, 117, 139, 190
laissez-faire 23, 31, 32-36, 38, 39, 50, 233
  and economic efficiency 32-5
law:
  and custom 236, 247-8, 254
  and family 67-70, 101, 184, 273-4
  and freedom 39-40, 51, 183, 194, 199, 224-5, 231, 233, 237, 239-43, 245-6
  and market economy 108, 113, 128, 140-2, 148, 155, 215
  and moral values xiv, 17, 18, 19, 21, 31, 32, 39-40, 46, 47-8, 55, 61-2, 86, 107
  and politics 187, 201, 215, 222
  and religion 17, 102
  authority and freedom under law 232, 233, 239-42, 250-1, 254
  Canon law 50, 101-2
  children and 61, 67-70 *passim*, 84
  Civil Law 71, 113, 240-2, 246

law—*contd*
  Common Law 37, 51, 56-7, 70, 102,
      139, 241, 143, 215, 237-8, 239, 329
    constitutional law 215-16, 217, 219,
      238, 239
    crime control 255, 257, 271-93 *passim*
    Criminal Law 39-40, 71, 113, 240,
      242, 246, 272, 274
    enforcement 278-81, 283
      through international tribunals
        226, 330-3
    in England 48, 50-1, 56-7, 59, 70,
      79-80, 101-2, 117, 139, 140, 143,
      185, 187, 188, 189, 197, 216, 219,
      225, 237-9, 240, 272-3, 279-82,
      286-7, 291, 329
    in Europe 50-1, 195, 330-2
    in France 70, 238-9, 272-3, 280, 286
    international 53-4, 58, 225-6, 244,
      302, 329-33
    in USA 244, 329, 331
    natural law 31-2, 37, 69, 184, 208, 302
    of property 44, 138
    Roman Law 12, 50, 68, 70, 139, 144, 243
    see also legislation; rule of law
  Law of Negligence 39, 113, 128, 241-2
  Law of Tort 39, 241-2
  Leavis, F.R. 152 (n.13)
  Leibniz, Gottfried Wilhelm 32, 49, 85
  Life *see* absolute values
  Limited Liability Act (1855) 140-1
  Lincoln, Abraham 169, 194 (n.1)
  Locke, John xvi, 49, 85, 130 (n.16), 167,
      181, 182, 184, 192, 203, 237
  Love *see* absolute values
  Lukes, S. xiv (n.5), 48 (n.2), 70 (n.5),
      74 (n.7)
  Luxemburg, Rosa 34, 139

  MacDonald, Ramsay 191
  Machiavelli, Niccolò 167, 178, 179, 192, 270
  Magna Carta (1215) 51, 117, 180, 185,
      238, 239, 242, 322
  Malthus, T.R. 30, 114, 208
  managerial class *see* class distinctions
  Mandeville 113
  market economy xiv-xvi, 3-4, 5, 8,
      14-15, 17-18, 21, 23-42 *passim*, 44-5,
      52-5 *passim*, 66, 69, 74, 76, 77, 80, 88,
      96, 104, 106-36 *passim*, 137-65 *passim*,
      166, 186, 189, 198-9, 200-8 *passim*,
      211, 212, 220, 232, 233-4, 245,
      249-51, 259, 260, 265, 267, 268,
      297-9, 301-2, 309, 316-28 *passim*, 334,
      335-6

market economy—*contd*
    and a caring society 28-30
    and authority and freedom 249-51
    and capital 115-17
    and moral value choices 112-13
    and the State and democracy 201-3
    distribution of income in 138-40
    global expansion of 316-21
    impact on structure of society 128-36
    nature of 108-10
    the moral dilemma 30-2
    see also laissez-faire; shareholder value
  Marx, Karl/Marxism xvi, 25, 28, 29, 34,
      35, 106, 114, 124, 130-1, 132, 133,
      135, 136, 139, 141, 144, 164, 167,
      189-90, 201, 202, 204, 206, 211-13,
      267, 299
    see also Communist Manifesto; Labour
      Theory of Value
  Maxwell, Robert 148, 214
  McCain, Senator Edward 321-2
  McKendrick, N. 152
  Memorandum of Association 141, 142
  mental illness 6, 288, 306
  Middle East 45, 46, 311-13
  Mill, John Stuart 31, 32, 110, 113, 167,
      184, 185, 189-90
  Milton, John 24
  monarchy 176, 225, 234, 238-9
  money 4, 21, 29, 31, 109-23 *passim*, 130,
      139, 144, 159, 162, 163, 170, 172-3,
      178-9, 188, 200, 207, 214, 288, 317,
      318, 322-3, 336
  moral values xii-xvi *passim*, 3, 4-5, 9-10,
      13, 16-19 *passim*, 21, 23, 28-33 *passim*,
      39-40, 43-9 *passim*, 61-5, 70-8 *passim*,
      80, 82, 85, 86, 89-104 *passim*, 107, 110,
      112-13, 114, 117, 118, 131-4 *passim*,
      136, 166-9 *passim*, 171, 176-9 *passim*,
      182-4 *passim*, 192, 193, 202, 203, 205,
      207, 211, 231-3 *passim*, 238, 242, 246,
      248, 254, 255, 258, 261, 283-4, 292,
      297-9 *passim*, 301, 304, 307, 320, 321,
      324, 333, 335
    and family discipline 70-1
    and political debate 45-51
    as determinants of behaviour 61-5
    as pillar of society 17-19
    from caring relationships 55-7
    in Plato 167-8
    significance of 44-5
  More, Thomas 24
  Mother Teresa 258

  National Audit Office 292

Index

national debt 119, 122
National Health Services Act (1948) 37
national identity *see* identity
National Insurance Act (1948) 37
nationalisation 206
nationhood xvi, 5, 7-10 *passim*, 16, 21-1, 26, 216, 325, 329
nation state 7, 8, 46, 329
  and European Union 50, 135
Netherlands, The 11, 135, 191, 222
Newman, Cardinal J.H. 25, 78 (n.2), 79, 124, 188
New Zealand 216
Norman Conquest 59, 219

Oakeshott, M. 84, 95
oligarchy 28, 172-3, 175, 186-7, 189-92 *passim*, 201, 301
opinion polls 178, 193, 196, 224

Paine, Thomas 196 (n.2)
peace studies 265 (n.3), 270-1
Peel, Sir Robert 276
'perfect competition' 108-9, 113, 127
Peters, R.S. 81, 83
Plato xii, xvi, 27, 28, 31, 46, 79, 83, 85, 117, 121, 130 (n.16), 167-78, 179, 183, 184, 185, 192, 193-4, 199, 201, 203, 211-13, 217, 219, 234, 237, 278, 299, 303, 322
  forms of government 170-6
  governance 211-13
  moral values and political philosophy 167-8
  selecting and educating leaders as statesmen 177-8
  the Athenian democracy 168-70
pluralist societies 13, 21, 267-9
Poland xvi, 122, 203
politics:
  alternate political systems 51-2
  and moral values 45-51
  elections 200-1, 219-20, 245
  Plato's political philosophy 167-8
  political change and universal suffrage 198-9
  political correctness 16, 62, 101, 251-3
  political courage 278-81, 284-5, 289-90
  political objectives 52-5
  role of political parties 220-4
  see also democracy; elections
Pollard, Sidney 120 (n.12), 141 (n.5), 145 (n.10), 161 (n.18)
Poor Law Amendment Act (1834) 188
Pope John Paul II 308 (n.3)

Popper, K.R. 135-6
poverty 4, 10, 14, 18, 24, 27, 32-3, 36-7, 38, 44, 123-5, 187-8, 198-9, 202-3, 208, 257, 258, 267-8, 277, 318, 319, 321
  poverty gap 267-8
property rights 12, 44, 68, 69, 129 (n.14), 328
Public Order Acts 246

rationality 161, 202, 207, 232, 235-6, 297-8, 300, 304-10 *passim*
reason 10, 74, 110, 169, 181-2, 184, 192, 202, 207, 235-6, 237, 251, 261, 300-1, 303-4, 306, 308-11, 336
  and religion 308-10
Reform Acts (1832, 1867, 1884) 184, 188
Reformation *see* religion
religion xi-xii, xiv, 16-18, 20, 24, 27, 29, 31, 32-3, 41, 46-7, 48, 49, 61, 72, 74, 85, 101-4, 252, 268-70, 299-301, 303-13, 334, 336
  and education 101-4
  and reason 308-10
  Christianity xi, 33, 46-7, 49, 102, 117, 182, 200, 303, 310-12
    Catholicism 24, 31, 66, 102, 121, 179-81, 252, 257
    Protestantism 24, 31, 66, 102, 179-81, 310
  fundamentalism 310-13
  Holy Books 17
  Islam 11, 20, 72, 102, 103-4, 117, 243, 269-70, 311-12, 327, 333
  Judaism 46-7, 202, 189, 311-12
  Reformation 24, 31, 50, 117, 178-81 *passim*
Renaissance 45, 49, 145-6, 167, 178-80
Representation of the People Act (1918) 184, 191
Rhodes, R. 209
Ricardo, David 31, 113
rights:
  and duties 14, 39, 100, 141, 194, 216, 217, 241, 245-7, 248, 265, 280, 301
  children's rights 67, 69, 70, 85, 256, 257, 264, 274, 285
  civil and social rights 12, 15-16, 18, 69, 182, 191, 194, 199-200, 206, 218, 232-3, 240-2, 247-8, 256-7, 274, 283, 302, 319, 328
  corporate rights and duties 115, 138, 139, 141, 147, 160, 213-14, 233, 249, 250-1, 324
  human rights 85, 107, 112, 209, 225, 244-5, 271, 281, 328, 331-2

rights—*contd*
  individual rights 107, 112, 184, 232,
    237, 240-5, 251-2, 256-7, 287, 302,
    303, 308
    and freedom 242-3
    and human rights 244-5
  political rights 16, 54, 167, 182, 184-5,
    187, 194, 199, 215-20 *passim*, 329
  property rights 12, 44, 58, 68, 69, 328
  women's rights 15, 19, 67, 233, 256-7,
    265
  see also accountability; freedom; free
    trade; legislation: Bill of Rights
Road Traffic Acts 39, 242
Romans, Ancient 12, 24, 45, 46, 50, 68,
  72, 138-9, 140, 144-5, 243, 258
Rousseau, Jean-Jacques xvi, 23, 27, 40-1,
  49, 55, 65, 85, 87, 92, 99, 104, 182,
  208, 237
rule of law 49, 225-6, 240, 255, 273, 293,
  301, 302, 328-30, 334, 336
Russell, Bertrand 257
Russia (Communist) 36, 73, 130 (n.16),
  133, 139, 191, 203-4, 205, 242

Sarin, R. 112 (n.7)
Sartre, Jean-Paul xii, 208
Schumpeter, J.A. 106, 114, 116 (n.8), 127,
  129 (n.14), 132-3, 134, 141, 144, 163,
  164, 165 (n.20), 205, 299, 322
Scotland 143, 270
self xiii-xiv, 5, 8, 27-8, 43-4, 66, 71, 75-6,
  89, 92, 95, 99, 103, 112, 169, 205,
  206, 231, 255, 260-1, 263, 301-2, 318,
  321
  'self instinct' 43-4, 52, 168
Shakespeare, William 10, 56
shareholders 18, 33-4, 35, 108, 128-9,
  140-3, 146-7, 148-51, 154-9 *passim*,
  161-2, 212, 213-15, 247, 322-3
  shareholder value xv, 3, 4, 9, 18, 21,
    33-4, 35, 38, 45, 54, 107, 108, 115,
    116, 120, 121, 124, 126, 128, 137,
    138, 147, 149, 153, 155, 157,
    161-2, 163, 164, 165, 210, 213,
    249, 250, 298, 316-17, 324
Shaw, George Bernard 41
Simester, A. 273
Slater, D. 107 (n.1), 131 (n.17), 207 (n.4)
slave trade, abolition of 188, 289-90
Smith, Adam 23, 31, 32, 44, 106, 110,
  113, 127, 141, 167, 170 (n.2), 184
social change:
  and education 78-81
  and the managerial class 140-4

social cohesion 3, 4, 12-17, 21-22, 28, 59,
  60, 75, 97, 102, 193-4, 196, 197, 209,
  211-12, 218, 226, 231, 245, 252, 258,
  259, 264, 266, 269, 278, 292, 297, 307,
  325-7, 335, 336
Social Conscience xiv, 3, 4, 13, 17-19,
  21-22, 37, 43, 45, 47-51 *passim*, 73-4,
  91, 101, 107, 109, 112-14, 116, 118,
  122-3, 127, 131-4, 136, 139, 145,
  148-51 *passim*, 165, 166-71 *passim*,
  176-8 *passim*, 193, 207-8, 224, 226-7,
  234-9 *passim*, 247, 250-8 *passim*,
  260, 271, 276-8 *passim*, 280, 283,
  298-302 *passim*, 304-8, 314, 321, 328,
  332-5 *passim*
  and accounting profession 148-51
  and authority 237-9
  and criminal behaviour 255, 262,
    276-8, 280, 283
  and custom 247, 250, 251-2, 253
  and freedom 193, 234-6, 239, 254,
    256-8, 321
  and government 224, 226-7, 278,
    321
  and intolerance 252-3
  and market economy 109, 113-14,
    116, 118, 122-3, 127, 132-4, 136,
    165, 166, 250, 298-302, 334
  and Marx 131
  and money 207-8
  and Plato 167-71, 176, 177-8
  and religion 101, 301, 307
  and Schumpeter 132-3
  and war 271, 332-3
  reality and influence of 304-8
social consequences:
  of economic recession 123-7
  of market imperfections 127-8
  of monetary inflation 117-23
social contract:
  and individual freedom 39-41
social fracture:
  conflict resolution 266-70
socialism xiv-xv, 25, 29, 34, 38, 43, 44,
  52-3, 103, 106, 117, 119, 131-3, 135,
  136, 139, 165, 190, 202-7 *passim*, 220
  and bureaucracy 203-5
  failure of socialist experiment 205-7
social justice:
  and intervention 35-9
social policy:
  and crime control 274-6
social structure:
  impact of market economy 128-36
  role of accounting information 153-6

social welfare:
    and government 189-90
    and political parties 220-1
Socrates 167
Sombart, R.A. 137, 145
sovereign authority xiv, 3, 4, 19-20, 28,
    43, 46, 47-9, 51-2, 59, 73-4,
    117 (n.10), 239, 242, 244, 253-4
    Social Conscience as sovereign
        authority xiv, 43, 134, 136, 166,
        171, 193, 328
    surrender to foreign bureaucracy
        324-8
    see also Divine Right of Kings
Stalin, Joseph 204
state intervention 23, 25, 29, 32, 36,
    37-9, 41-2, 113-14, 116, 135, 136, 250
    and free trade 113-14
stock exchanges 9, 33, 36, 109, 133, 143,
    152-3, 154, 155, 157, 158
St Thomas Acquinas xvi, 24, 31, 117
Sullivan, R. 273
Switzerland 194 (n.1), 195, 196, 204,
    212-13, 216, 269, 306, 331

Tawney, R.H., 31, 299
taxation 37-9, 119, 122, 125, 126, 129,
    133, 159, 185, 195, 218, 220, 243, 244,
    245, 249, 271, 286, 290, 325, 326, 329
television 93, 94, 284
tolerance 251-3, 288-91
    of criminal behaviour 277-8, 288-91
Tolpuddle Martyrs 187
Tonkiss, F. 107 (n.1), 131 (n.17),
    207 (n.4)
trade unions 25, 187, 190
Truth see absolute values
tyranny:
    and democracy 54, 172, 216, 326
    and freedom 176, 184, 197, 234, 254,
        321-2
    of bureaucracy 203-8, 222, 322
    of money 208, 213, 214, 322

ultra vires 142
Underdown, B. 210
unemployment 30, 36, 37, 41, 70, 90,
    120, 122-6 *passim*, 134, 191, 197,
    198-9, 277, 318
    redundancy 127, 150, 318, 319
United Kingdom (UK)/Britain xv, 4, 10,
    18, 26, 35, 36, 38, 40, 53, 58, 60, 100,
    121, 128, 189, 203, 210, 215-16, 219-20,

United Kingdom/Britain—*contd*
    225, 226, 238, 243, 244, 269-70, 286,
    291-2, 311-12, 319, 324-5, 329
    see also England; Home Office;
        legislation; Scotland; Wales
United Nations 53, 58, 271, 311, 330,
    333
United States of America (USA) 11, 13,
    20, 25, 38, 50, 58, 115, 123, 125, 131,
    134, 143, 164, 165, 183, 197-9 *passim*,
    201-4 *passim*, 206, 210, 214-15, 217,
    225, 226, 238, 239, 243, 244, 248,
    252, 253, 269, 270, 281, 311-13,
    320, 321-2, 325-7 *passim*, 329, 331,
    333
    American Bill of Rights (1791) 183
    McCarthyism 204, 252
    war on terror 12, 311, 331, 333
    see also Great Depression
universal suffrage 184, 185, 190-1, 193,
    198-201, 215, 322
    see also elections
usury 24, 31, 117, 138
Utilitarianism 110, 170 (n.2), 184, 185,
    190

Veblen, T.B. 137
von Clausewitz, C. 270

Wakker, P. 112 (n.7)
Wales 59, 143, 162, 187, 270, 281-2,
    291
war studies 270-1
Watson, James 73
Weber, Max 31
Wedgwood, Josiah 152
Welfare State xv, 4, 14, 18, 23, 26, 36,
    41-2, 52, 53, 125, 135, 188, 199, 206,
    268
    see also Beveridge
West Indies 60, 290
Whitehead, Prof. A.N. 168, 178
Wilberforce, William 188, 258, 289
Wilkins, Maurice 73
Williamson, O.E. 213
William the Conqueror 59, 219
Wittgenstein, Ludwig 58
World War I 36, 53, 191, 312
World War II 10 (n.3), 18, 53, 123,
    132 (n.18), 188, 204, 266, 271

Yamey, B.S. 145
Yom Kippur War 18

About the Author

MICHEL GLAUTIER is a graduate of the Universities of Manchester and London, and has a Doctorate in Management Sciences (with distinction) from the University of Paris. He has been on the Faculty of the Universities of Sheffield and Manchester, Professor of Accounting and Control at INSEAD, Fontainebleau, and at ESSEC, Paris and O'Bleness Chair Professor in Public Accounting at Ohio University. He has been Visiting Professor at several universities, including the University of Denver, San Diego State University, the University of Texas, Austin, and at the University of Western Australia. He has published widely and has had extensive experience as a business consultant.

He lives in Switzerland.